The Logic of
International Relations

Steven J. Rosen
Brandeis University and
Australian National University

Walter S. Jones
Nort...

Winthrop Publishers, Inc.
Cambridge, Massachusetts

Library of Congress Cataloging in Publication Data

Rosen, Steven.
  The logic of international relations.

  Includes bibliographical references and index.
  1. International relations. I. Jones, Walter S.,
joint author. II. Title.
JX1395.R56 1977   327   76–41293
ISBN 0–87626–506–9

Line illustrations by George Ulrich

Cover cartoon: LePelley in The Christian Science Monitor, (c) 1975
TCSPS

Cover photo: Gamma/Liaison; Michel Laurent/photographer

© *1977 by Winthrop Publishers, Inc.*
  17 Dunster Street, Cambridge, Massachusetts 02138

10 9 8 7 6 5 4 3

To Yem Ling,

who makes this world a better world;

and

to Sally and Doug,

*whose generation may have the final opportunity
to answer the question,
"Will man survive?"*

Contents

Contents

Preface

Readers of *The Logic of International Relations* will find in the second edition a substantial revision, with changes ranging in magnitude from the addition of a chapter (the perspectives of "America's Major Allies"), to thorough revisions, partial chapter revisions, and a mix of up-dating, re-drafting, and condensation. Conclusion of the manuscript marks a major victory over time and distance, since Steven Rosen served throughout this writing as Senior Research Fellow in the Department of International Relations at the Australian National University. Without the sponsorship of the Edward W. Brooke endowment at Northeastern University, a lengthy visit made by Walter Jones to Canberra would have been impossible; and without that opportunity for the authors to work together closely, small transgressions of time schedules would surely have grown so large as to have made impossible publication at this time.

In addition to debts incurred in preparing the first edition, the authors have benefited in a variety of ways from the helpful contributions of readers, critics, colleagues, and users of the first edition. Professor J.D.B. Miller and his colleagues in the Department of International Relations at the ANU afforded Steven Rosen generous support in time for contemplation and necessary travel, and in encouraging commentary on portions of the manuscript on which they are expert. They also provided Walter Jones with a peaceful refuge in which to think and write during December, 1975. Comments on the manuscript by Major Michael A. Freney of the Department of Political Science and Philosophy at the United States Air Force Academy contributed invaluably to some important conceptual reconsiderations, as well as to precision of detail. Opportunities created by Professor Robert K. Woetzel of Boston College, particularly at the Interuniversity International Seminar and at the Caribbean Conference of the International Criminal Law Commission, enabled Walter Jones to encounter personally some of the problems which are addressed herein and to improve the clarity of his thinking on them. General Indar Jit Rikhye, President of the International Peace Academy, twice opened wide the doors of the Academy during discussions of its role in international peacekeeping. A special debt of gratitude is due Mr. Alvin Zises of Boston, industrialist, philanthropist and donor of the Edward W. Brooke Professorship.

Production of the completed manuscript also had the advantages of the skills and inspiration of several people. Among them, the instincts and guidance of James J. Murray, III, President of Winthrop Publishers, sharpened many focal points and eased difficulties. Nancy Benjamin of Winthrop's production staff exceeded her normal duties on countless occasions to lend tender care to the phrasing, sensitivity, balance, and visual characteristics of the second edition. For her patience and forebearance, as well, we owe her gratitude. But mostly, Yem Ling, Sally, and Doug always fueled the spiritual flame which makes writing about the agonizing problems of public affairs so crucial, yet so rewarding. Because the appreciation of their contribution and of the friendships which this collaboration has forged will leave life-long remembrances of Christmas season 1975, the authors also owe a grateful acknowledgment to the Manley Ferry and to Martin Indyk.

For any shortcomings and imperfections which may have survived this outpouring of assistance, the authors bear full responsibility.

Steven J. Rosen
Walter S. Jones

Introduction

There are several questions of style and organization in this book that may at first seem odd and will be misleading without an explanation. The book begins in the first five chapters with an analysis of the world outlook of five key "actors" in the contemporary international system: the Soviet Union, the United States, the major Western allies, China, and a collective image of the Third World. We begin with an examination of how *each* point of view is influenced by concepts, values, national interests, and ideologics, rather than a statement of universal laws and regularities describing *all* actors, as is done in most texts. This emphasis on *perceptual analysis* is based on the belief that differences in national goals and perceptions are the origin of the two over-arching conflicts of our time: the dispute between East and West and the conflict between North and South.

For the fullest appreciation of the differences between perceptions of the international system, this book will use an experimental method of presentation. Instead of taking a detached, objective, "scientific" perspective and looking at each actor's view *critically*, we will try to step into each nation's shoes to look at the world from its *own point of view*. This is an exercise in role-playing, or more exactly, in role-writing, imagining first the outlook of a Soviet Communist, then seeing the world from an American point of view, then as a U.S. ally, then as a Chinese Communist, and finally from a synthesized Third World perspective. This differs greatly from the usual approach of newspapers, histories, and most of our sources of information, which stand above their subjects as "neutral and objective" observers. We believe that the task of understanding points of view that differ profoundly from our own is so difficult that it is necessary temporarily to suspend judgment to appreciate the perspective of the "other" from inside his own head, as best we can simulate it. To judge is to be separate from. We will try the Stanislawski theory of Method Acting: we will try temporarily to *be* the figure we wish to understand.

We must hastily interject several reservations and caveats at this point about our experiment. First, we will not present each perspective in the original words of national leaders, but rather interpret and organize their expressions and perspectives for an American audience. We believe that primary sources written for foreign audiences do not communicate successfully when taken into another context. Thus, the present authors are intermediaries between the various actors and the reader, and we will explain the five perceptual frames in their own terms. Original materials are available elsewhere.

Second, we will concentrate on idealized pictures of each actor, emphasizing values and professed beliefs. There is a danger here of mistaking mere rhetoric for the actual motives; we know that speechwriters often use idealistic disguises for less lofty goals such as the pursuit of power. The differences between nations are undoubtedly exaggerated when we concentrate on ideals, but they would be understated if, like most introductory texts, we concentrated instead on "universal" modes of behavior that ignore critical differences between actors. In a sense, we are choosing to err on the side of principles, drawing caricatures that highlight the unique and defining features rather than a completely proportioned portrait.

Third, we must concede that it is partly artificial to speak of *the* perceptual system of the United States or of its major allies or China or the Soviet Union or especially the Third World. Within each of these "actors" there are elites with differences of opinion regarding the national interest, the optimal course of strategy, and other issues. We will try to develop in each case a characterization that subsumes these differences, at least as far as the dominant elites are concerned. However, our analysis will give lesser effect to dissenting opinions within each "actor" that have not in the postwar period influenced policy directly and substantially. For example, in the American case our analysis will concern mainly the anti-Communist perspective that has in fact guided policy since 1948, and only in passing will we review various "revisionist" challenges to the dominant outlook. In other words, we are interested primarily in the various orthodoxies, not in minority views or factions that have been consistently out of power.

Fourth, we must explain one feature of our presentation that some may find controversial. We will give considerable attention to internal political features and problems of the various actors that shape their external outlooks. Conventional analysis draws a fairly sharp distinction between domestic politics and foreign policy, but many international relations specialists are finding this rigid boundary a hindrance to understanding the roots of international behavior. To a considerable degree, the foreign actions of a nation are continuations of essentially domestic processes and demands, and certainly international perceptions cannot be separated entirely from the broader value base that gives rise to them. Therefore, we feel justified in our emphasis on domestic matters at certain key points.

Fifth, our analysis takes the basic actor in international relations to be the nation-state. Some specialists believe that the nation is becoming less important as the key unit of analysis, and is being supplanted by the multinational corporation, the nongovernmental organization, and other "transnational" and supranational entities. We are sympathetic to this view, and later in this volume we will treat some of these actors at length. But we believe that the key actors in the cold war system are still nations and official bureaucracies, accounting for perhaps 80 percent of real power in international relations, while the other actors account for the balance. For the first section of the book, the basic unit of analysis will therefore be individual states.

Sixth, our concentration in this section on the cold war is not meant to imply that no change has taken place in the configuration of world politics in the last twenty-five years. The celebrated détente between the United States and the Soviet Union and China has indeed been a substantial relaxation of tensions, and the possibilities of direct military confrontation between the United States and either of the Communist giants are probably fairly low. But the cold war is still, in our view, one of the two major splits in the world (the other being the North/South conflict) and will be for at least several additional decades. The power of the Soviet Union and the United States is still opposed in nearly every corner of the world; and the two military alliance systems, Communist and anti-Communist, still dominate central stage in the global theatre. The superpowers continue to spend $200 billion per year preparing for war to deter each other, and the basic lines of global division still reflect essentially cold war coalitions. Thus, the relaxation of recent years must be seen as a modification of a continuing hostility, rather than a complete reconciliation between enemies. As regards the North/South conflict, this issue is growing rather than diminishing over time.

Finally, we must say a word about the political implications of perceptual analysis. It has been said that this method tends to be forgiving of sins, to view the behavior of each actor in the sympathetic light of his own values and experiences. Ultimately each actor is free of responsibility, each the victim of his respective misperceptions. We concede that an agnostic analysis of positions, giving the internal logic of each case and avoiding absolute and external judgments, may introduce greater moral ambiguities than fixing a single position from which to assess all the alternative views. We believe that these dilemmas of relativism and ambiguity are inherent in international relations, and that it is necessary to escape the comfort of one's own belief system. Relations between nations are in their very nature a meeting place of divergent perceptions.

The Logic of International Relations

Part One

THE LOGIC OF
NATIONAL PERCEPTIONS

1

The Soviet Perspective

The Soviet point of view has two core themes: a Russian theme as a *nation* with a long history of goals and conflicts before communism, and a Communist theme based on a universal *ideology*, which is a system of beliefs and values purporting to apply equally to all countries. The revolutionaries of 1917 were probably motivated more by Communist ideology than by Russian nationalism: one of their first acts was to sign away large portions of Russia (containing one-third of its population and three-quarters of its iron ore) in a very unfavorable German peace treaty at Brest Litovsk to preserve a kernel, however reduced in size, for the world's first Communist state. Russian national interests were subordinated to the Communist ideological goal of establishing a revolutionary base.

In recent years, the mixture of goals may have shifted to a greater emphasis on national interests and a reduction of communism's universal goals. More attention is given to the problems of Russian society and the demands of the Russian people, and less to world revolution. To understand the Soviet view, it is necessary to intertwine the basic tenets of Communist ideology with the historical interests of the Russian nation.

What is Communist Ideology?

Communist ideology is an analysis of the basic behavioral laws that underlie the spectrum of human relations and explain in an orderly way the otherwise unintelligible complexities of society. Karl Marx and Friedrich

Engels provided the basic analysis of capitalism and the state, and Vladimir Lenin, using Marx's "objective truth," contributed the main analysis of the international system.[1]

Fundamentals of Communism

Economic Determinism

Marxist–Leninist philosophy holds that the foundation of society is the economic system and the social relationships that it produces. Stalin said, "The basis is the economic system. . . . The superstructure consists of the political, legal, religious, artistic, philosophical views of society, and the political, legal, and other institutions corresponding to them." Communism is thus a branch of the materialist school of philosophy.

What distinguishes Marxism-Leninism as a materialist philosophy is its conception of *class relations* as the root of social interaction. In *The Communist Manifesto* Marx declared,

> The history of all human society, past and present, has been the history of class struggles.
> Freeman and slave, patrician and plebian, baron and serf, guild-burgess and journeyman—in a word, oppressor and oppressed—stood in sharp opposition each to the other.

This theory holds that in every organized society, one class controls the ownership of the *means of production,* and it uses political authority and all-powerful institutions to maintain this control. The ownership class extracts surpluses produced by the laboring masses. Society is a pyramid in which the broad working class at the bottom produces wealth for the privileged elite at the top.

Feudalism and Capitalism

This principle is seen in the feudal pattern of agriculture where ownership of land was concentrated in the hands of a small nobility, the "lords," for whose benefit it was worked by impoverished peasants. The laborers lived in shanties on a minimum subsistence, sustaining themselves from disaster to disaster. The lord lived in a baronial mansion in leisure, enjoying his daily diet of sport and cultivation of the arts. The landlords were not, of course, chosen by God; they achieved their position initially by conquests, foreclosure on usurious loans, and royal grants, and passed

---

[1] Alfred G. Meyer, *Communism* (New York: Random House, 1967), pp. 11–22, 51–58.

on their control through inheritance. Government was intertwined with feudal landownership: the lords gave a portion of their wealth and power to support the state, and the state used its physical force to guarantee the rights of property—that is, the position of the lords. The whole system was sanctified by the Church, the "opiate of the masses."

Industry, the second and more modern form of production, displaced feudalism. A new class of owners was created, the *capitalists*, whose interests were tied not to land, but to factories. In the capitalist mode, the bourgeoisie monopolizes control of machinery, assembly lines, and other modern means of production plus a financial infrastructure. Now, the labor power of the workers itself has become a commodity to be sold in the market to the highest bidder. By maintaining a surplus labor force— the pool of the unemployed—the price of labor (wages) is depressed. The industrial workers become proletarians where before there were serfs. The emergence of the capitalist mode of production shifted the center of power from landlords to industry. After a period of struggle, the bourgeoisie seized the reins of state from the landed gentry. Now the power of the state is used to provide infrastructure and supports for capitalist manufacture, trade, and finance. This is not to suggest that feudalism disappeared altogether; even today, in certain underdeveloped outposts of the imperial world, landlords collect rents of 60 percent and more. But the controlling interests of the "free market" industrial state are the capitalists.

Origins of the State

Economic exploitation creates *political* relations in society. "The state," Engels wrote, "has not existed from all eternity. There have been societies that did without it, that had no conception of the state and state power. At a certain stage of economic development which was necessarily bound up with the cleavage of society into classes, the state became a necessity owing to this cleavage." [2] Lenin added, "History shows that the state as a special apparatus for coercing people arose only wherever and whenever there appeared a division of society into classes, that is, a division into groups of people some of whom are permanently in a position to appropriate the labor of others." [3] The state, as Lenin concluded, "is an organ of class rule." [4]

[2] Friedrich Engels, *Origin of the Family, Private Property, and the State* (Moscow: Foreign Languages Publishing House, 1951), *Selected Works of Marx and Engels*, Vol. 2: 239.

[3] Lenin, *The State* (1919) (London: Lawrence & Wishart, 1939), *Selected Works*, Vol. 2: 644.

[4] Lenin, *State and Revolution* (New York: International Publishers, 1943), *Selected Works*, Vol. 7: 9.

Social Controls

This is not to suggest that the physical might of the state was the only or even the main means by which the elite protect their position. No social system, however oppressive, habitually uses force where there are less expensive and more efficient means of control available.

Coercion is the most visible form of control, but it is the least reliable. It requires vigilance and an elaborate network of enforcing agents who themselves are loyal to the system, and it raises a constant danger of rebellion. A social system that is forced to fall back on extensive coercion is on the point of collapse.

More efficient than coercion are *market* controls, meaning a structure of material rewards that is keyed to positive behavior, the carrot rather than the stick. Capitalism, for example, is a superior form of exploitation to slavery, because now the workers have the illusion of free choice. Their victimization is masked by what appear to be impersonal "market forces," rather than naked threats by identifiable enemies.

But the most effective form of behavioral control is neither coercion nor the market since both of these depend on external regulation of the individual. *Normative* controls work through education and social training to produce a set of norms and to identify expectations that act as internal regulators of behavior. Individual consciousness is patterned to fit the desired social model. "False consciousness" exists when deceptive morals, ideologies, and religions are used to mask injustice behind a façade of legitimacy and legality. Individuals are betrayed by their own education, and they come to revere the very institutions that exploit them.

In general, normative social controls, supported by a structure of market rewards for cooperative behavior, are capitalism's first line of defense. Only in the last resort is the brute force of the state necessary. Control of the state ensures the smooth operation of all three forms of control. Public law and administration are thus extensions of the relations of production.

The Meaning of Revolution

Marxism prescribes a revolutionary solution to the problem of class rule.[5] The aroused proletariat rips the instruments of control from the bourgeoisie and uses the state apparatus to seize the means of production, thus changing the entire basis of social relations. "Expropriation of the expropriators" gives land to the peasants, factories to the workers. A certain amount of violence may be necessary, since the ruling class will not

[5] Robert C. Tucker, *The Marxian Revolutionary Idea* (New York: W. W. Norton and Company, 1969).

give over its position voluntarily, but this is nothing next to the much greater violence of the everyday capitalist system. As Khrushchev said, "the use or nonuse of violence in the transition of socialism depends on the resistance of the exploiters, on whether the exploiting class itself resorts to violence, rather than on the proletariat." Communism does not romanticize violence, but it regards pacifism as bourgeois sentimentality. No matter how many crumbs the ruling class may let drop from its overloaded tables, the capitalist system will always rest on foundations of injustice and suffering, and it must be overthrown.

Marxism regards revolution not just as desirable, but also as *inevitable*. History is progressive, and each epoch represents an inevitable advance from the preceding period. Capitalism itself outdated all previous forms of social order; no poet could compose an ode to capitalism as flowery as Marx's celebration of its accomplishments. But capitalism rests on class exploitation, so while it is necessary and progressive, it is also unjust. Eventually, it produces the seeds of its own destruction. Mature capitalism is increasingly monopolistic and insatiable in its profit-hunger. Eventually, a point is reached at which the economy is saturated with enterprises, and the relentless search for investment opportunities drives the weaker capitalists back into the proletariat. The competition of the workers becomes more severe, driving wages down, and the misery of the proletariat grows.

Capitalism, which began as a progressive force leading humanity to the possibility of fulfilling all human needs through technology, becomes an obstacle to the next step. The army of the unemployed grows, production cannot be consumed, rates of profit fall, general desperation prevails. Capitalism has created the machinery to satisfy human needs, but it cannot use this machinery rationally. It is driven by its inner dynamic to amplify its contradictions until only revolution can rationalize society again.

Marx's prediction that capitalism would collapse of its own weight has not yet been fulfilled. While he apparently expected the collapse of advanced capitalist states by 1900, these centers have become progressively more secure. Meanwhile, revolution has occurred in the Soviet Union, China, Cuba, and North Vietnam, none of which had complied with the Marxist premise that mature capitalism must precede communism. How has this paradox occurred? In the Soviet view, the answer lies in the subtle ways in which capitalism manipulates the international system.

Lenin's View of the International System

Lenin extended Marx's analysis to a conception of international relations. Capitalism saved itself, according to Lenin, by reaching the stage of imperialism in which international dynamics temporarily ameliorate the conflicts at home. Borrowing from the English economist Hobson, Lenin showed that capitalism depends not only on oppression within the borders of the home state, but also on the external oppression of whole peoples in other parts of the international system. Lenin called this the "internationalization of the class system."

Searching for the Highest Rate of Return. One imperial drive given particular emphasis in Lenin's analysis is the search for the highest rate of return on capital. In the advanced stage of development, the centers of capital become saturated with investment, and the rate of return on new investment is relatively low. Less developed portions of the world still have not had their production raised to its full level of exploitive efficiency, so new capital realizes a higher rate of return. Capitalists therefore compete with each other for investment opportunities and concomitant "spheres of influence" around the world. Imperialism is, in this model, mainly a search for high-return investment opportunities for surplus capital.

Searching for Markets. Another factor that is cited by theorists of imperialism to explain the international nature of capitalism is the search for markets for surplus production. The capitalist system of production rests on a fundamental inefficiency in distribution. The workers must be paid less than the full value of their product if the capitalist is to retain a large share of production for profits. But this means that the workers are unable to buy all that they produce. Other markets must be found for the surplus product. So in addition to providing investment opportunities, colonies and spheres of influence can provide captive markets. This can be seen in many historical cases of colonial empires.

Controlling Raw Materials. A third reason for the internationalization of capitalism is the need to control the richest sources of raw materials wherever they exist. Monopoly capital minimizes the costs of production by suppressing wages *and* by developing the cheapest sources of supply. Thus, the bounties of nature located in the undeveloped world are important prizes for international capital.

In this way, the international class system reduces the poor nations of the world to the status of suppliers of raw materials and cheap labor, as well as captive centers of foreign investment and import dependency. The colonies must not be permitted to develop on their own, free of foreign control, but rather are kept as dependent subsystems in the empire of capital. As in the home system of exploitation, the capitalists reinforce their international position with a preponderance of physical might. Controlling the government of their own states, they use its power to secure their own positions. Naturally, this international system of exploitation is disguised by legal and moral principles that give a veneer of legitimacy to the capitalists' plundering. Much of international law, for example, was written by the imperial states to protect their position; an example is the

Treaty of Berlin (1885) in which the European powers delineated the legal borders within Africa.

The Growth of Imperialism. During the earlier period of this international system of exploitation, the capitalists were very crude in competing with each other for the most profitable prizes. In the days of colonialism, the capitalist states actually fought wars over who was to benefit from which subjugations. In the resulting colonies, bourgeois colonial functionaries developed a political system and an infrastructure (rails, ports, and so on) conducive to profitable investment.

In later years, this system has (with exceptions) become more subtle and durable. Direct control offended the national spirit of the subject peoples, so international capital has relinquished formal colonialism. Titular control has been passed on to the *national bourgeoisie,* a native class of capitalists comprising a subsystem of the international system. The native bourgeoisie are co-opted by giving them a small share in the profits of national exploitation (for example, the royalties from a mining investment). There is a pleasant illusion of self-determination. In case of trouble, the imperialists can use their overwhelming position in the international economic system to deny markets to any subject state that refuses to comply (the boycott of Cuban sugar by the United States, for instance), and the national bourgeoisie can be relied upon to put the recalcitrant former colony back on course. Very occasionally, it is necessary to use direct force to stop a revolution by those who see through this delusional system. In these and other ways, neocolonialism preserves and even extends the imperial system while giving the Third World a false sense of independence.

The development of the imperial system gives capitalism a temporary reprieve, postponing its inevitable collapse. A portion of the gains of imperialism has been passed along to the organized workers in the centers of capital, raising their living standard to prevent an alliance with the unemployed. This, combined with the promotion of racism and ethnic divisions, has enabled the ruling class to forestall revolution. In the poor countries, however, the class basis of the international system is only too visible. Hence, the paradox that revolution seems to be ripest where capitalism is least mature. Stalin explained this phenomenon in *The Foundations of Leninism:*

> Formerly, it was the accepted thing to speak of the existence or absence of objective conditions for the proletarian revolution in individual countries, or, to be more precise, in one or another developed country. Now this point of view is no longer adequate. Now we must speak of the existence of objective conditions for the revolution in the entire system of world imperialist economy as an integral unit . . . .
> Where will the revolution begin? . . .

9   The Soviet Perspective

Where industry is more developed, where the proletariat constitutes the majority, where there is more culture, where there is more democracy—that was the reply given formerly.

No, objects the Leninist theory of revolution (imperialism); *not necessarily where industry is more developed*, and so forth. The front of capital will be pierced where the chain of imperialism is weakest . . . . [6]

Recent experience has reinforced this picture. Revolution may come first in the most progressive states of the underdeveloped world, and the centers of capital may be the last, rather than the first, to fall. But eventually communism will be universal.

The State Withers Away

What form will communism take after the revolution against capitalism succeeds? Marx and Engels were not very specific on this critical question. Because of this ambiguity, it has been possible for Trotskyists and other so-called "independent socialists" in Western countries to build an anti-Soviet propaganda campaign that accuses the Soviet state of "betraying the revolution" and even being "non-Marxist."

One point in this anti-Soviet line is based on Engel's prediction in his *Anti-Duhring* that after the victory of the socialist revolution, the state would "wither away" and be replaced by a society without coercion. Obviously the Soviet state has not disappeared. But "Engel's formula had in view the victory of socialism in all countries or in most countries." The reality of today is that socialism is surrounded by a hostile "capitalist encirclement," so the country "of the victorious revolution must not weaken but must in every way strengthen its state, the state organs, the organs of the intelligence service, the army, if that country does not want to be smashed by the capitalist encirclement." [7] Those who make this criticism are simply "dogmatists" who won't face the most obvious realities. Stalin knew that the old Russia was repeatedly beaten by foreign enemies—the French and English in the Crimean War (1856), the Japanese in 1905, the Germans in 1917—exactly because of its political and industrial backwardness. The new Russia would use the most modern and practical means to ensure the survival of the first Communist advances in a still-capitalist world, and to protect the Russian nation.

"Democracy"

Western critics accuse the Soviet Union of suppressing democratic principles by not adopting the Euro-American concept of "electoral democ-

---

[6] Stalin, *The Foundations of Leninism* (New York: International Publishers, 1931).
[7] Joseph Stalin, "Reply to Comrades" (June 28, 1950), *Pravda*, August 2, 1950.

THE RUSSIAN UPHEAVAL OF 1917

racy" based on the ideas of John Locke and Jean Jacques Rousseau. But in the Soviet view, bourgeois elections are part of the state apparatus of capitalism. Even if balloting were conducted without deceit, and a decision were made by a voting majority, the outcome could not correspond to the objective interests of the masses anyway. False consciousness, perpetuated by class control of the mass media and the educational system, blinds the voters. Pious electoral candidates, most of whom are leading capitalists, further obscure the issue, often using a false demonology of "the Communist threat" to stir up fears. Marxist–Leninists reject this as a meaningless version of "democracy."

Real people's or worker's democracy in the Marxist–Leninist conception emphasizes the objective nature of the social system, rather than the formal decision process. Work is available to all in the Soviet Union, and slums and poverty, which are the hallmark of the Western so-called democracies, do not exist. The substantive question is whether a social system, especially in the ownership of the means of production, serves the interests of the masses. The meaning of social justice is not spurious procedural questions, but this question of real outcomes, substance rather than process.

Russian National Interests

We have seen in a selective discussion of key issues in Soviet ideology that Communist thought is an analytical scheme of universal applicability adapted to the specific situation of the first Communist regime. This adaptation imposed on Marxism–Leninism compelling issues of Russian *national* interest, since defense of Russia became the essence of defending communism. Stalin intertwined national and ideological imperatives in 1927 when he defined a "revolutionary" as "he who without arguments, unconditionally, openly, and honestly . . . is ready to defend and strengthen the USSR, since the USSR is the first proletarian, revolutionary state in the world." Moreover, "to advance the revolutionary movement is impossible without defending the USSR." [8] Thus, an historic accident married communism to the international position and national interests of a particular country.

Marx and Engels had been skeptical of nationalism and predicted its early demise as the interests of both the workers and the capitalists were internationalized. Polish and French workers would be united against capitalists of the two countries, and class, rather than nationality, would survive as the critical line of division. In this view nationalism is nothing more than a "false consciousness" dividing the proletariat.

But the first world war convinced Lenin that Communist ideology would have to adjust to the continued potency of the national idea. The workers of every country dropped all pretense of proletarian internationalism when war broke out and they marched blindly behind the various national flags. The Second International in 1907 had called upon all European socialist parties and trade unions to resist any international slaughter that would serve none but the competing capitalist interests. But these grand expectations were shattered in the summer of 1914 when not a single major socialist party in Europe opposed the war, and the German Social Democratic party, the leading Marxist group, voted unanimously for government war credits. The lesson for Lenin was that communism must join with nationalism rather than oppose it. [9] The power of this merger became visible thirty years later when Communist parties

[8] Stalin, "The International Situation and the Defense of the USSR" (August 1, 1927), *Sochineniya* (Gospolitizdat, Moscow, 1949), Vol. X, p. 61.
[9] Adam B. Ulam, *Expansion and Coexistence: The History of Soviet Foreign Policy 1917–67* (New York: Praeger, 1968), pp. 13, 18–19, and 24–25.

emerged from the second world war leading patriotic resistance movements in China, Indochina, Yugoslavia, Greece, and elsewhere.

The Russian revolutionaries of 1917 found themselves at the head not just of a nationalist movement but of a national *state*. They were an opposition party whose entire organization and philosophy had been geared to destructive action, suddenly in a position of responsibility rather than insurgency. Not just grand principles but physical Soviet realities had to be dealt with.

The first national issue was the challenge of *unifying* the vast Soviet land mass and the diverse peoples of the Soviet state into a cohesive nation under effective administration from Moscow. This would entail giant logistical difficulties under the best of conditions. Here, it was compounded by vexing nationalities problems, from oriental minorities in the Maritime provinces to Ukrainian separatism on the European border, with the Turkic peoples of Central Asia in between. "Russification" of the nationalities of the Caucasus and the Baltic littoral had resisted the best efforts of the Tsars. The first vital necessity imposed upon the Communist government was the amalgamation and federation of many separate pieces into a *Union* of Soviet Socialist Republics.

Also imposed upon the Soviet government was the necessity to insulate the state from excessive economic, cultural, and military *penetration* by the expansionist powers of Western Europe. The Communists used, from 1917–1940, an economic policy of autarky, a political policy of limited intercourse, and a strategic policy designed to equilibrate a European balance of power. Some Western observers dismissed these defensive maneuvers as the paranoia of Stalin overlaid on a traditional Russian xenophobia,[10] but the same actions can also be seen as a realistic response to a distinct external threat.

Another part of the historic Russian policy that preceded communism but has been continued is the *pursuit of influence* in critical border areas: Poland, the Balkans, the Bosporus and Dardanelles Straits, Manchuria, Finland, and elsewhere. The values in these policies are economic, strategic, and even cultural (pan-Slavism), in addition to the impetus of Communist ideology. Indeed, it is argued by some that the whole modern Soviet policy is nothing more than a continuation of the imperialism of the Tsars, even in Korea, Iran (Persia), and Mongolia.[11] The Balkan wars, the Crimean War, the Russo-Japanese War—all anticipated the broad pattern of Soviet policy in later years, except that the Soviet leadership has succeeded where the Tsars failed, as in achieving influence in Eastern Europe. Winston Churchill said that Soviet policy is "a riddle wrapped in

[10] Basil Dmytryshyn, *USSR: A Concise History* (New York: Scribners, 1965), pp. 143–53, 200–207, 247–59.

[11] Tsarist and Communist imperialism are compared in Michael Karpovitch, "Russian Imperialism or Communist Aggression," 34 *The New Leader* (June 4, 1951): 18.

a mystery inside an enigma. . . . But . . . the key is Russian national interest." [12]

The relative position of various national interests and ideological goals in Soviet foreign policy changes over time. But it surely cannot be said that the USSR is nothing more than "a conspiracy disguised as a state." Indeed, it is probable that Russian national demands have overshadowed questions of Communist principle, particularly in later years.

The Soviet View of the International System

The interplay of national and ideological themes in Russian policy can be seen in the Soviet interpretation of major events in international relations since 1917.

World War I and the Russian Revolution

Until 1917, the capitalist countries controlled the entire international system. All regions not part of the advanced capitalist world were dominated directly or indirectly by it, and exploited as subject markets and sources of raw materials. The capital-exporting countries divided the world among themselves, and periodic readjustments, sometimes involving wars, occurred. Russians call World War I "the Imperialist War," because they see it as having been a struggle between rival imperialists for the most desirable spoils.

The capitalist countries understood from the outset that the Bolshevik Revolution of 1917 posed a threat to their international system. Britain, France, the United States, and other imperialist powers sent an international army to join domestic counterrevolutionaries (the "White Armies") in a struggle that lasted from 1917 to 1921. (The United States played a relatively minor role, with 14,000 troops and 1000 casualties. The intervention is relatively unknown to Americans today, though it is well-remembered by Russians.) For a while, the tides of battle gave the imperial powers hope of preventing Russia's defection from the capitalist world, but heroic Red armies finally prevailed and revolution was secured. From the outset, the hostility of the capitalist world to socialism was manifest. But could it have been otherwise, when the very existence of the Soviet Union would only encourage other revolutionary movements?

The capitalists did succeed in preventing other revolutions from developing for many years by a combination of clever anti-Soviet propaganda and repression of revolutionary movements. The Soviet Union was an

---

[12] Winston Churchill, *The Gathering Storm* (Boston: Houghton Mifflin, 1948), p. 449.

"It's English, You Know!"

Source: Thomas Nast, 1885.

island in a hostile sea, and as such, needed to spend huge portions of its resources to keep up its defenses. Nonetheless, great progress was made from 1917 to 1940 in developing a revolutionary society in Russia, and in rebuilding the Soviet economy from the ravages of World War I.

World War II and Subsequent Hostilities

World War II erupted when a particularly virulent form of imperialism took hold in Germany, which had been a late starter in the imperialist division of the world and was determined to extend its hegemony at the

Participation of American armies in the 1918–19 invasion to overthrow the Bolshevik Russian Revolution is now virtually forgotten in the United States. But it is well remembered in the Soviet Union as proof of the innate hostility of capitalism to socialism. Here the bodies of 111 American soldiers killed in Russia lie on the Army Piers in Hoboken, New Jersey.

Source: The New York Times, November 23, 1919. Reprinted by permission of Wide World Photos, Inc.

expense of the other capitalist states, making war with the Western powers inevitable. The lunatic Hitler also proposed to lead a holy war against communism—that is, against the Soviet Union. The German-Italian-Japanese "Anti-Comintern Pact" led some of the Western powers to flirt briefly with the idea of neutrality, to "turn Hitler East" and "let the Nazis and Communists bleed each other dry." Harry S. Truman, then a U.S. senator, said on the occasion of the Nazi invasion of Russia, "If we see that Germany is winning we ought to help Russia and if Russia is winning we ought to help Germany and in that way let them kill as many as possible." (*New York Times,* June 24, 1941). But Hitler's expansionist aims forced the other capitalist states into a wartime alliance with the Soviet Union. The United States and Britain, still deeply anti-Communist and dedicated to the overthrow of the Soviet government, temporarily suspended this goal to deal with the more immediate danger of fascist Germany.

The Western powers did succeed, however, in shifting most of the burden of the European war to the Soviet Union. The great victory over fascism was paid for by Russian blood and by the heroic efforts of the Soviet people while the capitalist allies delayed opening the "second front"

The Logic of National Perceptions

on the West until 1944. Of the 22 million Allied lives lost in the war, an estimated 20 million were lost by the Soviet Union. By comparison, the United States, though it made an important financial and military contribution, lost only 300 thousand (1½ percent of the Soviet loss). The Nazi invaders destroyed and plundered over 1100 Russian villages and towns, razing many to the ground, while the Western allies suffered only minor damage. Many historians hold that the Soviet Union came very close to defeating the Germans single-handedly. Churchill said that Russia's fighting men "did the main work of tearing the guts out of the German army."

These great human and material sacrifices did bring some gains for Soviet revolutionary and national interests after the war. The Red Armies were decisive in liberating a number of countries from fascist occupation in 1945–46, particularly in Eastern Europe. Following the war, socialist governments were established with Soviet aid in Poland, Hungary, Bulgaria, Czechoslovakia, Rumania, Albania, and the Soviet-occupied sector of (East) Germany. Other Communist movements, with lesser amounts of Soviet aid, established socialist regimes in Yugoslavia and China. Within three years after the war, the Soviet Union had moved from isolation in a world of capitalist powers to partnership and leadership in a Communist bloc comprising half the world's population! Thus, the anti-Communist fanaticism of the fascists had a reverse effect.

As in 1917, the Western capitalist powers wasted no time developing a propaganda offensive against socialist gains. The establishment of Communist governments in Eastern Europe was characterized as "Soviet imperialism," while the restoration of capitalist forms in the West European countries was, of course, portrayed as the will of the people. The imperialists demanded that the financiers and landlords be returned to their "proper" position in the East European states, including even East Germany. The Soviet Union, it would seem, was expected to reproduce exactly the conditions that led to the two world wars and then sit back politely and wait for the next invasion. Instead, the Soviet Union committed itself to the establishment of a new order in Eastern Europe in cooperation with its new allies. The peoples of the Communist world were not deceived by Western propaganda, though the Western governments did succeed in reenforcing the false anti-Communist perceptions of their own peoples in some cases.

By 1950, the new imperialist NATO alliance system was developed against the Soviet Union and its allies. More than fifty hostile military bases were constructed by the Americans all around the Soviet periphery, reinforced by the American lead in the development of atomic weapons. This capitalist encirclement forced the socialist states to spend an inordinately large portion of their productive efforts on defensive capabilities to prevent imperialist adventures. It is ironic that the imperialists have managed to convince some people that the Soviet Union has aggressive designs, when it is the Americans who keep their bases far from home on the borders of the Soviet heartland, and not the other way around! Leonid Brezhnev, General Secretary of the Central Committee of the Communist Party of the Soviet Union, protested on March 30, 1971,

> The peoples will not be deceived by the attempts to ascribe to the Soviet Union intentions which are alien to it. We declare with a full sense of responsibility: we have no territorial claims on anyone whatsoever, we threaten no one, and have no intention of attacking anyone, we stand for the free and independent development of all nations. But let no one, for his part, try to talk to us in terms of ultimatums and strength.[13]

In the less developed portions of the world still under their control, the imperialists have intensified their exploitation of Afro-Asian and Latin American peoples and resources. These poorer countries have, in most cases, been given technical independence, but they remain under the control of neoimperialism through reactionary puppet governments, military interventions, and the manipulation of international markets. Within the capitalist countries, privileged segments of the working class have been given a small share in the wealth extracted from the Third World to buy their complicity in the imperial system.

The Soviet view finds the capitalist countries aggressive and the revolutionary countries defensive. The revolutionary movement is strong, but its final victory is postponed by the might of the imperialists. The Soviet Union has assumed the burden of defending the revolutionary advances that have been gained against imperialist reaction, while giving extensive aid to advance new anti-imperialist movements where they develop. The world system thus consists of an *imperialist bloc* led by the United States, a *socialist bloc* led by the USSR, and the *Third World nations* at various stages of development toward socialism but in many cases still dominated by the imperialists.

American Economic Imperialism

From the Soviet perspective, the United States is uniquely important in modern imperialism. American foreign investors play critical roles in the economies of over seventy-five foreign nations. The gross value of goods and services produced in foreign countries by American-owned facilities is over $200 billion per year. If we were to consider United States enterprises abroad as an aggregate, they would comprise the fourth largest "country" in the world, with a gross annual product larger than that of

[13] M. Gribanov, *Security for Europe* (Moscow: Novosti Press Agency Publishing House, 1972), p. 19. Originally stated at 24th Congress of the Communist Party of the Soviet Union.

any country except the United States itself, Japan, or the Soviet Union.[14] Some large American firms dwarf the national economies in which they operate. The annual sales of Exxon, for example, exceeded $42 billion in 1974, while the sales volume of General Motors was greater than $31 billion,[15] making each a larger economic entity than over one hundred states in the international system.

For some small countries, the operations and decisions of one or two large private investors are more important to national welfare than are the decisions of the highest domestic political officials, resulting in external control. The lust for overseas investments exists mainly because American investments in less developed countries return, according to Marxist computations, higher rates of profit than is normal within the home countries of the capitalists. This is, of course, a boon to the Americans, but a disastrous drain of wealth from the poor countries. United States investments in Latin America, for example, totaled less than $4 billion from 1950 to 1965. The returns on these investments that went back to the United States during this period were over $11 billion, almost three times as much.[16] For many individual countries, the outflow of profits *to* the United States is two to four times as great as the inflow of investment *from* the United States *every year*. This is one crude indicator of the exploitative character of the system of American economic dominance.

The highly favorable economic position of the American capitalists is secured and advanced by military force, just as the earlier imperialists used conquests and invasions to gain and protect a foothold for economic penetration. The United States protects its traders and investors by maintaining American armed forces in no fewer than sixty-four countries, truly a record in the history of empires. Naturally the hundreds of bases that are involved are rationalized in terms of "protecting" these countries from "Soviet imperialism" and "internal subversion," the American euphemisms for revolution. The American world system reaches farther and deeper than any previous imperial system in history, approximating a truly worldwide system of military, political, and economic control.[17]

The United States has achieved this dominant position by pushing aside older imperial systems, and also by extending the range of the imperial system beyond its former reach partly as a result of two world wars. The United States entered each of these wars only after the other major capitalist powers were already weakened, and it emerged with the most

---

[14] Leo Model, "The Politics of Private Foreign Investment," 45 *Foreign Affairs* no. 4 (July 1967): 640–41.

[15] *Fortune*, August 1975, p. 163.

[16] N. Simonia, *The Third World and the Struggle for Economic Independence* (Moscow: Novosti Press Agency Publishing House, 1972).

[17] V. Panov, *The Economic Weapons of Neo-Colonialism* (Moscow: Novosti Press Agency Publishing House, 1972).

intact economy. Meanwhile, it exacted colonial and other enriching concessions from its allies and defeated enemies. Indeed it even went so far as to colonize partly the European countries themselves. In 1963, the United States represented 72 percent of all foreign investments in Britain and American firms sold 75 percent of the accounting machines in France.[18] Of course, the Europeans are not quite as helpless as the smaller states, and they are attempting to counterbalance the weight of American economic power by developing institutions to defend their own interests.

In addition to assuming the colonial enterprises of the older capitalist states, the United States has also deepened its penetration of the world market areas that were formerly not fully exploited. This is reflected in the spread of foreign branches of United States banks all over the world. Table 1–1 shows how bank branches have grown, especially in recent years, and how this growth is due partly to a great increase in the number of countries in which United States financial institutions operate. Sometimes, the subject governments do not resist the invasion by United States interests but rather welcome it. This is partly because of the control of these governments already mentioned, but it is also because of the poverty of these countries from long years of exploitation. As a result of the extraction of capital from them for many years, they are not able to develop enterprises on their own, and consequently depend on outside aid. This makes them vulnerable to American firms looking for profitable investments, and of course it makes the future of these countries even more difficult.

Owing to these patterns of investment and ownership of foreign production, the American role in the world imperial system is huge and growing. American capitalist imperialism dominates the economic and political order in many countries, often *with substantially negative effects in the dominated countries.*

We turn now to a second Soviet proposition, that this imperialist behavior is rooted in the nature of American capitalism. This theory that *imperialism is caused by capitalism* distinguishes the socialist view from

TABLE 1–1   U.S. Bank Branches Outside the United States

	1918	1939	1950	1955	1960	1967	1975
# of Branches	61	89	95	111	124	298	732
# of Countries	16	22	24	26	33	55	n.a.

Sources: Through 1967, Harry Magdoff, *The Age of Imperialism* (New York: Monthly Review Press, 1969), p. 56. Copyright © by Harry Magdoff, and reprinted with permission of Monthly Review Press. For 1975, Andrew F. Brimmer and Frederick R. Dahl, "The Growth of U.S. Banking Abroad," *Journal of Finance* (May 1975): pp. 341–363, p. 346.

[18] Christopher Layton, *Trans-Atlantic Investments* (Boulogne-sur-Seine, France: The Atlantic Institute, 1966), pp. 13–16.

other critiques of American foreign policy. American liberals, for example, also tend to see United States foreign policy in a critical light, but trace its failings to excessive anti-Communist zeal, or to misperceptions of the objective situation in other countries, rather than to the basic nature of capitalism. If capitalism *inherently* tends to be imperialistic, the problem of imperialism will be more difficult to solve within a capitalistic framework than if the cause of imperialism is the more superficial issue of mistaken policies. Thus, the relationship between capitalism and imperialism is a critical difference between socialist views of American imperialism and other theories.[19]

 There are three needs that make capitalism externalize itself to imperialism in the Leninist view: (1) the need for *raw materials,* (2) the thirst for captive *export markets,* and especially (3) the search for secure, high-yield *foreign investment opportunities.* All three of these dynamics operate in the American case.

1. Raw Materials

The huge American industrial apparatus consumes immense quantities of raw materials imported from abroad, without which it would suffer a severe decline. While the United States was a net exporter of raw materials until 1920, since that year it has been increasingly dependent on imports, including reliance on foreign sources of vital petroleum fuels. Sixty-two industrial raw materials are listed by the Department of Defense as "strategic and critical materials," crucial for the warmaking ability of the United States, of which more than half of the annual consumption must be imported. For most of these materials, more than 80 percent of the supply is imported. It is obviously in the interest of American capitalism to secure these foreign sources of supply and to control the cheapest sources of raw materials. Both goals are served by American politico-military domination of the supplier countries.

2. Profits and Foreign Markets

Serious as it is, the raw material issue is a relatively small point compared to the other two themes of the Leninist analysis: the issues of controlling foreign *markets* and *investment* opportunities. The very *profits* of American firms are tied closely to the control of other countries. To assess this proposition, consider the relative magnitude of foreign sales by American producers compared to sales within the United States. Taking the total of exports and sales abroad by American-owned enterprises located outside the United States, the foreign market is equal to approximately 25 per-

[19] This critical distinction is developed in Robert Tucker, *American Foreign Policy and the Radical Left* (Baltimore: Johns Hopkins University Press, 1971).

cent of the total output of U.S.-owned farms, factories, and mines, and a somewhat higher percent of profits.[20] (Furthermore, while in 1961 American manufacturers exported $15 billion in goods and foreign affiliates of American industries sold $25 billion in goods, in 1970 the values increased to $35 billion in exports from the U.S. and $90 billion for sales by foreign affiliates. Thus in that decade exports increased by 133 percent, while the sales of foreign affiliates skyrocketed by almost 400 percent.[21]) A brief look at specific corporations reveals the extent to which individual manufacturers rely on foreign markets. To take some firms at random, 75 percent of Uniroyal's net income for 1970 came from abroad; Eastman Kodak, 19 percent; H.J. Heinz, 44 percent; General Motors, 9 percent; and F.W. Woolworth, 61 percent.[22] Orville Freeman, Secretary of Agriculture under Presidents Kennedy and Johnson, has said that "If American companies were deprived of their foreign earnings, the effect upon our economy would be devastating. Many companies would not be able to survive." [23]

3. Foreign Investment Opportunities

But even these figures understate the linkages between imperialism and class interests of American capitalists in the socialist view. An important additional point is the *concentration* of foreign interests compared to the domestic American economy. Forty-five firms control *more than half* of all United States foreign investments; 163 firms control more than 80 percent. Thus, the foreign operations of American capital are far more monopolistic than the domestic operations: the largest and most powerful corporations tend to have a disproportionate interest in the foreign market.

From the socialist perspective this is significant because concentrated economic interests are better organized and more influential politically than dispersed economic interests. Thus, a large industry that is concentrated, such as the General Electric Company, has more influence than a large industry that is dispersed, such as the retail drugstores, even though the total sales of all retail drugstores taken together may be larger than General Electric. The huge concentration of power in the foreign investment and export sectors gives added weight to these interests.

The Military-Industrial Complex

Another link between imperialism and the interests of capitalism is the military-industrial complex, even though it serves a domestic rather than

[20] Harry Magdoff, *The Age of Imperialism* (New York: Monthly Review Press, 1969), pp. 173–202, esp. 177–78.

[21] "The Multinational Corporation and the World Economy," Committee on Finance, United States Senate, 1973, p. 12.

[22] Ibid., from chart on pp. 14–15.

[23] *The New York Times*, March 5, 1972, p. III/16.

a foreign market. Military spending comprises another 10 percent of the profits of capitalism and again more for large firms than small ones. In addition, a large percentage of the United States labor force is involved in defense production. In 1969, more than three-quarters of factory jobs in San Diego and Wichita were defense-related. If we add defense to exports and foreign investments, and count only the largest firms, we may estimate that the world structure accounts for 35–40 percent of the profits of the top capitalist interests. The proposition is demonstrated: there is a clear linkage between capitalism as a socioeconomic system and the tendency to imperialism that is seen in American foreign policy.

How does this connection between the economic sectors of capitalism and the political policies of the United States government operate? There are both direct and indirect linkages. By studying the personal backgrounds, career origins, and bureaucratic job cycles of the 234 top American foreign policy decision-makers from 1944 through 1960, the years in which the American empire absorbed the older imperial structures and became the dominant force in the world system, it can be shown that a relatively small number of individuals circulated among the top policy bureaus during these years. Moreover, about 60 percent of these came from big-business, investment, and major law firm backgrounds.[24] There is an equally impressive circulation of personnel between the armed services and the top defense-supply firms. For example, more than 2,000 retired officers above the rank of colonel or naval captain are now in executive positions with the largest defense corporations. One linkage between imperialism and capitalism is the shared interests of the top capitalists and key government officials in the United States.

Another link is the influence that foreign-oriented capitalists are believed to exercise within the Congress and the American public. The Pentagon alone commanded in 1968 a force of 6,140 public relations officers assigned to sell the armed services point of view around the world. Of these, 339 were "legislative liaison" lobbyists assigned to the United States Congress. In addition, the private defense firms, the exporters, and the foreign investment interests all had lobbying and public relations operations of their own, including the employment of the most sophisticated Washington law firms to exercise influence with members of Congress.

Capitalism and National Interest

Another connection between the economic interests of capitalism and the political behavior of American officials operates through the perception of most officials that what is good for capitalism is good for America. In al-

---

[24] Gabriel Kolko, *The Roots of American Foreign Policy* (Boston: Beacon Press, 1969), pp. 16–26.

locating defense-spending, for example, members of Congress compete to get the juiciest prizes and largest military projects for their own districts. Mendel Rivers was the chairman of the House Armed Services Committee, which is supposed to keep military expenditures under control. Mr. Rivers' Charleston, S.C., district had an air force base, an army depot, a naval shipyard, a marine air station, the Parris Island boot camp, two naval hospitals, a naval station, a naval supply center, a naval weapons station, a submarine training center, a Polaris missile facility, an Avco plant, a Lockheed plant, a GE plant, and a Sikorsky installation. The annual military payroll in this district alone is $2 billion. It has been said that if any more defense plants were put in Charleston, it would sink.[25] Naturally, Representative Rivers was only too happy to go along with the military-industrial complex, justifying his position in terms of defending the "free world" (the international capitalist system) from "Soviet imperialism" (revolutionary movements against Western imperialism).

This is the theory of American imperialism as viewed by Soviet observers and socialists around the world. The United States is the dominant power in the global system of imperialism that exercises control almost everywhere outside the Communist world. Domination takes military, political, and economic forms, and is motivated by interests that are rooted in American capitalism. Thus, Lenin's perception that capitalism tends to produce imperialism because of foreign investment dynamics, the need for export outlets, and the search for cheap sources of raw materials describes, in the Soviet view, the reality of American behavior today. The theory of American capitalist imperialism is not just a rhetorical device employed by Soviet propaganda, but a real analysis of America's role in the world that is shared by Soviet Communists and other observers who consider themselves anti-imperialist.

While the theory of imperialism and the role of the United States in the international system dominates the Soviet view, two other questions must be raised: the position of Europe and relations with China.

The Soviet View of Europe

Europe is the most immediate geopolitical issue in Soviet foreign policy. The Soviet Union has been subjected to three major invasions from the West in the past 150 years—twice from Germany. Any Soviet government would have as a paramount interest the question of European security and defense. Today, these traditional issues are compounded because three (USSR, Britain, and France) of the world's six nuclear powers are European, and the line of division between the capitalist and socialist worlds

[25] *Newsweek*, June 9, 1969, p. 76.

runs right through the heart of Europe. On the Western side of the line of demarcation, the NATO alliance members maintain armed forces in excess of 5 million troops organized in twenty-four divisions, armed with 7200 nuclear warheads and an abundance of conventional air, sea, and land material. On the Communist side of the line, the Warsaw Pact nations maintain a defensive shield against this massive force. All of the world's largest economies (except Japan) are engaged in this massive confrontation of forces in Central Europe. Quite naturally, the issue of security in Europe looms large in the Soviet view.

From the beginning, the Soviet Foreign Ministry objected to the formation of the NATO alliance in 1949. The Soviet government favored an all-European security conference to conclude a nonaggression, collective security treaty instead of constructing two opposed systems of alliances. Signatories to the treaty would pledge themselves to refrain from attacking one another and renounce the threat and use of force. Hostile coalitions would be prohibited, and in the case of an armed attack on one or several of the signatories, the others would regard this as an attack on themselves and would render the necessary military aid. This system would be maintained by the setting up of political and military consultative committees.

The Western states consistently rejected this proposal, doubting Soviet intentions and, in the Soviet view, preferring to maintain the network of hostile and aggressive alliances in the hope of restoring capitalism in Eastern Europe or at least preventing the further spread of revolutionary movements. Thus, the socialist states were forced to form the Warsaw Pact counteralliance in their own defense. The defensive nature of the Warsaw Pact organization is shown by the provision that, in case of the discontinuance of the North Atlantic (Western) alliance, the pact would be invalidated automatically. Thus, according to the Soviet view, the responsibility for the system of cold war alliances lies with the West.

To accomplish the key Soviet goal of preventing an attack from the West in the absence of a European security system, three elements of Soviet policy are paramount:

1. Governments sympathetic to the USSR and socialist in orientation must be maintained in the belt of East European countries that lie between the Soviet heartland and the powerful countries of Western Europe, especially Germany (see Figure 1–1). (In the West, these East European states are considered a "buffer zone" of "satellite states.")

2. Germany, the most powerful and historically the most aggressive country of Europe, responsible for the terrible suffering and depradations of the war, must be neutralized as a threat. Germany cannot be permitted to reunify under a capitalist government that is still tied to the imperialist camp. Preserving the division of Germany into East and West is a necessary and expedient means of reducing the German threat. A government sympathetic to the USSR is maintained in the East.

FIGURE 1–1 Eastern Europe as a Buffer for Soviet Defense

3. The military powers of the West European countries must be counterbalanced by the military power of the USSR and the East European countries. This is the mission of the Warsaw Pact.

Soviet policy since World War II has achieved all three of these aims in Europe. As an outcome of the war, Poland, Czechoslovakia, Hungary, Rumania, Albania, Yugoslavia, and Bulgaria are now Communist countries, most of them reliable allies against the possibilities of a West-

The Logic of National Perceptions

ern invasion. The important location of Czechoslovakia, through which there is direct access to Soviet territory (See Figure 1–1), helps to explain why the Soviet Union invaded that country in 1968 rather than risk its move out of the Soviet camp and into a friendly relationship with West Germany. Such a turn would have jeopardized the entire Soviet–Eastern European defense system.

The problem of the immensely powerful country of Germany, once so threatening to the Soviet Union, has been reduced by permanent partition, and by the Soviet–American agreement at Helsinki in 1975, which recognizes as permanent the post–World War II boundaries. The division of Germany into two zones, originally a byproduct of a 1945 military convenience, had become a permanent reality prior to Helsinki. The USSR obviously cannot allow the zone under its influence (East Germany) to rejoin the Western half while West Germany maintains a capitalist social system and an alliance with imperialism. In addition, the Soviet Union strenuously opposes nuclear development in West Germany. An aggressive West Germany armed with atomic bombs would have nightmarish consequences not only in the Soviet Union, but also in Poland, Czechoslovakia, and other East European countries.

Finally, to secure control in East Europe and to counterbalance NATO, Soviet and other Communist forces in Eastern Europe are maintained at levels superior to Western ground forces. Communist divisions in central Europe have outnumbered those of the NATO countries since the second world war. While the West considers this a menace to the capitalist international order, in Moscow it is seen as a simple necessity for preserving the Socialist Commonwealth.

In recent years, a number of outstanding issues in the postwar division of Europe have been resolved. A spirit of détente has led to a gradual lessening of the implacable hostility of the Western states to the socialist side. A major event in this trend was the decision of Charles de Gaulle to withdraw France from the NATO integrated command, declaring as his intention the development of a united Europe from the Atlantic to the Russian Ural mountains. This paralleled a tenfold increase in trade between Eastern and Western Europe between 1960 and 1970—a trend that now has even affected American attitudes toward trade with the East.

The most significant development has been the conclusion of a treaty between the Soviet Union and West Germany in 1970, paving the way for the solution of all outstanding questions between these two crucial countries. The realistic *Ostpolitik* of West Germany has created the possibility of an acceptance of the de facto situation in Europe as the basis for new relations in this region. In particular, Germany accepted the Oder-Neisse line as Poland's western border with East Germany, and recognized the permanence of the two Germanies. The two signatories also pledged themselves to refrain from the use or threat of force and to guide their relations by the principles of the United Nations Charter.

The treaty was followed a year later (1971) by the signing of a four-power agreement on West Berlin by France, the United States, Britain, and the Soviet Union. The four-power agreement detailed a basis for relations between that city and West and East Germany, prohibited the use of force, and resolved many technical issues that had been barriers to the relaxation of tensions and the opening of borders for the freer passage of visitors. Although this agreement did not satisfy all sides, it did lay a realistic basis for the improvement of relations, bypassing the insistence on absolute principles that always leads to an impasse. Thus, some of the key issues in central Europe have been resolved by political moderation.

The Soviet Union has paralleled this "peace offensive" with a renewed call for a general European Security Conference. In 1966, at a conference in Bucharest, Rumania, the Soviet Union and six other socialist countries proposed the holding of an all-European conference on security and cooperation. It aimed at expanding nondiscriminatory East-West trade and at reducing military tension in Europe by gradual dissolution of military blocs, dismantling of foreign bases, withdrawal of foreign troops, and renunciation of the use of force.

At a subsequent meeting in Budapest in 1970, this proposal was expanded to emphasize economic, scientific, and environmental issues with a view to promoting political cooperation between the European states. And, most significantly, the Budapest Memorandum proposed the establishment of a permanent all-European political body to deal with questions of security and cooperation.

These proposals are greeted by grave doubts in the West, where they are perceived as a baited trap designed to weaken NATO and Western unity. There is also division of opinion in the West concerning the Mutual and Balanced Force Reduction talks, the European Security Conference and the resulting Helsinki Agreement, and Soviet–American discussions on reducing Washington's nuclear arsenal in Europe in return for a reduction of Soviet tank strength in Eastern Europe. Nevertheless, despite the temporary setback which Soviet-Cuban intervention in Angola caused for the growth of East-West détente, it is clear to all parties that, suspicions aside, a gradual lessening of tensions is indeed underway.

The Soviet View of China

The persistent conflict between the Soviet Union and China has assumed growing importance in the Soviet world outlook in recent years, contributing to the desire for reduced tensions in Europe. This antagonism is a very old issue, predating the introduction of communism. The historical fact of an expansionist pre-Soviet Russia relentlessly pressing eastward has naturally brought conflict between the two giants who share a

7,000 mile border. Issues dividing the USSR and China today include both ideological questions and historical national interests that would conflict regardless of ideology.

National Border Disputes

Western Region. The border may be separated into three general regions of conflict. In the Western region the 1,850 mile border between Soviet Central Asia and China's Sinkiang Province divides homogeneous ethnic minorities (Uighurs, Tadzhiks, Kazaks) whose movements do not always observe the legal boundaries. China conducts its atomic testing and some atomic production in Sinkiang, raising other special issues. The most serious problem from the Soviet point of view is that China controls the Ili Valley gateway to Turkestan, making the protection of Soviet Central Asia militarily difficult. This "Great Gateway of the Nations"— the Dzungarian Gates—was the route through which the hordes of Genghis Khan invaded Europe, and it has long been a problem of Russian (and later Soviet) defense.

Eastern Region. In the Eastern region the 2,300 mile border separating the Soviet maritime regions and Pacific ports from Chinese Manchuria is a special problem. These Soviet Far Eastern assets are vital commercial and military links, but they are logistically remote from the Soviet heartland and are difficult to defend. On the Chinese side of the border is the main Manchurian industrial region, which confers logistical advantages. China's claims for revisions of the existing line of demarcation, based on historical issues, would bring Chinese power right up to the city limits of Khabarovsk and in other ways substantially weaken the Soviet position. Therefore, the Soviet Union insists on the principle of sanctity of treaties, and denies the ambitious Chinese claims.

Central Region. In the remaining region, the 2,650 mile Chinese border with Outer Mongolia, the issue is not border delineation or the strategic balance, but the question of control over Outer Mongolia itself. This quasi-independent nation is now under Soviet influence. China asserts a historical right to suzerainty—a claim that the Soviets regard as pure troublemaking.

This 7,000 mile border cannot be directly defended mile by mile, so defense depends on a system of mutual threats and general military preparations. Hundreds of thousands of troops are arrayed on each side. Several skirmishes resulting in deaths occurred during the late 1960s and the early 1970s, and pessimistic predictions speak forebodingly of the potential for much larger encounters.

Ideological Disputes

In addition to this conflict of national interests, there are key *ideological* issues in dispute between the two Communist giants. Since the death of Stalin in 1953, Chinese propaganda has portrayed the Soviet Union as a "new imperialism" equally abhorrent to that of the Western capitalists. China has called for "alternative paths to socialism" in the Communist bloc, in which the central determination of bloc policy by the Soviet Union would be ended in favor of a concept of self-determination by each country. China has even laid claim to the mantle of ideological leadership, portraying Mao Tse-tung as a contemporary and co-equal of Lenin, while the present Soviet leadership is seen as a gang of bureaucratic hacks. Chinese propaganda has made virulent attacks of all kinds on the intentions and integrity of the Soviet Party.

The Soviets reject these principles as irresponsible and ill-founded claims motivated by wild ambition. Both "alternative paths" and Chinese leadership are invalidated by the simple reality that only Soviet might, backed up by the huge Soviet economy, can in fact defend the revolutionary states from capitalist encirclement and promote revolutionary gains in the Third World. Only Soviet nuclear power deters the American colossus—the Chinese capability could never do it alone. And only Soviet technology and production can supply the most advanced weapons and aircraft to aid the struggling peoples of Indochina and the Middle East. Thus, the Soviet Union is the shield and the arsenal of the revolutionary world.

In addition, the "alternative paths to socialism" slogan causes disunity in the socialist camp and creates a false ideal of relativism. The Soviets have never denied that revolutionary principles must adjust to the special conditions in each country, but they firmly reject the extreme "go-it-alone" lengths to which this idea is carried by China. The ideal form is collective determination of bloc policy by international party congresses, as practiced since 1945 and even earlier. The Soviet Union does not propose to rule by arbitrary and unilateral fiat, but neither does it propose to allow purely national interests within the bloc to rise above the collective interests of the bloc as a whole. The Brezhnev Doctrine pronounced in 1968 in justification of the Warsaw Pact's invasion and occupation of a liberalizing Czechoslovakia reaffirms the primacy of the collective socialist good over the particular interests of any single country within the camp. United, the socialist world will prosper; but divided it will fall to the hostile capitalist encirclement.

The Soviet Union itself, it is argued, must be the first among equals. The USSR was the first revolutionary state and spawned the others. The Soviet Communist Party is the direct heir of Lenin and is ideologically and materially best prepared for the leadership position. Thus, the Soviets reject the ideological as well as the territorial claims of the Chinese adventurists.

Summary of the Soviet View

The Soviet point of view is a combination of Russian national interests and Communist ideological principles. The contemporary international system is seen as largely unjust and threatening to the Soviet Union, whose main role is to defend itself and its allies and to combat international injustice.

The dominant theme in the Soviet view of the international system is the *theory of imperialism*. Capitalism, which is still the social system in most of the advanced and powerful countries, is supported by class exploitation, and imperialism is simply the international expression of this exploitation. Capitalist systems need empires that provide (1) raw materials, (2) markets for domestic exports and (3) high returns on investments. The imperialist states therefore dominate most of the poorer countries.

The Communist countries have defected from this international class system. As first and strongest socialist state, the USSR is the natural leader. The military might of the imperalists is such that direct challenge to the imperial system is not possible. But it is the obligation of the USSR to defend the Communist states that already exist from capitalist-inspired counterrevolution or invasion, and insofar as possible, to help other countries on the path to revolution. As the leading imperialist power, the United States has a special role in the international system. It controls more than half of the imperialist system of exploitation, and it is immensely powerful militarily. It maintains a vast network of alliances designed at the minimum to keep control of all countries not already Communist, and possibly even to "roll back communism" (that is, recapture the liberated countries for the imperial system). The United States is also important in that it is most skillful in hiding its true position behind moral and ideological disguises which continue to befuddle many non-Marxists.

The capitalist world encircles socialism, and only the Soviet shield protects and advances the world revolutionary movement. Yet a dissident faction within the socialist camp, led by China, would divide and disunify the revolutionary states and create an internal opposition to the Soviet leadership. Only the solidity of the Warsaw bloc in Eastern Europe prevents renewed aggression from the capitalist world. The unity of the socialist commonwealth must stand above the claims of factions within individual countries. Chinese adventurism must be opposed at every point, and the solidarity of the revolutionary world must be maintained. Only in this way can the final victory of socialism be achieved over the long run.

2

The American

Perspective

Ironically, it may be easier for American students today to entertain a friendly picture of the Soviet Union or China than to appreciate the role of an official of their own country. After a quarter century of inflated cold war rhetoric, there is a new willingness to take another look at the Communist side, but the failings of one's own country, denied by the official orthodoxy, seem all the more glaring. Yet perceptual analysis need not imply that every facet of a given perspective is "correct"—only that there is a strong internal logic that is consistent with the evidence when it is ordered in a certain way.

Roots of the American World View

Whereas Marxist thought begins with a theory of class conflict and revolution, the American world view turns on questions of political freedom and tyranny. "Freedom"—understood as self-determination, majority rule, and the right of dissent—is the highest goal in the hierarchy of core values. "Give me liberty or give me death," demanded Patrick Henry. When Americans evaluate other social systems, the first question they ask is usually the degree of freedom of speech and religion, the right to vote, and tolerance of dissent. Political liberty is put above economic well-being and questions of economic justice.

The relative unconcern of Americans for class injustices, compared to other peoples, has been traced to the lack of a feudal experience. Absentee landlordism and other abuses of feudalism left in many other countries a bitter heritage of class conflict which was much less pronounced here.[1] The promise of open land beyond the frontier before 1900 made America a "land of opportunity" where wealth was the direct reward for hard work and poverty the punishment for laziness or stupidity.[2] The early settlers who came to the New World sought not class revolution, but religious tolerance (for example, Puritans, Mennonites) and economic opportunity. Capitalism itself demanded a free market, entrepreneurial liberty, and political self-determination at least for the commercial classes.

These origins were consistent with the evolution of a philosophy of the "social contract." In this theory, the state is constituted by freely consenting individuals to protect the security and advance the common interests of society. Government "derives its just powers from the consent of the governed." Revolution is justified, not in terms of class upheaval, but as a legitimate response to political tyranny.

The principal danger to liberty is the inherent tendency of government to expand without limitation and to extinguish the rights of citizens. Power corrupts and absolute power corrupts absolutely. Tyranny is averted and governmental power is limited in the United States by constitutional restraints, majority rule, guaranteed minority rights, checks and balances between 80,000 separately elected governmental units, and the separation of executive, legislative, and judicial powers. Power is at every point balanced against power: civilian control of the military, judicial oversight of the constitutionality of legislative and executive actions, state versus federal authority, direct election of high officials, and other checks. The obsession of the entire design is eternal vigilance against despotism.

The American Image of International Relations

The problem of defending freedom against tyrannical tendencies exists not just within individual societies, but in international relations as well. The parallel to individual freedom in international society is the principle of national independence and self-determination, and the parallel to infringement of individual rights is the violation of territorial sovereignty and foreign interference in the internal affairs of a free nation. Civil freedom is threatened when uncontrolled authority expands to tyranny. Inter-

[1] The importance of a nonfeudal past is explored by Louis Hartz in *The Liberal Tradition in America* (New York: Harcourt, Brace, and World, 1955).

[2] The significance of the frontier is explored in Frederick Jackson Turner, *The Frontier in American History* (New York: Henry A. Holt, 1920). See also David Potter, *People of Plenty* (Chicago: University of Chicago Press, 1954).

national freedom is threatened when one nation or coalition undertakes to extend its power to the domination of others. In both cases, injustice begins when one power center upsets the natural balance of forces and seeks an unwarranted expansion.

Historically, internal and external tyranny are linked in the American view. Democratic governments and free peoples are thought to be naturally peaceloving, while tyrannies and dictatorships have an innate tendency to expand beyond their own borders to make demands on their neighbors. An unchecked tyranny in one country is soon a danger to the outside world.

The Image of the Aggressor

The image of the international Aggressor is a critical component of the American belief system. An image is a simplified representation of reality that serves as a mental ordering device. The Aggressor is a "bully" who employs military threats and actions to subdue weaker states and to seize from them any assets he wishes. He is immune to normal considerations of justice and regards international law and morality as mere "sentimentality." His appetite for expansion is insatiable, especially when motivated by a messianic ideology, and success in one conquest does not appease him but whets his appetite for more. He is cunning in the use of propaganda to conceal his intentions, and he regards agreements and treaties as mere expedients rather than obligations.

The only restaint that the Aggressor truly respects is physical opposition. If the world is to be ruled by reason and not by force, and if weak members of the international community are not to be left at the mercy of the strong, it is the special responsibility of the larger democratic states to oppose international lawlessness. The United States in particular is obligated by its vast resources and its historic ideals to play a role of leadership in guaranteeing minimum standards of international behavior.

The overriding theme of American diplomatic history during the twentieth century has been the search for an appropriate role. On the one side are the ideals of the American people and the perceived problems of the international system. On the other side are the limits of American commitment to external affairs. Repeatedly, the United States has been called upon to respond to aggression in other parts of the world, but the American people have continued to find the role of "world policeman" unnatural.

Aggression in the Twentieth Century

Before the first world war, the United States was relatively uninvolved on the world stage. Though potentially powerful, it was insulated from foreign conflicts by vast oceans on both shores, and the dominant position of the United States in the Western hemisphere assured safety within this zone. Moreover, the global system from 1815 until 1914 was relatively stable and did not demand active American military participation. The major European states that dominated the world system pursued essentially conservative policies of maintaining the status quo (though redistributive goals were pursued in relation to colonial issues), and the security of American interests was hardly affected by the tides of world politics.

American foreign policy during this period had three cornerstones:

1. *Isolationism*, which meant nonentanglement in the complex web of European military alliances and intrigues which were perceived as having little consequence for Americans.

2. The *Monroe Doctrine*, which meant an insistence on European nonintervention in the Western hemisphere, in effect declaring Latin America as the United States sphere of influence.

3. *Commercial expansion*, which meant full participation in free international trade and access to world markets while avoiding foreign conflicts.

In general, these principles asserted for the United States a major role as a world economic actor but a minor role in world political and military affairs.

This relatively harmonious world was thoroughly upset in 1914 with the outbreak of World War I. For the first time since 1815, a major actor (Germany) seemed bent upon fundamental redistribution and alteration of the European power balance, with vast consequences for the rest of the world. Within months, most of the big powers and their allies and colonies were drawn into the complex struggle, and a variety of regional antagonisms separate from the main issues were added to the conflict. The United States, protected by geographic position from the main issues and confused by the morass of charges and countercharges, claims and counterclaims, stayed out of the war for three years.

However, as the war progressed the early neutrality and isolationist attitude of Americans gave way to growing hostility toward the German movement and an increasing sympathy to the Allies, especially Britain. Ties of language and custom with England, as well as strong commercial links, made true neutrality impossible. Moreover, the struggle was increasingly viewed as a deeply moral issue of democracy and decency (England) versus dictatorship and barbarism (Germany). This image of the German Aggressor was promoted by British propaganda, and was taken up by President Wilson to build public support for entry into the war on the Allied side. When German submarines began sinking American commercial vessels with civilian passangers aboard, U.S. opinion was enraged and the image of the Aggressor was driven deep into the public consciousness. President Wilson's memorable war message on April 2, 1917, spoke directly to the key themes in the image. The war was caused by an attempt by tyrants to expand:

We have no quarrel with the German people.... It was not upon their impulse that their government acted.... It was a war determined as wars used to be determined upon in the old, unhappy days when peoples were nowhere consulted by their rulers and wars were provoked and waged in the interest of dynasties or of little groups of ambitious men who were accustomed to use their fellow men as pawns or tools.

The United States had tried to stand apart, Wilson declared, but had discovered to its sorrow that it could not escape the responsibility to oppose massive aggression.

A steadfast concern for peace can never be maintained except by a partnership of democratic nations. We are glad ... to fight thus for the ultimate peace of the world and for the liberation of its peoples, the German peoples included; for the rights of nations great and small and the privilege of men everywhere to choose their own way of life and of obedience.... America is privileged to spend her blood and her might for the principles that gave her birth and happiness and the peace which she has treasured.... The world must be made safe for democracy.

The United States would fight, not for narrow national interests, but for the restoration of an international system based on principles of justice and nonaggression.

We have no selfish ends to serve. We desire no conquest, no dominion. We seek no indemnities for ourselves, no material compensation for the sacrifices we shall freely make. We are but one of the champions of mankind.[3]

This break with historic isolationism sketched for the United States an active role in the defense of Western democracy.

The 1919 Settlement

The leadership of the United States in redesigning the peace after the German defeat in 1918 provides further clues to the operation of the Aggressor image in the American world view. Since Wilsonian thought traced the origins of German external aggression to roots of internal tyranny, the first task was to redesign the German political order. The Weimar Constitution, which was drafted largely by Americans and which borrowed heavily from Anglo-American constitutional experience, projected for Germany a model democratic system eliminating all traces of autocratic rule. Combined with a compulsory program of disarmament and

[3] Woodrow Wilson, *War Message*, 65th Congress, first session, Senate document number 5 (Washington, 1917), pp. 3–8.

arms limitation, it seemed to guarantee that Germany would not again attempt aggressive expansion.

On the international level, the Wilsonian design sought new systemic guarantees against potential future threats to stability. The idea of collective security was founded in the institutional form of the League of Nations (precursor to the UN). In effect, this modeled future international relations on the principle of an alliance of major powers permanently committed to oppose aggression.

Unfortunately, the League had little success in fulfilling these goals when new threats to international peace developed. Domestic political opposition and a resurgence of isolationism prevented the United States from actively supporting the League that Wilson had designed. Moreover, the major powers were not, in most cases, able to agree on joint policy toward expansionary movements, and it became clear that opposition to aggression on grounds of principle was less important to most leaders than the pursuit of more narrowly conceived national interests. The dream of collective security evaporated and international relations reverted to the more familiar pattern of power politics from which, in fact, it had never varied.

World War II

Within fifteen years of the victory in the Great War, three new Aggressors were moving to subdue new victims in a mounting series of crises. In 1931, militant Japan seized control of the crucial Manchurian industrial region at the expense of China. In 1933, Adolph Hitler used the ill-conceived Emergency Powers clause of the Weimar Constitution to overthrow the German Republic and establish the fanatical and aggressive Third Reich dictatorship. In 1935, Benito Mussolini led Fascist Italy into a war of conquest in Ethiopia. In 1936, Hitler remilitarized the Rhineland in preparation for war. In 1937, Japan extended its movement in China with an eye to total conquest.

President Franklin Roosevelt tried to warn the American people in 1937 that "the epidemic of world lawlessness is spreading." Despite these warnings, Americans remained firmly isolationist. Reluctance to get involved was based on retrospective doubts about World War I, including scandalous revelations about the activities of munitions profiteers and British propagandists in promoting the earlier war policy. In January 1937 a poll showed that 64 percent of Americans questioned thought that it had been a mistake to enter the previous war. Many Americans resolved not to be trumpeted into foreign troubles a second time, and the Neutrality Act of 1937 reflected this head-in-the-sand attitude.

Critical events in the deepening war crisis began in 1938. The German *Anschluss* absorbed Austria into Germany in March, signalling the opening of military advances in Europe. The democratic powers stood by helplessly while making indignant statements. When Hitler subsequently demanded that Czechoslovakia surrender the Sudetanland on the grounds that its population was German-speaking, the war alarm sounded across the continent. Czechoslovakia counted on its defensive alliances with France and Russia, while Hitler confidently expected that the Allies would balk at war.

In September, the United States requested, and Hitler and Mussolini agreed to, a big-power crisis conference at Munich, including the two Fascist leaders and the premiers of Britain and France (but excluding the Soviet Union) to discuss the Czech crisis and how war might be averted. At Munich, the democratic leaders took Hitler at his word that he would make no further demands if given the Sudetanland, and the allies abandoned Czechoslovakia to its fate. Prime Minister Chamberlain returned to London with the wishful declaration that he had achieved "peace in our time," on the grounds of Hitler's promise that this was "the last territorial claim which I have to make in Europe." These are now remembered as some of the most tragic statements in diplomatic history.

The Munich sellout is universally cited as the classic case of the attempt to "appease" an aggressor. The futility of this policy was immediately apparent when Hitler absorbed the remains of Czechoslovakia and went on to the invasion of Poland, which at long last triggered British and French resistance. Many historians believe, in the light of the documents that have since become available, that the allies could have stopped Hitler at the Sudetanland before he captured the Czech munitions industry and possibly could have deterred further expansionary moves. An additional cost of appeasement was the stimulus it gave to Soviet fears that the Allies were trying to "turn Hitler East" at Soviet expense, a perception that led to the infamous Hitler-Stalin nonaggression pact which temporarily took Russia out of the antifascist alliance. Americans took from this bitter experience a deeply imprinted skepticism about "appeasers" who would compromise with adversaries perceived as having aggressive intentions, a consciousness sometimes known as "Munich-mindedness."

As German armies rolled over Denmark, Norway, Belgium, Holland, Luxembourg, and finally France, and the nightmare of Nazi rule was rapidly extended across the continent, American isolationism began to give way to alarm. President Roosevelt reported to the American people that even the security of the United States itself was not absolutely guaranteed:

> Armed defense of democratic existence is now being gallantly waged in four continents. If that defense fails, all the population and all the resources of Europe, Asia, Africa and Australasia will be dominated by the conquerors. Let us remember that the total of those populations and their

resources in those four continents greatly exceeds the sum total of the population and the resources of the whole of the Western Hemisphere many times over.

Roosevelt asserted that, beyond considerations of our own security, "We know that enduring peace cannot be bought at the cost of other people's freedom." What was truly at issue was the ability of a tyrannical movement to aggress upon other peoples at will:

> Every realist knows that the democratic way of life is at this moment being directly assailed in every part of the world—assailed either by arms, or by secret spreading of poisonous propaganda by those who seek to destroy unity and promote discord in nations that are still at peace.
>
> During sixteen long months this assault has blotted out the whole pattern of democratic life in an appalling number of independent nations, great and small. The assailants are still on the march, threatening other nations, great and small . . . .[4]

The American people did not fully throw off the philosophy of isolationism and enter the struggle against fascist aggression until the Japanese surprise attack on the American naval and air base at Pearl Harbor on December 7, 1941. The purpose of the attack was to immobilize American defenses against Japanese seizures of American, British, and Dutch possessions in the Far East, but many Americans perceived the event as a step toward a move on Hawaii or even California. An enraged public gave overwhelming support to a declaration of war against Germany as well as Japan. But once in the war, broad principles of an allied defense against aggression took precedence over purely national concerns. For example, a frequent poll question during the war was, "If Hitler offered peace now to all countries on the basis of not going further but of leaving matters as they now are, would you favor or oppose such a peace?" Support for peace on these terms was generally below 20 percent. In many concrete ways, American war conduct manifested a broad commitment to principles of nonaggression and universal self-determination, rather than a pure concern with American self-interest.

The 1945 Settlement

Following the war, the United States and the Allies once again set about to secure the future international system. The German and Japanese political systems were redesigned by Occupation authorities along modern democratic principles, and the United Nations was founded to reestablish the machinery of collective security that had failed in the League of

---

[4] *Congressional Record*, LXXXVII (January 6, 1941), p. 46.

Day of infamy: Pearl Harbor. Explosion of magazine on destroyer Shaw in Japanese preventive attack to immobolize U.S. Navy during Japanese conquest of Asia and the Pacific.

UPI

Nations. Americans took the lead in proposing a reformation of the world system; more than half of the respondents in several Gallup polls favored the idea of a world government with the power to control the armed forces of all nations including the United States. The United States joined the UN immediately (whereas it had stayed out of the League) and was from the beginning one of its most active and supportive members. (See chapter 11.)

The greatest shift in American policy, then, was a strategic reorientation from isolationism to a permanent commitment to world responsibilities. In contrast to the almost complete disarmament after 1918, demobilization after 1945 left a standing army of more than one million and a global network of active American military bases. Americans had concluded from the experience of "coming to Europe's rescue" in two world wars that a position of responsibility in world politics was an inescapable obligation of the most powerful democracy, and that the interests of world stability and American security would be best served by involvement rather than by isolation. This shift in perception characterized mass opinion as well as the views of policy-makers. In various polls on isolationism since 1949, between two-thirds and four-fifths of respondents have favored the option of an active international role for the United States, working closely with other nations rather than taking an independent position. However, when the question is posed in the form, "Has this country gone too far in concerning itself with problems in other parts of the world?" opinion is more evenly divided.[5] It appears that the United States should, in the majority view, play an active role in defense of certain interests and principles, but should not attempt to be "policeman of the world." National exhaustion over the Vietnam War has served to deepen this sentiment.

Several points should be made about the terms under which the United States entered the world arena between 1914 and 1945. The tragic course of world history during these four decades convinced Americans that Europe had failed in its stewardship of world order. Twice the New World had been forced to rescue the Old from its own contradictions. The United States entered the world arena flushed with tremendous success at home in building the world's most dynamic economic and political entity and bursting with ideas for international reform. It had emerged from the two wars as the only major actor which had not been subjected to invasion, humiliating occupation, or the terror of aerial bombardment. The decisive role of its power in the two victories reinforced a sense of invincibility, built on the innate optimism of a people who had little experience with tragedy. America based its new image of "leader of the free world" on this foundation of pride and self-confidence.

It has been argued by Henry Kissinger and others that the unique innocence Americans brought to international politics has been a liability as well as an advantage. An optimistic people has a tendency to reduce burdensome complexities to simplistic explanations and easy formulas, and Americans have often compressed their understanding of difficult issues into very purified political and moral principles.[6] Not every conflict can be understood as a struggle between good and evil. In particular, the tendency to interpret the motivations of all adversaries through the lens of the Aggressor theory may distort reality and lead to false solutions. This is especially dangerous when America's response is founded on the anti-appeasement principle of countering perceived aggression by a strong

[5] See John E. Mueller, *War, Presidents, and Public Opinion* (New York: Wiley, 1973), p. 110.

[6] Henry Kissinger, *American Foreign Policy* (New York: W. W. Norton, 1969).

willingness to use force. The twin problems of accurately defining threats to the peace and formulating an appropriate response by the United States reached a more acute stage as the shape of the postwar world emerged from the fog of the victory over the Axis imperialists.

Origins of the Cold War

The settlement of 1945 that ended the violence of the second world war created at the same time the basis of the *cold war*. The United States and the Soviet Union ceased to be allies in the common struggle against fascism and initiated a prolonged competition for the political future of Europe, Asia, and the world. There are profound differences of opinion among informed Americans about the origins of the cold war, and alternative interpretations greatly affect the understanding of many other issues.

The alliance with the Soviet Union against Hitler was undertaken by the United States out of necessity. Before 1941, a deep-seated suspicion of Stalin and Soviet communism had severely restricted commercial and political relations with the USSR. These fears were amplified during the decade before the war by reports of massive purges in Moscow, the virtual extermination of several million farmers of the Kulak class, and other denials of human rights. Soviet foreign behavior was typified in the American mind by subversive activities of the Comintern that seemed to threaten the democratic states, by the hated Hitler-Stalin nonaggression pact, and by a brutal attack upon tiny Finland.

But the wartime alliance of necessity, once undertaken, generated a warmth between the two peoples and a respect in the United States for the deep commitment of the Russians in the struggle against fascism. Some American officials projected a new era of cooperation between dissimilar but friendly societies after the war, including cooperation in guaranteeing collective security through the Security Council of the United Nations. Other possible contingencies in relations with the USSR were not thoroughly examined by Washington before the end of the war, and little realistic and systematic planning was done for the design of the postwar world beyond the United Nations. In Moscow, however, some fateful and extensive decisions were being taken on postwar policy and actions. This difference in planning was later to produce a deep American shock at the Soviet design.

Some joint discussion of the postwar liberation took place at the Teheran, Yalta, and Potsdam Conferences. The three Big Powers—United States, USSR, and Britain—agreed on the following essential ideas: the Nazi war machine would be destroyed by Soviet armies moving from the East and U.S./British forces moving from the West. Temporarily, each of the allies would be responsible for establishing civil order in the territories it liberated, pending the assumed restoration of self-determination and free elections. Eventually, the occupation forces would withdraw and the various nations would resume their independent lives.

It was understood that, as a matter of simple realism, the Soviets could not be expected to tolerate potentially hostile alliances along their borders again, and that the new East European governments would have to respect this principle in their foreign affairs. An informal understanding provided this formula to guide political development during the transitional period:

Rumania	90 percent Soviet
Bulgaria	80 percent Soviet
Hungary	50/50 Soviet/West
Yugoslavia	50/50 Soviet/West
Greece	90 percent British

It was also understood that the Western European countries, including France and Italy, would not be under Soviet influence, but that Soviet security needs would have a large say in Poland and Czechoslovakia. Germany, the most serious problem, would be divided into four zones under American, Soviet, British, and French control, disarmed, and eventually reunified after pacification and political reconstruction. Other understandings applied to Korea, Japan, and other countries, and to the United Nations.

What was not intended in these agreements and definitely was not anticipated by the West was that the Soviets would leave the Red Armies permanently in control of the Eastern European states, creating a satellite chain linked by virtual puppet governments. Americans were outraged by the naked use of Soviet power to create colonies. In Poland, for example, the Soviets shocked world opinion by abetting the extermination of anti-fascist but non-Communist freedom fighters, and after they were destroyed, putting in their place an all-Communist government reporting directly to Moscow. In Czechoslovakia, a democratic coalition of Communists and non-Communist leftist parties was destroyed by a direct Moscow-ordered Communist coup. In Germany, the Soviet zone of occupation was converted into a permanent puppet state, and the agreed goal of reunification was scuttled. The idea of free elections was forgotten. "Across Europe," Winston Churchill declared to the American people at Fulton, Missouri on March 5, 1946, "from Stettin in the Baltic to Trieste in the Adriatic, an Iron Curtain has descended across the continent."

Behind that line lie all the capitals of the ancient states of central and eastern Europe. Warsaw, Berlin, Prague, Vienna, Budapest, Belgrade, Bucharest, and Sofia, all these famous cities and populations around them . . . . The Communist parties, which were very small in all these eastern states of Europe, have been raised to prominence and power far beyond their numbers and are seeking everywhere to obtain totalitarian control. Police governments are prevailing in nearly every case . . . .[7]

Even more alarming was the perceived effort of the Soviet Union to push forward this iron curtain and bring new lands under Communist control. Subversive activities were encouraged in France and Italy; claims were advanced against Iran; the Communist-controlled Viet Minh moved against French control in Indochina; threats were made against Turkey; and an insurgent movement was mounted in Malaya. In China, the Communists reopened their struggle against the Kuomintang government (see chapter 4). Throughout the world, insurgent parties fomented disorder and revolution in the name of communism. Many in the West concluded that the USSR sought not just security on its frontiers but expansion everywhere and possibly even mastery of the earth. (Dissenters argued that *not* every revolutionary event could be traced to a conspiratorial command center in Moscow.)

The Truman Doctrine

The case that finally produced a crisis atmosphere in Washington was that of Greece. There, the retreating Germans had destroyed railways, ports, bridges, communications facilities, and the network of orderly civil administration. More than a thousand villages were burned. By 1947 a majority of the children were tested as tubercular. In this atmosphere, rival Communist and monarchist factions of the former antifascist resistance were locked in civil war over the future of Greece. It was believed in Washington, though there were dissenters, that Stalin had given the go-ahead signal to the insurgents and that Soviet arms were flowing freely to the Communists in violation of the understanding that Greece was to be under Western influence.

This crisis had special significance for the assessment of Soviet intentions. If indeed this was a Soviet move against Greece, Russian expansionary goals evidently included political issues quite remote from critical zones of national defense. Stalin, on the one hand, seemed to have in mind much more ambitious plans for the destruction of capitalism in disregard of his agreements. On the other hand, some continued to see the Soviet Union pursuing essentially defensive goals, or at worst regional expansion along the familiar lines of Tsarist imperialism, rather than a truly global power grab in the name of communism. A great debate about Soviet motives and the wisest American response began in the United States.

The dominant school of thought, given its classic expression in the "containment" philosophy of diplomat and scholar George Kennan, was

[7] *The New York Times,* March 6, 1946, p. 4.

that Soviet policy served ideological imperatives demanding global struggle and opposition to capitalism. In July 1947, he explained,

> Of the original ideology, nothing has been officially junked . . . . The first . . . concept is the innate antagonism between capitalism and socialism . . . . It means that there can never be on Moscow's side any sincere assumption of a community of aims between the Soviet Union and powers which are regarded as capitalist.[8]

The responsibility to oppose this policy of limitless conflict fell to the United States which, Kennan said, must base its actions on the principle of containing Soviet power within its existing boundaries until internal changes within the Soviet leadership produced an abandonment of aggressive intentions.

> The Soviet pressure against the free institutions of the Western World is something that can be contained by the adroit and vigilant application of counterforce at a series of constantly shifting geographical and political points, corresponding to the shifts and maneuvres of Soviet policy . . . .

This point of view was shared by President Harry Truman, who incorporated it in his statement of the *Truman Doctrine* on March 12, 1947. The assumption of his speech was an analogy between Communist aggression and the Nazi aggression that preceded it: the "fundamental issue" in the war with Germany and Japan had been "the creation of conditions in which . . . nations . . . will be able to work out a way of life free from coercion." Now once again we had to be "willing to help free people to maintain their free institutions and their national integrity against aggressive movements that seek to impose upon them totalitarian regimes." Note the Wilsonian themes of aggressive dictatorship versus peaceful democracy in the following passage from Truman's address:

> The peoples of a number of countries of the world have recently had totalitarian regimes forced upon them against their will . . . . At the present moment in world history nearly every nation must choose between alternative ways of life. The choice is too often not a free one.
>
> One way of life is based upon the will of the majority, and is distinguished by free institutions, representative government, free elections, guarantees of individual liberty, freedom of speech and religion and freedom from political oppression.
>
> The second way of life is based upon the will of a minority forcibly imposed upon the majority. It relies upon terror and oppression, a controlled press and radio, fixed elections and the suppression of personal freedom.

[8] George Kennan (writing under the pseudonym "Mr. X"), "The Sources of Soviet Conduct," *Foreign Affairs* 25 (July 1947).

On The Threshold!

Source: Copyright © Gale in the *Los Angeles Times*.
Reprinted with permission.

TRUMAN DOCTRINE

    I believe that it must be the policy of the United States to support peoples who are resisting attempted subjugation by armed minorities or by outside pressures.

    I believe that we must assist free peoples to work out their own destinies in their own way.[9]

Note also that the United States will "support peoples who are resisting attempted subjugation by armed minorities. . . ." This suggests intervention against aggression *even when* the rebels are nationals of the same country, blurring the distinction between international aggression and civil war.

Critiques of the Truman Doctrine

    The Truman/Kennan perspective was criticized from several camps. The "realist" school, headed by Hans Morgenthau, accused it of "sentimentalism" and "moralism." The containment strategy was justified,

---

[9] *Congressional Record*, XCIII, March 12, 1947, pp. 1999–2000.

... not primarily in terms of the traditional American interest in the maintenance of the European balance of power, but in terms of a universal moral principle. This principle is derived from the assumption that the issue between the United States and the Soviet Union ... must be defined in terms of 'alternative ways of life' ... [and] proclaims the defense of free, democratic nations everywhere in the world against 'direct or indirect aggression' .... Thus the Truman Doctrine transformed a concrete interest of the U.S. in a geographically defined part of the world into a moral principle of worldwide validity, to be applied regardless of the limits of American interest and of American power .... As a guide to political action, it is the victim, as all moral principles must be, of two congenital political weaknesses: the inability to distinguish between what is desirable and what is possible, and the inability to distinguish between what is desirable and what is essential.[10]

Journalist Walter Lippmann, another realist, called the Truman Doctrine "a strategic monstrosity" which could not succeed in changing the situation in Eastern Europe. "No state in Eastern Europe can be independent of the Kremlin as long as the Red Army is within it and around it," he wrote. And the Red Army would remain as long as Russia was threatened with hostile encirclement across the military line of division in Western Europe. "The presence of these non-European armies in the continent of Europe perpetuates the division," he continued. The wise course of American response would be to offer the Soviets a mutual withdrawal, United States forces to leave the Western sector and Soviet forces to return to the USSR. "If the Red Army is in Russia, and not on the Elbe ... the power of the Russian imperialists to realize their ambitions will have been reduced decisively." The containment policy was seen as having exactly the opposite effect and therefore as an incorrect response to Soviet expansion.[11]

The "liberation" school of dissenters, headed by John Foster Dulles, took a position opposite to the realists. Dulles objected that containment was a passive policy which always left open the question, Which of us will be the next victim? It projected for the United States a static political role of allowing the Kremlin to determine the place and terms of conflict. "Ours are treadmill policies which, at best, might perhaps keep us in the same place until we drop exhausted." It was a law of history that "the dynamic prevails over the static," and the correct response to Soviet imperialism was not mere defense but an active offense. We could not just contain communism at its present boundaries but had to carry the struggle

[10] Hans J. Morgenthau, *In Defense of the National Interest* (New York: Alfred A. Knopf, 1950), pp. 120–21.
[11] Walter Lippmann, *The Cold War* (New York: Harper and Row, 1947), p. 61.

across the iron curtain to pursue the liberation of captive nations that have already fallen to Soviet imperialism.[12]

The third and final major school of dissent may be called the "dove" school in the parlance of later Vietnam debate. Climaxing in the unsuccessful 1948 presidential drive of former Secretary of Agriculture Henry A. Wallace, the doves argued that the containment policy itself endangered peace and provoked the very Soviet posture that it deplored. Wallace asserted that "a great part of our conflict with Russia is the normal conflict between two strong and sovereign nations and can be solved in normal ways. . . . When Britain competes for resources, we settle our differences as friends. When Russia competes for them, we sound a fire alarm and thank God for the atom bomb. Why?"

Wallace argued for cooperation in the UN rather than a worldwide anti-Communist military crusade. He predicted that containment would force the United States to support dictators everywhere in the name of defense: "Every fascist dictator will know that he has money in our bank. . . . Freedom, in whose name Americans have died, will become a catchword for reaction." [13]

Interestingly, a similar view was argued by Robert A. Taft, the leading conservative of the time, who objected to the North Atlantic alliance as "a treaty by which one nation undertakes to arm half the world against the other half," and predicted that "this treaty . . . means inevitably an arms race." Taft, like the doves, feared that "if Russia sees itself ringed gradually by so-called defensive arms, from Norway and Denmark to Turkey and Greece . . . . it may decide that the arming of Europe, regardless of its present purpose, looks like an attack upon Russia." [14]

The containment and liberation schools portrayed the Soviet Union largely in terms of the Aggressor image, while the realist and dove schools took a more limited view of the threat posed to the West by communism. To simplify and organize the key distinctions, the various views are condensed into a "hard" and a "soft" line in Table 2–1.

The magnitude of the Soviet threat has been a question of fierce controversy among American scholars and academic Kremlinologists. Inferences about Soviet motives have ranged from a portrayal of Soviet designs for world domination [15] to the view of a defensive Soviet Union acting more in fear of the West than in pursuit of an autonomous hege-

---

[12] John Foster Dulles, "A Policy of Liberation," *Life*, May 19, 1952, pp. 147–48.

[13] Speech by Henry A. Wallace at Madison Square Garden, New York City, March 31, 1947, printed in the *Congressional Record*, 80th Congress, 1st Session, Appendix, pp. A1572–73.

[14] Speech by Robert A. Taft, *Congressional Record*, 81st Congress, 1st Session, pp. 9208–10.

[15] Elliot Goodman, *The Soviet Design for a World State* (New York: Columbia University Press, 1960).

TABLE 2–1

	Hard Line	Soft Line
Russia's primary goal	Worldwide Communist expansion	National and regional defense
Communism	A centrally directed aggressive conspiracy	Only partly controlled by Moscow; not a monolithic bloc
New revolutionary crises	Most coordinated from the Kremlin	Most responses of local movements to particular conditions, aided but not controlled by Moscow
America's responsibility	Worldwide containment of Communist-led movements	Maintain European balance of power, but not play role of reactionary policeman of the world
Effects of U.S. alliances	Stalemate Communist aggressive moves	Stimulate defensive arms race and troop deployments on Soviet side

monial will.[16] In a survey of twenty-two major American writings on Soviet foreign conduct, nine authors were found to take *ultra-hard* positions (corresponding to the Aggressor image), seven *hard*, and six *mixed hard-soft*. None gave a *soft* or *ultra-soft* portrayal.[17]

In this survey, an *ultra-hard* view saw as Moscow's purpose a boundless expansion in pursuit of total worldwide revolutionary victory, accepting no restraint but those dictated by the ebb and flow of opportunity. The *hard* image saw the Soviet Union seeking a global improvement in its political, economic, and military position. Ideology to these authors played a secondary role in Soviet intentions, and the Kremlin's motivation for expansion outside areas of immediate national concern was considered moderate. The *mixed hard-soft* writers saw the Soviets as expansionist, but

[16] Denna F. Fleming, *The Cold War and its Origins* (Garden City, N.Y.: Doubleday, 1961).

[17] William Welch, *American Images of Soviet Foreign Policy* (New Haven: Yale University Press, 1970), especially pages 30–58. Welch selects Robert Strausz-Hupe, William R. Kintner, James E. Dougherty, and Alvin J. Cottrell, *Protracted Conflict* (New York: Harper and Row, 1963) to represent his *ultra-hard* image; Marshall Shulman, *Beyond the Cold War* (New Haven: Yale University Press, 1963), to represent his *hard* image; and Frederick Schuman, *The Cold War: Retrospect and Prospect* (Baton Rouge: Louisiana State University Press, 1967) 2nd. ed., to typify the *mixed hard-soft* image.

only as a continuation of the historic Russian reaction to repeated foreign invasion, and motivated by defensive concern for security rather than by dreams of a Soviet world state.

The majority of Americans followed President Truman's lead in taking the hard line. The Gallup poll asked, "As you hear and read about Russia these days, do you believe Russia is trying to build herself up to be *the* ruling power of the world, or do you think Russia is just building up protection against being attacked in another way?" In June 1946, just after Churchill's iron curtain speech, 58 percent favored the "ruling power" interpretation to 29 percent for the "protection" interpretation. By November 1950, after the adoption of the Truman Doctrine and the opening of the Korean war, 81 percent favored the "ruling power" theory to only 9 percent for the "protection" theory. In January 1948, 83 percent of Americans favored stopping all trade with Russia. The ratification of the NATO pact "to stop Soviet expansionism" was endorsed by 67 percent. On November 8, 1954, *Time* magazine defined the Communist idea of coexistence as "a period of deceptive docility while gathering strength for a new assault." Clearly, the great debate had been won by the containment theorists.

Deepening Hostility

Hostility between the United States and the Soviet Union deepened after the promulgation of the Truman Doctrine and the North Atlantic Treaty. A constant stream of negative headlines concerning events in the Communist world reinforced and strengthened the convictions of the containment model. The Soviets suppressed a liberalization movement in East Germany in 1953, in Hungary in 1956, and in Czechoslovakia in 1968, to mention only the large-scale coercive actions. Oppression against "captive peoples" was also perceived in China's forcible annexation of Tibet and Soviet policy toward non-Russian minorities within the USSR. These negative impressions were confirmed by millions of refugees who "voted with their feet" by fleeing communism to seek new homes in the free world. Three million left East Germany for the West (prompting the construction of the Berlin Wall by the Communists to stop the outflow); 180,000 left Hungary in 1956; a half-million came to the United States from Cuba. Even relatives of the ruling elite, including Stalin's own daughter and Castro's sister, have "defected" to the democratic world. Some of these migrants were motivated by economic considerations (foreign workers also came to Germany from Italy and Greece, without apparent political motivation, and more Puerto Ricans have come to the United States than Cubans), but many others described themselves as political refugees and reported events in their former countries as hostile to basic human rights. It appeared to the majority of Americans that these outer signs were the tip of an iceberg of repression, and that the Communists retained power only through the massive use of police coercion.

In addition to political repression, Americans saw the Soviet Union impose a system of economic imperialism on the "captive nations" after 1945. While the United States poured billions of dollars in Marshall Plan aid into the devastated economies of former allies and enemies, restoring Europe and Japan to economic health, the Soviet Union milked approximately $20 billion out of its zone of occupation, through four devices:

1. Billions of dollars in "war reparations" were assessed against East Germany, Hungary, and Rumania.

2. A "special price system" was imposed for trade within the Communist bloc, characterized by high prices for Soviet goods and low prices for exports by satellite nations. One result was losses to Poland of about $500 million in discounted coal exports to the USSR between 1946 and 1956.

3. "Joint stock companies" were established as a highly exploitive form of Soviet foreign investment in East European economies. Former German firms were expropriated by Russia under the Administration for Soviet Property Abroad, and their value was counted as Moscow's "investment" against which fair returns to Russia were calculated. Joint stock companies of this and other types transferred additional billions of dollars in value to the USSR.

4. Interdependence of production was forced on the satellite economies, restricting their trade with the West and giving priority to Soviet deliveries. Raw material dependency is illustrated by the case of Poland, which in 1957 imported from the USSR 100 percent of its oil, 70 percent of its iron ore, 78 percent of its nickel, and 67 percent of its cotton. From 1945 through 1956, exploitation of Eastern Europe was ruthless, though economic relations were more nearly equal after 1956.[18]

The Continuity of Policy: Korea and Vietnam

American policy remained firm and unvarying in its opposition to perceived Communist aggression for twenty-five years. The isolationist impulses were suppressed, and the most extensive commitments ever undertaken by a single power were honored. The essential continuity of the policy can be seen in a comparison of statements in the Korean and Vietnam wars, separated by a span of fifteen years.

[18] Zbigniew Brzezinski, *The Soviet Bloc* (Cambridge, Mass.: Harvard University Press, 1967), pp. 124–28, 282–87, and 376. See also Paul Marer, "The Political Economy of Soviet Relations with Comecon," in Steven Rosen and James Kurth, eds., *Testing the Theory of Economic Imperialism* (Lexington, Mass.: D. C. Heath, 1974).

President Truman explained the problem in Korea to the American people in bleak terms in an April, 1951 radio address:

The Communists in the Kremlin are engaged in a monstrous conspiracy to stamp out freedom all over the world. . . . The whole Communist imperialism is back of the attack on peace in the Far East.

Truman said that American strategy was based on the lessons of dealing with Communist aggression.

In the simplest terms, what we are trying to do in Korea is this: we are trying to prevent a third world war. . . . If [the Free World] had followed the right policies in the 1930's—if the free countries had acted together to crush the aggression of the dictators, and if they had acted in the beginning, when the aggression was small—there probably would have been no World War II. If history has taught us anything, it is that aggression anywhere in the world is a threat to peace everywhere in the world.[19]

Strikingly parallel themes were later used to explain the necessity for American military intervention in Vietnam. The important State Department white paper of 1965, significantly entitled "Aggression from the North: The Record of North Vietnam's Campaign to Conquer South Vietnam," portrays that struggle as a typical attempt at Communist aggression:

South Vietnam is fighting for its life against a brutal campaign of terror and armed attack inspired, directed, supplied, and controlled by the Communist regime in Hanoi . . . . Aggression has been loosed against an independent people who want to make their way in peace and freedom. . . .[20]

President Richard Nixon said in 1969:

If Hanoi were to succeed in taking over South Vietnam by force—even after the power of the United States had been engaged—it would greatly strengthen those leaders who scorn negotiation, who advocate aggression, who minimize the risks of confrontation. It would bring peace now, but it would enormously increase the danger of a bigger war later.

In both wars, the U.S. policy was based on four key propositions:

[19] Radio speech of President Truman on Korea, from *The New York Times*, April 17, 1951.
[20] U.S. Department of State, *Aggression from the North: The Record of North Vietnam's Campaign to Conquer South Vietnam* (Washington, D.C.: U.S. Government Printing Office, 1965).

4 Key Issues

1. Conflict is due to Communist aggression against the free world.
2. The Communist appetite for expansion cannot be appeased and will grow without limit unless checked.
3. The United States, as leader of the free world, is obligated to act as a counterweight to Communist aggression.
4. By fighting a small war now we avoid a bigger war later.

This was the stern formulation of American ideas from 1947 to approximately 1970.

Détente

Several changes in recent years have led to a revision of the American outlook and to a substantial reduction of tensions. First, the Communist bloc came to be seen as having several competing centers of power rather than a unified command center in Moscow. In particular, the growing Sino-Soviet dispute alerted the West after 1960 to the independence of China from Soviet control. The prevailing image of communism shifted from the fearful "monolithic" view to a more differentiated theory of "polycentrism." This implied the possibility of gains for the United States in a more fluid policy of dealing with different factions of the splintered Communist world.

Second, some amelioration was seen in the relentless hostility of Soviet intentions. After fifty years of revolution and rapid economic growth and ten years after the death of Stalin, the Soviet Union had grown "soft" and somewhat more satisfied with its own position in the world. The dominant elites in Moscow clearly favored coexistence with the West and minimization of the risks of war. Like the American government, Moscow was under continuing pressure from various industrial, regional, and consumer interests to hold down defense spending. The "hawk" group in the Politburo was on the decline, and new possibilities for cooperation with the West were open.

Third, the cold war itself came to be seen in less strident ideological terms. Whereas attention to Communist events in the early years had been highly selective, concentrating on negative news, later impressions included positive achievement in the USSR, China, and the East European states. Some observers saw a gradual process of "convergence" between the two economic systems, with the Soviets instituting managerial reforms known as "Liebermanism" and other tendencies toward free enterprise while the capitalist states accepted increased government planning and participation in their economies. Also, increased Western awareness of its own continuing injustices, such as the suppression of black people in the United States, weakened the moral righteousness of anticommunism.

Many people came to see the problem of dealing with the USSR as a practical balance-of-power issue instead of a battle between the forces of light and the forces of darkness. A less moralistic foreign policy permitted a more pragmatic exploration of options. As perceptions of the USSR shifted from the Aggressor image to more complex and less dangerous patterns of motivation, cooperative proposals were less vulnerable to charges of "appeasement" by domestic opponents.

In this atmosphere, the United States has opened a new phase in its dealings with the Communist world during the 1970's. Near normal relations have been resumed with China after twenty-five years of hostility. Several major agreements on arms control and political settlements have been reached with the USSR, notably the interim SALT I agreements and a settlement of the German borders. Western European trade with Eastern Europe increased tenfold during the 1960's, and American officials have projected even larger gains for U.S. trade during the seventies. Major officials have gone about proclaiming, "The cold war is over!", which, of course, cannot be taken literally, since $200 billion in defense expenditures is still devoted yearly to two competing alliance systems glaring at each other over military lines of division the world over. But it is clear that a new era of deëscalation is underway, however gradual and interrupted it may be.

By 1976, both internal and external events had come to bear upon the concept of détente. The Soviet-Cuban intervention in Angola, where a struggle for power followed independence from Portugal, set off a bitter battle between President Ford and Secretary of State Kissinger, on the one hand, and Congress, on the other, with respect to indirect American counterintervention in favor of Western-oriented Angolan forces. The rancor of the debate (which Congress won by denying supportive funds), coupled with firm public refusals of Soviet Party Leader Brezhnev to discuss the matter during Secretary Kissinger's visit to Moscow, cast a shadow over détente. This presented a severe embarrassment to President Ford during the presidential primary elections of 1976. Under attack from early Democratic front-runners Jimmy Carter (conservative and nationalistic) and Henry Jackson (consistently opposed to détente and in favor of expanding American military capability and deployment), and maneuvering to stave off Republican challenger Ronald Reagan's appeal to the right wing on foreign policy issues, Ford declared the deletion of "détente" from the American political lexicon. This change, then, resulted first from the embittered atmosphere of the Angolan affair, but principally from presidential electoral politics. Because the alteration of vocabulary meant little for the quality of Soviet-American relations (Brezhnev himself attributed it to electoral jitters), Secretary Kissinger told a Boston audience not to be surprised if, after several attempts to rename the environment, the same old word—"détente"—were to reappear.

The period of détente and renegotiation of relationships in the cold war

DÉTENTE

When two people agree not to harm each other today, or in the immediate future, this is cause for rejoicing. How much more satisfying, then, when two superpowers agree to the same thing. The rope of international tensions can be taut or slack; the thing to remember is that it is tied around all our necks, and when someone tries to drive a tank across it, or many tanks, he should be looked at peculiarly.

By permission of the artist, Edward Sorel. Originally published in the *Atlantic Monthly*, 1976.

has raised the question of what pattern will develop among the five major actors as Washington foresees the evolution of a five-power balance. Europe and Japan can be expected to act more independently of the United States, but American policy is based on the expectation that special relationships will continue to exist. The present European leaders favor a major Amer-

The Logic of National Perceptions

ican military presence as a counterbalance to the USSR on the continent, and Japan is expected to continue relying on the United States to maintain the balance of power in Asia. While there is domestic pressure to reduce America's world role after the Vietnam war, American leaders are firm in the commitment to remain in NATO and in the Pacific.

American relations with the USSR and China will, it is expected, continue to improve, but the United States will not take a position on either side in the Moscow/Peking rivalry. An effort to interlope in this quarrel might backfire, and the United States would not want to drive the Communist giants back into each other's arms. On the other side, while there might be some short term gains to the West if the Sino-Soviet dispute worsened, American officials believe that war between these powers would endanger American interests and the world. Thus, the delicate role of the United States is to take advantage of the split, avoid favoritism, and insofar as possible moderate the conflict to reduce escalatory tendencies. In general, the challenge of the future for the United States is the maintenance of stability among an increased number of independent power centers in world politics.

Rebuttal to the Theory of U.S. Economic Imperialism

One obstacle to improved relations is the contention of the Soviet Union and China that the United States is pursuing a design of world economic imperialism and hegemony. According to the neo-Leninist critics, the mature phase of capitalism is characterized by a saturation of the domestic market with surplus capital and by overproduction. The maintenance of the profit structure depends on penetration of foreign markets for high-yield investment opportunities, export outlets, and secure sources of the cheapest raw materials. For the United States, the necessary expansion has been justified behind a disguise of anti-Communism and defense of the free world. This is said to explain the basic dynamic of U.S. cold war policy and domination of much of the Third World. The neo-Leninist analysis, presented at length in the preceding chapter, is rejected by orthodox theorists on the following factual grounds:

 1. *Foreign investment profits are not higher.* American manufacturing investments at home between 1959 and 1969 averaged a 12.4 percent return, while investments abroad averaged 11.8 percent. Capital therefore could not be driven to foreign markets for higher profits. This is consistent with a study of British investments in India from 1800 to 1967, which found that they did not yield higher returns than domestic investment in the colonizing country.[21]

[21] Kenneth Boulding and Tapan Mukerjee, "Unprofitable Empire: Britain in India, 1800–1967," in Peace Research Society (International) *Papers*, Vol. 16, p. 11.

2. *American capitalism does not depend on foreign markets.* It is true that U.S. foreign investments have a book value of $170 billion, making them in the aggregate larger than any economy in the world except those of the United States, the USSR, and Japan. But these foreign assets were only 8 percent of the *domestic* book value of American corporations in 1968: big compared to most economies but small for the U.S. In 1968, only 6 percent of new investment went abroad. Looking at exports, foreign sales were only 8 percent as great as the value of goods sold at home. In most industries, exports are less than 10 percent of production. Foreign investment profits were only 9.3 percent of the total profits of American capitalism in 1968. These statistics do not support the view that the U.S. economy needs imperialism, large as American foreign investments are in an absolute sense.

3. *American capitalism does not depend on exploitation of the Third World.* Less developed countries are only a small portion of the market for U.S. foreign investment and exports, and they are gradually declining in significance (40 percent in 1960, 30 percent in 1969). American capitalism increasingly finds it more profitable to invest in developed countries (Europe, Japan, Australia, South Africa, for instance) than in underdeveloped lands. Therefore, it is not plausible to argue that American capitalism needs to dominate small countries or to retard their growth.

4. *Vietnam cannot be explained as economic imperialism.* The natural resources and market value of Vietnam or all of Southeast Asia could not begin to repay the costs of the war: $150 billion, ten years of war, and 50,000 American lives. The rice, tungsten, teak, and small offshore oil deposits of Indochina are relatively minor in value. American policy in Vietnam cannot be explained by the imperatives of capitalism. The stock market averages, which Leninists would have predicted to rise with the war, instead fell sharply, indicating that Vietnam was not good for business.

5. *There is not a clearly defined capitalist ruling class in America.* The neo-Leninist theory assumes that major multinational corporations are owned and managed by a small, definable class with vast influence in the American political process. In truth, the means of production are widely owned, including millions of successful small businesses. Even the large industries have widely dispersed ownership through shareholding. Sixty-seven percent of Americans—about 140 million—own stocks directly or indirectly (through pension funds, insurance companies, and other collective "institutional investors"). Thirty-five million Americans own shares directly in the stock markets. While there are some very large stockholders as well, to some degree America has achieved "people's capitalism." There is not a sharp line between rich and poor.

Moreover, the rich/poor division is just one way of slicing the pie in pluralistic democracy. Catholics are sometimes opposed to Protestants, men to women, black to white, Irish to Italian, farmer to worker, young to old, urban to rural, North to South, hawk to dove, among other divisions. Each conflict crosscuts the others, and instead of immutably opposed permanent classes, pluralism offers shifting coalitions and factions. Government is not the permanent agent of one class, but an arbiter standing above the various divisions favoring first one then another.

6. *Economic interests do not determine American foreign policy.* Even if the neo-Leninist can demonstrate a profit to someone in a market abroad, it does not follow that policy toward that country is guided by material gain. In general, security interests and ideological principles tend to override limited economic gains in the determination of foreign policy, according to the orthodox view. If, like many neo-Leninists, we discount Soviet imperialism as an official mythology created by U.S. propaganda, we must rely on exotic explanations such as economic determinism to explain American policy. But if we accept the reality of the Soviet threat, the primacy of security interests in determining U.S. policy is apparent. The theory of American economic imperialism is, in the dominant American view, a tired set of worn shibboleths to be mouthed without conviction by Soviet speechmakers on state occasions.[22] Americans look for a reduction in this kind of propaganda to confirm the relaxation of strident cold war policies on the Communist side.

Conclusion

The twentieth century has seen a radical alteration in the world position of the United States. It entered the epoch clinging to isolation, but was forced twice in twenty-five years to intervene in critical European conflicts that threatened world stability. After 1945, an obligation was accepted to play a permanent international role. But American responsibilities have continued to evolve as the conflict with the Communist world has lessened in intensity and as other Western nations and Japan have resumed some of their traditional influence. The United States can be expected to occupy a more moderate position in world politics in the future, avoiding the two extremes of isolationism, on the one hand, and world policeman, on the other.

[22] This analysis borrows heavily from Robert W. Tucker, *The Radical Left and American Foreign Policy* (Baltimore: Johns Hopkins University Press, 1971), especially pages 124–38.

3

The Perspectives of
America's Major Allies

The concept of a multiple-party balance in world politics, together with the burgeoning importance of nonmilitary components of power, calls for a review of the international perspectives of those states that are sufficiently modern to contribute independently to the balance if only they can remain free from foreign economic and military domination. These two conditions—modernity and the quest for autonomy—typify some of America's principal allies, particularly Japan, the European Community states, and Canada. Each of these has achieved a high level of industrial activity, a major competitive position in world economic affairs, and a sophisticated security system. Yet in both military and economic relations, each is intertwined with the interests and capabilities of the United States in a delicate balance between independent decision-making and domination from Washington and Wall Street. For each, accordingly, a world view is colored as much by the ambivalence of relations with closest friend as by fear of potential enemies.

Japan

A paradox of forces shapes the Japanese world view. On the one hand, Japan is intensely nationalistic, and has a proud history of cultural continuity and empire. Yet, on the other hand, Japan removed itself entirely from world affairs from 1640 to 1854, when it was "opened" by threat of force by the American fleet of Commodore Matthew C. Perry. After World War I Japan was humiliated by the refusal of the Western powers to include in the Covenant of the League of Nations a declaration of racial equality. In 1945, under relentless fire bombing and two atomic attacks, Japan was forced into unconditional surrender; and after six years of occupation by American troops, a peace treaty was arranged at the price of a series of military and economic agreements which compromised Japan's self-determination. Yet despite these restraints, in the years since World War II Japan has undergone a remarkable economic recovery unaffected by world economic fluctuations until after 1970. It is important to examine these events in Japanese history.

The Opening of Japan

Like China, Japan fell into the covetous orbit of American Manifest Destiny in the nineteenth century. As the China trade multiplied after 1844, American merchants eyed Japan as an additional source of Oriental goods, and as a supply station and refuge that would minimize the hazards of the long Pacific journey. Already, too, Americans had absorbed Japan in their missionary zeal. Popularized tales of Japanese treatment of ship-wrecked American sailors had prompted some Americans to brand the Japanese "enemies of mankind" who needed Western civilization. After two unsuccessful diplomatic efforts, in the wake of expansionism in the Mexican War and the acquisition of the Pacific coast, American national-ism and the idea of "opening" Japan converged. The departure of Perry's squadron was appropriately festive to the anticipated results; for it was to mark the first time Americans would deal directly with Japanese since the Napoleonic Wars, during which a few Americans carried on the trickle of Dutch trade which Japan permitted. Ironically, one of the sites of that trade was Nagasaki, the second of the two cities atomic bombed ninety-two years later by American B29s.

The Japanese entered reluctantly into a treaty with the United States in 1854 as an opportunity to learn industrial science. But if the commercial treaty opened the door to Japan, the immediate evolution of Japanese-American relations propped it back. For by 1858, while Japan had gained few concessions, Americans had acquired most-favored-nation status (auto-matic improvement of trading conditions if Japan were to offer more liberal terms to any other party), the right of extraterritoriality (Americans charged with crimes in Japan were to be tried in American courts by American laws), and the rights to teach Western religions and to establish religious institutions. As was the case in early Sino-American relations, then, the principal mark of these early dealings with the West was im-balance: Japan was assigned the obligations, while Americans gained the lucrative and enviable benefits.

Japanese Expansionism

Having emerged from isolation in the forty years following Perry's mission, Japan sought from 1894 to 1945 to expand its empire. Control of Korea, long an object of competition among China, Japan, and Russia, prompted the Sino-Japanese War of 1894–95, a war which Japan won because of its superior arms and modernization. Though Chinese interests were uprooted from Korea and Taiwan (Formosa), Japanese acquisitions on the Asian mainland were seized by Russia with the assistance of France and Germany. It was clear that if Japan were to achieve status as the dominant, modern Asian state, the influence of the Western states within the region would have to be restricted.

The peace was but a lull, as the Russo-Japanese War (1904–05) ensued, largely over competing claims to Manchuria and Korea. Again, however, a Western state's policy was to dominate the outcome. Having acquired the Philippines in 1898, the United States hoped that Asia and the Pacific would be stabilized by a Russo-Japanese stalemate. In view of Russia's apparent edge, President Theodore Roosevelt's policy was to encourage Japan to limit the Russian successes by dangling postwar rewards. But when Japan won decisive land and sea battles and appeared ready to seize Eastern Siberia (in fact, however, Japan was exhausted), Roosevelt saw urgent need for a peace that would ensure the stalemate that war apparently could not. While giving his assent in the Taft-Katsura Agreement (1905) to Japanese control of Korea, Roosevelt urged moderation of Tokyo's other expectations of indemnification. Though he did not force these compromises upon Japan, popular and editorial opinion focused national dissatisfaction with the peace treaty on anti-Americanism: American policy seemed to have betrayed the Japanese victory over a Western power. The flames of hostility were fanned by frequent reports of anti-Japanese racial violence in California, and by American policies which excluded Asian immigrants. With Russia vanquished and China quieted by Western colonialism, redress of grievances with the United States became the focal point of Japanese politics.[1]

The tenuous understanding, which was achieved through a visit of the American fleet, painted white, to Japanese ports and through executive agreements concerning immigration and mutual respect for Pacific territories, was broken by World War I. When at war's outset Germany vacated its China holdings, Japan moved swiftly to occupy them. Shortly thereafter, Tokyo issued to China the not-long-secret Twenty-One Demands (1915) which sought to enlarge Japan's influence throughout

---

[1] Raymond A. Esthus, *Theodore Roosevelt and Japan* (Seattle: The University of Washington Press, 1966); Howard K. Beale, *Theodore Roosevelt and the Rise of America to World Power* (Baltimore: The Johns Hopkins University Press, 1956), particularly chapter 5; and Charles E. Neu, *An Uncertain Friendship* (Cambridge: Harvard University Press, 1967).

China. Since wartime diplomacy did little to resolve these issues, their persistence accentuated the mutual distrust of the parties. At the Paris Peace Conference, its economy vibrant, its navy among the world's most modern, and its national spirit running high, Japan attached the China issue to a demand that the Covenant of the League of Nations, part of the Treaty of Versailles, include a declaration of racial equality. Without it Japan would not bow to President Woodrow Wilson's demand for a timetable for the return of Germany's former holdings to China. For their part, some European states rich in colonial holdings throughout the nonwhite world rejected Japan's demand. The Western resistance prevailed, leaving the China question unresolved but, worse, leaving the Japanese more convinced than before of the untrustworthiness of Western intentions.

The breakdown of trust was recorded also in a division of Japanese opinion concerning a role in the postwar world order. The civilian government and conservative elements readily subscribed to the Washington Treaties of 1922, which sought a permanent balance of interests in China and a restriction on naval armaments. But to expansionists and to the military, naval arms limitation and the new diplomatic regime for China constituted surrender to a Western design to regulate Japan's influence in Asia. The break resulted in the military becoming virtually self-governing. Thus the government was able in 1931 to deny that troops were moving into Manchuria even while the military was using a minor and deliberately provoked skirmish at Mukden as a pretext for the massive invasion of Manchuria and eventually China, Asia, and the Pacific. To the expansionists, this was a policy born of having been denied by habitual Western intrusion the prizes of conquest in 1885, 1905, and 1918. Consistent with this thinking were the decisions to withdraw from the Europe-controlled League of Nations, to create the Greater East Asian Co-Prosperity Sphere, and to join the Axis Alliance (1940) with Germany and Italy. These moves were additionally encouraged by the imperfections of American neutrality, the tendency to favor China, and Washington's economic sanctions against Japan. Prevention, then, or at least delay, of American intervention in the Asian war necessitated the Japanese attack on the American fleet at Pearl Harbor on December 7, 1941.[2]

The horrors of World War II in the Pacific concluded with several events that apparently indicated Western attitudes about the Orient. On the tactical front, as an alternative to the costly invasion of Japan, the U.S. chose to fire bomb Japanese population centers, a policy facilitated by the discovery of napalm (jellied gasoline), and to use the only two atomic bombs in existence to devastate the industrial cities of Hiroshima and Nagasaki. Two political decisions also stand out in Japanese memories.

[2] Herbert Feis, *The Road to Pearl Harbor* (Princeton: The Princeton University Press, 1950).

First, at the Potsdam (Berlin) Conference, held a scant three weeks prior to war's end, it was decided to force Japan into unconditional surrender and to reject an offer of surrender made through Moscow, which had as its sole condition preservation of the tradition of the Emperor's sovereignty. Second, the Soviet Union declared war on Japan on the day of the second atomic attack, giving Moscow five days of belligerency and almost no combat against Japan, but a claim to reparations despite five years of formal Soviet-Japanese nonbelligerency.

To the Japanese, the fire bombings were an unnecessary and heinous attack upon innocent civilian populations. These and the atomic bombings were wholly unnecessary in view of the offer to surrender on only a minor cultural condition. Since there was no strategic value to the use of atomic bombs, Japan already having been in virtual submission, these attacks are taken as evidence of an American intention to pulverize Japanese society, or to demonstrate American strength to the Soviet Union at great and indiscriminate cost to Japan. The opportunism of Soviet behavior was seen with equal suspicion. But one haunting question pervades all these suspicions: Would the West, and particularly the United States, have concluded the war in this manner had Caucasian rather than Oriental lives been at stake, and Western civilization rather than Asian?

During the occupation that followed, the Japanese faced not only national reconstruction, but also the revitalization of self-esteem under a victor whose intentions they had not trusted even in good times.

The American Occupation

The international climate in which Japan embarked upon restoration was one of utter turmoil. All Europe was in tatters; China was simultaneously in ruins and in civil war; and the Soviet-American wartime rapport had broken down immediately into a protracted Cold War. Japan would have to accept the United States as the sole occupying power despite the intention of the Allies to have a multilateral policy. It would also have to acknowledge the role of General Douglas MacArthur as the Supreme Commander for the Allied Powers in the Pacific, even though he personified the Allied conquest of Japan.

The Japanese were still less pleased with the American estimate that nearly a quarter-century would be needed to achieve the objectives of occupation: democratization of Japan; industrial restoration at a level below war potential; land reform and agricultural self-sufficiency; and societal purge of war criminals and imperialists. But, remarkably, nearly all of these had been achieved, or set in apparently irreversible motion, in little more than three years. Within that time General MacArthur had authorized the drafting of a new constitution, and by the end of 1948 he and others were publicly calling for an expeditious termination of the occupation.

Although the Japanese attributed the speed of success to their own forebearance as much as to American policy, they recognized that a prolonged occupation, if not oppressive, might be preferable to speedy independence. The cold war was underway; Korean reunification talks had broken down between Moscow and Washington; and the ideological balance of Asia seemed written in the forthcoming victory of Chinese communism over the Kuomintang (the Chinese Nationalist Party). Independence would mean dealing with the Soviet Union; balancing the interests of two Chinas; accommodating American economic and military might when its right of intrusion was no longer acknowledged; and surviving on industries which would be long on productive capacity but short on raw materials and energy sources. Now was scarcely a propitious time for new Asian ventures.

Again, however, the decision escaped the Japanese, as the occurrences within seven months of Mao's victory and the Korean War altered Japan's place in the American world scheme. No longer did the U.S. look upon Japan as a pastoral and self-sufficient island kingdom, but rather as a powerful, industrialized, and strategically located ally; an atomic fortress and haven for American investments; and a center of operations for American manipulation of the Asian power distribution. The cover of United Nations legitimacy in Korea could not conceal the fact that in its decision to contain communism in Asia, Washington had summarily transformed the purposes, the timing, and the consequences of the Japan occupation.[3]

The Pacific Treaties

Amidst these new circumstances John Foster Dulles began to negotiate the Pacific Treaties of 1951. Dulles' zealous anticommunism, heightened by events in China and Korea, seemed to ensure a revised role for Japan; his insistence on a "peace of reconciliation" rather than a "peace of retribution"[4] created a cordial negotiating environment. It was clear from the beginning, however, that within the framework of reconciliation, the United States would seek to acquire cold war access to Japanese territory, and would insist on including Japan in a growing chain of anti-Communist alliances. The peace of reconciliation would have to facilitate Washington's cold war strategies.

[3] Frederick S. Dunn, *Peace-Making and Settlement with Japan* (Princeton: Princeton University Press, 1963).

[4] As a young man, Dulles had been a member of the American Peace Commission at the Paris talks leading to the Treaty of Versailles. He came away from the conference with the conviction that the peace would not last because it was punitive, thus forming the basis for his later strategy of negotiating a Japanese peace treaty based on "reconciliation" rather than "retribution." See Townsend Hoopes, *The Devil and John Foster Dulles* (Boston: Atlantic-Little, Brown, 1973), especially chapters 2 and 7.

Of the four Pacific Treaties which resulted from Dulles' diplomacy, two pertained directly to Japan. (The other two linked the Philippines, Australia, and New Zealand to American alliances.) In the Peace Treaty, Japan was obliged to sacrifice virtually all territories acquired since 1895, and to enter into reparations negotiations with those Allied governments whose territories had been occupied by Japanese troops between 1931 and 1945. More important, however, were the clauses that prepared for Japan's inclusion in the American security system; as a consequence of these the Security Treaty went into effect simultaneously with the Peace Treaty. Both the Soviet government and the Chinese government of Mao were excluded from the Pacific Treaties.

In the early years of these agreements, great benefits accrued to Japan. Because of American willingness to bear the cost of Japan's security, the share of gross national product which would normally have gone to defense was invested instead in economic growth, leading to annual growth rates until 1971 of twice those of other industrial states. Favorable balances of trade and payments that accompanied this seemingly miraculous recovery enabled Japanese currency to share the spotlight only with German currency as the most valuable and desirable in the nonsocialist world. One measure of industrial growth is that from 1950 to 1973 Japan's gross national product multiplied more than eight and one-half times, most of that having occurred well after the postwar reconstruction and recovery (see Table 3–1). By comparison, during the same years the GNP of the United States multiplied approximately two and one-third times, and that of non-Communist Europe three times. By 1970, then, though Japan was not a militarily powerful state, its economic might had observers reassessing the ingredients of the world power distribution, and had induced scholars and statesmen to consider Japan an emerging superstate.[5]

But not all was well; for even as the Japanese economy surged upward,

TABLE 3–1   Japan's Economic Growth in GNP in Constant $US, 1973

1950	47.2 billion
1960	113.8
1965	181.9
1970	321.0
1973	414.3

Source: US Department of State Bureau of Intelligence and Research, *The Planetary Product*, 1973.

[5] For example, see Herman Kahn, *The Emerging Japanese Superstate: Challenge and Response* (Englewood Cliffs, N.J.: Prentice-Hall, Inc., 1971). See also Nobutaka Ike, *Japan: The New Superstate* (San Francisco: W. H. Freeman and Company, 1973).

external events imposed other burdens, many of which collided with the Japanese urge for more nearly self-determined foreign policies.

Relations with China

China's need for industrial goods and Japan's need for raw materials and markets create a remarkable trading partnership. Yet as Japan's ability to promote this relationship matured, American obsession with the isolation of China resulted in pressure to postpone massive Japanese trading with China. The Japanese interpreted this not only as an interference with national decision-making, but as an affront to national economic growth. They also viewed it as an American effort to use the isolation of China as an instrument for restricting Japanese competition with American manufactures. Furthermore, it was seen as a cause of unnecessary delay in normalizing the international relations of Asia, a delay from which Japan might suffer and for which it might be held responsible, despite its American origin.

Okinawa

Of the many territorial questions left over from World War II, none has been more excitedly symbolic to the Japanese than Okinawa. Even after conclusion of the Pacific Treaties, this large territory, regarded by the Japanese as virtually a fifth home island, had remained in American control, continuing as a major site for conventional and nuclear military strategies. Washington persistently rejected the growing demand for the reversion of Okinawa to Japanese sovereignty, particularly as the Vietnam War underscored the importance of Okinawa in American strategy. The question was further complicated in the United States Senate by powerful interests which insisted upon restricting Japanese textile exports to the United States as a condition for reversion of Okinawa.

American Military Bases

Under the terms of the Security Treaty, the United States maintained military bases throughout Japan. These bases were sources of particular resentment; they were viewed as remnants of the occupation, as symbolic of something less than sovereignty for Japan, and as a potential danger to Japan should the enemies of the United States take retaliatory action against the U.S. Most annoying to the Japanese was the continued use of their ports and territorial waters for servicing the nuclear submarine fleet, a presence that the atomic-bomb-conscious population detested. Successful efforts to negotiate the removal of nuclear weapons from the home islands and the requirement that the Japanese government be afforded the right of "prior consent" for the combat use of American bases on the home islands only partially allayed national dissatisfactions. A succession of American-oriented governments desperately sought compromise on these issues lest popular demand weaken the government and lead to a movement for national rearmament. With increasing fretfulness, a Japan restored to economic power and revitalized in national purpose reached for ways to effect a national role in a world in which it perceived its most troubling restraints to arise from its closest partner.

The Vietnam War

The enlarged military presence of the United States in Asia after 1965 brought new strains to Japan's foreign policy and to its internal politics. While the government tacitly supported the American commitment in Vietnam, the war became increasingly unpopular among Japanese. Particularly, it accentuated fears of Japanese involvement, should excesses of American strategy (such as B-52 launchings from Okinawa) result in retaliatory actions. The war also hardened the American position on the Okinawa issue, just as the balance-of-payments deterioration suffered by the United States during the war heightened American intolerance for Japan's export capability. Finally, to the extent that American involvement was motivated by the will further to isolate China and to contain its influence, the war threatened to prolong the hated restrictions on Sino-Japanese trade. Overlying all of these fears, however, was a prevailing apprehension that through its policy in Southeast Asia, the United States was attempting single-handedly to adjust the Asian power distribution in ways that would measure the benefits to the United States partly by costs to Japan.

Japan in a Changing World

From a century and a quarter of relations with the West, the Japanese had learned that international decisions concerning Asia tend to be made less by coordinated diplomacy than by the rush of events. Not inconsistently, then, as an opportunity for consideration of these issues seemed possible in the diminished fighting in Southeast Asia, the Japanese found their hopes dashed instead by new disrupting problems. At a time at which an independent role for Japan in Asian and world politics might have evolved, many of the basic assumptions on which Japan had built its political and economic policies were subverted.

The Nixon Doctrine. In its search for methods of face-saving withdrawal from Vietnam, President Richard Nixon's administration considered noninterventionary paths to Western-oriented political stability in the underindustrialized world. One such device was the Nixon Doctrine, first proclaimed during 1970.[6] Though its full meaning was never aired by the Nixon administration or its successor, its essence is that the United States will no longer intervene in civil or regional wars, but will provide arms and military information to help governments meet insurrections. The reaffirmation of the Japanese-American Security Treaty exempts Japan from the terms of the doctrine; yet its utterance nevertheless brings crisis to the politics of Japanese defense. What might the result be for the security environment of Asia and the Pacific? Is it now necessary for Japan to undertake a major remilitarization? Despite the formal status of the Security Treaty, do the Nixon Doctrine and the American withdrawal from Southeast Asia portend reduced reliability in the Japanese-American relation? Should Japan become a nuclear power?[7]

Regional events have compounded these security problems. The rapid changes in Southeast Asia from 1973 to 1975—particularly full American withdrawal and the exclusion of Western-oriented governments and factions from South Vietnam, Laos, and Cambodia—have opened a potential sphere of influence to which the Japanese government and investors have responded expeditiously. These opportunities seem offset, however, by the jeopardy to regional stability created by the precarious Soviet-American-Chinese triangle, and by the entry of India into the exclusive circle of nuclear powers (1974). At a time when the reliability of the American nuclear umbrella is in doubt, competitive ventures on an Asian continent of two regional nuclear powers (India and China) accentuate the urgency of whether Japan should "go nuclear." Long a heated issue in domestic politics between those who abhor nuclear strategy and those who consider it the only fruitful path to foreign policy independent of the United States, this topic is renewed by the Indian development.[8] To date Japan has not ratified the Nuclear Non-Proliferation Treaty (prohibiting the spread of nuclear weapons among its members), and is thus free from international legal constraint in this matter. The debate turns on constitutional questions.

In light of these events, and although Japan is in no immediate peril, the Japanese security formula is sufficiently eroded to require a major reassessment of the relationship with the United States. Will economic stability have to be compromised for a gross increase in military expenditures? The answer to that question has been consistently in the affirmative since 1970, as military expenditure has increased by nearly one-third (9

[6] Richard M. Nixon, *U.S. Foreign Policy for the 1970's*, Report to the Congress by the President of the United States, February 25, 1971.

[7] For a detailed consideration of the Nixon Doctrine's implications for Japan, see Robert E. Osgood, *The Weary and the Wary: U.S. and Japanese Security Policies in Transition* (Baltimore: The Johns Hopkins Press, 1972).

[8] Frank C. Langdon, "Japanese Reactions to India's Nuclear Explosion," *Pacific Affairs* 48 (Summer, 1975): 173–80.

percent increase per year) since that year. But to the Japanese the trend of this expenditure is less important than the perception that the precipitating disruptions result principally from American perfidy.

The First Nixon Shock. Events quickened after President Nixon announced in 1971 his intention to visit China the following winter. This decision, made without consulting Tokyo, took the Japanese by complete surprise. They could not comprehend even the remote possibility of Sino-American détente prior to complete resolution of the Southeast Asian war; and neither could they avoid suspicions about American motives in attempting to normalize relations with China even while forbidding Japan to modernize its relations, particularly with regard to trade. To make matters worse, if the U.S. ceased from isolating China and enacted the Nixon Doctrine simultaneously, were the imperatives for Japanese security multiplied? Were the concurrent changes of the security and political relations of Asia cumulative in the sense that the natural trading partnership between China and Japan might produce new forms of conflict? Once the national insult of the president's announcement had been digested, the anxiety took root of substantial change in Asia introduced unilaterally by the United States. The path to independent policy, so vivid only a few years earlier, now became cluttered by unforeseen, unknown, and menacing complications.

The Second Nixon Shock. Scarcely a month after the China visit announcement, the Nixon administration took steps to correct what it perceived to be the causes of economic recession, some of which were found in the international economy. Among other things, to reduce foreign competition in the United States, the government imposed for ninety days an additional tariff of 10 percent on all imported goods, with certain exceptions for underdeveloped countries and specially protected commodities. The Japanese interpreted this as an attempt to force a revaluation of their currency—a long-held objective in Washington—and as an assault on Japanese-built automobiles. A measure of the shock wave is that in 1970 U.S.-Japanese trade valued $10 billion, and had grown in 1973 to $19 billion. In all of its trading history, only with Canada had the United States previously done in excess of $10 billion business in a single year. Furthermore, for Japan the larger share of the total amount was in exports, enabling Japan to maintain an enviable balance of trade surplus.[9] Yet another

---

[9] Hisao Kanamori, "Future U.S.-Japanese Economic Relations," in Priscilla Clapp and Morton H. Halperin, eds., *United States-Japanese Relations in the 1970's* (Cambridge: Harvard University Press, 1974), pp. 58–78. For a summary of Japan's export distribution, see Ernest H. Pregg, *Economic Blocs and U.S. Foreign Policy* (Washington: National Planning Association, 1974), Report Number 135, pp. 124–26.

measure was the immediate effect of unemployment in the automotive industry.

By this act the United States had directly and boldly intervened in Japan's domestic and international economic policies as a reprisal for success, and as a measure for restricting Japan's ability to compete in the world's large industrial markets. Japan's postwar economic renaissance, generously supported by the United States as part of controlling the Asian power distribution during the Korean War and the cold war, was now too competitive. Once again, by unilateral American decision, the setting in which Japan would have to design its regional and world roles was fraught with the uncertainty of altered assumptions.

The Petroleum Crisis. Japan's economic stability was now subject to new pressures. Caught in global recession and inflation, forced by Washington to revalue their currency in a direction injurious to their prosperity, and once again conscious of their vulnerability to foreign economic decisions, the Japanese also saw domestic capital flow out to lucrative investment opportunities elsewhere. As a result of all these factors, they watched their remarkable growth rate slide toward zero, and their enviable payments surplus begin to dwindle.

Before effective changes could be made, the Organization of Petroleum Exporting Countries (OPEC) threatened Japan in 1973 with an oil embargo unless it either discontinued its relations and trading policy with Israel, or offered technological assistance to the OPEC members. Even after the embargo threat was withdrawn on the basis of an oil-for-technology agreement, the price of oil continued to rise to an intolerably high level, forcing Japan to petition the United States for a collective diplomatic offensive by the oil consuming countries.

But the humiliation of the petroleum crisis for the Japanese did not terminate with this reliance on Washington. Nor for Japan was the grave danger ended with removal of the embargo threat. There was deep concern for the purchase of Middle Eastern oil between 1973 and the development of alternative sources and adequate nuclear substitutes. In 1973, Japan was the world's sixth largest user of oil per capita, and eighth in total annual consumption, using one-third the amount consumed in the United States. (See Table 3–2.) Nearly three-quarters of all energy burned in Japan is oil; all of it is imported, approximately 80 percent from the Middle East. As early as 1972, it had been estimated that by 1985 Japan's annual consumption of energy would equal 40 percent of the total world use in 1970. In keeping with this prediction, the government had made plans for a twenty-fold increase in electrical generation from nuclear fuels. It was also exploring for oil with South Korea and Taiwan, arranging for petroleum exploration in Siberia under contract with the Soviet Union, and was discussing joint exploration with China.

TABLE 3–2   Comparative Energy Consumption, 1973, in Coal Equivalents, kilograms per capita

U.S.	11,960
W. Germany	5,792
UK	5,778
USSR	4,927
France	4,389
Japan	3,601
Italy	2,737
China	594
India	188

Source: *United Nations Statistical Yearbook*, 1974, pp. 359–62. Note that as per capita figures the absolute amounts of consumption are influenced by population. Note also that this is total per capita consumption, and is not restricted to industrial consumption per capita.

Japan's immediate response to the increased oil price was to expand industrial exports to the Middle East. Unable to compete with the United States and Europe in arms sales, however, Japan's ability to offset the rising price of oil was limited. Although it was able to increase the value of its exports to the region by more than five times in 1974, the first full year after the crisis commenced, the increased cost of petroleum importation, together with Japan's rising oil demand, resulted in a trade deficit with the Middle East of more than $11 billion, larger than that of any other state, and an increase of 320 percent over the preceding year.[10]

The combined effects of recent American economic and strategic policies and the petroleum crisis demonstrate the delicacy of Japan's transition from subordinate state to major power. On the one hand, Japan's apparent vulnerability has diminished the prospects of autonomous Japanese influence over Asia and in global politics. Yet, on the other hand, these disruptions have registered sufficient change in global relations to permit certain Japanese initiatives, including new patterns of foreign investment and joint exploration for petroleum. Furthermore, Tokyo has set out to conclude formal diplomatic relations with both Peking and Moscow, though early in 1976 the Kremlin broke off discussions because it thought Japan was hewing too closely to the Chinese view of intra-Asian relations. For its part, in efforts to repair relations with Japan as the principal American ally in the Pacific, the U.S. has been obliged to return Okinawa to Japan's sovereignty (1972), though Tokyo has formally acknowledged the utility of retaining non-nuclear American bases there.

[10] Atef Sultan, "Japan Sells Hard to Make Up Oil Deficit," *The Middle East Economic Digest*, December 5, 1975, pp. 5–9 and 29–30.

The Perspectives of America's Major Allies

Summary and Conclusion

Japan's transition from occupied state to a world power has had sudden last-minute diversions. Although, as Table 3–3 indicates, Japan's economic capacity as measured in gross national product is second only to the United States in the non-Soviet world and third in the entire world, the independence of its policies remains in doubt. Highly dependent upon external supplies of natural resources—particularly fuel—and upon stable external markets, the economy is ever-vulnerable to foreign pressures. By the same token, domestic and regional sensitivity to Japan's rearmament places severe constraints upon the likelihood of diminishing reliance upon the American security system in Asia, despite the growing fear that the American withdrawal from Southeast Asia and the declining American presence throughout Asia reduce the probability that the United States would go to the defense of Japan in case of nuclear or conventional war.

Matters are further complicated by Japan's awareness that the very success of the economy creates regional problems. Japan's status as the dominant economic power of Asia cannot go unnoticed by its neighbors, who will eventually compete for its markets and who are already aware of the political costs of Japan's burgeoning private investment in Asia and the Pacific.[11] Furthermore, it may be in their interest to restrict the availability of fuel to Japan. This raises still a new security imperative in view of Japan's heavy dependence on Middle Eastern oil; it could require more than a five-fold increase in naval strength to defend the seventy-five hundred mile sea journey from source to home.[12]

TABLE 3–3 Comparative Economic Capacities in GNP, 1973

	GNP ($US billions)	GNP per capita ($ US)
U.S.	1,289.1	6,127
USSR	624.0	2,499
Japan	414.3	3,766
W. Germany	346.6	5,590
France	257.3	4,948
China	181.3	202
UK	175.5	3,134
Italy	138.5	2,527
Canada	118.8	5,345

Source: Adapted from United States Department of State, Bureau of Public Affairs, *The Planetary Product*, 1973, pp. 21 and 24.

[11] Jon Halliday and Gavan McCormack, *Japanese Imperialism Today* (New York: Monthly Review Press, 1973).

[12] Jay B. Sorenson, "Japan: The Dilemmas of Security," *Asian Affairs*, July-August 1975, pp. 363–70, especially pp. 367–68.

The Japanese world view, then, is that of a nation that is developed economically, but that remains highly dependent upon the resources, markets, and stable economic policies of others in order to prosper. Most especially, the view is shaped by having arrived at the threshold of world power status at a time when the power distribution is changing rapidly, the role of the United States in Asia is unclear, and the conditions of security on which Japanese economic growth has been predicated are in upheaval. As a result, the national role remains undefined, and national politics is a battleground for decisions about changes in economic and military policies.[13]

Western Europe

Until a half century ago, world politics was Euro-centric. Europe was the center of the industrial revolution, home of the world's great financial capitals, site of the principal military and political rivalries, and the metropole from which vast empires were directed. Much of the world's population outside of Europe—in Africa and Asia—was under European domination; and still more in Australia, North America, and the Caribbean and the Near East owed their allegiances to one or another of the European powers. Even the American role in World War I, an intense but transitory plunge into global politics, did little to alter the fundamental structure of international politics. By refusing to join the League of Nations, the United States handed the management of international affairs back to the European governments. Neither could the defeat of Germany and the realignment of old empires change the fact that world politics revolved around Europe.

But the First World War set in motion certain inexorable trends. First, it gave Americans an external vision which they had not previously had, though in general their reaction was one of withdrawal. Still, the war demands on American industry produced a most modern and productive economy. Second, Russia's participation in the war ended with the Bolshevik Revolution in 1917, which gave birth to the Soviet Union and brought the Communist party to power. With a government dedicated to the transformation of a feudal society, massive industrialization, and the defense of state against capitalist encirclement, the Soviet Union meant change for Europe and the world. Third, in settling the issues involved in World War I, it was broadly acknowledged that imperialism and colonialism were major causes of war. The doctrine of national self-determination emerged and foretold the eventual collapse of the European empires.

[13] J. A. A. Stockwin, *Japan: Divided Politics in a Growth Economy* (New York: W. W. Norton and Company, 1975), particularly Chapter 12, "Issues of Foreign Policy and Defense."

In a real sense, then, World War I launched many of the forces that World War II concluded. While the Second World War left continental Europe in ruins, American industry had grown to unprecedented capability, as it had served all the allies including the Soviet Union since 1941. Similarly, while Western Europe depended upon the United States for reconstruction, the Soviet Union and the Eastern European states began a recovery of their own. Together, these events rearranged the international power distribution into one in which virtually all effective power was temporarily clustered around either the United States or the Soviet Union. Europe was cordoned into the Soviet-allied Eastern sector and the American-allied Western sector. World politics was no longer Euro-centric but bipolar, a configuration in which, far from being the pivotal point of global relations, Western Europe was an object of conflict between the two giants.

From this unaccustomed position, Western Europe looked to the United States for both defense and economic regeneration, objectives in which the United States readily assisted. Apart from America's European roots and heritage, the cold war confrontation with the Soviet Union dictated that the United States act to preserve democratic polities and free market economies wherever possible, particularly in Western Europe. This policy, though always expressed in ideological terms, had the firm support of American merchants and manufacturers, whose production surplus cried for external markets, and of American labor, which equally needed external buyers to maintain full employment. The investment community lent its support too, on the grounds that a reconstructed Europe would borrow American capital, and that a Western Europe staunchly defended from the menace of Soviet invasion would be a safe place for investment. The basic American cold war foreign policies, enunciated from 1947 through 1949, rose from ideological threat and from the convergence of these interests in the reconstruction of Europe. These included the European Recovery Plan (the Marshall Plan) of 1947, in which Washington committed almost $15 billion to Western Europe's revitalization; the Truman Doctrine (1947), which proclaimed Washington's intention to resist the territorial advance of communism, and on which the containment policy was based; and the institutionalization of European-American defense in the North Atlantic Treaty Organization (NATO) in 1949. Each of these moves presupposed a prolonged threat of Soviet aggression.

During the era of Europe's recovery and of agreement on the imminence of the Soviet threat, the cooperation forged by the Marshall Plan and NATO was constructive. But as Europe neared full restoration, and as the threat of war in Europe abated by the late 1950's, trans-Atlantic strains began to develop. Most of these occurred in the economic sphere, though there was a loss of harmony on security matters as well. Most important in both categories, however, was the uniting of Europe, a process of economic consolidation for more successful competition with the United States and revitalized Japan. As the states of Western Europe grew more interdependent after 1958, they asserted greater independence of the United States. American efforts to maintain the tenor of the trans-Atlantic partnership after the restoration of Western Europe fueled the potential conflict among allies.

The Uniting of Europe

When the European Recovery Plan was launched in 1947, the United States encouraged common economic planning among the aid recipients. The strategy for designing grant requests was for the European governments to study their common needs, design a policy among them, and submit a joint proposal to Washington. This was the beginning of co-operative economic planning, an idea that took firm roots by 1958. At that time, the economies of the region were rapidly fulfilling their recovery expectations, and the fear of invasion from Eastern Europe seemed remote. Now, however, though their individual economies were thriving (though not all equally), they realized their inability to compete with the United States. The American postwar starting point enabled the United States to outrace Europe in production of goods which sold better even in European markets than did European goods. Another reason for the noncompetitive position of the Europeans was that their national economies were too small to encourage the most efficient production. Furthermore, Europe was slow to develop its own capital market, and American money for multiplication of production facilities was scarce in this period, though it later became so abundant that its value dropped drastically. For all these reasons and more, the states of Western Europe seized upon the idea of a supranational economy, where the economic needs of the group would supersede those of any single state, and where trade among members would be facilitated while the entry of foreign goods would become more difficult.[14] (For a detailed discussion of international integration theory and the European experience, see Chapter 12.)

Because of its traditional reluctance to enter continental affairs and its unwillingness to join a French-inspired venture, the British government elected to take its own course. Hence as the European Economic Community (EEC, or European Common Market) was established by six Euro-

---

[14] For a review of the historical passage from cooperation to competition with an essentially European perspective, see Ernst H. van der Beugel, *From Marshall Aid to Atlantic Partnership* (Amsterdam: Elsevier Publishing Company, 1966), and Henry A. Kissinger, *The Troubled Partnership: A Re-Appraisal of the Atlantic Alliance* (New York: McGraw-Hill, 1965). For a study of European alternative strategies for effective global competition, see Alastair Buchan, *Europe's Future, Europe's Choices: Models of Western Europe in the 1970's* (New York: Columbia University Press, 1969), published for London's Institute for Strategic Studies.

pean states, the British set up the competing European Free Trade Area (EFTA). Together the Common Market and the EFTA included virtually all of industrial Western Europe. The EEC, with its larger industrial potential and its greater demand for industrial goods (particularly as EFTA became weakened by the declining British economy), was measurably the more successful of the two and, accordingly, the one which tended to widen further the trans-Atlantic division. France blocked Britain's attempt to leave EFTA and join the EEC in 1963 because of President Charles deGaulle's fervent desire "to de-Americanize" Europe, a goal which he deemed unreachable if Britain were to enter while retaining a special relationship with the United States. It was not until 1973 that Britain joined the EEC, together with Denmark and Ireland, leaving EFTA divided, but increasing the EEC from the Six to the Nine. Together, by 1973 the enlarged Economic Community (EC) had a GNP of over one trillion dollars and equivalent to 83 percent that of the United States. (See Table 3–4.) In addition, the combined economies of the EC outdistanced the United States in the production of such critical economic items as metal products and automobiles, though they generated only about half as much electricity as did America.

These observations do more than simply depict Europe's economic vigor. They also point to the ability of European manufacturers to compete with America, particularly in European markets. Furthermore, because the most productive members are also critical American military allies (notwithstanding France's withdrawal from the NATO integrated command in 1965), the data in Table 3–4 illuminate Europe's ability to resist American pressures in the security sphere as well as in the economic. Overriding these factors, however, is the most important one. Acting in

TABLE 3–4   US and EC GNP's, 1973

State	GNP $ US billion	Population (millions)	GNP/cap ($ US)
Germany	346.6	62.0	5590
France	257.3	52.0	4948
UK	175.5	56.0	3134
Italy	138.5	54.8	2527
Netherlands	60.0	13.4	4478
Belgium	46.1	9.7	4753
Denmark	28.3	5.0	5660
Ireland	6.6	3.0	2200
Luxembourg	1.8	.354	5085
Total EC	1,066.1	256.3	4146
U.S.	1,289.1	210.4	6127

Source: Adapted from U.S. Department of State, Bureau of Public Affairs, *The Planetary Product, in 1973.* pp. 21 and 24.

concert, the member states of the European Community comprise one of the most productive and therefore one of the most powerful and influential actors in the international system. Despite their individual problems, their disparities, their separate national identities, and the disagreements among them, it is as a composite actor rather than as individual states that they play a critical role in contemporary international relations as, together, they work to restore Western Europe as a principal world center rather than an area of Soviet-American competition, or as a handmaiden of American foreign policy. Thus it is the world perspective of this united actor that we explore here.

European-American Trade

The prime economic rationale underlying the EC is the theory of customs unions, which seek to expand trade among the members by eliminating tariffs and other trade barriers among them, and to guard against foreign imports by setting a common trade policy toward nonmembers. Through this device, the EC pursues economic stimulation by capturing a larger share of the European market, and by generating investment capital for expansion of production for external competition. The central objective is improved competitive position, though it was evident from the start that such competition would eventually run afoul of American economic nationalism. This was accepted by Europe as a natural extension of the cooperative recovery assisted earlier by the U.S.

While Europeans looked forward to trade equality with the United States and to the profitability of their customs union, Americans were quickly awakened to their potential losses. In a preventive step, Congress passed the Trade Expansion Act of 1962, which authorized the Executive branch to negotiate sweeping tariff reductions. To Europe the objective was self-evident: Americans, concerned that the toddling European Community might erode their lucrative export surplus, were searching for ways to reduce its competitive position. Because of these negotiations, and despite dire American predictions of trade loss, the *composite EC trade deficit* with respect to the United States has remained at approximately one and one-quarter billion dollars annually through 1973. However, in trade between America and the four most industrialized EC members, a modest European deficit in 1966 has spurted into a substantial surplus. Though the bulk of this is attributable to West Germany, only France has a deteriorating position in relation to the United States.

Europeans consider American efforts to manipulate the EC's trade balance, and particularly to undermine Germany's surplus, to be retaliations for Europe's success. This was especially pronounced in 1971 when the U.S. increased import tariffs by 10 percent in an attempt at economic stabilization. Because they considered this an assault on European competition and on the value of German currency, the EC Economic ministers jointly labeled the tariff increase a step short of an American declaration of trade warfare. They pledged that if the new and illegal tariff were not discontinued within ninety days, they would respond by increasing the barriers to American trade in Europe. A multilateral agreement on changes in currency valuations averted a showdown. The near-crisis demonstrated, nevertheless, the awareness shared by Europeans and Americans of the degree of damage which each can inflict upon the other in international trade. But from the European perspective, another issue fogs the route to full and equal competition: American ownership of European production through direct foreign investment.

American Direct Investment in Europe

The uniting of Europe commenced at a time when American investors were seeking external opportunities and when, in an effort to improve efficiency, industries were becoming multinational. Because the maturation of European customs unions threatened their exports, American manufacturers wished "to get behind" the tariff barriers presented by EFTA and the EC by buying and building plants in European nations as foreign subsidiaries. These would manufacture goods primarily for sale in Europe. Such goods, though bringing profit to American corporations, would be free of import duties in European markets. Subsequent increases in productivity would be financed not from fresh American capital, but from profit, the remainder of which would be repatriated and thereby removed from the European economy. The initial investment in this trend, recorded as capital leaving the United States, rose to such heights that the American balance of payments, already adversely affected by American commitment to Vietnam, slipped into severe deficit. President Lyndon Johnson responded by introducing a "voluntary restraints" program in which American firms were requested to moderate their foreign capital expenditures. But despite these pleas, by 1967 American firms controlled nearly 8,000 foreign subsidiaries, of which nearly half were in the EFTA and EC countries.[15] Of these, two-thirds were in Britain, France, West Germany, and Italy. The continuing outflow of capital for this purpose resulted in imposing mandatory controls in 1968.[16] Table 3–5 reveals the volume of direct American investment in the combined EC economy.

The prevalence of American capital and the extensive American ownership of European production have led to severe disenchantment among those Europeans who previously expected effective competition with the United States both inside Europe and out. Some have called upon Euro-

[15] Raymond Vernon, *Sovereignty at Bay: The Multinational Spread of U.S. Enterprises* (New York: Basic Books, 1971), p. 141.

[16] U.S. Department of Commerce, *The Multinational Corporations: Studies in U.S. Foreign Investment*, 1972.

TABLE 3–5 American Direct Investment in the European Community, 1960–1973 (in $U.S. billions)

1960	1965	1970	1973
$5.9B	$11.4B	$19.8B	$31.3B

Source: U.S. Bureau of the Census, *Statistical Abstract of the United States*, 1975.

Note: For the years 1960–1970, these figures represent Britain and the EC countries. Ireland and Denmark are not included. The amount for 1973, however, represents the full Nine.

peans to restore their own economic destiny by adopting American managerial techniques.[17] Others, as did French President Charles deGaulle, have insisted that the only path to effective competition is the "de-Americanization of Europe." Though this theme is not universally espoused among the EC members, it is widely felt that continued American domination of European capital and production not only defers equal competition, but actually places Europe in a position of dependency and colonization. This makes a double blow of American retaliations for Europe's success. Furthermore, since American firms have effectively penetrated the customs union and thus prevented European firms from dominating their own markets, the latter's share of European markets is too small to stimulate the most efficient production. As a result, the regional idea is rapidly giving way to the corporate demands for globalization of European industries. Thus more and more European industries, which were previously considered the foundations of regional integration, are going multinational instead.[18]

But intimidation in trade and ownership of production are not the only devices the United States uses to invade the autonomy of Western Europe. The military dimension of their relations, a cornerstone of their interdependence, is yet another device by which the imbalance of capabilities reduces Europe's progress toward regional self-determination.

The European Community and Trans-Atlantic Defense

If the emphasis of the European Community is on regionalism, then the underlying postulate of the Western security system is Atlanticism. And if the United States relates to the European Community in the economic sphere as an overbearing competitor, then it presents itself to the European members of NATO as a dominant partner, unsure of its objectives, but

[17] J.-J. Servan-Schreiber, *The American Challenge* (New York: Avon Books, 1968).
[18] Raymond Vernon et al., *Big Business and the State: Changing Relations in Western Europe* (Cambridge: Harvard University Press, 1974).

resistent to change in its stature. As in the economic sphere, the EC members acknowledge their reliance on the United States, but deplore the political and economic consequences of imbalance. Is American control of trans-Atlantic defense policy an instrument for preventing marked alteration of political and economic relations? Is it a means by which Washington and its economic interests pursue economic Atlanticism as an alternative to effective competition from a united Europe? Is European integration feasible in the presence of a NATO as presently structured? Is NATO integrative of Atlanticism, but disintegrative of Europeanism? [19]

Despite the clear European dilemma on the security issue, however, there is among the NATO partners considerable fragmentation of perception. All suffer a degree of torment concerning the acknowledged superiority of the Warsaw Pact's conventional capability over that of NATO. In consequence, any American political activity, particularly in the United States Senate, aimed at reducing American forces in Western Europe is viewed as a threat to regional security. Nevertheless, the Europeans differ in their attitudes about the imminence of threat from the East. The more liberal elements argue that the Soviet Union's demands for a stable European balance have been satiated and that with increasing concern in the Kremlin for the Sino-Soviet border in Asia, the likelihood of war in Europe is tiny. The more conservative opinion, however, suspects the tranquility of Moscow's European policy of comprising a wary, lurking presence, poised for any weakness in Western defenses which might invite a Soviet initiative. The Soviet Union, this opinion insists, is sufficiently powerful in both its nuclear and conventional arsenals to protect its Asian border against any threat from China and, at the same time, to act adventurously in Europe.

Only the French seem, at least on the surface, to have resolved the dilemma of reliance on American forces, on the one hand, and the desire for independence from American political and strategic policies, on the other. In 1965 France withdrew from the integrated command of NATO (though not from NATO itself) and ordered all of the alliance's installations out of French territory. It is almost certain, however, that this action was more symbolic than significant. France has continued to serve as an observer of NATO's affairs, and there is an obvious necessity for the NATO governments to defend France against external attack whether or not Paris participates in the institutional arrangements of the alliance. France, nevertheless, has basked in the self-satisfaction of having expelled a major instrument of what it considers to be American domination of Western Europe.

More typically, however, the NATO members have attempted to resolve cooperatively the dilemma of Atlanticism and Europeanism. Within

[19] Francis A. Beer, *Integration and Disintegration in* NATO (Columbus: Ohio State University Press, 1969).

The Christian Science Monitor

Le Pelley in The Christian Science Monitor © 1975 TCSPS.

Europe, for example, both Britain and France have undertaken independent nuclear policies, each premised not on the thought of destroying a potential enemy, but on developing the capability to inflict intolerable harm, a policy of minimal deterrence. These national developments have resulted in public debate about the creation of an Anglo-French deterrent, a prospective policy of combining British and French nuclear capabilities under a planning system which will reduce the dependence on American strategy. Furthermore, the Eurogroup within NATO continues to press collectively for a greater European voice in the strategic planning of NATO, an effort designed to take maximum advantage of the American commitment while at the same time minimizing European servitude to

The Perspectives of America's Major Allies

Washington's objectives for the alliance. None of these efforts, though, can deal effectively with a confrontation with the conventional strength of the Warsaw Pact without American participation. Americans, then, ask the question, "How much longer must we bear the cost of Western Europe's defense even while suffering from increasingly effective European economic competition?" Simultaneously, Western Europeans are asking, "How can we reduce our reliance on the United States without emasculating the alliance to the point at which the balance of forces across all of Europe is irreparably damaged? And how can we promote Europeanism without eroding Atlanticism to the point of inviting American retaliation and coercion?" To Americans, the costs of NATO are asymmetrical because they carry the bulk of the economic burden. But the Western Europeans believe they assume the social and political costs of the reliance on Washington. For as long as the relative costs are perceived and measured differently, the dilemma of Atlanticism and Europeanism will persist, and the Western perception of the international system will continue to focus most nervously on the dangers imposed by its closest non-European friend.

Canada

If there is one indicator that differentiates the relations of the United States with Japan and Western Europe from those with Canada, it is proximity. Like its Asian and European counterparts, Canada shares an extensive economic and security relationship with the United States. But that relationship has the added features of a 3,000 mile undefended border and a long tradition of intimate economic cooperation facilitated by closeness. Though until the end of World War II Canadian economic and political relations were more closely tied to the United Kingdom, the prevalence of the American economy since the war, and the aggressive diffusion of American capital, have reversed this course. At present, the trading relation between Canada and the United States reaches an annual value exceeding that of any other bilateral economic relation in history; such has been the case for over a decade. Canadian export trade with the United States in 1973 comprised over 14 percent of the Canadian gross national product, and its imports and exports combined represented fully 28 percent of the 1973 GNP.

These figures only begin to suggest Canada's total economic capacity, which at present ranks ninth in the world by gross national product and third by GNP per capita. Also, its capacity is increasing because of its vast mineral reserves. Supporting a population of only 22 million in one of the world's largest territorial masses will enable Canada to preserve its natural resources longer than most nation-states, though at the present rates of extraction the petroleum and natural gas reserves (presently known) will have been depleted within twenty-five years.

But despite these apparent foundations for national autonomy, the geographical closeness of the United States has fostered a pattern of investment, trade, and managerial control leading to what some call partnership and others label a colonial relationship. Still others are tempted to refer to an integrated Canadian-American economy, though such an observation ignores the asymmetry of benefits that befalls the United States. The conditions that surround the effort to establish full economic, cultural, and political sovereignty out of this lopsided partnership govern the Canadian world perspective.

Domestic Influences Affecting the Canadian World View

Canadian domestic politics is divided along several firmly drawn lines. Most significant among them is the ethnic distinction between the dominant Anglo-Canadians and the French Canadians, who are concentrated in Quebec Province. Although French Canadians consider themselves a nation within a nation, only at the extreme is French Canadian nationalism separatist. They are deeply persuaded that as a minority they have been exploited and oppressed by the English. Nevertheless, in their external outlook they are concerned for Canada's economic independence from the United States. As a self-proclaimed oppressed minority, they were unusually sympathetic to young Americans who emigrated to Canada rather than serve in the armed forces in Vietnam, and whose criticism of American foreign policy and of "the American establishment" accentuated the appetite for Canadian autonomy even more than for Quebec's secession.

For their part, the Anglo-Canadians have been slower to recognize the costs of economic ties to the United States, having for so long depended upon American capital for industrialization. Those who inhabit the industrial heartland, however, which for the most part is centered close to the American industrial complexes along the Great Lakes, have developed a new self-consciousness regarding managerial control, and are now eager to establish full Canadian economic sovereignty by reducing American ownership of the nation's industry. It is this geographic distinction which forms the second line of division among Canadians in determining the world outlook.

A third important line of difference in Canadian politics is that between continentalists and nationalists. Continentalists have resolved in their minds the partner/colony debate by declaring their preference for an economy integrated with that of the United States for the maximum profit of Canada. This view is now held most notably by mineral exporters who find that national pricing systems put them at a disadvantage with respect to prices that can be earned in the United States; and among those who re-

An American antiwar protest in Montreal, 1972.

Montreal Star—Canada Wide.

side at the industrial fringes, who believe that national investment policies favor the industrial heartland and retard the economic development of their own regions.

The nationalists, however—the growing number of Canadians who believe that American investment and ownership have already exceeded the desirable level—avidly support policies drawn to safeguard Canada from further encroachment, policies that will reduce American industrial ownership of Canada. It is principally the convergence of this sentiment among the Anglo-Canadians who comprise the new entrepreneurial class (and who yearn for national scientific and technological development) with the more traditional French Canadian nationalism that has led to the now widely recognized "new era" in Canadian-American relations.[20] The new

[20] Robert Gilpin, "Integration and Disintegration on the North American Continent," *International Organization* 28 (1974): 851–74. See also John Sloan Dickey, "Canada Independent," *Foreign Affairs* (July 1972): 684–99; and Gerard F. Rutan,

Anglo-Canadian nationalists, amply and vigorously represented in government, particularly deplore the deleterious effects upon Canada of American legal control over foreign subsidiaries in Canada. The government recognizes this problem of "extraterritorial control" as a political intrusion more costly than mere foreign ownership.[21] It is with these thoughts in mind that the nationalists have sharpened their focus of the Canadian world view on the economic relationship with the United States, though security, ecological, and cultural problems also exist.

Trade

As we have noted, trade between Canada and the United States is of extraordinary volume, both in industrial products and in natural resources. The Canadian subsidiaries of American-based multinational corporations add imports of their own to the vast northward flow of finished consumer goods and military hardware; and Canadian firms, American-owned or not, ship goods to the United States. As a result, the total volume of Canadian-American trade increases annually. Principally because of the export of Canadian natural resources to the United States, the value of Canada's exports to the U.S. exceeds the value of goods imported. The result is a Canadian balance-of-trade surplus. (Canada does likewise with respect to Britain, its second largest trading partner.) Perhaps more striking is that the surplus is rising even while Canada's *global* balance of trade is suffering an ever-widening deficit, as is indicated in Table 3–6.

But despite the apparent enviability of this position, the maintenance of a trade surplus with the southern neighbor has not been without high costs. In the long run perhaps the greatest cost will be premature depletion of natural resources. More immediately, however, Canadians are concerned with the American political and corporate controls to which their economy is susceptible. Particularly in the automobile industry, for example, stimulation of production occurred only by an Auto Pact (1965), in which Canada sacrificed tariff revenues in return for anticipated employment benefits and lower consumer prices. But employment has been subject to economic fluctuations in the United States and to the decisions of the multinational auto companies to relocate production. Furthermore, subsequent investment has come largely from profit, rather than from fresh capital flowing from the United States. At the intergovernmental level, in order to minimize Canada's trade surplus with respect to the United States, American policy on automobile trade ensures that in this single commodity, Canada will have a fluctuating deficit. Finally, Canadians fear

"Stresses and Fractures in Canadian-American Relations: The Emergence of a New Environment," *Orbis* 18 (Summer 1974): 582–93.

[21] "Foreign Ownership and the Structure of Canadian Industry: A Report of the Task Force on the Structure of Canadian Industry" (January 1968): 310–45.

TABLE 3-6 Direction of Canadian Trade, 1969–1973 (in $U.S. billions)

	1969			1973			1969–73 Change in Balance
	Imports	Exports	Balance	Imports	Exports	Balance	
U.S.	9,543.9	9,798.7	+254.8	16,510.6	17,115.8	+ 605.2	+238%
UK	731.6	1,029.8	+298.2	1,005.5	1,588.7	+ 583.2	+196%
World	14,310.9	13,529.2	−781.7	26,213.6	24,020.9	−2,192.7	−280%
U.S.% of Canada's World Trade	67	72		63	71		

Source: Adapted from *Direction of Trade, Annual, 1969-73*, p. 156, a publication of the International Monetary Fund and the International Bank for Reconstruction and Development.

88

that in their efforts to negotiate conditions that will enhance the industrial sector, they may be forced by Washington into a continental policy in natural resources which will both accelerate the depletion of reserves and further erode national autonomy.

Thus, behind the Canadian trade surplus lurk the dangers of such extreme reliance on a single partner for both import and export markets, and the problems of external investment and foreign industrial ownership which give rise to these external controls.

Direct Private Investment

During the lengthy period of British influence in the Canadian economy, private investment was mostly of the portfolio type—that is, purchase of stocks and bonds on securities markets. As the era of American domination began in 1950, however, with investments rising from approximately $5 billion to $25 billion in twenty years, the pattern shifted from portfolio investment to purchase of Canadian firms and mineral deposits, and construction of foreign subsidiaries of American firms. In the immediate postwar years and in the early years (1955–1965) of concerted Canadian industrial development, government planning took for granted that this direct private investment was profitable for several reasons. It brought needed managerial skills as well as capital; it hastened industrialization and the ability to exploit natural resource reserves; it created profit and increased employment; and it generated public revenue as well as export surpluses. The rapid and sustained increases in the gross national product and in per capita income seemed testimony to the wisdom of an open policy on direct private investment from the United States.

As Canadian economic nationalism began to rise, however, this policy was reappraised. Between 1964 and 1967, for example, Canadians who thought that there was enough American capital in their economy rose from 46 percent to 67 percent of those questioned. Clearly the national population had awakened to how much the partnership with the United States was decaying into colonial subordination. Table 3–7 dramatizes the basis for this fear. By 1972, only 37 percent of Canadians polled felt that they shared with the United States an economic partnership, while 34 percent felt that they had become colonized. Only 34 percent felt that dependence on the United States was good for Canada; 53 percent thought it bad.[22]

---

[22] For an extensive statistical study of Canadian attitudes toward American domination, see John H. Sigler and Dennis Goresky, "Public Opinion on United States-Canadian Relations," *International Organization* 28 (1974): 637–68. For a briefer survey pertaining specifically to attitudes on foreign investment, refer to John Fayerweather, *Foreign Investment in Canada: Prospects for National Policy* (White Plains, N.Y.: International Arts and Sciences Press, 1973), Chapter II, pp. 13–72.

TABLE 3–7   Foreign and American Ownership of Selected
Canadian Industries, 1971

Industry	% Foreign Ownership	% American Ownership
Motor vehicles and parts	95.7	95.6
Industrial electrical equipment	95.7	89.6
Iron mining	86.2	85.8
Rubber products	92.4	82.9
Petroleum refineries	99.9	72.0
Synthetic textiles	85.0	71.5
Oil and gas wells	82.6	65.0
Pharmaceuticals	82.2	68.6
Soap and cleaning compounds	92.5	62.1
Industrial chemicals	79.9	58.9
Aircraft and parts	91.6	48.3
Fruit and vegetable canners	67.4	62.3
Major appliances	58.5	58.5

Source: Adapted from 1967 Report of Corporations and Labour Unions Return Act as quoted in the Report of the Standing Committee on External Affairs and National Defence, on investigation into Canada-US relations (The Wahn Report), and as produced in Malcolm Levin and Christine Sylvester, *Foreign Ownership* (Don Mills, Ontario: General Publishing Co., Ltd., 1972), p. 74.

After decades of satisfaction with the profitability of American investment, national preoccupation turned to the sordid side. This spirit led to the report of the Gray Task Force in 1972, which focused as much on the costs of dependence as upon the benefits. In a marked departure from traditional assumptions, the Gray Report concluded that most of the profit which accrues to Canada is actually drawn *not* from American investment capital, but from the American corporations' ability to exploit Canadian resources.[23] If this is the case, then the wise course for Canada is to distinguish between investment policy as a capital venture and foreign ownership and, thereafter, to restrict foreign direct investment to a level below 50 percent ownership or control. As early as 1970, a plurality (though not a majority) of Canadians polled reported that they would approve a policy of restricting American ownership to 49 percent in any industry *even if* it meant a reduction in the national standard of living!

The Gray Report was followed only months later by an extensive government report on Canadian relations with the United States entitled *Options for the Future*, a statement on foreign affairs by Mitchell Sharp, Minister for External Affairs.[24] Major portions of this report deal with the question of whether asymmetrical interdependence with the United States

[23] Gray Task Force Report, *Foreign Direct Investment in Canada* (Ottawa: Information Canada, 1972).

[24] Published as a special issue of *International Perspectives* (Ottawa: Information Canada, Autumn, 1972).

automatically raises threats to Canada's economic sovereignty. The report suggests that in both trade and investment policies, Canada henceforth use as a measure of permissible relations the benefit to Canada and Canadians. Since then, Parliament has entertained a variety of proposals for screening investments by foreign sources in accordance with the requirement that a project strengthen the Canadian economy without further deteriorating national control over economic activity. Recognizing that excessive nationalism might damage the economy by repelling useful investments, the government seeks a policy that will run a delicate line between destructive nationalism and equally destructive continentalism.

Natural Resources

Canada's richness in natural resources permits a favorable trade balance with the United States. Though fuel products (including uranium) comprise the bulk of such resources, Canada is also plentiful in metal deposits. The United States is the largest customer, to the extent that by exporting half of its annual gas and oil production, Canada fulfills about 6 percent of the total American demand.[25]

In an era of fuel shortages and gloomy predictions about exhaustion of resources, it would seem that it is the United States that is dependent upon Canada in this regard; and on the surface this is accurate. From the Canadian viewpoint, however, this is but part of the story. As we saw in Table 3–7, the mining and refining facilities of Canada are heavily in foreign—and particularly American—control. As a result the profit from these enterprises contributes little to the Canadian economy, but is repatriated (sent back) to the United States. Moreover, the rate of production is determined less by Canadian public policy than by American demand and American corporate decisions. Of paramount importance is the tendency of Canadian fuel production to become enmeshed in American foreign policy. The OPEC threat of a total oil embargo as a lever on Israeli-American relations in 1973 heightened Washington's interest in a continental oil policy which would formally subordinate Canadian national policy to joint Canadian-American determination. Coupled with gradual depletion of Canada's reserves, such overtures threaten Canadian autonomy.

Security

Although the current principal Canadian-American links are economic, they were originally forged around the need for a continental defense policy during World War II. That partnership was epitomized by including Canada in the Hyde Park Declaration of 1941, which meant a

[25] Ted Greenwood, "Canadian-American Trade in Energy Resources," *International Organization* 28 (1974): 689–710, at p. 703.

The Perspectives of America's Major Allies

common production effort with the United States and Britain to meet wartime industrial and munitions needs. Later Canada became an active member of the North Atlantic Treaty Organization, though it declined to participate in the Inter-American Treaty of Mutual Assistance, the military wing of the Organization of American States. The continental radar defense system, NORAD, is a joint Canadian-American undertaking of long standing, as are several bilateral defense planning boards.

Despite this cooperation in common security matters, Canada has steadfastly refused to endorse the entirety of American defense strategy. Ottawa was one of the first Western capitals to break with Washington over both Korea and Vietnam; it sold wheat to China and the Soviet Union during the era of containment; it opened diplomatic relations with China during the Vietnam War (though at a point at which this act probably facilitated American withdrawal from Southeast Asia and aided Sino-American normalization); and while reducing its commitment to NATO, Canada became one of the main contributors to United Nations armed peace-keeping expeditions. It is evident that one of the central tenets of Canadian defense policy is to distinguish between Canadian-American relations on continental and on extracontinental matters, respectively.

This independent attitude results not simply from a different ideological view of the world, or from disavowal of a global role. It rises instead from the will to conduct foreign policies from which Canada will prosper quite without the constraints of the American world view. It assumes that transnational economic relations are more effective governors of the international system than are ideological confrontations and arms races. This attitude has enabled the Canadian government to reduce military expenditures over the last decade both in absolute number of dollars and as a percentage of GNP. Built into this policy is the realization that threats to Canadian security are extremely remote. Canada grows less responsive to what it considers excessive sensitivity in the United States to apparent threats to the security of North America and to the common economic interests of the U.S. and Canada.[26]

Conclusion

As one of the world's most productive states, Canada has all the ingredients of independent and prosperous foreign policies, and of continued national economic growth and autonomy. At present, however, neither of

[26] For more thorough treatments of Canada's quest for autonomy see Peter C. Dobell, *Canada's Search for New Roles: Foreign Policy in the Trudeau Era* (London: Oxford University Press, 1972); Kari Levitt, *Silent Surrender: The Multinational Corporation in Canada* (Toronto: Macmillan of Canada, 1970); and William Henry Pope, *The Elephant and the Mouse: A Handbook on Regaining Control of Canada's Economy* (Toronto: McClelland and Stewart, 1971).

these goals is held in the tight control of Canadian decision-makers, inasmuch as the resources and production facilities on which each relies are controlled by foreign interests, mostly American. Since this degree of external control raises the specter of foreign interference, the Canadian world view is one that is especially wary of the motives, needs, and machinations of its neighbor to the south, a neighbor which is friendly but rapacious; tolerant but ambitious beyond its means; libertarian in philosophy but determined that the foundations of its global supremacy will not be eroded. It is because Canada is so closely tied to those foundations, and because its quest for autonomy is perceived by the U.S. to contribute to their erosion, that the Canadian perspective on the international system is tinted by a growing sense of association with the dependent middle-ranking powers. Also, there is a commensurate sense of separation from the United States to the extent that the United States insists on those modes of interdependence that prevent Canada from achieving a full sense of autonomy in a world which it finds otherwise comfortably peaceful.

Conclusion

In a world of nuclear superpowers and economic upheaval caused by the new roles of the mineral-rich states, it is understandable that the American student of international affairs should overlook the diversity of perception among even those states that are most interdependent. It is not the purpose of this chapter to argue that the Western alliance is in imminent danger of collapse or that the foundations of cooperation within it have deteriorated beyond repair. It is intended to demonstrate, rather, that the volume of political and economic transaction which occurs among the Western allies in North America, Western Europe, and Asia creates internal problems, difficulties that are not related to attitudes concerning the Soviet Union or China or the Third World. Close mutual identity fertilizes inequalities, stimulates demands, and breeds resistance. As the conditions of world order enable America's industrial allies to reduce their dependence on Washington, they find themselves confronting an ally which, through the power of military and economic preponderance, wishes to forestall those changes in conditions that would advantage its allies but disadvantage itself. Because their own global perspectives differ vastly from those of the United States, these allies struggle to avoid subordination to American foreign policy.

4

The Chinese Perspective

The world perspective of the People's Republic is based on a fusion of two great forces: a *national* force flowing from China's long history, and an *ideological* force of Marxism-Leninism-Maoism. Both elements must contribute to an analysis of contemporary policy and outlook. The national force is a consequence of a continuous political experience spanning two thousand years. But the infusion of Communist ideology has modified and reshaped China's self-perception and the image of the outer world. Perhaps the historical force accounts for three quarters of the perspective of the present leadership and the ideology of communism for most of the remaining quarter.

China's history falls broadly into three periods: (1) the long classical epoch of imperial greatness (the "Middle Kingdom"); (2) a century of degradation and Western domination from 1840 to 1945; and (3) the modern period of national revolution and rebirth. It is impossible to understand China today without at least a general comprehension of these three periods.

The Middle Kingdom Period: Classical China

Classical China was a vast empire comparable to the great Roman Empire in the West, but persisting over a longer historical period. Most of the people under the direct sovereignty of the "Middle Kingdom" were ethnic Chinese (that is, Han Chinese), but this included a multitude of regional, cultural, religious, and linguistic differences. Chinese were as different from each other as the European peoples, and their integration into a single political unit was one of the great feats of early social engineering that is still not completely understood.

One factor behind this vast system of central government may have been that China required for its survival a vast irrigation network to control the twin problems of flooding and drought that are characteristic of its rivers. The basic requirements of agricultural production depend on rigorous social controls to ensure orderly development of hydraulic works over the huge territory. Because of their mutual water needs, the diverse lands of China joined politically.

This is not to suggest that China was a fully integrated society. Local potentates known as "warlords" wielded great power in their regions throughout Chinese history, and during long periods the emperor ruled only at their discretion. When the imperial center was weak, the warlords carved out zones of control and reduced the emperor to a powerless figurehead dependent on the warlord armies. Only when the imperial court was strong, free of corruption, and skillful in building necessary coalitions could the power of the warlords be reduced and the central government be able truly to rule. In a sense, the empire was a syndicate of local organizations; tension always existed between the central and regional powers.

The authority of the emperor was legitimized by the belief that he ruled by divine sanction as the Son of Heaven occupying the celestial throne. Emperors were dethroned throughout Chinese history, but this was explained by the convention that they had lost the mandate of heaven, as evidenced by the success of their enemies, and the divine sanction had therefore passed to the new rulers.

The officially encouraged culture of China was essentially conservative. It emphasized the Confucian virtues of obedience and "filial piety," a system of moral obligations guiding all social behavior. Individuals had their meaning mainly as members of the nuclear family or the community, and through other group identities. Within these units every individual had some importance; outside them the individual was nothing.

The educational system emphasized knowledge of the classic writings. It was more concerned with the development of values than with the acquisition of functional knowledge; and advancement in society, to the extent that it depended on education, stemmed more from command of the ancient texts than from expertise.

All segments of Chinese thought, even reformist and revolutionary, were portrayed as conservative and restorative of the principles in the venerated classics. Reforms were rationalized as reinterpretation of the great books, said to be more consistent with the original intentions of the texts than existing practices (comparable to the U.S. Supreme Court's stimulation of social change by reinterpretation of the Constitution). This system of reverence for the classical texts served as a stabilizing element in Chinese history. It encouraged a profound respect for literacy; scholar/administrators were revered and powerful men, and the inventor of writing was deified. The nation was guided by the accumulated wisdom of a thousand years.

The Chinese believed themselves to be the center of world civilization, having relatively little contact with other peoples except weak states on the periphery of the empire. Many of these were periodically conquered by China during expansive phases, only to regain independence when the warlord struggles reduced the emperor's ability to exercise control in the outlying regions. (This expansion and contraction of China over time makes it difficult to define today exactly what the boundaries of the classical kingdom were. China's proper "historical borders," over which there is now so much contention, depend on the historical dates chosen as the base years.)

Under the *tribute system*, the rulers of the peripheral societies kept themselves in power by acknowledging the superiority of the Chinese emperor, sending gifts and offerings of homage. These gifts were not significant in economic terms, but they reinforced the Chinese national self-image as the "Middle Kingdom" at the center of known civilization. Non-Chinese were regarded as "barbarians." A new envoy would arrive with a caravan of gifts for the emperor, kneel before the Son of Heaven three times in the act of kowtow, and present the tribute. This ritual set the tone for the entire relationship between China and other peoples, one not of equality but of dominance and submission. China saw little need for the outside world and therefore sent forth few explorers, traders, or conquerors.

The Century of Humiliation: The Meeting with the West

This stable, conservative, and self-confident Chinese society was in for a rude awakening when it came into contact with the dynamic societies of Europe and North America. The Chinese were very poorly prepared for this experience, and the shock of it has reverberations still.

The first Europeans came to China to spread Christianity and to find trading opportunities. The missionaries carried the word of God to heathen peoples, proselytizing, spreading human kindness, and fighting such savage practices as the binding of girls' feet. The traders were more frankly self-interested. They wanted Chinese silk, spices, and other goods, and proposed to find markets for their own products.

Both the Christians and the merchants discovered that their arrival stirred relatively little interest in China. In other parts of the world, explorers had been revered as gods or at least as men of extraordinary power and inventiveness, but in China they were received as envoys from inferior civilizations. Early Chinese maps portray entities called "England," "France," "America," "Portugal," and so on, as small islands on the fringes of a world with a huge China at the center. The advanced products of Europe that so dazzled other peoples were received unexcitedly in China. The Son of Heaven wrote to the king of England in 1793:

> The virtue and prestige of the Celestial Dynasty having spread far and wide, the kings of myriad nations come by land and sea with all sorts of precious things. Consequently, there is nothing we lack, as your principal envoy and others have themselves observed. We have never set much store on strange or ingenious objects, nor do we need any more of your country's manufactures.[1]

Christian missionaries were tolerated but also were regarded as a nuisance.

China may not have been much interested in the Europeans, but the Westerners coveted China. By 1715, the British had established the first commercial base at Canton, and they were soon joined by French, Dutch, and American traders who, under close Chinese control, were confined to tiny enclaves and hampered by travel and other restrictions. Europeans were required to deal exclusively with a government trade monopoly, and Chinese were forbidden to teach them languages. Naturally, the traders grew increasingly unhappy with these restrictions, and energetic representations were made to the emperor, but to no avail.

Perhaps the most serious problem to the traders was the relative lack of interest in Western products. To buy from China they had to sell in exchange something that the Chinese wanted. The Europeans discovered that there was one major marketable product. Its nature and the fact that its open sale was encouraged may surprise the modern reader. The product was opium.

Opium had been known in China for many years, but as in Europe and America, its sale and use were prohibited. Before the Europeans stimulated the trade, opium addiction was a minor problem, partly because Chinese cultural traditions discouraged personal hedonism and antisocial behavior. But after the European trade reached its peak, in some communities as much as 50 percent of the population was addicted. The imperial government tried repeatedly to stop this traffic by decree, but with little effect. In 1729, at the time of the first decree, importation was approximately 200 chests of pure opium per year. By 1830, this had grown to about 19,000 chests, and by 1838 to 30,000 chests. European persistence joined with ineffective decrees and corruption among Chinese officials to encourage growth of the drug trade.

The Opium War

The encounter of China with the West culminated in the Opium War in 1839, when a serious effort was finally made to halt the corrupt trade. A Chinese official named Lin Tse-hsu, commissioned to control the contra-

---

[1] Quoted in John K. Fairbank and Ssu-yu Teng, eds., *China's Response to the West: A Documentary Survey* (Cambridge: Harvard University Press, 1954), p. 19.

band, ringed the commercial enclave at Canton with troops, seized $11 million worth of opium, and drove the drug traffic out of Canton altogether. The British government, construing this as aggressive interference with freedom of international trade, promptly initiated a battle that resulted in the destruction of the Chinese forts at Canton and the signing of the Treaty of Nanking in 1842. In military terms China's losses were minor. But a handful of barbarians employing the mere gadgetry of their inferior civilizations had been able to humble the great Chinese empire. As one Chinese official said at the time to the British, "Except for your ships being solid, your gunfire fierce, and your rockets powerful, what other abilities have you?" [2]

The Opium War was the first in a long series of national defeats that lasted from 1840 to 1945, the Century of Humiliation. During this hundred years the power of the celestial throne was destroyed and China found itself increasingly the victim of external enemies—Europe and Japan—and internal dissolution—the warlords.

The Opium War itself led to major losses. In the Treaty of Nanking, China was forced to give Hong Kong to Britain "in perpetuity," to reopen Canton and the opium trade, to pay $21 million in reparations (a huge amount, equivalent to the American federal budget at the time), and most important of all in the long run, to give four more "treaty ports" to the Europeans. Treaty ports were put under the direct control of the Europeans; they were "extraterritorial," meaning that even civil laws were to be enforced by European courts. (In Cushing's Treaty of 1844, the United States was granted similar rights.) These "unequal treaties" led to many insults, including lax treatment of Europeans convicted of crimes against Chinese and even a sign in a park in Shanghai prohibiting Chinese and dogs.

China went into steady decline after the Opium War. In 1858, there was another skirmish in which British, French, American, and Russian negotiators, backed by thirty gunboats and 3000 troops, forced open eleven more ports to trade. Worse, they demanded for the first time access to the interior, meaning penetration from the coastal areas into the vast heartland. Now all of China would be open.

The T'aip'ing Rebellion

Another step in the decline was the T'aip'ing Rebellion, a civil war which occurred during the same years as the American War of the States, 1861 to 1865. In the American war about 400 thousand died; in China the losses were closer to 20 million. The Rebellion was a mass uprising led by a zealous Christian who had been converted by a missionary and believed that God whispered to him at night to redeem the nation. The T'aip'ings

[2] Quoted in John Stoessinger, *Nations in Darkness* (New York: Random House, 1971), p. 14.

favored communal forms of social organization and production, a kind of peasant communism before Marx.

At first the Europeans looked with interest on the Rebellion, thinking that its avowedly Christian leadership might have beneficial results. With European neutrality, the rebels almost succeeded in destroying the Manchu Dynasty. But late in the struggle, the Western governments concluded that the fanatical zeal of the T"aip'ings might make them more difficult to deal with than the corrupt officials of the imperial court, and they aided the emperor in putting the rebels down. The war ended with the imperial government weakened, the peasant movement destroyed, and the Europeans strengthened. The very power of the Manchu Dynasty to survive thereafter depended directly on the Europeans.

Chinese society entered a period of self-criticism. How could China prevent total colonization by Europe? The policy of clinging to the great traditions and refusing to acknowledge the inevitability of change had failed. China had scorned Western technology, but a handful of foreigners had reduced China to submission. This point was driven home in 1894 when Japan, which had met the Western challenge by adopting Western economic and industrial values, seized the peninsula of Korea from China. In a mere quarter century Japan had modernized its economic and military capacities while China had declined. The contrast was particularly humiliating.

Rebirth and Revolution: China Fights Back

Only with the victory of Chinese communism in 1949 can the control of China from the outside be said to have ended. But even during the latter half of the subjugated period there were significant attempts at national self-assertion.

The Boxer Rebellion

The first of these was the Boxer Rebellion in 1900. The Japanese victory over China (1894–1895), the spread of European commercial exploitation, and the growth of Christianity outraged national sensibilities, and some nationalists believed that the only recourse was a popular uprising against the white devils. In 1900, large numbers of young patriots joined in a rebellion by the Society of Harmonious Fists, otherwise known as the Boxers. Attacks on converts to Christianity, on missionaries, and especially on European commercial and industrial interests aroused the Europeans to resist. Here was a struggle between Chinese who felt that they were defending national independence and Europeans who thought of themselves as defending the rights of free trade and protecting their citizens. The

Chinese were enraged by the unceasing advances of foreign profiteers and missionaries. The Europeans were enraged by the assassination of the German minister and other wanton acts of violence against Western civilians and their Chinese friends. The United States demanded "speedy suppression of these rioters, the restoration of order, the punishment of the criminals and the derelict officials, and prompt compensation for the property destroyed." [3]

The Boxer Rebellion was counterproductive and stimulated foreign exploitation rather than stopping it. An eight-nation European force crushed the rebellion and looted the city of Peking. The collaboration of the Chinese government with the Boxers destroyed the remnants of foreign cooperation. Westerners now proposed the wholesale dismemberment of China into "spheres of influence" under the control of the various European powers. But the British and the Americans were opposed to the spheres-of-influence concept and insisted on the Open Door, under which there would be freedom of trade in all parts of China—that is, everybody would share equally in the rape of the Chinese people.

Instead of outright colonization, France got rights at Kwangtung, Kwangsi, and Yunnan in the South; the Russians got control of the railroads in Manchuria; the Germans got rails and mines in Shantung; Britain extended its holdings opposite Hong Kong and got development rights in the Yangtze Valley; and Japan got trading concessions in Fukien Province. American traders, who had no exclusive trading areas, moved gradually inland, assisted by the navy's right to patrol the Yangtze River.

Sun Yat-Sen and the Republic of China

The rebellion of the Boxers failed, but the revolutionary spirit spread and deepened. In 1911 a nationalist rebellion by followers of Dr. Sun Yat-sen, the father of modern China, succeeded in overthrowing the Manchu Dynasty, which was by then thoroughly discredited. But the revolutionists had seized a rump government. Real power had gone to the warlords, who filled the vacuum created by a weak center. Sun Yat-sen was quickly replaced by warlord puppet Yuan Shih-k'ai, who suppressed Sun's Nationalist Party (the Kuomintang). Sun fled the country, the party went underground, and the ideals of 1911 were temporarily defeated.

The Russian Revolution in 1917 revived the cause of Chinese nationalism. When European revolutions failed to materialize and Russia found itself an island in a hostile capitalist sea, the Soviet leaders looked to the possibility of a friendly China with great interest. In 1922, the Russians offered to Sun Yat-sen substantial aid for his Kuomintang party. The Russians conceded that "the conditions necessary for the establishment

[3] Quoted in O. Edmund Clubb, *Twentieth Century China* (New York: Columbia University Press, 1964), p. 27.

of either socialism or communism do not exist in China." In exchange, Sun admitted the Chinese Communist Party into the Kuomintang. Russian aid reawakened hopes of national rebirth.

Sun Yat-sen's death in 1925 occasioned the rise of a powerful new figure in the leadership of the Kuomintang: Chiang Kai-shek. Chiang was later to lead the most corrupt elements in China in their struggle to cling to power, but in this early period he was an important figure in the Chinese nationalist movement.

Chiang Kai-shek

Chiang organized and led a military campaign to break the power of the warlords in order to reunite China and set it on the path to national development. In this so-called "Northern Expedition," portrayed in the American movie "Sand Pebbles," Chiang's armies swept the country and destroyed or absorbed the power of the warlords. In some cases, notably Shanghai, the Communists were the main patriotic force, and they simply turned the keys to the city over to Chiang when they arrived. With the success of the Northern Expedition, a major step in the renewal of China had been taken.

Chiang rewarded the Communists for their efforts by turning on them in the middle of one quiet night in 1927, having them dragged from their beds and shot in the streets. He did not want any competitors for power in the system of personal control he was to create. In one sweep, the membership of the Communist party was reduced from 50,000 to 10,000.

The Rise of Mao

In 1928, a new figure emerged to save the Chinese Communist Party, a previously minor functionary named Mao Tse-tung. In five years of difficult organizing (1928–1933), he built a party of 300,000 and a Red Army to oppose the KMT (Chiang's Kuomintang). However, Mao's forces were no match for the huge Kuomintang, and in 1933, 400,000 KMT troops killed 60,000 Red soldiers, still another defeat for revolution in China. The surviving elements of the Red Army made the famous Long March to sanctuary in the mountains.

No ordinary retreat, this was a 6000-mile forced march by 90,000 men and women which took more than a year, while they evaded KMT harassment on all sides. It was one of the great feats of military history and is celebrated in poems and operas throughout China today. Only 20,000 troops reached Shensi, but a kernel of the Red Army survived to fight another day.

Another element entered this complex picture in 1931. While the struggle unfolded between opposing Chinese forces, foreigners were continuing their rape of China. As late as 1936, foreign interests still con-

What's unusual about this 1935 Kuomintang government currency?
It is printed in English on one side, reflecting the dominant position
that foreign businessmen held in the Chinese economy.

trolled 95 percent of China's iron, three quarters of its coal, half its textile
production, most of its shipping, the bulk of public utilities, and much of
its banking, insurance, and trade. Half of the industrial workers in Shanghai were employed by foreign firms.[4] This foreign control continued right
up to World War II.

Japan

Japan had a relatively small piece of the exploitive action in China.
Japanese militarists, backed by the booming industrial revolution and the
dynamism of Japan's economy, determined in the late twenties that Japan
needed an empire of its own to assume its proper place in the sun. In 1931,
Japan invaded Manchuria to gain position in the Chinese industrial heartland. The invasion came by way of the Korean peninsula (controlled by
Japan as a result of the Russo-Japanese War of 1904–1905) and achieved
a foothold for further expansion to create the so-called "Greater East Asia
Co-Prosperity Sphere," that is, the Japanese empire in Asia and the Pacific.

Chiang paid relatively little attention to the Japanese threat, concentrating his attacks on the Communist forces. This choice discredited him
in the eyes of former allies in the nationalist movement, and in 1936, he
was kidnapped by some of his own Manchurian officers who demanded a
more active resistance to Japan. To gain his own release, Chiang agreed

---

[4] Jan Prybyla, *The Political Economy of Communist China* (Scranton, Pa.: International Textbook, 1970), p. 58.

to form an uneasy united front with the Communists to resist the growing Japanese advance.

Soviet Involvement

It may be wondered why the Chinese Communist Party was willing to form even a temporary alliance with the KMT, considering the 1927 bloodbath and the deep bitterness between the two factions. One major consideration was Russian pressure. Soviet observers doubted that revolutionary conditions were ripe in China, and regarded an effective struggle against Japanese expansion as a more immediate issue. Not least important in this Russian opinion was the threat Japan, if not checked, might pose to Eastern Russia itself. Soviet aid to China, which until 1941 was far more significant in amount than American aid, therefore went mainly to Chiang. By 1941, this amounted to $250 million in military loans, 885 planes, provisions for 24 Chinese divisions, 4,000 Soviet advisers, and several hundred Soviet pilots. Virtually all of this went to the KMT, and on a number of occasions Soviet supplies were used by Chiang against Communist forces. Representations by Mao to Moscow demanding a larger share of these supplies were ignored. And still the Chinese Communists acceded to the demand for a united front.

A main theme of the second world war in the Asian theater was the Japanese attempt to colonize all of China. American support for the Chinese resistance, climaxed by the dropping of atomic bombs on two Japanese industrial centers, finally achieved the defeat of the Japanese militarists in 1945. China's darkest hour had ended, but disorder and administrative chaos followed the Japanese withdrawal. The Soviet Union, expecting the restoration of effective KMT government in the recovery, lost no time in looting the industrial wealth of Manchuria, transporting whole Chinese factories back to Russia. The Russians urged the Chinese Communists to join a coalition with the KMT as the only effective means of gaining access to a portion of political power. This coincided with the American view, as expressed in the mission of General George Marshall, that further struggle between the KMT and the Communists would be useless and fratricidal, and that a coalition should be constructed to speed national recovery.

The Rise of the Communist Party

But this time the Chinese Communists had higher hopes and different intentions for an independent strategy. Mao knew that the administrative structure of the KMT was shattered by the war, and that popular support for Chiang had evaporated. The Communists had emerged from the war in many areas as the heroes of the anti-Japanese resistance. The seeming selflessness and patriotism of the Communist forces in wartime were contrasted in the public mind with the image of the Kuomintang as a self-seeking party of corrupt officials and landowners clinging to their own position in society. When the Communists entered a village, they turned all land over to the peasants. When the KMT reentered, the initial act was often land repossession. The difference was not lost on the peasants.

In the civil war that raged from 1945 to 1949, the position of the KMT steadily declined. Whole divisions of Chiang's soldiers, including even their officers, deserted to the Red Army. To the end, the Russians continued to write off the Communist case as hopeless, and continued their relationship with Chiang. But the fierce determination of Mao's forces led to the final rout of the KMT in 1949. Chiang fled with the remnants of his army to the island of Taiwan (Formosa), subdued the people of that island when they resisted, and established a new but much reduced dominion behind the shield of the U.S. Seventh Fleet, which since 1950 has protected the KMT from attack from the mainland. In the view of mainland Chinese, this United States act was an unjustified intervention denying the Chinese people the right to complete their own revolution and preserving the insulting fiction of a rump "government in exile." Nevertheless, with the flight of the KMT the Century of Humiliation was concluded, and China was reborn as a free and self-determined nation.

The Chinese World Outlook

The world outlook of Communist China since 1949 has been deeply influenced by this history. Unlike the Soviet Union or the United States and its principal allies, China's soul has been seared by exploitation, humiliation, and oppression. The seemingly endless waves of foreign conquerors passed through China within the memory of the current generation of leaders.[5] The difference between the sturdily independent and self-sufficient China of today and the pathetic and degenerate China before is obvious even to its enemies. Without exaggeration, the absolutely overriding consideration of Chinese foreign and domestic policy has been the restoration and preservation of China as a powerful and independent nation invulnerable to external conquest and domination. This goal has required both objective and subjective changes, including the revival of self-confidence. But there is no disagreement among modern Chinese leaders concerning the paramount necessity of national defense and self-sufficiency. The enemies of China must be kept at bay—and doing so means, as we shall see, deflecting threats from the world's three richest powers: the United States, the USSR, and Japan.

The intensely nationalist outlook of the Communist leadership dictates

[5] It is interesting that no recent American president has felt compelled to learn the Russian language—let alone Chinese. Nor has any Soviet premier been known to speak Chinese or English. But Chou En-lai was fluent in both Russian *and* English.

an emphasis on defensive, China-centered priorities in international relations. We can infer the following hierarchy of priorities in the formulation of Chinese foreign policy since 1949:

1. Defense against external military attack or domination.
2. Prevention of foreign nonmilitary interference in Chinese domestic affairs.
3. Renunciation of the unequal treaties lingering from the Century of Humiliation.
4. Reintegration of outlying and alienated territories (for example, Tibet) and, insofar as possible, recovery of territories lost to foreign powers.
5. Restoration of Taiwan from the KMT and its incorporation in the national administrative structure.
6. Reestablishment of international respect and assumption of a leading role in regional and international affairs.
7. Opposition to imperialism throughout the world and support of revolutionary movements.
8. Reformation of the international system in accordance with the Five Principles of Peaceful Coexistence.

Each of these principles requires a brief elaboration.

1. *National defense* on the basis of self-sufficiency is a most demanding requirement for a nation in China's position. China perceives itself to be threatened by both the United States and the Soviet Union, and to a lesser extent by the resurgence of Japan's power and stature. Peking has often proclaimed the Soviet Union to be its main menace and the greatest threat to world peace. The Chinese economy has made impressive achievements since 1949, but it is still inadequate to support simultaneous arms races with the world's three leading economies. Chinese steel production is only one-sixth that of the United States and perhaps 7 percent that of the United States, the USSR, and Japan taken together. Oil production is 7 percent of the United States, electric generating capacity 5 percent, cement production 20 percent, railroads 10 percent, and so on. China's air force consists of less than half as many combat aircraft as the United States; of course, these planes cannot match the technological level achieved by an economy ten times its size. China's navy is insignificant by modern standards, and its atomic weapons deployment, while important, is less than 1 percent of the U.S. nuclear arsenal. Comparisons with the USSR or Japan along some of these dimensions would be only slightly more favorable. The huge population of China (900 million) and its extensive territory (about equal to the United States) have not yet been marshalled into modern military or economic capabilities.

This weakness is particularly dramatic when measured against China's military needs. The 7000-mile land border separating China and the Soviet

Union (including Soviet-influenced Outer Mongolia) is the world's longest hostile border, and is considered indefensible mile by mile. On the East, the Chinese navy cannot defend the seaward approaches on the Yellow Sea, the East and South China Seas, or the Straits of Taiwan. Even the Indian borders on the southwest demand extensive defensive preparations. Under these circumstances, China must rely for its defense on primitive nuclear deterrence and on the reluctance of its opponents to undertake an invasion. It is not difficult to understand the obsession of China's leadership with security and defensive preparations.

2. *Preventing external nonmilitary interference* has not been so difficult to achieve. The traditional foreign interests were simply evicted after the revolution from their commercial and industrial positions. Foreign investments were expropriated, including, for example, $196 million in American holdings and larger amounts for other countries. Most remaining foreign residents were pressured to leave the country, and a deliberate policy of national isolation was adopted. In effect, China virtually sealed its borders and cut its commercial lines to much of the outside world.

There were some important exceptions to this curtailment of external interference, particularly involving the Soviet Union and India. Soviet leaders took advantage of Chinese weakness immediately after the civil war to demand certain concessions in exchange for Soviet aid. These included the so-called Sino-Soviet "mixed companies" to develop Chinese oil and mineral resources, airlines, railroads, and other facilities. These gave Soviet personnel direct influence over and access to internal Chinese affairs. One form of Soviet behavior particularly disturbing to the Chinese was covert support given to Uigur separatist elements in Sinkiang. After 1955, the joint stock companies were phased out, but subversive activities in remote regions have been more difficult to uproot, particularly as Sino-Soviet relations have worsened (see later discussion).

China perceives India to have interfered in Chinese internal affairs with regard to Tibet. One of the first acts of the People's Liberation Army after the revolution was the repossession of Tibet on October 7, 1950. India, part of whose territory abuts Tibet, refused to recognize Chinese suzerainty and gave various forms of covert aid to Tibetan autonomists. In April 1954, the Indian government seemed to recognize the Chinese claim in an agreement referring to "the Tibet region of China," but this did not settle the issue. In 1958, Prime Minister Nehru of India announced, and then cancelled under Chinese pressure, a visit to Tibet to symbolize support for Tibetan nationalists. This was one element sparking a Tibetan revolt against China in 1959, a revolt quickly suppressed by the Chinese authorities at a cost of 65,000 Tibetan lives. India is known to have allowed the shipment of supplies to the Tibetan guerrillas, and various dissident Tibetan elements fled to India after the revolt. In these ways, India has supported Tibet against China.

The issue of Indian interference is complicated by territorial issues on the remote Indo-Tibetan border in the lofty Himalayas. This region is so desolate that it might seem to be of little interest to anyone. But a Chinese arterial road in Tibet passes through a portion of the area that each claims. Indian claims rest on a Sino-Indian treaty of nineteenth century vintage. China views this document as an unequal treaty of a bygone era, without legal or moral force today, and rests its own claims on historical boundaries. This dispute led to a brief but bitter Sino-Indian border war in 1962, which resulted in a reaffirmation of the Chinese claims. Despite the remoteness of the territory, however, the dispute continues.

3. The third principle of Chinese foreign policy, the *renunciation of unequal treaties*, is also illustrated by the above example. One of the first acts of the victorious Maoists was to announce a reexamination of all treaties concluded by the Manchu and Nationalist governments in order to decide whether to revise, renegotiate, abrogate, or recognize their contents. Though a natural part of national reassertion is reasonable from China's perspective, many of its treaty partners regarded unilateral Chinese abrogation as a violation of the legal sanctity of treaties. This issue was particularly thorny when, as in the Sino-Indian conflict, treaty renunciation included a demand for the recovery of lost territories.

4. *The recovery of lost territories* naturally puts China in conflict with other nations, many of whom gained during the Century of Humiliation. The regions listed by various Chinese accounts as lost are shown in Table 4–1. Interestingly, the Chinese Communist claims are generally supported by the Kuomintang government of Taiwan.

Many of these claims are stated only in principle, and do not represent active demands of the Chinese government. Some are impractical, and others have been rendered obsolete by changing historical conditions. In many respects, the boundary lines claimed represent the maximum extent of the former Chinese empire at its greatest reach. Seemingly, Peking would not be justified in regarding the furthest outlying territories as "Chinese" any more than Italy could demand rightful restoration of the former Roman empire or Turkey demand the reincorporation of all the peoples it once ruled. The conquests of one epoch cannot be regarded as natural possessions in another. But many of the Chinese claims do have a reasonable basis in national history and were in fact severed by conquest. These the Chinese government regards as reasonable targets for repossession.

5. *The reincorporation of Taiwan* is a special issue different from other territorial demands. In this case, both the mainland Communists and the Kuomintang government of Taiwan agree that the island is rightly Chinese (though some of the native Taiwanese, who comprise 85 percent of the island's population, demand national independence); the two Chinese sides disagree about who rules China itself. Nationalists on Taiwan refuse to accede to demands for reincorporation. Peking regards the issue of Taiwan as one of the paramount challenges for Chinese policy in the future.

TABLE 4–1   Historic Losses of Chinese Territory

Territory	Recipient	Year
1. North-East Frontier Agency; Assam	Britain	After 1820
2. Left Bank of Amur River	Russia	1858
3. Maritime Territory	Russia	1860
4. Tashkent Region	Russia	1864
5. Bhutan	Britain	1865
6. Sakhalin	Russia-Japan	After 1875
7. Ryukyu Islands	Japan	1879
8. Indochina	France	1885
9. Siam	Independence	1885
10. Burma	Britain	1886
11. Sino-Burmese Frontier Region	Britain	1886
12. Sikkim	Britain	1889
13. Taiwan and the Pescadores	Japan	1895
14. Malaya	Britain	1895
15. Korea	Japan	1895 and 1905
16. Ladakh	Britain	1896
17. Nepal	Britain	1898

Adapted from: Robert C. North, *The Foreign Relations of China,* 2nd ed. (Belmont, Ca: Dickenson Publishing Company, 1969), p. 55n. Copyright © 1969, 1974 by Dickenson Publishing Company, Inc., Encino, Ca. Reprinted by permission.

Could Peking retake Taiwan by force? The Communist Chinese leadership would have to weigh many elements in any decision for direct military action. One factor would be the likely reactions of the United States and Japan. On one hand, if the U.S. Seventh Fleet were interposed between the mainland and Taiwan, a seaborn invasion would have to run over American naval and air power, risking a confrontation of unpredictable proportions. If, on the other hand, the relaxation of tensions between China and the United States were to lead the Americans to decide that the Taiwan issue is an internal Chinese affair, such action would run a lower risk of engaging the United States. In this case, China would have to weigh the effects on Sino-Japanese relations of a successful military action against Taiwan. One possible consequence would be a Japanese determination to rearm to balance the growth of Chinese power. The degree to which China will fear Japanese rearmament depends on a broader framework of analysis of Sino-Japanese relations.

The Taiwan issue is the principal barrier to normal Sino-American relations; and it has evolved no further than the statement made at the end of President Nixon's ice-breaking trip to China in 1972. In the Shanghai Communiqué which ended that visit, China reaffirmed its insistence that:

> The Taiwan question is the crucial question obstructing the normalization of relations between China and the United States; the Government of the People's Republic of China is the sole legal government of China;

"The olive was delicious, but I can't eat another thing either."

Le Pelley in The Christian Science Monitor © 1975 TCSPS.

Taiwan is a province of China which has long been returned to the motherland; the liberation of Taiwan is China's internal affair in which no other country has the right to interfere; and all U.S. forces and military installations must be withdrawn from Taiwan. . . .

For its part, the United States declared that it:

. . . acknowledges that all Chinese on either side of the Taiwan Strait maintain there is but one China and that Taiwan is a part of China. The

The Logic of National Perceptions

United States Government does not challenge that position. It reaffirms its interest in a peaceful settlement of the Taiwan question by the Chinese themselves. With this prospect in mind it reaffirms the ultimate objective of the withdrawal of all U.S. forces and military installations from Taiwan. In the meantime, it will progressively reduce its forces and military installations on Taiwan as the tension in the area diminishes.[6]

Even if China were to disregard the attitudes and actions of interested third parties, it would still have to weigh the immediate military implications of action against Taiwan. Invasion would depend on the limited airlift and sealift capabilities of the mainland forces, and would require the most hazardous of military operations: an opposed landing on a hostile beachhead. The Nationalists are heavily armed with tanks and sophisticated defensive aircraft, and have a well-trained army of over a half-million men. Even with supporting bombardment to cut into the defensive capabilities of the KMT, a Communist invasion would be extremely costly. The defenses of Taiwan are impregnable to invasion at any reasonable cost to Peking.

Peking's second option is aerial bombardment to subdue the island. The history of strategic bombing suggests strongly that this strategy has almost always been less successful in crushing opposition than most of its proponents expect, as illustrated in the German bombing of Britain in World War II and the American bombing of Vietnam. In the Taiwan case, conventional bombers would be opposed by the sophisticated air defenses provided to the KMT by the United States, including both antiaircraft emplacements and defensive fighters. Nuclear bombardment would undoubtedly be more effective, but this would run a high risk of engaging outside powers. Also, there is doubt that China would use an "overkill" capacity against the island. As one American commented, "Who would clean up the mess?"[7]

So long as Taiwan is united in its opposition to Chinese reincorporation, it appears that there is no effective means of action available to Peking to achieve this goal. One possibility that might change this assessment in the future would be the development of serious internal dissension on the island, especially the emergence of a successful Taiwanese opposition to the KMT. Internal subversion on Taiwan, combined with a growth of mainland capabilities, could lead to new opportunities. On the other side, the acquisition of nuclear capabilities by the KMT, a possibility that cannot be excluded, would multiply the defensive capabilities of the island.

6. *China's search for renewed international respect* has been substan-

[6] *Peking Review* 15, number 9 (March 3, 1972, pp. 4–5, as reprinted in Gene T. Shiao, editor, *Sino-American Détente and Its Policy Implications* (New York: Praeger Publishers, 1974), pp. 298–301.

[7] Drew Middleton, "Taking Taiwan by Force: What Peking Must Weigh," *The New York Times*, March 9, 1972. p. 5.

tially rewarded in recent years. The visit of the American chief of state in 1972 was regarded as a cardinal achievement in China. That President Nixon, overseer of the world's largest empire in the Chinese view, would come to see Mao and Chou in their own capital tended to confirm the "Middle Kingdom" self-perception of China as the historical center of the earth. The subsequent seating of China in the Security Council of the UN institutionalized the new Great Power image of China. As early as 1958, Mao wrote:

> I consider that the present world situation has reached a new turning point. There are now two winds in the world: the east wind and the west wind. There is a saying in China: 'If the east wind does not prevail over the west wind, then the west wind will prevail over the east wind.' I think that the characteristic of the current situation is that the east wind prevails over the west wind; that is the strength of socialism exceeds the strength of imperialism.[8]

Whether or not the east wind will prevail over the west wind, there can be no doubt that China has come back from its meek and degraded condition of only a few decades ago.

7. *China characterizes its own global role as anti-imperialist supporter of Third World revolutionary movements.* The world's subjugated peoples must go through two stages to free themselves from domination and oppression, the stages of *national* and *social* revolution. *National* revolution is the overthrow of colonialism and foreign control over territory and resources, including the economic mechanisms of neoimperialism. *Social* revolution means a change in class ownership of the means of production, taking control from the landlords and capitalists and giving it to the workers and peasants. Many countries are experiencing the stage of national revolution, while few have as yet reached the stage of social revolution. China has had much experience with both.

It is an old self-imposed obligation of China, as a Great Power, to "protect the weak and lift up the fallen." Chinese assistance to the world anti-imperialist movement is the modern expression of this ideal. China is a natural leader of the Third World, as a non-white state which is one of the most advanced revolutionary nations in the world, having passed through the national revolution stage well into social revolution.

China has made unique contributions to the Marxist-Leninist-Maoist theory of revolutionary struggle, and sets the example for a new kind of politico-economic development by going directly from the stage of feudal agriculture to the stage of socialist industrialization without the historically intervening stages of industrial and financial capitalism. Thus, its experience may be a useful model for developing nations at a backward stage (see

[8] Mao Tse-tung, "Imperialists and all Reactionaries are Paper Tigers," reprinted in *Current Background*, no. 534 (November 12, 1958), p. 12.

chapter 5). But China rejects the idea of big power "leadership," which it suspects as a disguise for new forms of imperialism, and instead seeks a spirit of Third World unity and co-equality. Thus, China counts itself as a socialist member of the Third World movement against exploitation, and as a particularly successful case of self-help in the struggle to regain national independence and achieve economic development with social justice.

Lin Piao (who later fell into disfavor with the Chinese leadership for other reasons) characterized the present stage of the world struggle against imperialism in his famous metaphor of the countryside and the cities. Mao Tse-tung's strategy of revolutionary struggle in China had achieved success by establishing revolutionary bases in the rural districts and from there progressively encircling the cities. Lin extended this to a theory of the world system. "Taking the entire globe," Lin said, "if North America and Western Europe can be called 'the cities of the world,' then Asia, Africa, and Latin America constitute 'the rural areas of the world.' " Revolution would come first to the countryside and eventually to the cities in a process of the global encirclement of the centers of imperialism.[9] This expectation is quite the opposite of Leninist theory, which predicts revolution in the most advanced industrial countries first.

8. The final point in codifying the eight priorities of Chinese policy is reformation of the international system to achieve the *Five Principles* of peaceful coexistence. These principles are a statement of the characteristics that relations between different peoples and social systems should have after exploitive linkages have been destroyed. First enunciated in a joint statement with India on June 28, 1954, the Five Principles (also known as the *Panch Shila*) consist of:

1. Mutual respect for each other's territorial integrity and sovereignty
2. Mutual nonaggression
3. Noninterference in each other's internal affairs
4. Relations based on equality and mutual benefit
5. Peaceful coexistence

These principles would prohibit aggression, territorial seizures, subversion, and other acts prohibited under customary international law, but they would also exclude certain forms of behavior traditionally considered allowable in international law but here identified as inconsistent with equality and mutual benefit, such as highly exploitative forms of foreign economic activity. President Nixon and Premier Chou En-lai incorporated the Five Principles in their joint communiqué after the 1972 state visit.

But what of Peking's relations with the three countries that figure most prominently in the Chinese perception of the world system: the United States, the Soviet Union, and Japan?

[9] Lin Piao, "Long Live the Victory of People's War," *Peking Review*, Aug. 4, 1965.

Chinese Relations with the United States

Until recently, China and the United States had regarded each other as implacable enemies since the Communist victory in 1949. Many Americans perceived the triumph of the Red Army in the most negative light, and from the beginning of the new regime they were determined to oppose Communist power in the region. For example, here is how one middle-of-the-road American publication—*Life* magazine—characterized the closing days of the Civil War which, in the Chinese view, ended the Century of Humilation:

> Gradually the Red hordes pressing toward the Yangtze were eliminating the tired armies of Chiang Kai-Shek, changing China from a self-governing land into a Soviet satellite and impressing its 450 million people into the intellectual puppetry of Karl Marx.[10]

(On the "Soviet satellite" claim, see discussion of Sino-Soviet dispute below.) In the Chinese self-perception, the revolution represented rebirth, yet to the Americans, China "fell," was "lost to the Communist," "collapsed," "went down the drain," and so forth. In a 1951 National Opinion Research Center poll, 58 percent of American respondents said that the United States should give aid to the Kuomintang to launch a new attack on the mainland to restore Chiang Kai-Shek, while only 24 percent were opposed. But American aid to Chiang, including the interposition of the Seventh Fleet, confirmed China's fears of the hostile intentions of the United States. Why else would the Americans want to support this corrupt vestige of the past?

Misperceptions and hostilities were magnified during the Korean War. The U.S. government perceived the invasion of South Korea by the North Korean army on June 25, 1950, as an act of international Communist aggression planned in Peking and Moscow. The involvement of China in the early stages of the war was in fact minimal, and here as elsewhere American perceptions of the "Chinese threat" were meaningless in Peking. When American armies responded with a counterinvasion of North Korea in October, the pious mask of anti-Communist hypocrisy was torn away. Korea, like Formosa, had been taken from China by Japan during the Century of Humiliation (in two stages in 1895 and 1905) and subsequently was used by Japanese imperialists as the invasion route to Manchuria and North China in 1931 and 1939. It naturally appeared that the United States was seeking to gain control of this vital salient off the Manchurian industrial heartland.

This perception was reinforced on November 20, 1950, when the U.S. Seventh Division reached the North Korean border with Manchuria, seem-

---

[10] "Red Shadow Lengthens Over China," *Life*, November 29, 1948.

China Before the Revolution.

Source: Philip Dorf, *Visualized World History* (New York: Oxford Books, 1952). Copyright © 1952 by Oxford Book Co., a division of William H. Sadlier, Inc. Reprinted by permission.

ingly poised to invade China. Six days later, a force of 200,000 Chinese counterattacked across the Yalu river and drove the American and allied forces back.[11] The United States took the issue to the Security Council of the United Nations, then a puppet of American policy, and on February 1, 1951, China was officially branded an "aggressor against the United Nations," in the Korean War. The United States had even gone so far as to threaten China with atomic attack should it attempt to evict the imperialists from Korea. The Korean experience also demonstrated to the Chinese the extent to which the United Nations was an instrument of American power rather than an independent and objective international organization.

The Chinese perception of American hostility was further confirmed by Washington's opposition to legitimate revolutionary aspirations in Indochina. As early as 1949, America gave financial aid to France to secure its colonial hold on Indochina and oppose the patriotic forces led by the Viet Minh. When the French position collapsed at Dienbienphu in 1954 and France sued for peace at Geneva, the United States moved in to take

[11] Allen S. Whiting, *China Crosses the Yalu* (New York: Macmillan, 1960).

France's place as the dominant power in Indochina, even though this had not been an area of American involvement in the past.

A puppet government of former French collaborators was devised, and American military and financial "assistance" was used to put a new face on colonialism. Opposition to supposed Chinese influence in Hanoi provided the rationale for the new American policy, and Indochina became another base for the American encirclement of China. From South Vietnam, anti-Chinese influences were extended to Thailand and Cambodia, with each of which China had enjoyed fairly good relations previously. Here again the United States demonstrated its hostile intentions by supporting corrupt and oppressive regimes that declared themselves to be hostile to China.

It seemed to the Peking leadership that everywhere they looked the United States had allied itself with anti-Chinese forces: in Indonesia, Malaysia, the Philippines, Taiwan, Korea, Vietnam, Laos, Cambodia, Thailand, India, all far from the continental United States and clearly not traditional areas of American concern. In no way could the security of the continental United States be imagined to hinge on any of them. And yet the United States invested vast sums and spent scores of thousands of lives to secure political satellites on the Asian periphery, just as the British and Japanese and Germans had acted to subdue Asian peoples in earlier periods. The United States inherited Formosa and Korea from Japan, Vietnam from France, and the Philippines from Spain. While the United States played a relatively minor role during the Century of Humiliation, in later years it assumed the conquests of the older empires to become the home base of world reaction. In this perception the Chinese and Soviet views are much in agreement.

While United States propaganda portrays China as an aggressive country interfering in the affairs of other nations, various Chinese publications show maps of the Chinese motherland encircled by hostile American military bases pointed at its heart. China has no military bases outside its own territory, while American troops have operated in Korea, Indochina, the Philippines, Taiwan, Japan, Thailand, and other countries. Who, it is asked, is truly the aggressor?

In recent years, Sino-American relations have moved into a phase of détente and gradual reduction of tensions. The United States has softened its anti-Communist obsession, and this has led to an easing of conflict with China in Taiwan, Korea, Indochina, and elsewhere. Harsh and fanatical portrayals of China in the American press have been replaced by a more balanced view, and Americans no longer automatically perceive gains for the Chinese people as losses for themselves. China, for its part, has somewhat relaxed its fear of American attack and is exploring avenues for improved relations. The visit of President Nixon was an historic step in this direction, as was the less celebrated visit of President Gerald Ford in 1975. But the future limits of Sino-American friendship will be determined by the amount of military and political support that the United States commits in opposition to China in Asia.

Many Western observers argue that the fears of the Chinese leadership have shifted almost entirely away from the American threat to the Sino-Soviet dispute. The reduction in Sino-American tension seems to correlate with the escalation of hostilities with Moscow. More generally, however, the Chinese willingness to host American presidents and to discuss the future of Taiwan—processes that began even before the departure of American troops from Vietnam—seems to signal not only a tolerance of American policy, but an active desire to keep it in Asia as a deterrent to Soviet expansion. It may be that if the American phase of the Vietnam War had any benefits for major-power politics, it was that the United States and China developed a new understanding of the limits of one another's foreign policies which permits them not merely to "bury the hatchet," but to strike a mutually satisfactory compromise in Asia in the face of Soviet policy. In any case, it is evident from the outspoken and repeated declarations made by high-ranking Chinese officials during the 1975 visit of President Ford that Moscow has replaced Washington as China's main preoccupation.

Conflict with the Soviet Union

Conflict between China and Russia has historic roots. Both Czarist and Soviet Russia benefited at Chinese expense during the Century of Humiliation, including a part in the ruthless economic exploitation of China and the seizure of extensive territories (see Table 4–1). Some of these holdings were conferred by notoriously unequal treaties from 1858 to 1881.[12]

In addition, partly with the help of the United States at the Yalta Conference in 1945, the Soviet Union exercised control over the rail system in Manchuria and in other ways exploited China and its economy.

The newly victorious Chinese Communist Party expected in 1949 that there would be a willingness in Moscow to renegotiate these unjustifiable relationships in a spirit of Communist fraternity. The two giants were natural allies in a world still dominated by the coalition of capitalist powers. China did not expect full restoration of alienated territories, conceding, for example, that the loss of Vladivostok would by then be an intolerable sacrifice for the Soviet Union. But China expected at least symbolic recognition of Chinese claims, and wherever possible some restoration of lost territory. In addition, China expected some financial and

[12] W. A. Douglas Jackson, "Borderlands and Boundary Disputes," in E. M. Bennett, ed., *Polycentrism: Growing Dissidence in the Communist Bloc* (Pullman, Wa.: Washington State University Press, 1967), p. 42.

military aid from the USSR, partly in repayment for the seizure of Manchurian industrial facilities by departing Soviet forces in 1945–1946.

With these assumptions in mind, Mao Tse-tung made a highly unusual three-month visit to Moscow in December 1949 immediately after his victory. In a prolonged and dramatic series of negotiations, he presented the Chinese case to the Soviet leadership. Surely this was an epic development in the history of the Communist movement. There stood Mao Tse-tung and Joseph Stalin, at the pinnacle of power in two of the world's great nations, celebrating the greatest revolutionary achievement since 1917. Surely between them they could adjust the seemingly trivial issues dividing natural allies.

On the basis of what is now known, it can be said that the conflicts between China and the Soviet Union were a great deal more profound than the Western world realized at the time, and that boundary conflicts were overlayed by substantial *ideological* disagreements. Stalin greeted Mao as an architect of revolution accepting the homage of a follower from a minor province. Khrushchev later revealed that Stalin had treated his guest in a domineering and demeaning manner, refusing to respond seriously to the rightfulness of Chinese demands.

Stalin took as given the primacy of the Soviet party in the world Communist movement, and seemed to expect China to fall in faithfully behind the Soviet advance guard. He regarded loyalty to the Soviet party as the cardinal obligation of Communists everywhere, since defense of revolution required first of all international solidarity and discipline. The requirements of the socialist bloc as a whole stood above the demands of individual countries. The Soviet Union was the source of all revolutionary inspiration, as well as the sword and shield against the threatening capitalist world. Furthermore, Mao was reminded of his great debt to the Soviet Union for its support during the war years.

This outlook must have been highly objectionable to the Chinese leader. The Soviet contribution to revolutionary success in China had been minimal—in fact, Soviet support flowed mainly to Chiang until the very end of the civil war. Had the Chinese party leadership accepted the advice of Stalin in 1945 to forego revolutionary struggle during the years of Chiang's greatest weakness (after the Japanese collapse), there might never have been revolution in China. Now the Soviet party demanded the right to dictate the future course of action for a regime that it did not create and in fact came very close to opposing!

This objection to Soviet leadership would become even stronger in later years, when the demands would be made by younger party hacks and bureaucrats who, unlike Stalin, did not themselves participate even in the Russian revolution. Why should Mao and Chou En-lai, who achieved success only after thirty years of bitter struggle, accept domination by such men? Some of them had only read about revolution in books, while Mao's own brother, sister, and first wife had been killed by the Kuomintang.

Mao left Moscow with a very disappointing package. On only one territorial issue was there any concession by Stalin—a phased return of Port Arthur, acquired in 1945. On the issue of economic aid, the Russians pledged only $300 million for five years in high-interest loans, less than the United States gave to France to support the war in Indochina. Other assistance included joint Sino-Soviet companies for the exploitation of oil and mineral resources, with Soviet control of 51 percent of the stock. These terms seem more like the neoimperialist concessions that capitalist powers took from colonial enclaves than fraternal expressions of support.

The Soviet response to Mao's visit showed to the Chinese the clear domination of Soviet national interests over the dictates of Communist ideological principles. While Soviet ideologists mouthed the tenets of Marxism-Leninism and the platitudes of revolutionary solidarity, their actions showed that Communist Russia was not really very different in its basic outlook toward China than Czarist Russia had been. Communism meant about as much in Russian behavior as Judeo-Christian principles do in American foreign policy, it seemed.

By now, the Sino-Soviet dispute is an open quarrel, and the main issues in the Chinese position are familiar. The policy of the Soviet Union, according to Chinese observers, is not truly socialism but rather "social imperialism"—socialism in word but imperialist exploitation in deed. The Soviets have betrayed the cause of anti-imperialism and have, in fact, become a new bourgeoisie oppressing the workers and peasants and dominating a new economic empire. Typical of duplicity in Chinese eyes is the Soviet position toward peoples' revolutions:

> The Soviet leaders want revolutionary people to employ milder forms of struggle against counterrevolution, but they themselves use the most savage and brutal means to deal with revolutionary people. . . . Is it a "milder form" when you send large numbers of armed troops and policemen to suppress the people of different nationalities in your country? Is it a "milder form" when you station large numbers of troops in some Eastern European countries and the Mongolian Peoples Republic to impose tight control over them, and even carry out military occupation in Czechoslovakia, driving tanks into Prague? And it is a "milder" form when you engage in military expansion everywhere and insidiously arrange all manner of subversive activities against other countries? [13]

Some Western observers believe that the Sino-Soviet differences may adjust over time, and that the conflict between capitalism and democracy, and communism and revolution, may outlast this quarrel between the two socialist giants. Even at the height of their quarrel during the Vietnam war years, they arranged for Soviet transshipment of war supplies to Hanoi over Chinese rails, though with many restrictions. Issues of competing national interests and differing ideological interpretations might be for-

[13] Editorial distributed by Hsinhua, the Chinese press agency, March 17, 1971; quoted in *The New York Times*, March 18, 1971, p. 1.

gotten if either of the Communist powers were threatened from the capitalist world, for example by Japan or the United States. However, if national interests rather than ideologies predominate in determining the actual behavior of states, we may expect that the enduring problem of a contested border between these two major powers will perpetuate the Sino-Soviet dispute long after the cold war is forgotten.

Whatever its future, conflict with the USSR is the major threat to Chinese security today. Ever since the Warsaw Pact invasion of Czechoslovakia in 1968 and the attending Brezhnev Doctrine which limits the sovereignty of the socialist states, China's fear of Soviet aggression has been extreme.[14] After all, one-third of the Soviet armed forces are arrayed along the Chinese border, in addition to a considerable portion of Moscow's strategic and nuclear capabilities. If the Russians succeed in reaching a mutual force reduction agreement with the NATO powers in Europe, still more deployments would be freed from the European to the Asian sectors of Soviet military preparation. Who can be certain that the Soviets will not consider a preemptive nuclear attack on the Chinese atomic production facilities in Sinkiang, or that the Soviets will not attempt to foster subversion among dissident populations? (China has a relatively homogeneous population—94 percent Han Chinese and only 6 percent minorities—but the minorities occupy a disproportionate share of territory, comprising over a third of the Chinese land mass.) To meet these and other military demands, it is imperative for the Chinese government to seek détente with other potential opponents, insofar as relations can be improved at reasonable cost of other objectives. One relationship that is especially affected by the Sino-Soviet dispute, and that is a particularly thorny issue for China in the future, is Japan.

Relations with Japan

Japan is one of the powers that benefited most from China's subjugation during the Century of Humiliation. The invasions and conquests of 1894, 1931, and the second world war brought to China the harshest consequences of Japanese militarism, and many living Chinese remember well the cruel behavior of the Japanese army. Chinese fears were not completely erased by the defeat of Japan in 1945. The prolonged boom has moved the Japanese economy to the third position among industrial powers, behind the United States and the USSR but well ahead of China.

It is true that Japan has not manifested overt militarism and the spirit

[14] At least one observer holds that the Brezhnev Doctrine drove China out of isolation and that, because Peking considered the Doctrine a threat to Chinese independence, "the natural response was to seek détente with the United States." See Kenneth W. Rea, "Peking and the Brezhnev Doctrine," *Asian Affairs*, September-October 1975, pp. 22–30.

of forceful conquest during recent years, but this cannot be excluded for the future, and a renewal of Japanese militarism would be much more dangerous under modern conditions. Japanese foreign economic expansion has continued, though it has shifted from military to commercial forms. Japanese raw material hunger and the mercantilist export push have taken Japanese business in much the same orbit that the Greater East Asia Co-Prosperity Sphere was to have achieved through military invasions. South Korea, the Philippines, South Vietnam, Thailand, Malaysia, Australia, Taiwan, and Singapore are among the nations that have been penetrated by vigorous Japanese capital. Furthermore, the 1960 mutual security treaty between Japan and the United States has made Tokyo in many respects an arm of the U.S. military machine. For all these reasons, relaxation of tensions between China and Japan, much as it is desired because of the Sino-Soviet dispute, is hindered by many problems.

On the positive side, several considerations have improved the prospects for reconciliation in the Chinese view. The Japanese constitution of 1946, adopted under the American occupation, forbids military preparations for war purposes. This has been interpreted by Japanese governments as prohibiting offensive but not defensive levels of military deployment. It is true that this constitution could be amended through Japanese political processes, but there remains considerable opposition to announced plans for increased budgets for a build-up of conventional forces. There is also much opposition to the acquisition of nuclear weapons, which would be otherwise possible in technological and economic terms. In 1973 Premier Tanaka publicly stated during a visit to the United States his government's intention not to embark on a nuclear course. Thus, the strong antimilitarist tilt of Japanese politics since 1945 gives some comfort to former and potential future victims.

Chinese propaganda has at times portrayed Japan as a natural ally of China and a fellow victim of the superpowers. "U.S. imperialism is the common enemy of the Japanese and Chinese peoples." The "unequal treaties" affecting Okinawa and the Bonin Islands have been compared to the concessions that were exacted from China. More recently, Chinese overtures to Japan have suggested a mutual interest in restraining the extension of Soviet power in the Asian theatre. Chou En-lai indicated to Japanese Premier Kakuei Tanaka in 1972 that he could even imagine circumstances under which China would come to Japan's aid, possibly alongside the United States, in the event of a Soviet attack. Chou also indicated that, instead of fearing a proposed doubling of the small Japanese military expenditure on the so-called Self-Defense Forces, China actually welcomed a "reasonable growth" of Japanese strength as a potential counterweight to the Soviet Union's "aggressive designs" in Asia.[15]

[15] William Beecher, "Chou is Said to Have Given Japan Military Assurance," *The New York Times*, December 14, 1972.

Chou En-lai, Mao Tse-tung, and Japanese Prime Minister Tanaka exchange gifts at close of historic meeting which preceded by a few months Japanese diplomatic recognition of the Mao government.

AP Photo.

Japan must weigh the advantages of a Chinese alliance against other considerations. While Japanese business is enthusiastic about expansion of trade with China, there is also major interest in obtaining Siberian oil and timber from the USSR in exchange for Japanese financing of large development projects in Soviet Asia. Undoubtedly, Japan would have preferred to establish formal relations with both Peking and Moscow, and in 1975 attempted to do so. But Soviet dissatisfaction with the terms of Sino-Japanese relations, terms which the Kremlin considered anti-Soviet, forced the cancellation of Soviet-Japanese negotiations in early 1976 and resulted in Japan's decision to pursue normal relations with China. This choice was predicated on the gamble that informal relations with Moscow, conducted under an Interim Agreement of 1956, would enable economic relations to proceed uninterrupted. Nevertheless, too close a relationship with China might imperil Japan, which is within easy range (500 miles) of fifty-five Soviet air bases. In the absence of the American nuclear umbrella (see preceding chapter), no combination of Japanese and Chinese forces now foreseeable would be sufficient to spare Japan.

Still, Sino-Japanese rapprochement is a welcome development in both countries. From the Chinese point of view, it reduces the likelihood of the opposite development—Japanese collusion with the Soviet Union, the

United States, or even Taiwan. It is likely that relations between Japan and China will continue to improve in the future.

Conclusion

The Chinese perspective on the international system is primarily defensive, originating in memories of the Century of Humiliation and fears of hostile encirclement today. The international system is fraught with the dangers of capitalist imperialism, social imperialism, and neocolonial economic forms of exploitation. The restoration of China depends on internal solidarity and strength and a careful balancing of external forces. Insofar as possible, China is committed to the promotion of revolutionary conditions in other countries as well as aid to anti-imperialist forces. But the cardinal principle of revolution is, in the Chinese view, self-defense. Each people must struggle for its own national and social liberation for the final defeat of imperialism and the establishment of the Five Principles of peaceful coexistence.

5

The Third World
Perspective

The term *third world* connotes a different meaning today from its early use in the 1950's. When the cold war was at its height, the term identified an informal coalition of "neutral" countries aligned neither with the Western powers (the "first" world) nor the Communist bloc (the "second" world). Today, it is no longer the real or imagined ideological unity of Third World countries that makes it possible to speak of them collectively, but rather their shared poverty and underdevelopment. The term is now used interchangeably with "developing nations" or "less developed countries" (LDC's).

The international system is stratified fairly sharply into these two classes of nations: the rich and nearly rich, and the very poor. All the countries of Latin America, Africa, the Middle East, and Asia together produce less than a third of what the United States produces alone and less than half of the Western European figure. With much larger populations, their income per capita is only one-thirteenth of that in the developed world, and perhaps one-twenty-fifth of that in the United States. Moreover, the gap between the rich and the poor is not closing but widening (see Figure 5–1). Per capita income in Latin America has been growing by less than 1.5 percent per year, compared to 2.5 percent in the United States and 4.0 percent in Europe.

When we speak of poverty in the Third World, it should be distinguished from deprivation in the industrialized nations. The poverty of American cities, for example, harsh though it is, is softened by many features not found in the slums of the developing countries: hot and cold

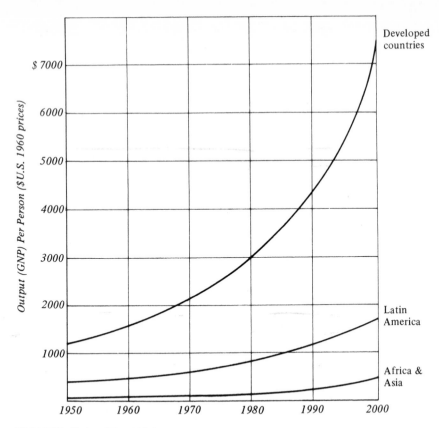

FIGURE 5–1 The Widening Gap

Source: Barbara Ward, J. D. Runnalls, and Lenore D'Anjou, editors, *The Widening Gap* (New York: Columbia University Press) Frontispiece. Reprinted by permission.

running water, sewers and toilets, electrical appliances, a diversified diet including at least occasional meat, sometimes even an automobile. By way of contrast, hundreds of thousands of people in Calcutta, including whole families, live, sleep, and die in the streets and in doorways, literally competing with rats for food. Poverty in the United States is dramatic if we compare it to the wealth of the majority of Americans. But the American poor would be considered very fortunate by most of the peoples of the developing countries.

The Faces of the Third World

The common theme of the Third World is the struggle for development. But within this unifying focus we should recognize broad differences among the hundred LDC's along a number of dimensions.

Resources. The poor countries vary greatly in the natural resources with which they are endowed. Some, like the Sudan, lack many raw materials and are hampered in their development by the relative barrenness of the earth itself. Others, like Nigeria, are richly endowed with the blessings of nature and need only to find the social and political means to utilize their gifts.

Population. Less developed countries (LDC's) also vary in the concentration of their human populations. Some are teemingly overpopulated; tiny Java (Indonesia) has one-third the population of the United States. Others are sparsely populated; oil-rich Libya is almost empty; Tanzania cultivates only one-third of its arable land. Some are largely urban societies, concentrated in and dominated by the cities. Others are agricultural societies or even nomadic wandering cultures. Some are huge in territory, such as India and Brazil. Others are countries of postage-stamp dimensions, such as El Salvador, Lebanon, and Gabon.

Ethnic Divisions. Third World countries differ greatly in their ethnic composition and in the unity or diversity of their peoples. Some, like Chile, have relatively homogeneous populations. Others are sharply divided into two or three ethnic groups among whom there may be deep conflicts; for example, the struggle in Nigeria between the Ibos and the Hausas and Yoruba erupted into civil war in the late 1960's. Others are composed of a multiplicity of peoples held together by slender threads of common interest. An example is India, whose people speak the following languages: Hindi, Urdu, Bengali, Punjabi, Tamil, Kanarese, and Telugan, as well as many dialects. So incomprehensible are these peoples to each other that the national tongue is English, the former colonial language. Thus some Third World peoples are highly unified and ready to face national economic problems, while in others sharp ethnic divisions consume much of the national energy.

Political histories. The nations of the Third World also have very different political histories. Some were colonies until recently (for example, Morocco, Kenya), while others have not been subjected to direct foreign control for many centuries (Thailand). Some are ancient countries which have existed as political entities longer than the United States (Iran), while others are new political creations recently formed by colonial masters for their own administrative convenience (Nigeria) or new federations of formerly separate peoples (Malaysia).

Modernizing and traditional cultures. Some peoples hew closely to ancient traditions, have a low consciousness of nationalism, and are concerned mainly with age-old problems of village and religious life. In other societies, the traditional order is under challenge by a modernizing elite, some variety of participatory revolution is underway, and national identities are superseding antiquated principles of social organization. Literacy rates vary widely in developing countries.

Governments. Governmental types include traditional ruling elites and monarchies, elected regimes on the Western democratic model, military juntas that have come to power by coup d'état, and revolutionary movements. Within each type we may crudely distinguish a corrupt form, in which the ruling parties pursue self-aggrandizement, from a progressive form, in which government is responsive to the larger public good.

Economies. Economies vary from those highly dependent on imports and exports (Chile) to others for whom foreign trade is relatively secondary (India); from societies in which income is distributed very unequally (Saudi Arabia) to highly egalitarian cases (Cuba); from primarily agrarian (Sri Lanka) to substantially industrial (South Korea); from stagnation (Afghanistan) to rapid growth (Brazil); from capitalist (Argentina) to socialist (North Vietnam); and along many other dimensions.

The Meaning of the Third World

Given this long list of differences, it is fair to question whether there is in fact "a" Third World. It is obvious that no completely unified image can be drawn of these highly diverse and noncomparable countries. But increasingly the leaders of the developing countries themselves have adopted this terminology and the perspective that it implies. In conferences at Bandung, Indonesia in 1955, in Cairo in 1962, and in Algiers in 1973, a symbolic unity has been projected by increasing numbers of developing nations. Coalition politics and bloc voting are becoming more organized and sophisticated at the United Nations, the General Agreement on Tariffs and Trade negotiations, the International Monetary Fund, and elsewhere. Unity within diversity is the broad theme of these collaborative efforts.

Moreover, the analysis of international relations requires some sacrifice of the full richness of detail of the real world for the sake of a comprehensive view. The concept of the Third World is a mental ordering device to reduce the infinite complexity of international politics to a manageable and parsimonious set of terms. The shared goal of "catching up" with the developed countries provides the core of a common perspective, and it is reasonable to accept a general analysis of "the" Third World without the cumbersome requirement of restating these reservations at every point.

Conventional vs. Radical Theories of Economic Development

The key question in an analysis of the Third World is *the cause and cure of underdevelopment*. Why are some countries impoverished while others enjoy high standards of living? There are two sharply conflicting causal theories of underdevelopment. The *conventional* theory, favored in the Western countries and in the less developed countries closely associated with the West (such as Brazil or Indonesia), blames poverty on the *internal* conditions within the poor countries which prevent them from achieving the advances accomplished by the developed countries. The *radical* theory, favored by revolutionary thinkers and the more militant voices in the Third World (such as Cuba and Libya), blames poverty on *international* conditions of exploitation of the poor countries by the developed nations. The conventional theory sees the rich countries trying to help the poor "lift themselves up by the bootstraps," while the radical theory sees the rich countries profiting at the expense of the poor through foreign investment and trade.

The Conventional Theory of Development

According to the conventional theory, the process of economic growth and development in the LDC's has been arrested because of low rates of *productivity* combined with high levels of social waste and inefficiency. The Western standard of living is high because the modern high-technology worker produces a great deal in eight hours. Conversely, the LDC worker produces less though he labors longer hours because he works inefficiently with primitive tools and methods. For example, the American farm laborer works on the average more than one hundred acres, while the LDC farmer averages less than three acres. Furthermore, the American squeezes two or three times as much annual yield out of each acre by using advanced methods of fertilization, irrigation, and scientific farming. The result is that the American farmer is able to feed about fifty people, while the LDC farm worker feeds fewer than two. The higher rate of agricultural productivity in the Western countries allows a surplus to be invested in industrial development, while retarded agricultural production in less developed countries slows economic growth and drains the labor force.

The Western worker is more productive, not because of image or superior genes, but simply because he has machinery and automation to multiply the results of his labor. U.S. production consumes about 22,000 pounds of coal equivalent energy annually per capita, while in India the comparable figure is 380 pounds per capita. Western productivity is based on using artificial means to multiply the efficiency of human workers.

The LDC's cannot match the mechanization of the West because of a shortage of capital. It is estimated that the average American worker is supported by $30,000 worth of capital equipment in addition to a substantial investment in education ("human capital") and economic "infrastructure" (roads, railroads, telephones, harbors, and so on). The most basic question for the conventional theorists, then, is how and where the LDC's can raise the *capital* necessary to increase productivity to lift themselves from the cycle of poverty.

The basic source of capital for all economies is production itself. Capital is a *surplus* of production, a portion that is not exhausted by personal consumption but rather *saved* and *invested*. If 200 bushels of wheat are produced by a peasant family and only 100 are immediately needed to sustain the lives of the producers, the other 100 can be sold or traded for tools and tractors (capital goods) that would enable the family to increase its production, say to 300 bushels, the next year. The second year, perhaps 150 of the 300 bushels could be converted into "producer's goods"—that is, invested—to raise production still higher in the third year. Thus, the theory of *self-sustaining growth* holds that eventually a point is reached when productivity gains become normal as a result of constantly increasing investment. Under these circumstances, it becomes possible to achieve permanently expanding capitalization and also rising personal consumption.

The problem, according to the conventional theorist, is that economies reach this point of "take off" to self-sustaining growth only under conditions of rapid capital accumulation. But most of the LDC's have been able to achieve only modest rates of saving and investment because of poverty itself and various forms of waste and inefficiency. Even where surpluses might be generated, they tend to be squandered on unnecessary forms of consumption rather than on growth-oriented investment. Four kinds of waste significantly retard development: (1) runaway population growth; (2) excessive military expenditures; (3) needless luxury consumption; and (4) official corruption.

1. Population Growth

Population is growing much faster in the LDC's than in the developed countries (see Table 5–1). Developed countries grow by about 1 percent per year. In contrast, Africa grows more than three times as fast—3.4 percent annually, and some populations are expanding even faster. Latin America will increase its population by 150 percent between 1970 and 2000, while Europe will grow by only 25 percent during these years.

The LDC's have twice as much of their population under ten years of age as the developed countries. Because infants and young children consume but do not produce, they act as a drain on economic growth. It is estimated that a country with a 3 percent population growth rate must invest 6 percent of its production each year just to keep up with the increase, without achieving *any* expansion of per capita income.

TABLE 5-1   Where Population is Growing Fastest

	Population (millions) 1950	1970	Increase by 2000	Projected Population (millions)
Latin America	162	283	75%	652
Africa	217	344	59%	818
Asia	1,355	2,056	52%	3,778
Oceania	13	19	46%	35
North America	166	228	37%	333
Russia	180	243	35%	330
Europe	392	462	18%	568

Source: United Nations Statistical Yearbook, 1972.

Interestingly, the LDCs' total economies grew *faster* than the developed countries from 1963–73: 5.8 percent of GNP per annum compared to 4.9 percent. But because the rich countries had less than half the rate of population growth (1.0 percent compared to 2.5 percent for the LDC's), the *rich* countries gained in terms of *per capita* growth. Per person, GNP expansion was only 3.2 percent in the LDC's compared to 3.9 percent in the developed countries, and the latter, of course, started very far ahead.

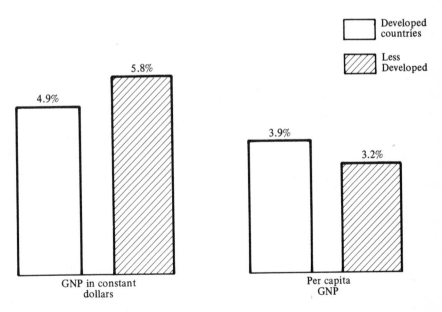

FIGURE 5-2   Economic Growth of Developed and Less Developed Countries, 1963–1973

Thus, excessive population growth in the LDC's retards their development and widens the gap between the rich and the poor.

Why is the population explosion occurring in the Third World? The cause is *not*, as many people believe, an increase in the birth rate; this has remained relatively stable. Rather, a decline in the death rate has been achieved by improved public health, medicine, and nutrition. Historically, the rich countries have compensated for longer life expectancy by cutting the birth rate correspondingly. Families are smaller among middle class people in industrial societies. The LDC's are caught in a transitional bind. They have reached the point in modernization where the death rate drops, but not yet the point where the birth rate goes down. Thus, their population growth is much more rapid than it once was, and far exceeds the population growth of the richer countries.

Efforts by some LDC's to solve this problem through birth control and family planning have not, on the whole, made a great impact. Many peoples consider large families a blessing, or have religious objections to birth control, or are culturally ill-suited to the faithful use of birth control methods. Some novel approaches have had a limited success. In India, payment of a small reward (less than $5) has induced men who already have several children to undergo voluntary sterilization. In China, strong urgings to young people to postpone marriage until twenty-five or thirty have been somewhat successful. Various medical innovations now in the stage of experimentation in several countries may achieve a real breakthrough. But in many countries, population growth is not being arrested, and economic stagnation is a result.

2. Excessive Military Expenditure

A second form of waste that erodes the small increases in production that the LDC's are able to achieve is military expenditure. Many developing countries spend a large portion of their scarce resources on the maintenance of armed forces. Developing countries imported over $38 billion in military goods from 1964–1973. Imports of armaments from the developed countries have risen steeply over recent years (see Figure 5–3), and many LDC's are now armed at levels that would have been considered impressive even for industrial states forty years ago. Some of the most remote countries of the world are heavily armed and various regional antagonists now glare at each other through the sights of sophisticated artillery and from the windows of advanced combat aircraft. Third World leaders seem to be squandering their meager surpluses on guns instead of butter.

India is often cited in this regard for its defense budget of approximately $2 billion per year. From the economic point of view, most of this is waste. A two-week skirmish with Pakistan in December of 1971 over conflicting boundary claims in Kashmir resulted in $260 million direct costs to India, plus $500 million in refugee expenses, and $65 million in

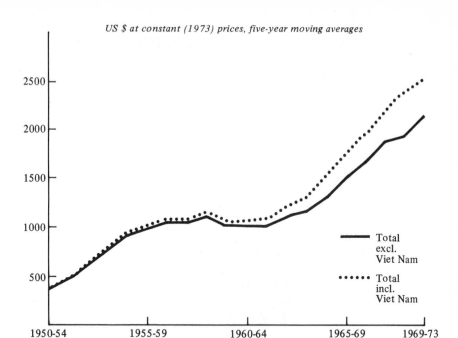

US $ at constant (1973) prices, five-year moving averages

Total excl. Viet Nam

Total incl. Viet Nam

FIGURE 5–3   Total Exports of Major Weapons to Third World Countries

Source: SIPRI, Arms Trade with the Third World (Stockholm, 1975).

lost agricultural and industrial production in the Punjab district alone. Had the war not been of unusually short duration, the costs could have been higher. Afterward, India, faced with the danger of future conflict with a Pakistan seeking revenge, expanded its air force and navy at staggering economic cost. New civilian investment could be increased by more than 25 percent (more than all foreign aid) simply by diverting these military expenditures back into the economy. But there is no real prospect that any Indian government will do this.

Why do less developed countries "waste" so much on military expenditures despite pressing human needs? Some have profound conflicts with neighboring states over borders, while others have acute internal divisions. Ethnic minorities and secessionist movements may threaten to split off from the national body. Dissident revolutionary or counterrevolutionary movements and insurgencies may threaten the position of the ruling elite. (See chapter 10 for an inventory of conflicts.) Beyond these demands of political realism, military expenditures may be motivated by considerations of sheer prestige and organizational and career imperatives of the armed forces themselves. A powerful army, it is thought, is an indispensable attribute of nationhood.

Quo Vadis?

LePelley in The Christian Science Monitor. Copyright © 1973 TCSPS.

The result of all these pressures is that military expenditures are growing more rapidly in the LDC's than in the rich countries. From 1963 to 1973 military expenditures grew by 7.2 percent annually (in constant prices) in the developing countries, compared to 2.0 percent in the developed countries. The number of soldiers under arms grew by 3.8 percent annually in the LDC's while there was no growth in the armies of the wealthy nations.

Moreover, military expenditures are increasing more rapidly than general economic growth in the LDC's (see Figure 5–4). The effect is that an expanding share of national income is wasted on armaments. Thus, military expenditures are a severe drain on economic growth. In 1972, less developed countries spent almost two and a half times as much on military budgets as they received in foreign economic aid ($30 billion vs. $13 billion). Another disturbing comparison is the armed forces versus other social outlays. LDC's spend on armies more than they invest in education ($30 billion vs. 23 billion in 1972) and almost four times as much as they put into public health ($8 billion).

Some of the LDC's are trying to recover a part of this economic waste by involving the armed forces directly in development projects. In Peru, Cuba, and Tanzania, for example, soldiers provide a backup migratory labor force for the harvest, the building of dams, harbors, and roads, and for other projects. Experiments have been conducted in some places to have the armed forces grow their own food. Military organization may be a form of social mobilization for economic development, as peasant boys are taken out of the relative stagnation of the traditional village and given modern organizational and production skills and a national orientation. However, while these efforts may reduce the net loss, military expenditures are still a poor priority from an economic viewpoint.

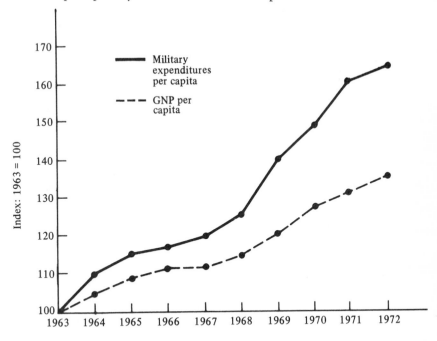

FIGURE 5–4   Growth of Military Expenditures in Developing Countries Compared to GNP

Source: U.S. Arms Control and Disarmament Agency, *World Military Expenditures, 1963–1973* (Washington, D.C.: U.S. Government Printing Office, 1975), p. 14.

3. Luxury Consumption

In many poor countries, the abysmal poverty of the masses contrasts sharply with the astronomical wealth of a handful of landlords, maharajahs, princes, or industrial barons. "Stratification" (unequal distribution) of wealth is much sharper in the LDC's than in the wealthy nations. For example, in Colombia the top 5 percent of the population get 42 percent of the income, compared to only 16 percent in the United States. In more than half of developing countries, less than 10 percent of farms have over half the cultivable acreage. In general, the percentage distribution of income is less equitable in the LDC's (see Table 5–2).

It might be thought that concentrations of wealth could be invested in economic development. But the rich throw away much of this potential through luxury spending on automobiles and baronial estates, instead of putting it to developmental purposes. Wealthy classes in the Third World tend to emulate privileged Americans and Europeans. In addition some send sizable amounts abroad to avoid taxes and possible confiscation. The "Swiss banks" factor is said to have drained more than $3 billion out of Latin America alone in unauthorized outflows during the 1960's. Keeping this money at home for useful investment could have replaced about one-third of foreign aid. Clearly, luxury consumption by the rich and nearly rich is a serious drain on economic development.

4. Corruption

A final waste factor is the corruption of public officials, an especially acute problem in some developing countries. While in the United States more than 90 percent of the taxes that are due (after loopholes) is successfully

TABLE 5–2 Percentage Distribution of Income in Selected Countries

Country	Bottom 40%	Middle 40%	Top 20%
India	11	25	65
Mexico	10	30	60
Sri Lanka	13	31	57
Colombia	15	29	56
Guatemala	14	31	55
Sweden	13	41	47
Norway	16	39	45
United Kingdom	17	39	45
United States	17	41	42

Source: Thomas E. Weisskopf, "Capitalism, Underdevelopment and the Future of the Poor Countries." Reprinted with permission of Macmillan Publishing Co., Inc. from *Economics and World Order* by Jagdish Bhagwati. Copyright © 1972 by Macmillan Publishing Co., Inc.

collected, in some LDC's the actual collection rate is below 50 percent. The state treasury—one of the main instruments of development—is depleted by tax evasion. In addition, allotments from the treasury are eroded by the corruption of project administrators at every level. A flood of resources put into the pipeline at one end can come out the other end reduced to a trickle. Sometimes, corruption takes the form of "legitimate" expenditures such as luxury cars for officials and expense accounts.

Another form of waste that we may list under corruption is lavish expenditure on prestige projects whose only function is to satisfy the needs of the ruling elites. Examples include opulent presidential palaces, ostentatious airports used only by the rich, and other relatively private luxuries. Taken together, these various forms of corruption are a significant drain on the process of capital accumulation.

Foreign Aid and Investment

As we have seen, the LDC's are typically low-income agrarian societies which devote the greater portion of their economic activity to subsistence production. Industrial development and agricultural mechanization are the keys to economic expansion, but these are inhibited by a shortage of capital rooted in low productivity. What small capital surpluses that do accumulate are depleted by population growth, military expenditures, luxury consumption, and corruption. The basic solution, in the conventional view, is to find new sources of capital and to use more effectively the capital that is available.

This is where the international system can help, in the conventional view. While LDC's are suffering from a scarcity of capital and technology, these assets exist in surplus in the developed countries. Can the rich states, at reasonable cost to themselves, stimulate the systems of the poor states by injecting economic nutrients at critical points? Can we devise an effective means of capital transfer to "prime the pump" of development, without making unreasonable demands on the benevolence of the prosperous peoples? Three forms of assistance from the developed nations to the LDC's have dominated the theory and practice of the conventional view: (1) foreign aid; (2) foreign investment; and (3) technical assistance.

Foreign Aid

Foreign aid is a transfer of resources from the state treasury of a prosperous nation to one or more developing nations, either in the form of direct funding or in commodities and goods subsidized by the donor. Foreign aid can take the form of outright grants or long-term, low-interest

Squalor in the Third World: A family's fight for survival in Bangladesh, 1974.

Photographer/Michel Laurent. Gamma/Liaison

loans. Also, we may differentiate between bilateral (country to country) and multilateral (such as UN or World Bank) forms of giving. Another distinction that we should introduce is military versus economic aid. Some observers leave military assistance out of the development category, while others say that it helps by freeing domestic resources for productive investment. Taking all these categories together, many billions of dollars have been given to LDC's by the United States and Canada, Western Europe, the Soviet Union, and other developed countries.

Developing nations have increasingly taken the view, at the United Nations Conference on Trade and Development and elsewhere, that foreign aid is not charity but an obligation of the advanced nations that are favored by the global division of wealth. UNCTAD has fixed a standard of 1 percent of national income as the target for giving by the developed countries. The United States, which alone has given more than twice as much aid as all other donors combined since 1945, still falls short of this goal, giving less than two-thirds of 1 percent in recent years. This is a poorer showing than some European nations which, despite much lower absolute donations, do approach the target figure.

Opulence in the Third World: Wealth from oil exports in Kuwait, 1975.

Photographer/Bernard Gerard. Gamma/Liaison

Moreover, after giving more than $125 billion in bilateral economic and military assistance since World War II, plus substantial amounts of Food for Peace and multilateral aid, the American willingness to contribute is declining. Increased awareness of unanswered social needs within the United States had led to demands by Congress and the public that resources be used to solve domestic problems first. Aid appropriations are a favorite target of the taxpayer revolt. In addition, some liberals have begun to oppose foreign assistance as a potential "foot in the door" for American interventionism, while conservatives are offended by hostility toward the United States among the more than seventy-five developing countries that have shared this largesse. Some U.S. economists have come to see aid as a worn-out formula that doesn't work. Billions of dollars were poured into the Alliance for Progress in Latin America, for example, without achieving the decisive development breakthrough that had been promised by President Kennedy. In general, the American disillusionment with aid makes expansion of giving by this country unlikely.

Other industrial nations may be expected to increase their donations. Germany and Japan are under special pressures to expand foreign aid, as both have enjoyed booming economies and large balance of payments surpluses while spending relatively small portions of national income on defense (thanks to the U.S. security umbrella). Japan, as the third largest economy, is expanding its giving along the Asian periphery, while Germany is developing a program coordinated with its trade policies in the Middle East and in Africa. Other European nations give substantial aid to former colonies and other trading partners in the LDC's. U.S. bilateral aid was 59 percent of the Western total in 1961, but only 34 percent in 1973. (See Figure 5-5.)

In an interesting recent development, some of the larger and more advanced developing nations have themselves begun giving to other LDC's. China, though beset with its own staggering problems of economic development, has become a major donor of aid, much of it in the form of grants and very low interest loans. In 1970, China, whose very name until recently connoted poverty, committed $709 million in economic aid compared to $204 million by the Soviet Union. Peking's aid went primarily to Zambia and Tanzania (for a critical railway that will free Zambia from dependence on trade routes through white-dominated southern Africa), Pakistan, Guyana, North Vietnam, North Korea, and Chile. Other

FIGURE 5-5 The Declining Role of the United States as a Foreign Aid Donor

Source: Based on Report by the Chairman of the Development Assistance Committee, *Development Co-operation, 1973 Review* (Paris: OECD, 1973), p. 181.

The Logic of National Perceptions

developing countries giving foreign aid include India and Brazil. India's aid to Bangladesh and other neighbors runs to tens of millions annually—over $200 million in 1972. Brazil, its own economy booming in the early 1970's, gave aid to Bolivia ($14 million in 1971), Uruguay, Guyana, and Paraguay.

Unfortunately, increases by all these donors will not be sufficient to meet the capital needs of the less developed countries during the balance of this century. Some economists believe that the LDC's could usefully absorb five or ten times as much outside capital as will be available. The present prospect is a general decline in the significance of foreign aid, compared to population and growth needs.

Foreign Investment

Because the flow of governmental foreign aid is not on the recommended scale, conventional theorists look for other forms of capital transfers from developed to less developed states. Long-term private investment by profit-seeking firms offers the greatest possibility of expanded resource flow. Billions of dollars move through the money markets of the United States, Western Europe, and Japan every day, and if even a fraction were directed to the Third World, the effect would be substantial. But the share of global foreign investment going to developing countries has in fact been declining as the wealthy nations focus their trade and investment increasingly on each other. The problem for the conventional approach is to attract new interest from global business to invest in developing countries.

This positive attitude toward foreign capital, advocated by Western-oriented governments such as Indonesia, Brazil, and Taiwan, is directly opposed to the radical ideology of states like Libya and Cuba, which depict foreign investment as a form of neocolonialism (see below). Even the Western-oriented states share some fear of the multinational giants like General Motors whose $31 billion in annual sales dwarfs the GNPs of more than 100 countries. But conventional theorists argue that controlled foreign investment is a proven stimulus to rapid growth, as demonstrated in South Korea, Brazil, Nigeria, and other countries. To get more foreign investment, many countries maintain public relations offices and consulates in the major capital centers (New York, London, Paris, and Tokyo, for instance) and publish advertisements and lavish inserts in the world financial press (such as *Wall Street Journal*, *Fortune*) singing the praises of investment in their economies.

Advocates of increased foreign investment, such as former Brazilian Minister of Planning Roberto Campos, enumerate the following advantages of foreign capital.[1]

---

[1] Roberto Campos, "Economic Policy and Political Myths," in Paul E. Sigmund, ed., *The Ideologies of the Developing Nations* (New York: Praeger, 1967), pp. 418–24.

1. *Jobs:* Most positions created by foreign firms go to indigenous workers. For example, U.S. multinational enterprises operating in the LDC's employ over three million locals as against only 25,000 American nationals located abroad.

2. *Technology:* The foreign firm brings the most advanced methods and technologies, acting as an agent for the transfer of new knowledge. This spills over to local subcontractors as production is integrated in the local economy.

3. *Import substitution:* Foreign investment often helps the balance of payments of the less developed country by enabling it to produce for itself what it once imported.

4. *Market access:* The foreign firm brings international market connections conducive to a continued inflow of capital and the expansion of export opportunities.

5. *Efficiency:* The profit incentive is keyed to cost reduction and maximal use of resources. The foreign investor has a natural motive and the managerial skills to organize local people and information in the most cost-effective and productive way.

6. *Demonstration effect:* Local enterprises may be induced to utilize the techniques and management ideas of the efficient foreign branch to maintain their competitive position.

7. *Planning:* The international investor is in an excellent position to assess the comparative advantages of local production in world markets, and he may aid in the identification of ideal lead sectors for planned national economic development.[2]

For all these reasons, the politically more conservative voices in the Third World reject the isolationist course of a closed door to Western capitalism.

Technical Assistance

A third form of international aid to the developing countries is technical assistance. Most of the world's research and development is conducted in the rich countries. If the results of technological advances are not to be confined to the privileged peoples and if the benefits of scientific discovery are to be shared by all of humanity, a means must be found to facilitate what has been called the *transnational migration of knowledge.* Examples of technical assistance include the Atoms for Peace program, under which the United States has given small atomic reactors and fissionable materials to more than fifty countries to promote peaceful applications of nuclear technology; the arid zone research program, under which the United States supports research on desalinization of sea water by ad-

[2] Harry G. Johnson, "The Multinational Corporation as an Agency of Economic Development," in Barbara Ward, Lenore D'Anjou, and J. D. Runnalls, eds., *The Widening Gap* (New York: Columbia University Press, 1971), pp. 242–51.

vanced means; and most significant of all, scientific advances in agriculture known as the *Green Revolution*, which brings to developing nations modern cultivation techniques and new seed strains that make possible a dramatic increase in farm productivity.

Using the new methods of the Green Revolution, the output of grain cereals (rice, maize, wheat) can be multiplied without any expansion of acreage or the labor force. For example, high-yielding dwarf variety wheat, pioneered in Mexico, has a genetic potential double or triple that of the best yielders among older, tall-strawed varieties.[3] With American help, this advance has been introduced, along with necessary supporting improvements in fertilizer, insecticides, weed killers, irrigation, and machinery on the Indian subcontinent.

The results have been spectacular. India increased its wheat production by 80 percent in four years, Pakistan by 60 percent in two. These two nations have long been known as major food deficit sufferers, dependent on charitable imports. Now they are approaching not only self-sufficiency but even surplus and a capacity for export. Some Indian experts predict that they will exceed American production by 1980.

A similar advance in high-yielding dwarf variety rice—IR8—has ended the Philippines' historic dependence on rice imports. Transfer of the Philippine advances to Sri Lanka increased that nation's production by 26 percent in three years. Many other countries are benefiting from these hybrid grains, including Afghanistan, Burma, Indonesia, Iran, Laos, Malaysia, Morocco, Nepal, Tunisia, Turkey, and Vietnam.[4] It is also known that the Green Revolution is finding its way into the Communist world.

These impressive achievements have vast political and economic consequences. A few years ago, leading demographers were predicting a global food crisis caused by population expansion. It is not clear whether this problem is now solved or only postponed, but the present trend seems to be towards food self-sufficiency. This trend will reduce external dependence and relieve balance-of-payments problems. Internally, productivity increases may support advances in industrialization. Many of the now-advanced nations squeezed their initial surpluses out of agriculture to finance industrial development, and we may expect this pattern to be repeated in the LDC's. Thus, the Green Revolution may promote a more dynamic political and economic prospect for the developing countries.

There are, however, some costs that must be accounted for in the balance sheet of the Green Revolution. The intensive use of chemical fertilizers and insecticides raises ecological issues that are now familiar in the wealthier nations. Fish and wildlife are endangered, and the runoff carries

---

[3] Norman Borlaug, "The Green Revolution, Peace, and Humanity," *Population Research Bulletin* selection # 35, Jan. 1971.

[4] Lester Brown, "The Social Impact of the Green Revolution," *International Conciliation* no. 581 (Jan. 1971).

excessive nutrients and poisons to the oceans, whose ability to sustain pollution is not infinite. The vulnerability of the new strains to disease requires increasing dosages of insecticide, with the long-term danger that new insect varieties will develop that are resistant to all known poisons.

There are also social problems associated with the Green Revolution. Advanced agriculture is based on the substitution of capital for labor to pay for machines, seeds, fertilizer, insecticides, and irrigation systems. As agriculture becomes capital- rather than labor-intensive, small farmers are squeezed out and larger landholders absorb smaller ones. Agricultural employment may be reduced as productivity increases. Thus the effect of the Green Revolution is to widen class disparities rather than to narrow them, increasing the characteristic problem of stratification that we noted earlier. The initial beneficiaries of the Green Revolution may be the already prosperous rather than the suffering poor. But advocates of the conventional theory argue that the flood of benefits will inevitably trickle down to the lower classes, and that the solution to maldistribution effects is rational planning by governments rather than forgoing the possibilities of the new approach.

Summary

In broad outline, the conventional theory sees the root of underdevelopment as internal stagnation, and the solution as international aid from the advanced countries. The key forms of international help are foreign aid, foreign investment, and technical assistance. Only with vigorous and benevolent intervention by the prosperous nations will the sharp international cleavage between rich and poor be reduced.

The Radical Theory of Development

The radical theory of development fundamentally disagrees with this conventional view regarding both the cause and cure of underdevelopment. To the conventional theorist, the *cause* is internal inefficiency and the *cure* is outside help from the developed states. To the radical, the cause is international *exploitation* by exactly these developed "friends," and the cure is a fundamental change of international relations between the poor and the rich. Indeed, the very medicine proposed by the conventional theorist—foreign investment, trade, and aid—is considered the root of the disease by the radical, for whom investment, trade and aid are extractive mechanisms that systematically siphon away the wealth of the LDC's.

The two schools disagree on basic assumptions regarding the global inequality of life. To the conventional theorist, the rich are ahead of the poor because of uneven endowments of intellectual capacity, dedicated effort, and managerial skills. To the radical, the Western peoples achieved their advantage, "not by the laws of the market, but by a particular sequence of world conquest and land occupation."[5] It follows from the conventional view that when the poor make up the gap in productive skills (with the help of foreign aid, and so on) the economic gap will close. It follows from the radical view that only cutting the international relationship will end the unjust division of the world's wealth.

The conventional view posits an essential similarity between the development problems of the LDC's today and the problems successfully mastered by the now rich states in earlier periods. It says in effect, "Just as the United States and Europe developed yesterday and Japan and Mexico are developing today, so will you, the late starters, develop tomorrow." Development is portrayed as a linear process in which every economy passes through certain known stages of economic growth.[6]

Radical analysis rejects this portrayal of the LDC's. The economies of the big capitalist states started as largely autonomous markets under domestic control, though international trade and investment were conducted within careful limits. The economies of the Third World, however, enter the modern development epoch as mere subsystems of global capitalism, having long ago been penetrated by foreign interests and been made economic satellites of the dominant states of the North. The global system consists of a "center"—Europe, America, and Japan—and a "periphery"—the dependent economies of Latin America, Africa, and Asia. The basic economic institutions of the dependencies were formed in response to the insistent demands of the industrial world, rather than in relation to local needs and interests. The typical dependency economy is geared to the export of commodities needed by the industrial center and the import of products from the center. This is known as the pattern of "foreign-oriented development," in which external rather than domestic influences shape the society, economy, and political structure.

What produced this lopsided and unnatural development, so heavily dependent on foreign interests? In the earliest period, it was caused by massive raw material hunger on the part of the industrial nations. The underdeveloped regions, subdued and controlled by the superior military force of the center, were reduced to cheap suppliers of raw materials, useful mainly for their wells or mines or tea or rubber. Cuba became a sugar plantation, Bolivia a tin mine, the Arab world an oil field, Southeast Asia a rubber plantation, Gabon (in Barbara Ward's phrase) "a faint appendage to a mineral deposit." In many cases, local impulses to produce industrial goods for home consumption were quelled by the dominant

---

[5] See Ward et al., *The Widening Gap*, pp. 152–64, where the two views are eloquently contrasted.

[6] See Walt W. Rostow, *The Stages of Economic Growth* (London: Cambridge University Press, 1960).

foreigners, as the dependency was needed as a secure market for exactly these products from the center. Thus, foreign domination served to channel LDC economic activity into a high degree of forced specialization.

In general, *one* main export item accounts for a much higher portion of foreign sales by poor nations than by rich nations—46 percent compared to 17 percent. Thus, it is fair to say that the typical LDC is a one- or two-product exporter, while the typical developed nation has a diversified economy.[7] Venezuela exports 90 percent oil; Colombia depends on coffee; Cuba has not escaped sugar dependence; two-thirds of Chilean exports are copper. Should the mineral be exhausted (as is happening to Bolivia) or a cheaper source be found for the national product (such as the seabed?), or should changing consumer preferences reduce demand, dependent LDC economies could be destroyed. What if people stop drinking coffee? In other words, highly specialized economies are dangerously subject to the vicissitudes of the world market.

The "Terms-of-Trade" Problem

The export commodities in which the LDC's specialize tend strongly to be "primary products"—minerals, fuels, and crops taken more or less directly from the earth with minimal processing. Approximately 80 percent of the exports of poor countries in 1973 were primary products, compared to about 20 percent for rich countries. Conversely, 80 percent of the exports of the rich countries were manufactures, compared to only 20 percent for the poor countries. The poor sell to the rich raw materials and buy from them finished goods.

This commodity composition of trade adversely affects the developing countries. One reason is the tendency of primary-product export prices to fluctuate substantially and sometimes extremely in world markets, as illustrated in Table 5–3, while the prices of industrial product imports tend to rise relatively consistently over time. One hundred pounds of Burmese rice, for example, fetched $7 in 1968 but only $3 in 1971. This means that to pay for a $5000 imported International Harvester tractor, Burma had to sell thirty-six tons of rice in 1968. In 1971, the same tractor cost at least the equivalent of eighty-three tons of rice and probably more because of inflation in the price of the industrial product. Of course, in a boom year the price fluctuation may be quite favorable. In 1974, at $17 a hundredweight, Burma had to export only fifteen tons to earn $5000. But when a large portion of the labor force and economic activity of a small country is tied to the export of a single product, the wild "boom and bust" cycles illustrated in Table 5–3 are socially hazardous and detrimental to orderly economic development.

[7] Thomas Weisskopf, "Capitalism, Underdevelopment, and the Poor Countries," in Jagdish Bhagwati, ed., *Economics and World Order* (New York: Macmillan, 1972), p. 73.

TABLE 5–3   Price Fluctuations of Selected Primary Commodities

Nigeria cacao (100 pounds)		*Brazil coffee (100 pounds)*	
1968	$31	1968	$32
1970	43	1970	44
1972	30	1971	34
1974	59	1973	53
Chile copper (100 pounds)		*Malaysia rubber (100 pounds)*	
1968	$47	1968	$17
1969	61	1969	22
1972	44	1972	15
1973	71	1973	35
Philippines copra (100 pounds)		*Burma rice (100 pounds)*	
1970	$ 8	1968	$ 7
1972	5	1971	3
1973	10	1974	17

Source: International Monetary Fund, *International Financial Statistics*, August 1975.

Moreover, the price fluctuations of primary commodities do not necessarily average out over time to a general rate of increase comparable to the incessant inflation of industrial goods. Indeed, Third World economists such as Raul Prebisch and leading Marxists such as Arghiri Emmanuel have argued that there is an inherent inequality in international trade, and as a result the prices of primary products tend to "decay" over time relative to industrial goods.[8] That is, the prices of primary commodities have not risen as rapidly as finished industrial goods, and in some cases they have declined absolutely. Figure 5–6 compares the "terms of trade" for developed and less developed countries by using indices based on export prices divided by import prices. The figure shows that, particularly during the 1950's and early 1960's, market prices strongly favored the advanced industrial exporters to the disadvantage of the less developed primary exporters, and that even by 1973 substantial losses in LDC terms of trade had not been recovered. (See also Figure 5–7.) The United Nations Conference on Trade and Development estimated the magnitude of terms-of-trade losses to the LDC's at $13 billion for a six-year period from 1961 through 1966. This drain, significantly, results *not* from explicit imperialism and exploitation, but rather from the quiet operation of market laws seemingly beyond anyone's control, so-called objective world market prices. Billions of dollars are implicitly taken from the poor and given to

[8] Two recent classics developing this view from different perspectives are United Nations Conference on Trade and Development, *Towards a New Trade Policy for Development* (UN: 1964), universally known as the Prebisch Report, and Arghiri Emmanuel, *Unequal Exchange: The Imperialism of International Trade* (New York: Monthly Review Press, 1972).

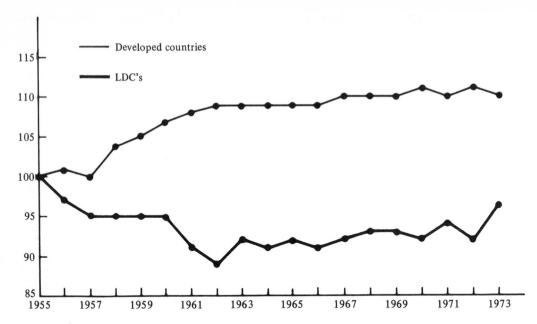

FIGURE 5–6 The Terms of Trade: Unit value index of exports divided by unit value index of imports

the rich through the impersonal mechanism of freely negotiated international trade pricing. Even the Soviets were accused by Ché Guevara of using these unfair world market pricing advantages.

Productivity increases. The terms-of-trade factor puts the LDC's in a position that cannot be compared to that of the rich states in an earlier period. The now advanced states achieved rapid increases in productivity during their "takeoff" stage, and these are regarded as the key to their success. But today, the primary price decay erodes productivity gains. Malaysia, for example, increased its rubber exports almost 25 percent from 1960 to 1968—from 850 to 1100 thousand tons—while reducing its plantation labor force significantly. This is a notable gain in productivity. But its *income* from rubber sales *declined* by about 33 percent during these years as prices fell. In effect, productivity increases were passed along to foreign consumers in the form of lowered prices, rather than to Malaysian workers in the form of higher wages and living standards. The terms-of-trade problem can be a treadmill on which it is necessary to run faster and faster just to stand still.

Inelastic demand. Explanations of this phenomenon are based on disadvantages of primary products against finished goods. One is the relative "inelasticity of demand" for primary goods—only so many bananas

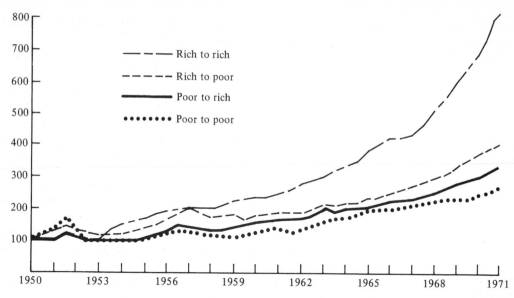

FIGURE 5–7   Export Value Indices for Developed and Developing
Countries, 1950–1971

Source: World Bank Group, *Trends in Developing Countries 1973,* Table 5–5.

will be consumed no matter how many are produced, tending to reduce
prices after the market is saturated.

Unorganized labor.   Another factor is the position of labor in the
LDC's compared to the industrial countries. Workers in the advanced
states are relatively well organized into trade unions, and can command a
share of the gains from productivity increases. The comparative weakness
of labor organizations in the LDC's, however, allows productivity gains
to be taken by management in the form of profits or to be passed on to
consumers in the form of lower prices. Productivity gains in the center are
taken at home, but productivity gains in the periphery tend to flow
away—to the center—in the form of lower prices or in profits remitted to
foreign owners. The deck is stacked in favor of the already developed world,
and mere productivity advances of the type advocated by the conventional
theorists will not change the unfavorable rules.

The Radical View of Foreign Investment

While the conventional theorist views the multinational corporation as
an agency for the transfer of capital and technology for the betterment
of the developing countries, the radical theorist sees it as an instrument of

foreign control extracting exorbitant profits. U.S. investment, for example, puts about $1 billion in new capital into the LDC's annually, but takes out each year $2.5 billion in profits—in effect substantially *decapitalizing* the host countries. Moreover, each incoming dollar buys four times that amount of control over the local economy, since foreign firms borrow from local banks about $2 for every $1 of new money that they bring in, plus the reinvestment of a fourth dollar of local earnings from past investment. The result is a geometric rate of expansion of foreign economic penetration. It is estimated that American foreign holdings in all countries grow in value by $8 billion yearly from reinvestment alone, with no real contribution of funds from the United States. In Latin America, U.S. investors have taken out more than three times as much as they put in since 1945, and yet the book value of American holdings continues to grow. Profit rates in some sectors are still increasing despite the imposition of restrictions by many countries. United States returns on direct investment in Latin American mining and smelting went from 9 percent in 1951–55 to 11 percent in 1956–60, 15 percent in 1961–65, and 23 percent in 1966–68.

Multinational firms use several devices to evade legal restrictions on excess profits. For example, one foreign subsidiary of a multinational conglomerate typically buys some of its intermediate components from other branches of the same parent located in other countries. The internal "prices" of such sales may be manipulated by the parent for optimal bookkeeping results, taking losses in one subsidiary where profits are restricted and showing them in another where they are not. Other devices include the manipulation of royalties, management fees, and other internally negotiated "costs." The multinational enterprise has a variety of options to remit profits without defying legal limits.

Another objection to foreign capital is its effect on the social and class structure of the host society. The foreign firm is at first typically an isolated enclave of modern economics in a sea of underdevelopment, but eventually a network of subcontractors extends the patterns of dependency outside the company gates. Often the multinational guest dwarfs all local enterprises— the sales revenue of the United Fruit Company, for example, exceeds the entire national budgets of Panama, Nicaragua, Honduras, Guatemala, and El Salvador. The pure economic power of such an entity opens the doors of the middle and even the top strata of the official bureaucracy and creates at the same time a dependent class of local merchants and bankers. In addition, the foreign firm develops a special relationship with certain privileged sections of the labor force, sometimes by paying wages slightly above the depressed local rates. United States firms in northern Mexico, for example, are able to pay 75 cents an hour, which is more than three times the local average but at the same time only a third of the rate in nearby southern Texas. Local workers are co-opted by the competition for these prized jobs. In effect, foreign capital creates satellite classes whose interests are tied to the *dependencia* syndrome.

Even if the economic and social effects of foreign investment were entirely positive, patriots of developing countries could be expected to resist the control of national industries by foreign interests. In Malaysia in 1968, for example, the share of foreign-controlled subsidiaries and branches was 75 percent of rubber plantations, 54 percent of other agriculture, 69 percent of mining, 49 percent of manufacturing, 30 percent of construction, 60 percent of wholesale and retail trade, 28 percent of other industry and 57 percent of all industries as a whole. Such unrestricted penetration by outsiders gives foreign investment the image of neocolonialism, whatever the economist may conclude from the arithmetic of cost-benefit calculations.

Objections to Foreign Aid

It may seem surprising that even foreign aid is regarded with suspicion in the radical theory. If we concede that dependence on foreign capital and primary product exports is disadvantageous, wouldn't it seem to follow that aid as a form of capital transfer would give the recipient some relief?

There are several objections to this simple view. First, most foreign aid consists not of simple grants but of interest-bearing loans that must be repaid. The typical less developed country runs a chronic payments deficit because of the unfavorable balance of trade and the drain of excess profits to foreign firms. Borrowing foreign "aid" to make up the gap in current bills leads to mounting indebtedness and simply defers the day of reckoning, accumulating losses to be repaid in some future golden age. Borrowing from Peter to pay Paul (or "rolling over" the debt) does not break the pattern of dependency, but reinforces and perpetuates it. Foreign debt service cost the developing countries 11 percent of their export earnings in 1971 and will go to 20 percent by 1980. Some countries are especially hard hit—foreign debt service preempted over one-sixth of Egypt's total public revenue in 1972.

The emergence of LDC dependence on aid makes these nations vulnerable to political influence in new ways. For if aid is terminated, not only is development slowed, but even bare necessities that are imported will be halted, the nation will face a balance of payments crisis, and the economy will be capsized. Chile was faced with such an "invisible blockade" when the government of Salvadore Allende moved in directions perceived as hostile by the U.S. On the other side, obedient dependencies are permitted to have periodic debt crises during which the rich states generally allow payments moratoria for short periods to allow the LDC's to "catch their breath." Thus, the accumulation of foreign debt creates new forms of dependence. This problem grows in significance as indebtedness mounts. Figure 5–8 shows that the foreign public debt of the Third World quadrupled in twelve years, while that of the developed world stood still.

A second objection is that radicals object to the political conditions under which aid is given. More than half of American aid, for example, went to a handful of client states of dubious political character in the radical view: Vietnam, Laos, Taiwan, Thailand, Philippines, Spain, Portugal, Greece, and Turkey. These states also get the most favorable terms, including a high proportion of straight grants. Aid is given by the United States in the name of promoting international "stability"—that is, reinforcing the very relationships that keep the LDC's enslaved. Aid is part of the web of imperialism.

Third, the principal economic benefits from aid go not to the developing countries but to agricultural and industrial interests within the advanced countries themselves. Most aid is "tied" to purchases from the donor country, resulting in substantial sales for industries such as capital goods, fertilizers, defense, and railroad equipment. More than 90 percent of American foreign aid is spent within the borders of the United States. Purchases financed by aid account for more than $1 billion per year in United States industrial exports and an equal amount in agricultural exports. Indeed, PL 480, renamed the Food for Peace program by Presi-

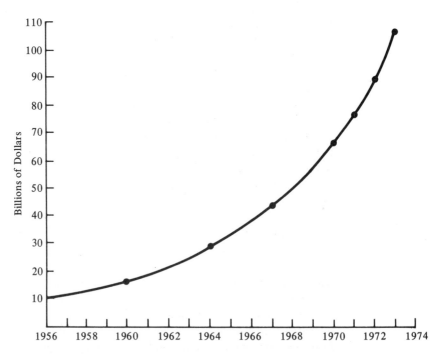

FIGURE 5–8   External Debt of Developing Countries

dent Kennedy, was originally called the Agricultural Surplus Support Program. Significantly, United States agricultural and industrial lobbyists generally give their firm support to maximum congressional appropriations of foreign assistance. On the Department of Commerce assumption of 60,000 jobs for every $1 billion in industrial exports, we may estimate that well over 100,000 American workers owe their employment to foreign aid.

Subsidized sales to LDC's under the aid program also have the effect of creating permanent trade links and a market infrastructure. Replacement parts will later be needed. Aid is the foot in the door for other forms of economic penetration.

Even the celebrated Green Revolution does not escape suspicion in the radical theory. We noted earlier that scientific agriculture may actually increase class conflict by concentrating land ownership. It also tends to increase reliance on machinery, chemical fertilizers and insecticides, and large investment of capital, much of which must be imported. Thus, even domestic agriculture begins to depend on foreign factors. Over a third of nitrogen, phosphate, and potash fertilizers must be imported as consumption increases. American exports of tractors and agricultural supplies are in fact booming as a result of this new development. Radical analysts are divided as to whether the food production advantages of the new methods are sufficient compensation for this new form of trade dependence.

Alternative Futures

If reliance on foreign investment and aid is rejected as the solution to the development problem of the Third World, what are the alternatives? A majority of the developing peoples now live under governments describing themselves as "socialist" in orientation, but what does this mean in international relations beyond the symbolic hostility to "capitalism"?

The Chinese Model

Some voices in the developing countries, such as the ruling party in Tanzania and the Maoist groups in Latin America, cite values in the Chinese experience for other poor countries. Before the Communists took power, the industrial and commercial sectors of the Chinese economy were thoroughly penetrated by foreign influence, to the extent that paper and metal currency was printed in English on one side. As late as 1935, we noted in chapter 4, foreigners controlled 95 percent of China's iron, three quarters of its coal, half its textile production, and most of shipping, public utilities, banking, insurance, and trade. Most industrial workers were employed by foreign firms, and the Chinese social structure showed many of the typical symptoms of what we now call the dependency syndrome. The corrective steps taken by the Communists after 1949 were harsh, but they succeeded in cutting the ties of dependency and putting China on a self-reliant path of rapid development. China in effect virtually sealed its borders to capitalist trade and investment and adopted an economic policy of isolation and autarky for twenty years.

Could the Chinese example of the "closed door" and almost total self-reliance be imitated by other LDC's? Probably not. China is a world in itself, a nation of 800 million people providing a huge internal market with diversified resources and productive potentials. The thirty less developed countries of sub-Saharan Africa *taken together* have less than 25 percent of this population base; individually, most developing countries are much smaller. Most economists agree that the cost of isolationism to a small country would be a substantially reduced rate of growth, if not economic collapse.

Regional Integration

Another solution for small nations is forming regional economic groups to consolidate the economies of several neighboring states into one larger entity. Present experiments in economic integration among developing countries include the East African Common Market, the Arab Common Market, the Central American Common Market, and the Latin American Free Trade Association. Degrees of integration range from the free trade area (where tariffs on trade among members are eliminated), through the customs union (where a common external tariff is added to the free trade area) to the common market (where labor and capital as well as goods and services are permitted to move freely). Later steps in economic integration may include monetary union (a common currency), the merger of tax systems, and finally a single national budget including a shared defense budget. Each stage of economic integration has political costs as well as benefits (see chapter 12), and inevitably some elites gain from a merger while others lose. The success of developing nations in achieving regional integration is partly a function of the relative strength of these forces.

Another obstacle to regional economic integration is the fear that the costs and benefits of cooperation will be distributed unequally. Experience has shown that without special preferential measures favoring the less developed members of a group, the benefits of integration are likely to be concentrated in the more advanced countries, while a disproportionate share of the costs will be borne by the less advanced ones. In theory, this inequality could be relieved by asymmetrical tariff policies providing a higher degree of protection for a prolonged transition period for the less developed states, as well as directly subsidizing their development in key sectors. But in practice, even the more advanced members of a regional grouping tend to experience developmental strains, and national priorities rather than mutual interests tend to prevail. Moreover, the economic systems of neighboring states may have a limited potential for integration. States whose previous economic development was geared to the export of highly specialized products to the developed countries may find the expansion of trade with fellow developing countries difficult. The noncomplementarity of LDC economies explains their tendency to concentrate the volume of trade on distant, more advanced partners rather than on their neighbors.

Another obstacle to integration is the national pride of newly independent countries and the mutual hostility of some adjoining states. Integration requires a sacrifice of unrestricted autonomy in favor of joint decision-making, and this in turn requires mutual trust and a willingness to accept a shared fate.[9] Many developing countries, especially those which gained independence within the past two decades, seem to prefer a go-it-alone strategy. Indeed, intra-African economic integration has declined rather than increased since the collapse of the colonial empires, and dependence on the center paradoxically has increased. During the colonial period, integration was forced on diverse neighbors by their European masters, such as the French-imposed West African Customs Union and the Equatorial African Customs Union. Britain established a common market, a common currency, and common railways and other services in the East African colonies of Kenya, Uganda, and Tanganyika. Since independence, these cooperative arrangements have been largely dismantled. The lines of commerce and communication from most developing nations flow not to their neighbors, but to the nations of the center, like spokes to a hub.[10]

Commodity Producer Cartels

In reality, many developing countries seem destined to play the role of primary product exporters for years to come, given all the obstacles to radical alternatives such as the Closed Door or regionalization. Means of stepping up the pace of economic development will have to be found within the present framework of commodity specialization. For this reason, some leaders of exporting countries are looking for progress in the formation of agreements among producers of primary products to regulate and improve the prices of their commodities.

The outstanding example of success for such producer groups is, of

[9] D. C. Mead, "The Distribution of Gains in Customs Unions between Developing Countries," *Kyklos* 21: 713–34; R. F. Mikesell, "The Theory of Common Markets as Applied to Regional Arrangements among Developing Countries," in R. F. Harrod and D. C. Hague, eds., *International Trade Theory in a Developing World* (New York: Macmillan, 1963), pp. 205–29.

[10] Dharam P. Ghai, "Perspectives on Future Economic Prospects and Problems in Africa," in Bhagwati, ed., *Economics and World Order*, pp. 265–66.

course, the Organization of Petroleum Exporting Countries (OPEC) which succeeded in raising the basic price of a barrel of oil from $2.18 in 1971 to $11.25 in 1975—an increase of 416 percent. Despite a drop in the volume of exports following the price increase, the OPEC countries earned $100 billion in oil revenues in 1975 compared to $8 billion in 1970. Petroleum exporters with large populations, such as Nigeria, Indonesia, and Iran, suddenly have the capital resources to finance development at a greatly expanded pace. Exporters with small populations, such as Saudi Arabia, Kuwait, and the United Arab Emirates, not only can afford rags-to-riches luxuries at home, but also are able to accumulate huge and unprecedented financial surpluses with which to influence other countries and even the great powers. The entire world watches as Saudi Arabia, once described as "rushing madly from the eleventh century into the twelfth," banks a $20 billion *surplus* in one year, while Great Britain, on whose empire the sun was never to set, is at its feet.

Could this model of successful collusion among oil exporters (a *cartel*) be duplicated by producers of copper, cocoa, coffee, and the like? Members of the Intergovernmental Committee of Copper Exporting Countries, the Union of Banana Exporting Countries, the International Tin Council, and at least a dozen other commodity groups hope so, but professional observers disagree on their prospects. Five conditions determine whether a cartel will be durable and effective:[11]

1. *Price elasticity of demand*. Demand must be relatively unresponsive to price. If a commodity is important to consumers, and substitutes for it are not readily available, then price increases can be imposed without a severe loss of sales. This is the case with oil, and it is also believed to be true of minerals such as copper and aluminum and some foods such as coffee. Other products, such as natural rubber and bananas, have more elastic demand and cannot increase in price without also curtailing sales.

2. *Limited number of producers*. A relatively small number of producers controlling a relatively large share of total world exports in a commodity is ideal for collusion. This condition is met by at least eight major commodities in which the top four LDC producers account for over half of world exports. Moreover, there must be high barriers to entry against new producers—that is, it must be difficult for new competitors to break into a market by underselling the cartel price. This also is true for many commodities, whether because of the limits of raw material sources, climatic and soil conditions, the start-up costs of production, or other factors.

3. *Shared experience of producers*. Producing states must be aware of their interdependence and be willing to cooperate and act as a limited

[11] Adapted from Stephen D. Krasner, "Oil is the Exception," *Foreign Policy* (Spring 1974).

economic coalition. This condition also is met by producers of several commodities, though in other cases the necessary basis of shared values is less evident.

4. *Consumer resistance*. The probability that a cartel will be successful is reduced if consumers are organized for effective resistance. In the petroleum market, the position of the major oil companies is believed to have facilitated collusion among the exporting countries. Other commodity markets lack such middlemen to act as "tax collectors," and the probability of resistance may be higher.

5. *Ability to take a long-term perspective*. A cartel member must be prepared to accept short-term costs for long-term gains. The market may contract severely as buyers resist the inflated price and "draw down" their inventories. The oil exporting states were in a good position to curtail production, as they could live for some time on substantial capital reserves previously accumulated. Also, the production of oil is not labor intensive, and relatively few workers were idled by the deliberate slowdown. Countries with small financial reserves and high proportions of the labor force dependent on export production are in a poor position to pay the short-term costs of cartelization. The temptation to cheat may be irresistible for poorer cartel members, who will be able to take advantage of the situation by price-shaving. In no other commodity are producing countries in as strong a position to accept short-term costs as in oil.

Is cartelization of other primary commodities, then, probable or improbable? The evidence is ambiguous, but some Western observers believe that the developed world will face "one, two, many OPEC's" [12] and some Third World leaders believe that this is the first opportunity for the developing countries truly to redress the global inequalities between rich and poor. Advanced states are being forced to consider a range of defensive measures to protect themselves from price-gouging by cartels. Some have proposed expanding "buffer" stockpiles and diversifying sources of supply of primary commodities as measures to prepare for economic warfare. Consumer coalitions would be constructed to oppose the producer cartels. In the extreme case of economic strangulation of the industrial states by a hypothetical long-term oil embargo, some have raised the possibility of direct military intervention to assure access to supplies and possibly to reduce prices if they reached "impossible" levels.

Others reject this economic warfare model, and call for cooperation between producing and consuming states to raise the income of primary producers with minimum disruption to the international economy. Third World spokespersons particularly believe that the global redistribution of wealth is long overdue, and that increases in prices of exports of develop-

---

[12] See especially C. Fred Bergsten, "The Threat from the Third World," *Foreign Policy* (Summer 1973), and his "The Threat is Real," *Foreign Policy* (Spring 1974).

ing countries will be a principal means of achieving this. They reject the charge that the new price of oil is artificially high; rather it is the old price that was artificially low. The rich countries have become habituated to a terms-of-trade structure that must be changed, and they are finding the transition painful. Americans have become accustomed to a situation in which their standard of living, measured in per capita GNP, is twenty-three times that of the developing countries. Now the developing world has an effective means of changing this balance of wealth, admittedly at some cost to the developed world, and they are unmoved by cries that "you're bankrupting us."

The Soviet Union may be expected to support the Third World on this issue. The USSR is the world's leading producer of petroleum, and is a fairly substantial exporter to East and West European countries as well. The change in the price of oil achieved by OPEC resulted in direct gains to the USSR of about $2 billion per year in export earnings, partly at the expense of the East European Communist states. The Soviet Union is a major primary product exporter, and it would be strengthened by further revision in the terms of trade, while the NATO allies and Japan are the world's major raw materials importers.

The United States is in a less favorable position, but still is better situated than Europe or Japan. The U.S. imports about 15 percent of the critical industrial materials it consumes, compared to about 75 percent for Europe and Japan. And while the absolute volume of imports is high, dependence is concentrated on other developed countries rather than on Third World sources. The leading suppliers of nonfuel raw materials to America are Canada, Australia, Rhodesia, South Africa, and Brazil. As commodity power becomes more important in international relations, the U.S. can be expected to upgrade its alliance with these states. In only a few minerals—notably bauxite (aluminum), manganese, tin, and natural rubber—is supply significantly centered in the Third World, and for these, alternative sources of supply and substitute materials are available at some cost of transition. Moreover, the U.S. is itself the leading exporter of another category of primary commodities: wheat and other grains. As "the world's breadbasket," the U.S. has gained substantially from the inflation of world food prices. Indeed, increased agricultural export revenues almost cancelled out the increased costs of imported oil in the U.S. balance of payments from 1973 to 1975. Overall, the United States is less vulnerable to "resource warfare" than are other industrial states.

Ironically or tragically, some of the countries that have suffered most from the burden of OPEC oil prices have been other developing countries that import petroleum. India and Brazil, for example, each paid over one billion dollars more for oil imports in 1974 than in 1972, while the Philippines' bill went up $500 million. These figures vastly exceed the grant foreign aid that these countries received even in boom years, and they have plunged many non-oil LDC's into ever deeper debt to finance critical imports. Compensatory aid given by the OPEC states is substantial, but is mainly in the form of loans (especially in the case of non-Arab recipients), widening the cycle of dependency. And while advanced industrial states can offset part of the higher cost of oil by expanding military and other exports to the OPEC states, this market is less accessible to developing-country exports. Thus, while the "Group of Ten" leading Western industrial states (taken together) were still in balance of payments surplus in 1975, the non-OPEC developing countries had a current account deficit of $35 billion.

Only about one-third of this deficit can be attributed to the increased cost of oil. Other factors include the reduction of LDC exports to the rich states because of the general world recession, higher prices for non-oil imports (including grain purchases from the U.S., Canada, and Australia), and the weakness of primary product prices. But those who argue that OPEC oil prices are a case of "the poor robbing the poor" point to comparisons between oil and other forms of perceived "exploitation" of the developing countries. Non-oil LDC's paid the OPEC states over $10 billion more in 1974 for about the same volume of oil imported in 1972, an amount which exceeds the profits of all foreign investors and multinational corporations in these countries in the best years. It is also more than the cost each year of the terms-of-trade decay of non-oil commodities since 1950 as computed by the United Nations. Thus, one could argue quantitatively that "oil exploitation" of non-OPEC states is a greater problem than foreign investment or the terms of trade. This view is not accepted by the great majority of Third World spokespeople and writers, who continue to regard OPEC's success as their own. Indeed, there is some hope that OPEC states will use some of their surplus revenues to support the position of other commodity producer cartels, especially to increase their capacity to absorb the short-term costs of cartelization. In this way, the OPEC strategy could be widened to a general economic offensive for the Third World.

The Power of OPEC

Whether or not imitations of OPEC are successful, oil will continue to have some unique attributes of supreme importance to the structure of international relations. Oil is the lifeblood of modern industrial society, and any substantial interruption of its supply can bring a halt to industry, commerce, transportation, and heating in colder climates. The loss of other imported raw materials and fuels could bring serious inconvenience and even ruin to limited sectors of Western society, but only the loss of oil could bring complete strangulation of economic life. Thus, the threat of an oil embargo is a uniquely potent weapon that oil exporters can wield against importers.

A second noteworthy attribute of oil is its money value. The revenue of the trade in oil swamps that of all other raw materials and fuels combined, and oil has a much greater impact on the balance of payments of importing countries than any other raw material or fuel. Moreover, some of the largest oil exporters have tiny populations and a limited capacity to absorb imports. These OPEC "low absorbers"—Saudi Arabia, Kuwait, Qatar, and the United Arab Emirates—therefore have huge balance-of-payments surpluses. Saudi Arabia, for example, increased its international financial reserves from $2.5 billion in 1972 to almost $25 billion in 1975, and is expected to continue this unprecedented rate of accumulation. The OPEC group together had a $65 billion current account surplus in 1974, and despite a breathtaking buying spree in 1975, succeeded in reducing this surplus only to $36 billion. The build-up of OPEC funds is expected to reach a peak between 1978 and 1980 that is variously estimated between $150 billion (UBAN Arab Japanese bank statement in 1975) and $650 billion (World Bank estimate in 1974). Even the lower figure exceeds the total book value of all U.S. foreign investments, direct and portfolio, and the higher figure is in the magnitude of the market value of all shares of all companies listed on the New York Stock Exchange at the end of 1975. The legendary wealth of the Rockefeller family, estimated at about $2 billion and formerly thought to confer nearly limitless political influence, is a mere pittance compared to the bank reserves of the king of Saudi Arabia, whose *income* is $2 billion per month. Moreover, the power of the petrodollar surpluses is self-multiplying: OPEC surpluses mean deficits for other countries, which mean the need to borrow, which means increased influence for the lenders. And the OPEC "low absorbers," with two-thirds of the exporting countries' proven reserves and half their current output, have only 12 million people. Suddenly, the desert sheikhs of the Arabian Peninsula control the largest accumulations of capital ever assembled in so few hands, and the leaders of government and industry in the greatest states of the Western empire now rely upon their good will.

The Limits of Oil Power

What are the *limits* to the power of the embargo (the supply problem) and the petrodollars (the financing problem)? The power of embargo is limited by problems of collusion, targetting, and countermeasures.

1. *Collusion.* No single state acting alone, not even Saudi Arabia, can significantly affect world oil supply if the other OPEC states use their "shut-in" or excess capacity to expand exports in compensation. Thus, an

effective embargo requires the collusion of at least four or five of the largest exporters. And producers with relatively large populations and revenue needs, such as Iran, Iraq, and Nigeria, depend on the income from oil and would suffer from participation in an embargo. Therefore, the embargo option in all but very extreme cases is limited to the "low absorbers." As these all happen to be Arab states, one (and probably only one) scenario for collusion is plausible: an embargo in support of the struggle against Israel.

2. *Targetting.* But Israel does not obtain oil from the Arab states. Even if the non-Arab exporting countries that do supply it, including Iran, could be induced to participate, the United States has undertaken to assure supply to the Jewish state (whose imports are in any case quite small compared to world consumption). Thus the Organization of Arab Petroleum Exporting Countries (OAPEC) would be forced into a "secondary boycott" against the U.S. and other states to change their policies toward Israel. But the United States, Israel's primary supporter, is relatively invulnerable to an Arab embargo. The U.S. imported 40 percent of its oil in 1975, but only a quarter of this came from Arab sources. Thus, 10 percent of U.S. oil, or 4 percent of total American energy consumption in all forms, came from the Arab states, a relatively small figure compared to the other capitalist states. And the loss of Arab oil, if confined to the U.S., could be compensated by stepped-up imports from non-Arab states (whose shut-in or unused export capacity substantially exceeds the volume of OAPEC exports to the U.S.). If neither Israel nor the U.S. is a vulnerable target, an OAPEC embargo would have to be turned on Europe and Japan, which are vulnerable. But these states are of secondary importance to the Arab-Israel conflict. Moreover, many states, such as Japan and France, have developed extensive bilateral ties with individual Arab states and have supported many Arab demands in international forums. Thus, OAPEC would hurt its friends more than its perceived enemies.

3. *Countermeasures.* In addition to the limits of collusion and targetting, an effective embargo would risk severe countermeasures by the affected states, especially the U.S. The idea of military action in case of a devastatingly effective embargo has been the subject of sensational speculation in the world press, encouraged by ambiguous remarks of American officials. While there would be many tactical and strategic problems for the U.S. in such an action, it cannot be ruled out. The examples of the U.S. in Vietnam and the USSR in Czechoslovakia show how bold and relentless the great powers can be even when there are many arguments for restraint. Moreover, a state of economic warfare may evoke many countermeasures and undesired effects even without military force. It will strengthen the Communist states against the West, which would not be in the interests of the conservative dynasties of the Middle East, and will renew or deepen the world economic crisis to the detriment of many

countries. The strategy of the embargo is a very limited option, and one that would be embraced only if the oil states were backed to the wall by extreme threat, provocation, or humiliation.

The use of *petrodollars* for influence has more varied and subtle possibilities. An accumulated surplus of $250 billion by 1980—the most reasonable estimate—will mean a global network of lending and investing relationships that will confer upon the "low absorber" states many opportunities for quiet persuasion. The Gulf states will control a significant portion of the world's liquid assets available for international transfer.

But financial influence alone also has limits. OPEC can offer money, but not the technology or managerial skills of the Western capital-exporting states. Moreover, the quantitative magnitude of the "low absorbers'" surplus, while impressive, should not be mistaken for control of the world's money markets. Yearly accumulations of $30 to $40 billion by OPEC countries must be compared to total non-Communist world savings annually of $500 billion. The OPEC share is 6 to 8 percent—though the effect is amplified somewhat because the low internal needs of the OPEC states make these savings more portable. And the cumulative surplus of OPEC in the peak year ($250 billion) will not compare to the total stock of financial assets in the U.S., Japan, Europe, and Canada ($6,000 billion in 1980). The OPEC share will be only 4 percent, though rather more if we consider only capital available for export.

The petrodollars will have a major influence on small states, but lesser impact on the great powers. And it is expected that, over time, the larger industrial states will attract a growing share of OPEC investment. It is estimated that in the United States alone, the demand for capital and credit for industry, housing, and government deficits during the decade 1976–85 will exceed the domestic supply of investment resources by $1,500 billion, or six times the total OPEC surplus. The Persian Gulf states are proving to be very conservative investors and are likely to prefer established banks, blue chip stocks, and the securities of well established governments. This fiscal conservatism, combined with the capital hunger of the advanced states, suggests that the petrodollars are more likely to fall into an orderly system of routine "recycling" than to be used arbitrarily and capriciously for political pressure.

It is beyond dispute that the success of OPEC has enhanced the prestige and influence of the oil producers. Nations fortunate enough to sit over deposits of "black gold" can no longer be taken for granted by their trading partners and allies. But there is a tendency to become intoxicated on such large numbers and to imagine the OPEC states as having capabilities, including destructive capabilities, that they do not possess. Even the most blessed of the OPEC states will be middle powers in economic terms and relatively small powers in military terms (with the possible exception of Iran, a middle power) for the foreseeable future.

Conclusion

The radical theory of underdevelopment seeks its cause in international mechanisms of unequal trade and foreign investment. The conventional theory explains it in terms of the impediments to development within the social and economic structures of the developing countries themselves. But there is a convergence in the perspectives of the two schools on several concrete policy issues in international relations. Perhaps the foremost element of agreement is that the international trade position of the LDC's must be improved, and that primary product prices are a key element in this. Thus, the example of OPEC is equally important to countries with very different political orientations.

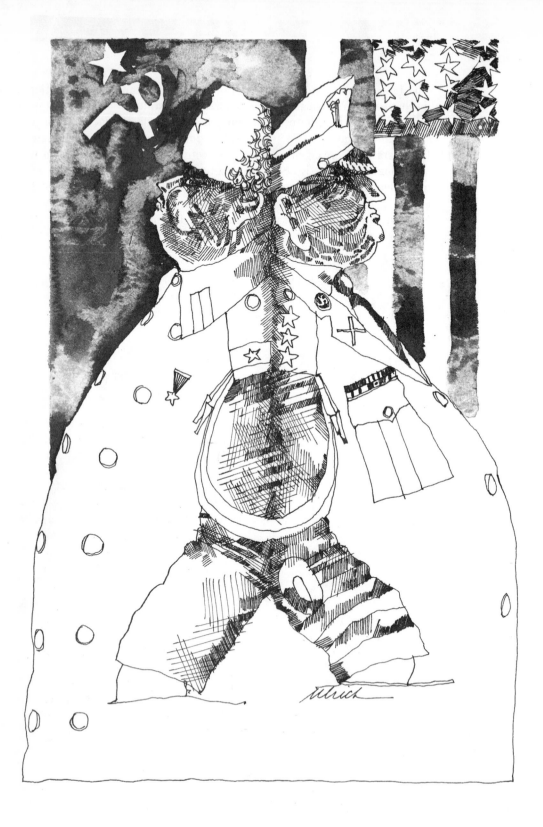

6

Perceptions in
International Relations

We have reviewed the perceptual frames of five major actors in the international system today—the USSR, the United States, America's major allies, China, and the Third World. The *Soviet Union* sees the world divided into two innately hostile camps of *capitalist* and *socialist* states, with itself as the progenitor and protector of the socialist camp and the United States as the world headquarters of antirevolutionary reaction and imperialism. The *United States*, on the other hand, sees Soviet communism as an inherently expansionist totalitarian ideology threatening to engulf weaker nations of the Free World, except for the protective umbrella of American power; this gives the United States the responsibility of countering aggression. *America's allies* perceive themselves to be threatened less by communist menace than by subordination to the United States as modern economic colonies. *China* sees this U.S.-Soviet cold war as a thin disguise for two competing imperialisms, capitalist and socialist, both trying behind masks of protective benevolence to expand their domination of the world's peoples. China sees itself as the true home of people's revolutions and as a model for national development in a world of equals without superpowers. The *Third World* countries have little direct interest in these East/West conflicts and are as a group more concerned with the North/South conflict of colonialism, economic dependency, and an international environment hostile to the political and economic development of the small powers.

Each of these *perceptual systems* is supported by an array of data and historical analyses. Each seems to its proponents so well supported by facts that it needs no further substantiation. Each perceptual system regards the others as inaccurate and dishonest. Proponents of the other points of view have a misperception, a limited perception; or they are dissimulators who know the truth, but for ulterior motives pretend to have a different perception. In short, laymen and national policy-makers believe their own perceptual systems to be true and those of opponents at least partly false.

How is it possible for each perceptual system to persist in resisting change when confronted with contradictory information by other points of view? Why don't the nations of the world sit down and iron out their differences, work out each other's misperceptions, and resolve at least that portion of their conflicts that is rooted in misunderstanding? Why don't we get down to the *facts* and replace all this confusion with an understanding of *reality?*

To answer these questions, it will help to understand some of the propositions in the *theory of international perceptions*—propositions adapted from social psychology and applied to the study of international relations.

Facts

In everyday life, we generally assume that our understanding of reality flows directly from the nature of that reality itself. It is common sense that certain things are facts while the opposite assertions are not, and that if we can ascertain the facts, certain conclusions will follow. The purpose of *information-gathering,* for both the scientist and the decision-maker, is to determine the facts from which knowledge of reality can be drawn.

Perceptual theorists do not accept this simple conception of knowledge. To them, knowledge has a *subjective* as well as an *objective* component: the facts do not speak for themselves, but are given meaning by each interpreter from his own analytical point of view. The conclusion that follows from facts depends on the interpretation that the facts are given.

Furthermore, facts do not spring up from reality to meet the eye but are, rather, particular pieces of information from reality that are *selected* by an observer as having importance while other pieces of information are *rejected* as lacking importance. Reality consists of an infinite amount of potential information, from which only a tiny part is taken as a set of facts. For example, in writing the history of a war the historian must select from countless data a small portion to report. Millions of individuals are involved in billions or trillions of acts; billions of decisions are made by participants; the patterns of interaction are beyond imagination. The historian must select from all this a few pieces of information which seem summarily to describe the interactions and succinctly explain their causes.

Students of history and historiography know only too well that the facts do *not* speak for themselves.

David Easton has summarized this view of facts in a terse definition: A *fact is but a peculiar ordering of reality according to a theoretic interest.*[1] That is, the facts themselves are imposed on "reality" by the observer, rather than the other way around; and the very nature of the "facts" themselves depends on the questions that the observer chooses to ask. Since each perceptual system asks its own questions, observers of divergent viewpoints naturally arrive at different answers or facts.

To illustrate: from the Soviet point of view, data about the profit structure of American corporations is a body of facts that one must have to understand the international system; from the American point of view, it is off the point entirely. If one is given twenty minutes to explain the cold war and spends fifteen on the nature of American investments, that person will be regarded by a Soviet listener as having given "the facts," but by an American listener as having evaded them. To the American, the real facts have to do with Soviet aggression and American response, and cases of Soviet behavior will be pertinent. "Facts" are thus subjectively defined and are themselves a phenomenon of perceptions. Perceptions cannot be corrected when confronted with facts if the facts themselves are perceptions.

Newsweek International—Ranan Lurie, reprinted with permission.

[1] See David Easton, *The Political System* (New York: Alfred A. Knopf, 1953).

Values, Beliefs, and Cognitions

Perceptual theorists distinguish among three components of perception: values, beliefs, and cognitions. A *value* is a preference for one state of reality over another: health is better than illness, green is prettier than blue. Values do not specify what *is* but rather what *ought to be.* Values assign a relative worth to objects and conditions.

A *belief* is a conviction that a description of reality is true, proven, or known. Often it is based on prior reception of information from the environment ("I have learned that . . .") but it is not the same as the data themselves. It is an analytical proposition that relates individual pieces of data into a "proven" pattern: democratic governments are less warlike than totalitarian governments; imperialism is the mature phase of monopoly capitalism. A belief is not the same as a value. One might believe that communism brings a higher rate of economic growth, and that capitalism has a better record of protecting individual freedoms. Given these beliefs, one must decide which is better, capitalism or communism, according to one's own values. Which is worth more, economic growth or personal liberties?

A *cognition* is data or information received from the environment: Russia is giving warplanes to Syria. Cognitions are key elements in establishing perceptual systems and in changing those systems. The concept of changing national perceptions refers to introducing cognitions that will revise beliefs and values. If we held a conference between the major cold war actors to iron out their differences and "misperceptions," our purpose would be to influence perceptions by introducing new information. We would try to change stubborn beliefs and values that cause conflict by confronting each side with new cognitive data.

Unfortunately, it has been found in a variety of studies that at all levels of human behavior, deeply held values and beliefs are highly resistant to change through new cognitions. Social psychological research data support a theory of "cognitive dissonance." Briefly stated, this theory holds that when a deeply held value or belief is contradicted by a new message from the environment (a "dissonant" cognition) the message (fact, cognition) will be rejected and the value or belief retained. This may not take the form of outright rejection of the discrepant message. It may take the alternate form of reinterpretation of the datum to make it consistent with the existing belief. But the effect is the same: the individual's value and belief system protects itself from external alteration.[2]

We might relate this phenomenon to the idea of an "economy of

[2] See Leon Festinger, *The Theory of Cognitive Dissonance* (Stanford: Stanford University Press, 1962).

thought." It is very "expensive" to carry about in one's head all the information supporting one view and its opposite. Mental economy requires that we have a filtering system to fit a single reality to our preconceptions, so that we are not constantly revising our basic perceptual systems with all the readaptation and adjustment that that would require. Political organizations choose as their leaders individuals with known points of view which concur reliably with those of the membership. If national leaders were relatively free to revise their perceptual frameworks, they would not be reliable. Hence, the rigidity and predictability of the leadership's perceptual system is an asset to the group. The leader should not be quicker to change than are his constituents.

The constituents, on the other side, must not be overly vulnerable to perceptual change from external influences. If foreign leaders could appeal "over the head" of a national leader to his own constituents, they might manipulate these persons to their own advantage. For this and other reasons, it is functional for each nation to have its own system of "authorities," public officials who determine the overall national interest with regard to other nations. These same public officials play a major role in channeling the cognitions which reach their "publics." Many studies have shown that individuals will accept or reject the same information depending on whether it comes from a positive or negative prestige source. Thus, constituents choose their leaders for the relative inflexibility of their perceptual systems, and the leaders process incoming information in such a way as to maintain the existing perceptual system of the constituents. The national belief system is stable and resistant to change.[3]

For all these reasons, we can safely assume that national perceptual frameworks will usually survive challenges from other nations and new experiences. They may make superficial or cosmetic improvements to adjust to new realities at times, but fundamental change is a long-term process. The vehicle of national policy is steered by looking in the rearview mirror; nations are influenced more by where they have been than by where they are going. American policy is still responding to the failure of isolationism and the ill wisdom of Munich. Soviet policy is still responding to the terrible invasions of the two world wars and to a threadworn theory of capitalism that is now a hundred years old. China is still responding to the Century of Humiliation. And the Third World is still obsessed with colonialism. Perhaps in fifty years we will be ready for 1978.

[3] Compare Herbert Kelman, ed., *International Behavior: A Social Psychological Analysis* (New York: Holt, Rinehart and Winston, 1965), especially "The Effects of Events on National and International Images" by Karl Deutsch and Richard Merritt; Ole Holsti, "The Belief System and National Images," *Journal of Conflict Resolution* 6 (1962): 244–52; Kenneth Boulding, *The Image* (New York: Harper & Row, 1960); Robert Jervis, *The Logic of Images in International Relations* (Princeton: Princeton University Press, 1971).

We have seen that international events are selectively perceived by key actors, and that every "reality" has multiple meanings depending on the perceiver. This principle can be seen sharply in a comparison of two big power interventions in the middle 1960's: the United States intervention in the Dominican Republic in the spring of 1965, and the Soviet military intervention in Czechoslovakia in August 1968.

The United States sent 25,000 Marines into the Dominican Republic to prevent that country from shifting leftward; three years later the Soviet Union opened a military invasion of Czechoslovakia to forestall that country's drift toward political liberalism. The Dominican Republic is in the traditional American "sphere of influence" in the Caribbean, while Czechoslovakia is a key element of the traditional Soviet sphere in Eastern Europe. Thus, to many outside observers the two events were a clear demonstration of the "dual imperialisms" philosophy of the superpowers, dividing the world up between them and intervening freely in the affairs of lesser states in their respective hegemonies. But to the superpower leaders themselves, these events had very different meanings and each justified its own behavior profusely and insistently as different in kind from the lawless interventionism of the other. Perceptual analysis provides a key to understanding these two cases.

The Dominican crisis arose from a conflict between a right-wing military government and a rebellion by supporters of ousted civilian President Juan Bosch. Bosch had been the first freely elected president in thirty-eight years following a long period of dictatorship, but he was evicted from office by a military coup after only nine months. The crisis of 1965 erupted when a "constitutionalist" movement attempted to restore him to office and to remove the generals. American officials on the scene and in Washington perceived the rebellion as a Communist conspiracy using the good name of Bosch as a mere convenience. Although this characterization was disputed by many observers, President Johnson felt obligated to dispatch the Marines to Santo Domingo to "prevent another Cuba" in the Caribbean.

By what right, we may ask, did the United States intervene in what were manifestly the internal affairs of the Dominican Republic, regardless of how American officials might have felt about events there? It was conceded that the rebellion itself was composed entirely of Dominican citizens, making the American action a foreign intervention in a *civil* war. This accusation was quite important to the American self-image, because the United States counts itself a strict adherent to the principle of nonintervention in the internal affairs of other countries, which is codified in the United Nations Charter, the Charter of the Organization of American States, and elsewhere in international law.

American officials responded that while all the rebels were indeed Dominican, the rebellion was nonetheless part of the *international* Communist conspiracy and was, in the words of the legal adviser to the State Department, "an attempt by a conspiratorial group inspired from the outside to seize control by force" and was thus "an assault upon the independence and integrity" of the Dominican Republic.[4] It follows that the American intervention was justified to "protect" the Dominican people.

The Soviet reaction to the American intervention was swift and indignant, and accorded with the strong reactions of many non-Communist governments. Soviet Ambassador N. T. Fedorenko said at the UN on May 1, 1965, "There can be no justification for the invasion of the territory of a sovereign state by the United States armed forces, . . . a cynical violation of the elementary norms of international law." Fedorenko specifically rejected one argument in defense of the American action that will be important in our analysis later: the American assertion that intervention was justified by the principles of the "Inter-American System" as enunciated by the United States–dominated Organization of American States. OAS resolutions had affirmed and validated the American contention that communism was inherently a foreign threat to Western hemispheric nations, and on several occasions the OAS had endorsed American military interventions in Latin American countries to oppose developments perceived as Communist inspired. The Soviet spokesman objected that the American position amounts to a belief that:

> the right to decide the fate of the Dominican Republic rests only "partly with the people of that country and partly with their neighbors". . . . Such statements are incompatible with the obligations of the United States under the United Nations Charter, which prohibits any interference in the internal affairs of other countries. . . . The question of internal organization and regime is purely an internal affair of the Dominican people themselves and they alone . . . have the right to decide it without any pressure or interference from outside.

The United States, Fedorenko insisted, cannot act in Latin America "as if it was [sic] in its own private domain, . . . as if it were a question of Alabama or Mississippi."[5]

Thus, in the Dominican case, the United States invoked certain regional principles that allegedly supersede the usual rule of noninterference in the internal affairs of other countries, while the Soviet Union rejected these claims and stood firmly on traditional international law and standards of decent behavior. Three years later, these positions were exactly reversed

---

[4] Statement of Leonard C. Meeker, "Legal Basis for United States Actions in the Dominican Republic," reprinted in Abram Chayes, Thomas Ehrlich, and Andreas F. Lowenfeld, *International Legal Process*, vol. 2 (Boston: Little, Brown, 1969), p. 1182.

[5] Fedorenko remarks as reprinted in Thomas M. Franck and Edward Weisband, *Word Politics* (New York: Oxford University Press, 1972), pp. 97–102.

in the case of the Soviet invasion of Czechoslovakia, and the statesmen of the two countries demonstrated an extraordinary rhetorical dexterity in reversing roles and taking opposite parts without embarrassment. This time it was the Soviet Union which asserted a special regional right to intervene in the internal affairs of a sovereign country, and the United States which was outraged at a naked display of international gangsterism.

The crisis in Czechoslovakia materialized when the Communist government headed by Alexander Dubĉek began to move, in domestic and foreign policies, in directions that differed in basic orientation from the philosophy of the Soviet Union as leader of the Warsaw Pact nations. Just as the United States had feared "another Castro" in the developing Dominican crisis, the USSR came to fear "another Tito" in Czechoslovakia, meaning an independent Communist regime that could not be counted upon to contribute to "regional stability" and that might ally itself with hostile extraregional powers (that is, NATO). To prevent this, several hundred thousand troops of the Soviet Union and other Warsaw Pact nations entered Prague in August 1968 to dismantle and replace the Dubĉek government.

American officials, reflecting opinion in most of the world, labelled the Soviet action an outrage. Secretary of State Dean Rusk insisted that "a small country"' is entitled to "live its own life" without having the will of a dominant neighbor forced upon it. American spokesmen portrayed the Czech events as a plain act of foreign interference, comparable to the Nazi invasion of Czechoslovakia in 1938.

The Soviet rebuttal began with the proposition that the Dubĉek government had become a conscious or unconscious agent of capitalist imperialism. Antisocialist forces were seeking to sever Czechoslovakia from the socialist commonwealth. And while these antisocialist forces were Czechoslovak nationals, giving the conflict the appearance of an internal affair, Russia claimed to possess "irrefutable data concerning ties between the internal reaction in Czechoslovakia and the outside world . . .," according to Soviet UN representative Jacob Malik.[6]

Furthermore, the Czech government was responsible "not just to its own people, but also to all the socialist countries," *Pravda* argued. Czechoslovakia occupies a crucial geopolitical position in the European balance of power, and "weakening of any of the links in the world system of socialism directly affects all the socialist countries, which cannot look indifferently upon this."[7] Thus, in effect the Soviet argument invoked the very same regional right to intervene that it had rejected in the Dominican case.

American spokesmen were equally inconsistent. American officials rejected most strenuously the assertion that there are special rules within the "socialist commonwealth" that supersede the universal principle of noninterference, even though the United States had asserted precisely

[6] UN Security Council, Doc. S/PV 1441, August 21, 1968, p. 32.

[7] *Pravda* statement reprinted in *The New York Times*, September 27, 1968, p. 3.

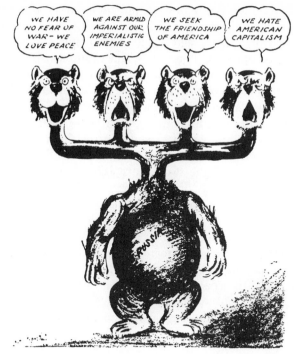

Four-headed Bear

Source: Goldberg in the *New York Sun,* 1946.

such a special relationship for the Organization of American States in the Dominican case. "No matter what the intimacy of one country with another," a United States delegate at the UN argued, "neither may claim a right to invade the territory of its friend. . . ."[8] And yet the American nations could, in the American view, determine that no more Communist governments would be tolerated in the Western hemisphere, *even if such governments were established by purely internal processes.*

Thus, the two superpowers sharply reversed their positions in the two cases, depending on perspective and policy considerations. The Soviet Union rejected the idea that "the right to decide the fate of the Dominican Republic rests only partly with the people of that country and partly with their neighbors," but at the same time asserted that the Czech government "is responsible not just to its own people but to all the socialist countries." The United States asserted that the Organization of American States, as the institutional expression of the "Inter-American System," could make determinations regarding the internal movement of members

[8] Statement of the U.S. representative to the UN Special Committee on the Principles of International Law on Legal Aspects of the Invasion and Occupation of Czechoslovakia, September 12, 1968, in *U.S. Department of State Bulletin,* LIX, October 14, 1968, p. 394.

toward Communist government, but the Warsaw bloc could not exercise the same rights in the name of the "socialist commonwealth."

Underlying these disagreements of principle are critical differences in political perception. On one hand, American officials see the "Inter-American System" as a free association of self-determined nations, while the "socialist commonwealth" is a mere collection of satellites and puppets of the USSR. Soviet officials, on the other hand, see the Organization of American States as a formal expression of the historical fact of American imperialism in Latin America, while the socialist community is an alliance of progressive states under the leadership of the USSR. Thus, even if detailed cognitions of the two events were identical, interpretation would involve conflicting sets of prior contextual beliefs and values. To Americans, a shift toward communism would be a loss of freedom, while Soviets would see a progressive and even inevitable development. However, Americans regarded the liberal movement of the Prague regime away from Soviet-style orthodoxy as progressive and hopeful, while Soviet observers saw regression toward capitalism. Thus, officials of the two countries would reject the contention that their positions in the two cases were contradictory.

Each side could also defend its actions by pointing to certain factual differences that favor a given perception. The Soviet intervention interrupted the otherwise peaceful evolution of Czechoslovakia, while the smaller United States force helped to end a fratricidal civil war that was already underway. The United States intervention was followed by reasonably free elections, while the Soviet intervention was followed by continued repression. On the other side, there is a pattern of United States economic domination in the Dominican Republic, while economic relations in Eastern Europe actually favor Czechoslovakia over the USSR. Also, Czechoslovakia is vital to the Soviet defense network, while the Dominican Republic is a minor matter for the United States—raising the argument that the Soviet intervention might have been more justifiable in the name of necessity. Facts of this sort can be raised to justify the rationalization of each side that "our case is different." The unflattering parallels that we have drawn can be rejected by either side, and the perceptual framework can remain invulnerable to empirical or logical refutation. This comparison of two cases shows that an intelligent perceptual structure is highly resistant to change even in the face of direct contradiction.[9]

The Special Problem of American Perceptions

Many Americans are sympathetic to the idea that leaders of other countries tend to look at the world through ideological lenses and perceptual

[9] For an extended comparison of the Dominican and Czech interventions, including thorough documentary citations, see Franck and Weisband, *Word Politics*.

distortions, but reject the view that such an analysis can be applied with equal validity to the American case. Is it not true, they ask, that the United States has a free press in which diverse opinions and outlooks are represented? Virtually every point of view, no matter how silly or outrageous, has its own magazine or publication in the fantastic array of printed materials available. This contrasts sharply with the situation in the Communist countries and in most of the Third World, where available information sources tend to be monopolized by the political party in power and only a single point of view is available. It would seem that the "free market of ideas" in the United States would make Americans less vulnerable to self-deceptions and rigid ideological distortions of perception.

There is ample justification for this expectation, and it must be conceded that American policy mistakes are freely criticized at home as well as abroad, while dissent in some other countries is partially or completely suppressed. Alternative perceptions and policies are openly discussed within the domestic political structure of the United States, and misperceptions are quickly unmasked by domestic critics. Thus, the mechanisms of potential self-correction seem to operate much more effectively in America.

At the same time, it is undeniable that certain crucial American misperceptions have managed to persist over very long periods of time despite their repeated "correction" by intelligent and responsible dissenters. For example, the American image of China as a satellite of the Soviet Union dominated the perceptions of foreign policy decision-makers until at least 1960, long after this misperception should have been adjusted by available information. Dissenters who questioned the orthodox point of view in the early years after the Chinese revolution had their patriotism and loyalty to "the American cause" seriously questioned; only the bravest voices were willing to continue their dissent from the official mythology. That other pictures of China could be obtained in small dissenting magazines and publications is interesting but not as meaningful as Americans like to think. The dominant misperception of China was reinforced by all the major publications and broadcast media—the overwhelming volume of information supported the official view. Thus, the "free market of ideas" is not a guarantee against false orthodoxies and misperceptions, though it does help to keep alive other points of view.

Another hazard of the American self-perception is the easy assumption that what Americans think is typical of "world opinion." The people of the United States, like peoples elsewhere, are prone to the delusion that when an opinion prevails among everyone they know, it is equally popular elsewhere. Americans are particularly subject to this error, because of their self-conception as "the leaders of the Free World." Scientific sampling of public opinion in different countries shows, however, that the particular outlook of the Americans is not universally popular, and that there are many issues on which American public opinion is inconsistent with opin-

"Psst—Want To See Some Poems?"

Copyright © 1961 by Herblock. From *Straight Herblock* (Simon & Schuster, 1964).

ion abroad. For example, the Gallup organization conducted an eleven-nation public opinion poll in November of 1967 on the United States policy in Vietnam. It found that outside the United States the military escalation policy of the United States government was almost universally unpopular, while in the United States the majority of opinion favored even greater escalation. In nine of the eleven "Free World" countries polled, American *withdrawal* was overwhelmingly the favored option, while in the United States 53 percent favored *even greater escalation* and only 31 percent favored withdrawal (see Figure 6–1). On this issue, apparently, the American people isolated themselves from "world opinion" and deluded themselves that they were the shield of the "Free World." It is reasonable to conclude that Americans, despite a remarkably free press and apparent good intentions, are no less prone to errors and misperceptions than are other peoples, and that they as much as others should listen carefully to the opinions both of acknowledged friends and of perceived enemies.

Conclusion

We live in a world of nations created in response to revolutionary ideals that inspired their founders and continue to motivate subsequent genera-

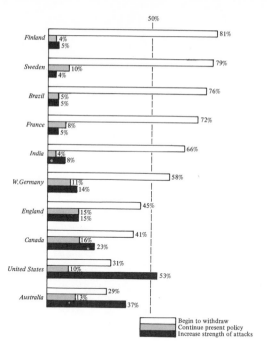

FIGURE 6–1   Eleven-Nation Gallup Poll on Vietnam

Source: Gallup Opinion Index no. 29, November 1967. Reprinted by permission.

tions. The American founding fathers, the early Soviet Bolsheviks, the Chinese Maoists, and the various inspirational heroes of the Third World countries all bequeathed to their followers a special sense of creative mission and a feeling of obligation to carry forward the advances of their revolution. Like the missionaries of more religious times, each nation sends forth its young people into the outside world to convert the heathen and spread the Gospel. This messianic spirit can be a constructive and energizing force, but when it is overlayed by misperceptions and self-delusions, it can become a dangerous basis for international relations. In the incisive words of Hans Morgenthau, here is the image of ideological warfare in the modern world:

> The claim to universality which inspires the moral code of one particular group is incompatible with the identical claim of another group; the world has room for only one, and the other must yield or be destroyed. Thus, carrying their idols before them, the nationalistic masses of our time meet in the international arena, each group convinced that it executes the mandate of history, that it does for humanity what it seems to do for itself, and that it fulfills a sacred mission ordained by Providence, however defined.[10]

[10] Hans Morgenthau, *Politics Among Nations*, 4th ed. (New York: Alfred A. Knopf, 1967), p. 249.

Part Two

THE LOGIC OF POWER

7

Power

The previous chapters have been concerned with values, perceptions, and goals of key actors in the contemporary international system. The present chapter and those that follow focus on the instruments of foreign policy and the ways that systems of international relations constrain the abilities of states to achieve their goals. We move from the level of analysis of *actors* to the level of *systems* and interrelationships. The first question is the nature of power and capability in the international system.

The Nature of Power

What is the nature of power in international relations? We may define power broadly as *the ability of an international actor to use its tangible and intangible resources and assets in such a way as to influence the outcomes of events in the international system in the direction of improving its own satisfaction with the system.* This definition points out some of the important features of the relationship of influence among actors. First, power is the means by which international actors deal with one another. It is a collection of possessions, but specifically a collection of possessions which creates an ability. Second, power is not a natural political attribute, but a product of material (tangible) and behavioral (intangible) resources, each of which has its unique place in the totality of the actor's power. Third, power is a means for achieving influence over other actors who are competing for outcomes favorable to their own objectives. And fourth, the use of power, when rationally designed, is an attempt to shape the outcomes of international events for the specific purpose of maintaining or improving the actor's satisfaction with the international political environment. Such satisfaction is normally a measure of the degree to which the influential foreign policy-making elite elements of a national society perceive their needs and objectives to be served by the prevailing international norms.

These characteristics of power suggest still others. It is important, for example, to think of power as having an *instrumental* character. Power is a means to ends, an instrument for achieving subsequent objectives. The possession of power is meaningless if in its application it is unable to bring about results which enhance the actor's satisfaction. Furthermore, one must consider the *relative* character of power. When two states compete over an international objective, their abilities to exert power may be roughly equal (a *symmetrical* power relationship) or severely unequal (an *asymmetrical* power relationship). Thus, it is important when assessing the power of an actor to ask the question, "Powerful relative to whom?" or "Powerful relative to what?" We know, for example, that in 1935 Italy was sufficiently powerful to overrun Ethiopia, as it pressed its First World War vintage weapons against a primitive society. But the same Italian armed forces were virtually impotent in the face of the modern allied assault eight years later.

More modern military examples have dramatized still another peculiarity of power: *the use of power may have diminishing returns.* In South Vietnam, for example, the United States used virtually all military means short of nuclear warfare to bring about a North Vietnamese withdrawal. Yet for all its fire power the U.S. failed to achieve its objective. The North Vietnamese and Viet Cong, infinitely less powerful militarily, were able to seize upon national will and deteriorating support for the war in the United States and among Washington's allies to achieve politically what they could not achieve militarily: governmental self-determination and the expulsion of American force. The diminishing returns of American fire power, together with the superior nontangible resources which the Vietnamese were able to utilize, redressed the apparent asymmetry of their relationship. Some forms of power are impotent indeed!

But as vivid as such military examples may be, not all power relationships are measured in armaments. In fact, it should be said categorically that *power is not force*, and the ability to exert power is *not* limited to forceful situations. Indeed, international actors exercise power almost unceasingly; yet rarely, given the huge volume of international transactions, do they resort to force. Force, then, is an extreme use of power. Though the frequency of forceful operations may tempt us to think otherwise, the use of force in international relations is an aberration of the normal power relations of states. Force should be thought of as residing at the extreme end of a continuum of choices available to an actor when its agents consider influencing the outcomes of events.

At the other extreme of that continuum is *persuasion*, or the achievement of influence by the power of reason. Regrettably, it is appropriate only to those international situations in which two actors have a close similarity of objective, or in which one asks but a small alteration in the policy of another in an event which is not crucial to the latter. Beyond this rare case, the achievement of influence depends on the relative availability of positive and negative *sanctions*, which may be extended to affect the behavior of the other party. When the sanctions are positive, they may be regarded as *rewards* or as *inducements* to concur in the policy or objectives of the sender. One government, for example, may offer a major trading concession to another in exchange for its support on another issue. When such enticements fail, the same government may resort to negative sanctions, to *punishments* or *deprivations*, to alter the course of another's policy. It may threaten to rupture diplomatic relations, to discontinue trade, or to carry out any of countless other deprivations which will have a negative consequence for the receiver's international satisfaction. Or in situations crucial to its satisfaction an actor can threaten or use *force*. Force, then, is the result of an escalation of the power relationship of actors.

The choice of any of these methods of using power depends on several factors in the relation of the parties. Foremost among them is the importance of the outcome to each party. A government will not threaten nuclear war over small issues or issues of marginal importance. In addition, the choice of methods depends in part on the access which one actor has to another. Specifically, if the relationship is one in which there is a general agreement on the composition of international satisfaction, then persuasion and rewards will normally be adequate. Equally important, however, is the degree of similarity in their respective interpretations of the specific issue with respect to their satisfaction. The United States and Britain, for example, since World War II have enjoyed an extraordinarily high degree of mutuality on general issues of international satisfaction. Yet they broke sharply over the British role in the Suez War of 1956, an occasion on which the United States resorted to diplomatic embarrassment —public deprivation of concurrence—in order to alter the course of British policy. In some cases the access problem has another dimension, one in which a government is simply unable to reach another. This was particularly true of the Cold War years when, in order to exert power over American allies, the Soviet Union had to contend with American responses; and to reach the governments of Eastern Europe the United States was faced with Soviet counteractions.

In all of these situations, it may be concluded that one actor has power over another when it enjoys the superior position in an asymmetrical power relationship. In all cases, diplomatic effectiveness is linked to the capabilities which underlie policy. In cases of ultimate confrontation, it is linked to the state's endowment of military capabilities.

The Ingredients of Power Potential

Studies of power in international relations recognize that power is a mixture of capabilities derived from both domestic sources and international activities. Furthermore, such studies recognize that power comes from three sources: *natural, sociopsychological,* and *synthetic.* The importance of each varies according to the type of international transaction and to the choice of power exercise which has been selected as a matter of national policy. Needless to say, the greater the degree of conflict and the more coercive the intentions of the actor, the more intricate the combination of power ingredients which will have to be brought to bear.

Natural Sources of Power

Among the natural sources of power, *geography* is among the more important. Decades ago geography was widely regarded as the most important single ingredient of power, though this theory has faded considerably in the era of instantaneous warfare. Nevertheless, geography and territorial position are among the most enduring determinants of national power. They determine the extent of the land mass, which affects both the ease (size) and the difficulty (length of hostile borders) of national defense. The vast extent of the Russian land mass frustrated and devoured invading armies throughout the suffering history of that country, causing the defeat of Napoleon in 1812 and of Hitler nearly 150 years later. But just as sheer size can multiply the defensive capabilities of a state and reduce its vulnerability to enemies, so too can lengthy borders be detrimental to strategic planning and military costs. Both China and the Soviet Union, for example, which share the world's longest hostile border, are acutely aware of the additional costliness which those borders present to the defense of each. Similarly Israel, surrounded by hostile boundaries easily traversed by tanks and infantry, and further weakened by its tiny size, is severely hindered in national defense by the natural aspects of geography. In contrast, Switzerland is safeguarded by mountain barriers to land invasion; and the United States is safeguarded by 3000 miles of ocean on the east and 6000 on the west, which separate it from major potential antagonists.

It has been demonstrated that the frequency of wars correlates with the number of borders a nation shares, an observation which has led to the theory of *geographic opportunity.*[1] It was once fashionable in the study of international relations to search for simple geopolitical "laws" that delineated national power for all times. Three prominent examples:

[1] James Paul Wesley, "Frequency of Wars and Geographical Opportunity," *Journal of Conflict Resolution* 6, no. 4 (December 1962): 387–89.

1. Sir Halford Mackinder's "Heartland" formula in 1904: "He who rules Eastern Europe commands the Heartland of Eurasia; who rules the Heartland commands the World Island of Europe, Asia, and Africa; and who rules the World Island commands the World." [2]

2. The dictum of Alfred T. Mahan, an American theorist of the late nineteenth century, that control of the seas is decisive in the global balance. [3]

3. Attempts to explain the sweep of Russian imperialism as a search for warm water ports open in winter.

While there can be no doubt of the importance of seapower, warm water ports, and control of Eastern Europe, efforts such as these to derive immutable geopolitical laws from specific historical instances are prey to the fallacy of the single factor. No monocausal theory can account for the richness of military and political geography. This is not, however, to deny the critical importance of special geopolitical assets such as the Suez and Panama Canals, the Persian Gulf, the Straits of Gibraltar, the Dardanelles, and the Straits of Malacca.

But even geographic features of power are not limited in their significance to security. Just as warm water ports may house major naval facilities, so too do they facilitate international trade, support oceanic and suboceanic research, and provide other services vital to national enrichment. By the same token, territorial size not only figures in the equation of national defense, but determines in part the resources which will sustain a population at peace, and which will contribute to the national economic well being. Any of these factors may play a major role in national cohesiveness, the stature of the nation in the international community and, in general, the satisfaction of the population with international events and its ability to foster that satisfaction.

As suggested in the discussion of geography, a second critical component of power is *natural resources*. Relative endowments of natural resources and raw materials may affect the power of a nation significantly, though here again we should not assume an inflexible connection. There is no doubt that plentiful natural resources have helped to create the superpower status of the United States and the Soviet Union and may some day do the same for Brazil. Nations rich in raw materials are less dependent on the outside world and hence less vulnerable to negative sanctions (blockade, boycott, and so on); at the same time they are better able to apply both positive and negative sanctions to opponents. The wealth conferred by natural resources may be held out as a reward, or it may be with-

[2] Sir Halford Mackinder, *Democratic Ideals and Reality* (New York: Holt, 1919), p. 150.

[3] Alfred T. Mahan, *The Influence of Sea Power Upon History* (Boston: Little, Brown, 1890).

held as a form of persuasive deprivation. Ultimately, it may be used to expand the military potential of the state as the highest negative sanctioning (warmaking) capability.

An extraordinarily instructive example of the ability of natural resource richness to affect world politics even to the point of altering its course is found in the recent policies of the oil-producing underindustrialized states. Through rapid and very large increases in the price of crude petroleum, and by acting collectively through the Organization of Oil Exporting Countries (OPEC), most of them have had such huge accumulations of trade surplus and foreign currencies ("petrodollars") as to be able to finance rapid development and to upheave the international monetary system to the decay of former imperialistic patterns. In addition, the coincidence of these events with exacerbation of Arab-Israeli tensions resulting in war in 1973 enabled the Arab members of OPEC to use the threat of

Economic elements of power in international relations: Saudi Arabian delegates to a conference at Algiers in 1975 at which the OPEC governments agreed to pace oil production according to the needs of the industrial states.

Photographer/Gilbert Uzan. Gamma/Liaison

oil embargo and the actual reduction of petroleum exports as an instrument to force many industrialized states to alter their political and economic relations in the region. (See Chapters 3 and 5.)

However, this should not obscure the fact that there are many poorly endowed nations which have great power and richly endowed countries which are weak. Japan, for example, imports most of its critical raw materials and yet has been one of the most important economic and military powers of the twentieth century; Indonesia, blessed with huge reserves of minerals, has played an insignificant role on the world stage. A nation that effectively mobilizes its economic and industrial capacities may adjust to a scarcity of raw materials by importing primary products and exporting finished goods. Critical strategic materials can be stockpiled against the possibility of wartime blockade, and natural and synthetic substitutes can be devised in case of shortages.

Quite aside from the warmaking capability which natural resources may impart, such richness is a vital part of national power. It is not because petroleum enables the OPEC members to wage war, for example, that they have been able to adjust the global power distribution by cooperative oil export policies. Instead, it is because of the covetousness of the industrialized world for those riches that they have been able to adjust international trading relations and thus to accelerate economic development. The sheer volume of international trade in raw materials dramatizes the amount of dependency which may lie behind trade. Also, it indicates the extent to which abundance in natural resources can enhance the ability of a state to influence other parties and, finally, to influence the outcomes of international events even without overt force. Only in extreme cases of the need for sanctioning capability must natural resources be correlated to military preparedness.

A third natural component of power is *population*. In general, large populations are capable of a variety of social functions and services. They are able to promote industrial vitality, make maximum use of resources, and support large military components. Yet there are major exceptions to the rule that size and power are directly correlated. Indonesia, for example, with 130 million people in 1973 cannot be ranked in modernity and power with West Germany (62 million), nor can India (603 million) be imagined above Japan (111 million). Table 7–1 reveals the disparity between population size and economic modernity as measures of power. The contribution of population to power depends not exclusively on size, but on the social, economic, and psychological consequences of size as well. Among these qualitative factors are level of technical skill, productivity per capita, level of social and political development, and effective coordination of human and material resources. Unskilled, starving, and ineffectively governed populations such as that of India cannot marshall into effective power their other resources. China, where population size has

TABLE 7-1 National Ranking in 1973

By *Population* (millions)		By *GNP* (billions)	
1. China	898.6	1. U.S.	$1,294.9
2. India	603.3	2. USSR	697.0
3. USSR	249.7	3. Japan	408.1
4. U.S.	210.4	4. W. Germany	346.6
5. Indonesia	129.9	5. France	258.0
6. Japan	110.6	6. China	181.0
7. Brazil	103.0	7. UK	170.1
8. Pakistan	65.4	8. Italy	137.0
9. W. Germany	62.0	9. India	73.4
10. Nigeria	58.9	10. Brazil	62.0
11. UK	56.0	11. Indonesia	12.5
12. Italy	54.8	12. Nigeria	10.6
13. France	52.0	13. Pakistan	6.3

Source: World Military Expenditures, 1963–1973 (Washington: U.S. Arms Control and Disarmament Agency, 1974).

traditionally been a barrier to modernization of power potential, has only now begun to coordinate its human resources to the point of turning them toward effective development of the state.

Social and Psychological Components of Power

Just as the size of the national population has significance for power, so too do the images, attitudes, and expectations of peoples. Among the most critical is *national self-image*, which contributes acutely to the concept of the role that the nation ought to play. Ideals, even when perverse, govern foreign policy in large measure. Such slogans, for example, as White Man's Burden, Manifest Destiny, World Policeman, and others not only express a mood about national expectation, but form a social framework in which national policy is set. Such policies may be more a manifestation of mood than of rational choice.

Images of others are an equally important part of the policy-making framework. When national peoples hold the governments and peoples of other nation-states in high regard, their attitudes about foreign relations are ones of tolerance and forebearance; when they view the second party with mistrust, suspicion, and fear, their expectations about foreign policy are reactive at best. Social-psychological research has amply demonstrated that demands on foreign policy stem significantly from perception and from attitudes which peoples hold toward others.

All of these images are products of *political socialization*, the process by which the individual acquires political attitudes. And just as national peoples prepare themselves through fear, affection, and propaganda to trust some governments and distrust others, so too do they prepare themselves to measure the potential impacts of international events. Political information is also measured against these ingrained "mind sets" which socialization provides, giving rise to *images of situations*. Not all events are crises, and not all events evoke severe responses. The reaction to an event is a product of salience, a product of the immediacy of the event's consequences. If an event touches closely upon the interests of an individual and threatens to have some immediate impact, the reaction will be pronounced; if it and its probable consequences seem remote, the reaction will be moderate. Clearly, when a salient event is initiated by a national actor whose intentions are feared or distrusted, the tendency of a government to prepare a forceful response is understandable. Similarly, in such circumstances the social-psychological mood of the body politic is elevated, with the result that great demand is placed upon foreign policy, and there results a tolerance for adventurous response. This is all a result of the mental and emotional interpretation of information.

Political socialization is a continuous process, though ideas that are firmly fixed are difficult to erase or even alter. Nevertheless, it is not uncommon for events to change in significance. In the United States, for example, it seemed likely that the emnity toward China, firmly established in 1950, would take decades or even generations to reverse. Yet a single presidential visit to China unleashed a remarkable groundswell of reversed opinion, with the result that normalization of relations was able to occur in a matter of only months. In another familiar case, the American attitude about continued warfare in Southeast Asia turned around sharply between 1968 and 1972, to the point at which there was public demand to discontinue the American involvement even without having achieved minimal objectives. Policy-making in Washington could not for long resist this new element in the opinion structure, and was forced to implement a policy of withdrawal, a policy which only a few months earlier was officially regarded as defeatist and treacherous. It became clear to major decision-makers, however, that the ability of the government to continue the exertion of power was limited by the political consequences of resocialization, by the political meaning of a new national mood about the war.

All of these images of self, others, and situations contribute to yet another component of power: *public support and cohesion*. Support of government and popular unity are critical morale factors in national power. Internal divisions consume political and military resources to secure domestic cohesion, and they pose the danger of a "fifth column"—a domestic faction unifying itself with a foreign enemy. For example, some Ukrainian separatists joined the Nazi invaders of the Soviet Union in the hope of liberation from Russian domination. A relatively unified population such as the North Vietnamese, on the other hand, is capable of great exertions.

Unity does not mean unanimity on all questions, and controversies may be tolerated, particularly in domestic questions. But there must be a clear disposition to support the government in the foreign arena; in the popular American phrase, "politics should stop at the water's edge." Adversaries must be denied the possibility of appealing to the population· over the heads of the national leadership.

Unity also does not necessarily mean how "democratic" a government is. It is not consistently true that democratic regimes have enjoyed more popular support in foreign affairs than authoritarian governments. Germans rallied behind Hitler from 1936 to 1945 despite the avowedly dictatorial quality of his government, while the French were on the whole less unified in support of their democracy. The popularity of a government is difficult to measure from the outside—for example, the Castro government of Cuba is considered highly popular by some observers and highly un-

Leadership and power: Churchill, Roosevelt, and Stalin at Yalta, 1945, at a summit meeting in which they laid plans for concluding the war in Asia and commenced plans for the postwar occupation of Europe.

U.S. Army photograph

190   The Logic of Power

popular by others. What counts in conflict is the effective disposition of the population to mobilize resources and undertake sacrifices proportionate to the perceived importance of the outcome. Thus *unity* and *public will* are the indispensible catalyst for transforming potential power into useful power.

Finally among the social determinants of power is *leadership*. The quality of leadership is the most unpredictable component of national power. Leadership orchestrates the other components, defines goals in a realizable manner, and determines the path of strategy.

China exemplifies the extent to which a change in leadership alone can mobilize the other latent energies and capacities of a nation, transforming it from the weak victim of a succession of international predators to a self-sufficient power able to exercise considerable influence in foreign affairs. The same population with the same territory and endowment of natural resources can be weak and disunited or strong and dynamic, depending on the quality of leadership.

Sometimes the rise of a unique individual at a particular moment catalyzes other historical forces to change the trend of events. Napoleon, Bismarck, Hitler, DeGaulle, Stalin, Castro, Mao—these are visionary and sometimes charismatic leaders who changed the equation of international power and the course of international history. Some believe that the role of the individual "hero" in history has been falsely glamorized and overstated, and that events are decided more by systematic factors in national capability than by such "idiosyncratic" elements as individual personalities. And yet who does not believe that an incredible determination to resist in a bleak hour when Britain stood alone was not roused by Winston Churchill's defiance of the Nazi behemoth: "We shall fight on the beaches, we shall fight on the landing grounds, we shall fight in the fields and in the streets, we shall fight in the hills; we will never surrender." Leadership cannot create power out of air, but it can dip into untapped reserves of national creative energy. Sometimes a single statesman makes the difference.

The Synthetic Components of Power

In addition to the natural and sociopsychological determinants of power, there are some which are synthetic. These involve the skillful use of human and other resources in such a way as to coordinate, develop, and prepare for readiness the ability of the state to put its power into motion. Most important are *industrial capacity* and *military preparedness*.

Industrial capacity is virtually synonymous with major power status in the twentieth century. Modern war requires both a sophisticated manufacturing capability and huge economic resources. The victory of the Allied powers in the second world war, for example, may be traced to the ability of Soviet and American assembly lines to turn out artillery pieces, tanks, and aircraft in greater numbers than the German and Japanese factories. The economic costs are staggering: the individual American soldier today is supported by annual equipment expenditures of almost $25,000; United States outlays in Vietnam averaged several hundred thousand dollars for each Communist soldier killed. Modern warfare is mechanized, expensive, and technologically complex, and the ranking of nations by gross national product approximates closely their ranking in military power.[4] (See Table 7–2.)

Quantitative studies of power and capability have tended to confirm the importance of industrial capacity as the single most important determinant of power.[5] One found that the wealthier state or coalition won thirty-one of thirty-nine international wars from 1815 to 1945, suggesting that an advantage in industrial capacity brings victory in four of five cases.[6] This reduces the warmaking function from heroic exploits of brave men to mundane statistical comparisons of numbers of ironworkers, ball

TABLE 7–2   Ten Major Military Powers, 1973, by Annual Military Expenditure

1. USSR	$ 86.0 billion
2. U.S.	78.5
3. China	15.0
4. W. Germany	11.8
5. France	9.3
6. UK	8.5
7. Italy	4.1
8. Poland	3.9
9. Canada	2.4
10. India	2.3

Source: U.S. Arms Control and Disarmament Agency, *World Military Expenditures, 1963–1973* (Washington, D.C.: U.S. Government Printing Office, 1974).

[4] Indeed, one study found that perceptions of laymen regarding the power rankings of nations correlate highly with GNP—people expect rich nations to be stronger. Norman Alcock and Alan Newcombe, "The Perception of National Power," *Journal of Conflict Resolution* 14, no. 3 (November 1970): 335–43.

[5] F. Clifford German, "A Tentative Evaluation of World Power," *Journal of Conflict Resolution* 4, no. 1 (March 1960): 138–44; Rudolph Rummel, "Indicators of Cross-National and International Patterns," *American Political Science Review* 68, no. 1 (March 1969): 127–47; Bruce Russett, *International Regions and the International System* (Chicago: Rand McNally, 1967); and Harvey Starr, *War Coalitions* (Lexington, Mass.: D.C. Heath, Lexington Books, 1973).

[6] Steven Rosen, "War Power and the Willingness to Suffer," in Bruce Russett, ed., *Peace, War, and Numbers* (Beverly Hills, Calif.: Sage Publishing Company, 1972), pp. 176–78.

bearing output, efficiency of the airframe industry, and so forth. Military might today depends as much on the managers as on the generals.

Power and the Ability to "Win" in War

We have identified several elements of national power potential: geography, natural resources, industrial capacity, population, governmental support, and the quality of leadership. All are important, but industrial capacity is the outstanding *economic* variable and the quality of leadership is the most important *political* factor. Each state has a certain innate capacity to exercise influence on the world stage, and leadership determines the extent and purposes for which this capacity will be used.

The exercise of power takes many forms in international relations. Economic rewards and punishments may be used to elicit favorable responses from other nations. Cultural influence may be extended through the transfer of products, mass media, student exchanges, and published materials. Public opinion in other countries can be influenced through direct propaganda efforts such as the U.S. Voice of America program and the large foreign radio transmission programs of the Soviet Union, Egypt, and other states. The international sale of armaments provides the exporter with a variety of positive and negative sanctioning powers, as shipments can be expanded or withheld. Power within international organizations and alliances may take the form of skillful lobbying and bargaining. Influence operates by various means, and it should not be assumed that the exercise of power most often involves the application of physical force. Most typically, force is used when one actor, unable to compromise on the outcome of an issue, perceives that it must deprive the opponent of alternative solutions.

Still, force tends to have overriding importance in international relations. Arab states may attempt to revise their borders with Israel through diplomatic persuasion, propaganda, economic sanctions, and a host of other means, but in territorial conflicts, war is often the ultimate means. Especially in the international arena, where institutional means of conflict resolution are yet at a low level of development and peace-enforcing authority is weak, the potential influence of an actor is critically dependent on its capacity to wage war in the regions in which its values are deeply engaged.

We may conceptualize war as a distribution mechanism making allocations of scarce goods to competing parties. The two sides make mutually exclusive claims to a given position or resource (such as a piece of territory or control of the instruments of state) and war decides who is to get what. The "decision rule" that operates in making a settlement is to award to each side a "share" of the disputed values that corresponds to its relative war power. War establishes a *ratio of power* between the contestants, and political bargaining allocates the prize according to this formula. In the words of General Maxwell Taylor, a peace settlement "simply records the assumed balance of power at the moment."

It is crucial, therefore, to understand the nature of power in war. The factors of power potential are translated into effective war power in terms of two specific warmaking capabilities: *strength*, by which we mean the ability to impose sanctions or destroy the assets of the adversary, and *cost-tolerance*, by which we mean the willingness to tolerate deprivation or the destruction that the enemy imposes on one's own assets. Our relative power in war is a function of my willingness to tolerate the harm that you are able to impose, versus *your* willingness to tolerate the harm that I am able to impose. Thus, the power to "win" wars is based on political as well as military factors.

The Importance of Cost-Tolerance

The visible side of war is the mutual imposition of negative sanctions by two parties, tempting the observer to view the power relationship mainly as a function of relative strength. But the critical role of cost-tolerance cannot be overlooked. A party inferior in strength and yet superior in *cost-tolerance* may paradoxically be more powerful than a strong opponent less willing to suffer. This was precisely the case in Vietnam, where the physical might of the United States vastly exceeded that of the Communists, yet the total power equation was much more nearly even or tilted to the weaker side. Ho Chi Minh predicted, "In the end the Americans will kill ten patriots for every American who dies, but it is they who will tire first." This was also the model of Algeria, where the deep commitment of the nationalists enabled them to withstand the immense sanctioning power of France longer than the less committed French were willing to accept much lower costs delivered upon them by the Algerians. A study of forty wars found that almost *half* were won by the party that suffered *more*.[7]

Revolutionary strategists, who see themselves fighting the might of global imperialism, have put special emphasis on the idea that courageous hearts can compensate for the opponent's superior strength. The power of the anti-imperialist is the willingness to die; the Arab commandos call themselves *fedayeen*—"the sacrificers." Chinese strategists, too, emphasize the military importance of revolutionary commitment and determination.[8]

[7] Ibid.
[8] See Robert North, *The Foreign Relations of China* (Belmont, Calif.: Dickenson Publishing Company, 1969), pp. 34–35.

And an Irish revolutionist said, "It is a question which can last longer, the whip or the back."

This vision of war has been compared to torture. The victim is on the table, and the question is whether his will can be broken by torment. Sometimes the resistance of the victim is actually stiffened by his suffering; German terror bombing of London had this reverse effect—what Toynbee has called "the stimulus of blows." [9] A more recent example is the American bombing of North Vietnam, reported as follows by James Cameron:

> So far from terrorizing and disrupting the people the bombings seem to me to have stimulated and consolidated them. By the nature of the attacks so far, civilian casualties have not been very great, but they have been enough to provide the government of the Vietnam Republic with the most totally unchallengeable propaganda they could ever have dreamed of. A nation of peasants and manual workers who might have felt restive or dissatisfied under the stress of totalitarian conditions had been obliged to forget their differences in the common sense of resistance and self-defense. From the moment the U.S. dropped its first bomb on the North of Vietnam, she welded the nation together unshakeably. [10]

The revolutionary's conviction that the will to resist can overcome immense disparities in material strength is often questioned by orthodox strategists. To a claim that Communist cost-tolerance in Vietnam was a bottomless pit, for example, Henry Kissinger is said to have replied, "Every pit has a bottom." While it is evident that in his devotion to a cause the revolutionary may survive overwhelming odds, it is clear that Kissinger is also right: more often than not, the weaker party will yield, and only in the most exceptional case will cost-tolerance advantages be sufficient to endure a wide disparity in strength. The nation with a superior industrial capacity starts with a long lead in war power.

Measuring War Power

How do we determine which of two adversaries is more powerful? How is it possible to say that one nation is a "major power" and another weak, given the complexities of the power relationship? How can decision-makers

[9] Arnold Toynbee, *A Study of History* (London: Oxford University Press, 1934), vol. II, pp. 100–12.

[10] James Cameron, *Here is Your Enemy* (New York: Holt, Rinehart and Winston, 1966), p. 66.

reasonably estimate their national power potential in relation to a certain opponent, to chart a strategic course in the face of many uncertainties? Karl von Clauswitz observed that in war ". . . all action must . . . be planned in a mere twilight, which . . . like the effect of fog or moonshine, gives to things exaggerated dimensions and an unnatural appearance." [11] Systematic planning requires reasonably reliable bases on which to estimate the probabilities that a given course of action will have a predictable outcome. How can national leadership measure the balance of war power and plan accordingly?

There are many inherent uncertainties and difficulties in assigning specific weights to the various factors in war power, particularly in advance of actual fighting. The cost-tolerance factor is wholly psychological and subjective, and there is no empirical referent simply visible to both parties by which the willingness to endure negative sanctions can be estimated reliably in advance. The revolutionary says that he will fight forever; Henry Kissinger says that every pit has a bottom. Who is right?

Even purely physical capabilities in war are exceedingly difficult to estimate. Simple magnitudes of hardware must be assessed. How many X-type tanks equal a Y piece of artillery, and under what conditions of development? Obviously, opinions will vary. Even the gross defense expenditures of an opponent may be difficult to estimate. It has been shown, for instance, that different methods of computation by "reliable" analysts yield estimates of Soviet defense expenditures as a percentage of U.S. defense expenditures ranging from 28 percent to more than 100 percent for the same year.[12] Still more difficult to estimate is the skill of a nation in the use of its available forces.

If the *present* power ratio between two parties is not easily measured by either, the projection of trends to predict probable future power relations is even more difficult. To assess present and future conditions, each party must make complex calculations based on arbitrary assumptions. Policy must be planned on the basis of *perceptions* of present factors and *expectations* of the future. The result is a highly conjectural process of reasoning in which it is necessary to rely on "guesstimates" at critical points to reach general and usable conclusions on which to base policy. How do you weigh the imponderables? Of making the final decision to attack Pearl Harbor, the Japanese war minister said, "Once in a while it is necessary for one to close one's eyes and jump from the stage of the Kiyomizu Temple." [13] Warner Schilling says that the Japanese:

[11] Karl von Clauswitz, *On War* (Baltimore: Penguin, 1968), p. 189; originally published in 1832.

[12] Lynn Turgeon, "The Enigma of Soviet Defense Expenditures," *Journal of Conflict Resolution* 8, no. 2 (June 1964): 116–20.

[13] Quoted in Stanford Studies in International Conflict and Integration, *Annual Report to the Ford Foundation* (Stanford, Calif.: Stanford University Press, 1961), p. 4.

went to war with a beautifully complex plan of attack but without a clear answer to the single question of how they were going to win. There was, to be sure, the expectation that the U.S. would shortly decide that the costs of defeating Japan were not worth the gains and would therefore seek a compromise peace. But the Japanese did not give this critical hypothesis any real analysis. It was a hope nourished from despair at the alternatives.[14]

Strategic Decisions Under Conditions of Risk

At each stage of strategic analysis, opinions diverge whether optimistic or pessimistic assessments are warranted. Alternative pictures of the situation confront decision-makers with a range of power ratios from which they must choose. Should President Johnson have listened in 1965, for example, to the Joint Chiefs of Staff, who told him that the Communists could be defeated in Vietnam within two years, or to the CIA, which gave him a much gloomier prediction?

Research findings are highly contradictory on whether most statesmen, like Johnson in the Vietnam case, choose optimistic estimates or darker ones. While one study has found that social groups tend to overrate themselves and underrate their opponents,[15] another found quite the opposite: that "armed services inevitably overstate the military capabilities of the opponent. . . ."[16] Still a third study found that aggressors sometimes recognize the potential superiority of their opponents, they perceive this edge more clearly than do the defenders and take the risk that it will not be used.[17] The inconclusiveness of this evidence underscores the subjective component in framing assumptions about going to war.

It is likely that a full study of strategic planning in past wars would show that decision-makers tended to use optimistic rather than pessimistic

---

[14] Warner Schilling, "Surprise Attack, Death, and War," *Journal of Conflict Resolution* 9, no. 3 (September 1965): 389.

[15] Bernard Bass and George Dunteman, "Biases in the Evaluation of One's Own Group, Its Allies, and Opponents," *Journal of Conflict Resolution* 7, no. 1 (March 1963): 16–20.

[16] Samuel Huntington, "Arms Races," in Carl Friedrich and Seymour Harris, eds., *Public Policy 1958* (Cambridge: Harvard University Press, 1958). ". . . In 1914, for instance, the Germans estimated the French Army to have 121,000 more men than the Germany Army, the French estimated the German Army to have 134,000 more men than the French Army, but both parties agreed in their estimates of the military forces of third parties."

[17] Bruce Russett, "The Calculus of Deterrence," *Journal of Conflict Resolution* 7, no. 2 (June 1963): 97.

assumptions *if* both were based on equally plausible information. Effective leadership will concede critical objectives only when there is no reasonable hope of successful struggle. The rational strategy for mobilizing public will and forging national unity is to use the more optimistic estimates, provided that they are equiprobable with pessimistic alternatives.

Sometimes, of course, the use of hopeful estimates is mere grasping at straws. When the overwhelmingly superior Athenians demanded that the Melians surrender during the Peloponnesian War (431–404 B.C.), the Melians chose to resist:

> We know that the fortune of war is sometimes more impartial than the disproportion of numbers might lead one to suppose; to submit is to give ourselves over to despair, while action still preserves for us a hope that we may stand erect.[18]

This was a very unfortunate decision. The Melians were easily defeated and the grown men were all put to death, while the women and children were taken as slaves.

Another case of the "grasping-at-straws" syndrome was the following reasoning by a Spanish commander about to sail with the Armada to its defeat at the hands of the British Navy, destroying Spain as a global power (1588):

> It is well known that we fight in God's cause. So when we meet the English, God will surely arrange matters so that we can grapple and board them, either by sending some strange freak of weather, or more likely, just by depriving the English of their wits. If we come to close quarters, Spanish valor and Spanish steel—and the great mass of soldiers we shall have on board—will make our victory certain. But unless God helps us by making a miracle, the English, who have faster guns and handier ships than ours, and many more long-range guns, and who know their advantage as well as we do, will never close with us at all, but stand aloof and blow us to pieces with their culverins, without our being able to do them any serious hurt. . . . So we are sailing against England in the confident hope of a miracle.[19]

This too, proved to be a very unfortunate line of thought.

These are the extreme cases. Ordinarily, optimistic planning is based

[18] Thucydides, *The Peloponnesian War* (New York: Modern Library, 1951), pp. 330–37.

[19] Quoted in Bernard and Fawn Brodie, *From Crossbow to H-bomb* (New York: Dell, 1962), pp. 67–68.

Army Medical Examiner: "At last a perfect soldier!"

Antiwar cartoon by Robert Minor in *The Masses,* 1915. Reproduced in *Comic Art in America* by Stephen Becker (Simon & Schuster, 1959).

not on wild fancy but on seemingly reasonable estimates, such as the expectation of the Joint Chiefs in 1965 that the North Vietnamese could not long withstand strategic bombing by the United States and deployment of a half-million well-armed American troops. Doubters may offer gloomier projections, but they cannot prove their case over the optimists. The final decision is always in some measure a leap of faith. Hitler bet that the British and French would not intervene in Czechoslovakia; he was right. Acheson and Truman bet that the Chinese would not intervene in Korea; they were wrong. Certainty is much easier looking back than for the decision-maker forced to rely on advance projections.

Overrating your own power means relatively underrating your opponent. In World War I, for example, both the French and the Germans expected quick victories within a matter of weeks; both were disappointed. In Vietnam, each side long believed that the other would eventually yield, so that victory purely was a matter of time. The Communists seemed to have in mind the example of Algeria or the victory over the French at Dienbienphu, while the Americans based their policy on the model of postwar Greece and Malaya, where guerrillas were defeated.

We noted earlier that the function of a war settlement is to allocate values in proportion to war power. Since the two parties have different pictures of the power ratio in advance of the fighting, they propose to each other different settlements. Each considers that the other is offering too little. The Americans reasoned in Vietnam, "Why should we accept a Communist-dominated coalition government when they will be unable to force one on the battlefield?" The Communists reasoned, "Why should we give up our political goals as the Americans demand when the trend of battle is sure to favor us?" The disparity in power perceptions ensures conflicting *political* demands.

Some theorists have argued that were it not for the disparity in power perceptions, it would not be necessary to *fight* wars at all. Having a common assessment of the power ratio, the parties could simulate the war decision by making the same settlement in advance, without the bloodshed.[20] Both sides would be favored by avoiding violence if the same distribution could be achieved without it. Some parties might fight anyway without expecting victory, in despair at the alternatives or in "confident hope of a miracle," or at least to make it expensive for the aggressor; but in most cases rational decision-makers would make the settlement without pointless violence.

The poverty of this theory is evident: *it is never possible to know the outcome with confidence in advance.* Opinions will differ about what resources the enemy has, what resources the enemy will use, how much outside help each side will get, whether the enemy will tolerate a given level of costs, exactly what the enemy intends to do, and which of several conflicting statistical estimates is correct.[21] Georg Simmel, the pioneer sociologist of conflict, concluded that, "The most effective prerequisite for preventing struggle, the exact knowledge of the comparative strength of the

---

[20] See, for example, Raymond Mack and Richard Snyder, "An Analysis of Social Conflict," *Journal of Conflict Resolution* 1, no. 2 (June 1957): 217.

[21] Compare Fred Ikle, *Every War Must End* (New York: Columbia University Press, 1971), especially chapter two, "The Fog of Military Estimates."

two parties, is very often obtainable only by the actual fighting out of the conflict." [22] It is unfortunate that, as Harold Lasswell said, "No medium of exchange [can] be devised which [will] bear the same relation to estimates of fighting power as monetary metals do to estimates of economic value."[23] War itself must sometimes resolve diverse perceptions of the power ratio.

Wars end when the parties arrive at a common picture of their relative power *and* a common assessment of appropriate settlement claims.[24] There is negotiating on these questions *within* each nation as well as between nations. Internal debate may split between "superpatriots," who want to fight on for national honor regardless of the odds, and "traitors," who are accused of being overly eager to throw in the towel and surrender. A leader making peace on less than perfect terms must sell both the settlement and his version of the battlefield situation to his own people.

One of the functions of international mediation is to help national leaders find domestic support for imperfect settlements. When a significant portion of the politically active population believes that the war situation is not as dire as claimed by the leadership, and/or that the leadership is making a needlessly unfavorable settlement, the basis may be molded for a later political reaction against the settlement. One of Hitler's main appeals was the claim that the nation had been "sold out" in 1918 and his demand that the Versailles treaty be repudiated as a document of shame. A stable settlement means that the agreement, however unfavorable, must be accepted as realistic.

Some kinds of warfare lend themselves to clear settlement more readily than others. In pre-Napoleonic wars, common symbols were available as manifestations of potency visible to both sides—for example, possession of a specific fortress or strategic position. When one side gained possession of these symbols, it was clear to leaders and followers on both sides that the issue was concluded.[25] In modern war, struggle engages whole societies, and victory and defeat are not so clearly marked. The victor is the side that wins the last battle, but which battle is the last is not so obvious. One exception to this problem might be a nuclear war, where the conclusion would be only too decisive.

[22] Georg Simmel, "The Sociology of Conflict," *American Journal of Sociology* 9, (January 1904): 490–525.

[23] Harold D. Lasswell, "Compromise," in *Encyclopedia of the Social Sciences*, vol. 4 (New York: Macmillan, 1930), p. 148.

[24] See William T. R. Fox, ed., *How Wars Are Ended*, the November 1970 issue of the *Annals of the American Academy of Political and Social Science*.

[25] See Lewis Coser, "The Termination of Conflict," *Journal of Conflict Resolution* 5, no. 2 (December 1961): 347–53. Many of the ideas in this chapter were developed in this seminal article. See also Anatol Rapoport's introduction to Karl von Clausewitz, *On War* (Baltimore: Penguin, 1968), p. 19.

Wars end when mutual rejection of claims is not worth the costs of continued fighting to either side, in light of the available strategic estimates.[26] As the power estimates of the two sides become congruent, their offers of settlement converge. In Vietnam, the United States at first offered the Vietcong a deal that amounted to its dissolution as a political force,

"... Or do you want *me* to do the talking?"

Copyright © 1949 by Herblock in *The Washington Post*. Reprinted by permission.

[26] Compare Paul Kecskemeti, *Strategic Surrender* (New York: Atheneum, 1964), esp. pp. 5–30.

while the Vietcong offered to preside over the dismemberment of the Saigon regime. As the two sides' optimistic hopes of decisive victory were frustrated, they came closer together. The immediate function of war, then, is to provide empirical evidence to adjust divergent assessments of relative power in order to permit the parties to develop similar perceptions of reality upon which they may base an agreed settlement. The purpose of fighting is not ordinarily to destroy an opponent completely (the "Carthaginian peace") or to deprive him of residual strength and render him helpless and defenseless.

Wars seldom go this far. It is not usually necessary to destroy an opponent to change his opinion or values, or to cancel his objectives. World War II, which was fought to "unconditional surrender," is a notable exception. So too might be a decisive Arab military victory in the Middle East, *if* the Arab objective is obliteration of Israel. Wars begin with a determination on the part of each group to convince the opponent of its version of the power ratio. The ideal strategic goal in war is to bring the enemy's power estimate to the point at which he will agree to the settlement that you seek. Full victory is obtained by one side if it can bring the other's perception all the way around to its view.[27] Typically, however, there is a process of mutual adjustment and compromise, where neither side can enforce its version of reality completely.

Changes in Capability and the Outbreak of War

Wars occur more often during historical periods in which there are major shifts in the balance of capabilities. New distributions of strength need to be tested to ascertain their limits. Spurts in industrial development, resource discovery, inventions, and other developments in military power correlate with the frequency of international conflict.[28] Herman Kahn has estimated that fundamental advances in weaponry, which once occurred every 500 years, now occur about every five years.[29] This accelerated development, coupled with the global diffusion of arms technology, may explain the frequency of wars in modern times (see Table 7–3), even though the Soviet-American strategic arms race has stabilized the relations of the superpowers.

[27] See Robert North et al., "Capability, Threat, and the Outbreak of War," in James Rosenau, ed., *International Politics and Foreign Policy* (New York: Free Press, 1961).

[28] See E. Chertok, "Sources of International Tension," 3 *Bulletin of the Research Exchange on the Prevention of War* no. 17 (1955): 20.

[29] Herman Kahn, *On Thermonuclear War* (Princeton: Princeton University Press, 1960).

TABLE 7–3   Sixty-five Wars, 1945–1976 (July)

War	Began	War	Began
Syria-Lebanon	1945	Goa	1961
Indonesia	1945	Angola	1961
China	1945	Yemen	1962
Malaya	1945	West New Guinea	1962
Indochina	1946	Portuguese Guinea	1962
Greece	1946	Algeria-Morocco	1963
Madagascar	1947	Cyprus	1963
India-Pakistan	1947	Malaysia	1963
Kashmir	1947	Somalia-Kenya	1963
Philippines	1948	Zanzibar	1964
Israel	1948	Thailand	1964
Hyderabad	1948	Mozambique	1964
Burma	1948	Dominican Republic	1965
Korea	1950	India-Pakistan	1965
Formosa	1950	Indonesia	1965
Tibet	1950	Biafra	1966
Kenya	1952	Israel	1967
Guatemala	1954	Czechoslovakia	1968
Algeria	1954	Malaysia	1969
Sudan	1955	El Salvador	1969
Cyprus	1955	Chad	1969
Sinai	1956	Northern Ireland	1969
Hungary	1956	Ethiopia (Eritrea)	1970
Suez	1956	Cambodia	1971
Lebanon	1958	Bangladesh/Kashmir	1971
Cuba	1958	Burundi	1972
Vietnam	1959	Arab-Israel	1973
Himalayas	1959	Iraq (Kurdish)	1974
Rwanda	1959	Cyprus	1974
Laos	1959	Angola	1975
Congo	1960	Timor	1975
Colombia	1960	Lebanon	1975
Cuba (Bay of Pigs)	1961	Spanish Morocco	1976

Changes in the distribution of power will occur also after a war is settled. A good settlement should allocate values in such a fashion that future shifts in the power ratio between the two parties will not cause one side to re-ignite the struggle for a better distribution. In other words, the settlement should reflect not only the momentary balance of capabilities, but also reasonable estimates of future trends. A peace arranged by Jovian between Rome and Persia in 363 A.D., while not completely satisfactory to either party, so closely approximated the power relationship that it enabled the two sides to avoid further struggle for one and a half centuries. Interestingly, the balance broke down when a minor border skirmish in 502 showed Persia to be stronger in relation to Rome than either of them had expected. Further fighting was then resorted to as a test of limits of the new power ratio.[30]

The Management of Power

In our discussion of power we have given primary emphasis to the threat or use of force as a means of influence. The dilemma is that nations continue to find military capabilities useful and necessary instruments of diplomatic action, as evidenced by constantly expanding defense budgets in many countries, even while technological changes make the use of violence ever more horrible and cataclysmic. In ancient and medieval warfare, a battle might rage all morning between two mercenary armies, pause for lunch, then resume with equal ferocity in the afternoon, leaving at the end of the day losses of perhaps twenty men and a donkey. In modern trench warfare, on the other hand, the gain or loss of a few hundred yards may cost 10,000 lives in an hour. This accounts for the dramatic increase in casualties in conventional warfare during the first quarter of the present century (see Figure 7–1). Modern nuclear warfare has the potential to tower above these numbers, as exemplified in the 100,000 deaths which resulted from the atomic bombings of Hiroshima and Nagasaki in 1945. Recent advances in both explosive might and delivery accuracy would enable a missile-launched thermonuclear war targeted to major population centers to kill millions of people instantly.

Clearly controls must be established over the use of force, both to prevent the outbreak of war and to limit the scope and intensity of struggle once begun. International relations scholars look to three basic ideas for the control of power in the next hundred years:

1. War prevention through regional and global *balances of power* between quarreling states, such that resort to war is made unprofitable even though disagreements continue.

2. War prevention by *balance of terror*, a variant of the balance-of-power concept, in which technologically developed adversaries have the capability for mutually assured destruction through finely targeted instantaneous warfare. Aggression is deterred by the certainty of intolerably destructive retaliation.

3. War prevention by further *institutionalization of mediation* and

[30] Vern Bullough, "The Roman Empire vs. Persia, 363–502: A Study of Successful Deterrence," *Journal of Conflict Resolution* 7, no. 1 (March 1963): 55–68, esp. 58–60 and 62.

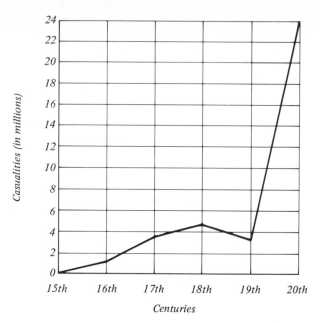

FIGURE 7–1 War Casualties in Europe, 1500–1925

Graph based on data from Pitirim Sorokin, *Social and Cultural Dynamics,* vol. III, (New York: Bedminster Press, 1962). Originally published in 1937.

other means for the nonviolent resolution of international conflict, ultimately including a central peacekeeping authority and the disarming of nation-states.

Because the first two of these address the practical problem of deterrence in a world of heavily armed states acting autonomously in their respective interests, most contemporary scholars and statesmen consider them the most realistic option for the foreseeable future. Though inordinately expensive and consumptive of natural resources, they respond to the decentralized and hostile environment in which political differences are acted out. Replacing this model of international relations with one built upon intergovernmental institutions capable of establishing and enforcing an equitable distribution of values in the manner now served by war and deterrence, is a process long held in infancy. To some observers it is an impossible dream. To others who look beyond unstable peace to the survival of humankind and the betterment of its condition, it is the endurance of the nation-state system which is the impossible dream if such a system is to balance precariously among fifty or more nuclear powers deeply divided by ideological, territorial, and economic conflicts. If, since World War II, national governments have given us two wars per year, why must one presume that the costly pursuit of peace through competition is superior to the quest for peace through cooperation?

The remainder of this section explores war and peace through the balance-of-power and the balance-of-terror approaches. Part Three will consider the quest for peace and stability through political transformation of the international system.

8

The Balance
of Power

Historians, statesmen and students of international relations often assert
that the only way to keep peace is through a careful balance of power.
What do we mean by this commonly used expression "balance of power"?
It connotes not only military and deterrent capabilities, but the entire
structure of *power* and *influence* which governs the relations of states.
Balance of power is concerned, therefore, not solely with the ability of states
to threaten their neighbors or to dissuade others from planned policies;
rather, it encompasses all of the political capabilities of states—coercive
and pacific—by which the delicate balance of conflict-without-war is maintained.

Meanings of "Balance of Power"

Among laymen and scholars alike, the expression *balance of power* has
many uses. Consider four such uses in these sentences:

1. "There is a balance of power between India and Pakistan."
2. "The balance of power favors the United States."
3. "The balance of power has shifted in favor of Israel."
4. "Britain was the crucial actor in the nineteenth-century balance of
power system."

Clearly, there are several different meanings here. The first statement

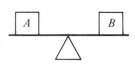 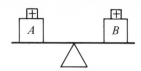

(A) Two-party Equilibrium   (B) Equilibrium Maintenance

FIGURE 8–1

infers that *equilibrium* exists between two parties. Further, the relations of the respective parties with outside states, particularly the nuclear superpowers, are nearly equal, thus preventing the occurrence of disequilibrium by the unilateral addition of external strength. In short, the equilibrium in the relations between India and Pakistan exists because neither has significantly more power or influence than the other; neither can distort the balance. Figure 8–1 (A) shows the situation that exists; (B) shows the maintenance of equilibrium by the equal use of influence upon outside states.

The second statement carries a sharply different implication. To say that the balance "favors" one party over the other is to introduce a *disequilibrium*. Though this meaning is most frequently used to describe the balance of military forces, in its broadest usage it says that the United States holds the upper hand over some other party, and is able to rely upon greater military, diplomatic, and other resources. Throughout most of the cold war, for example, the United States and the Soviet Union, while perhaps not absolutely equal in military potential (the United States probably always had superior military technology), had practical equivalence. Yet the United States had a vast edge in influence and in ability to work its will through its economic resources. Hence, despite "mutual superiority" in arms and a balance of terror, the balance of power has traditionally favored the United States. "Balance of power" defined as disequilibrium is diagrammed in Figure 8–2.

Now let us look at the third sentence: "The balance of power has shifted in favor of Israel." This sentence connotes either a shift from equilibrium to disequilibrium, or a shift in predominance from one party to the other. Acquisition of a new weapons system by Israel might have a

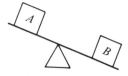   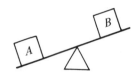

(A) Disequilibrium Favoring *B*   (B) Disequilibrium Favoring *A*

FIGURE 8–2

major impact upon the Middle Eastern balance, as might the stature of Israel by a diplomatic victory. Recognition by West Germany, for example, improved Israel's access to military and industrial goods, and gave it a new and powerful friend whose influence it might utilize. Similarly, although the 1967 Arab-Israeli War was preceded by regional equilibrium, Israel's victory significantly upset military and political relations in the Middle East and among the major powers, who had to apply their influences anew to reestablish equilibrium. Figure 8–3 depicts the two patterns of shift in balance.

The fourth statement implies still a different meaning, this time not describable by the simple balance beam. "The balance of power system" was a specific historical event in a Euro-centric world from the seventeenth century to the outbreak of World War I. In this system, states behaved in certain ways (described below), with one state conserving its influence for the sole purpose of maintaining equilibrium.

In summary, then, in place of a concise definition of the balance of power, we may say that it is a concept of many meanings, particularly equilibrium, disequilibrium, and shifts in dominance, as well as a particular historical systemic principle. This chapter examines the various ideas behind the term "balance of power." It is particularly concerned with balance as a system of keeping peace.[1]

(A) Equilibrium Shift to Disequilibrium

(B) Disequilibrium Shift to Opposite Disequilibrium

FIGURE 8–3

[1] For thorough discussions of the several, and often confusing, meanings of balance of power, see Inis L. Claude, Jr., *Power in International Relations* (New York: Random House, 1962), particularly Part I; and Ernst B. Haas, "The Balance of Power: Prescription, Concept, or Propaganda?" *World Politics* 5 (1953): 442–77. A third useful source is Hans J. Morgenthau, *Politics Among Nations*, 4th ed. (New York: Alfred A. Knopf, 1967), pp. 161–63.

Political Assumptions Underlying Balance of Power

Before examining the components of the balance of power, it is useful to clarify five features about the international system, regardless of its historical era or its structural form. First, as in all other relations of two or more parties, *the potential for conflict is permanent.* Throughout the history of the multistate system, governments and peoples have differed as to means and ends, their differences often resulting in crisis. Even at the subwar level, divergent objectives and disputed means have perpetually threatened conflict. There is no justifiable reason to expect the potential for conflict to abate. Accordingly, the best we can do is to explore the elements of the balance of power to assess the capability for reducing the frequency and/or intensity of international conflict.

The second important feature of international politics is the *permanence of power,* and with it the ability of states to promote their external objectives. Since power is intrinsic to political relations, no international system is imaginable without it. The object of the balance of power, therefore, is not to eliminate power, but to *manage* or *control* it in such a way as to make it constructive rather than destructive, a stabilizing factor rather than a destabilizing one.

The third inherent feature of world politics is the *relativity of power.* Although a state may consider itself powerful, it cannot rely upon its power unless perceiving it to be great relative to that of an adversary.

A fourth fundamental notation about the international system is the *variety of sources of power.* Though we seize in this nuclear world upon military yardsticks, power still arises from several combined and coordinated sources. Some of these are natural (resources, population); others are social and psychological (social cohesion, mass perceptions); and still others are synthetic (governmental efficiency, military preparedness, economic vitality). To assess the balance of power and its practical effects upon the stability and instability of interstate relations, we must be able to assess the *full power potentials* of competing states, not merely their respective military capabilities. We must know something about their respective wills to use power, their determination to maintain peace at the expense of other interests, and their willingness to risk war for individual objectives.

Finally: except in abnormal circumstances, the *acquisition of power is designed as a means to subsequent objectives.* The measured and judicious use of power, therefore, is the currency by which governments influence others. This currency, said to be to politics as money is to economics, may be expended in many ways. Some of these are peaceful, such as persuasion or rewarding another party for acquiescing in policy. Others are coercive: deprivation of rewards (terminating trade or diplomatic relations, for example), threat of force, visible deployment of force (as in "gunboat diplomacy"), or the actual use of force in either limited or general warfare.

Balance of Power as an Analytical Device

In light of these observations, "balance of power" may be presented as an analytical concept for exploring the practical effects of equilibrium and disequilibrium in world politics, and for assessing the consequences of power shifts. It becomes an analytical device rather than a form of advocacy, prescribing no particular model(s) for world peace. Instead, it searches out the conditions of order and disorder in international relations, concentrating on the sources and consequences of balance and imbalance.

The role which a state plays in a global or regional balance of power is determined by its capabilities and intentions (see chapter 7). In its external relations, a government makes what are presumably rational and calculated determinations of the costs and benefits of specific policies as related to specific objectives. From these formulae it sets the course of foreign policy, and by them it determines the state's role in the balance of power. "Will we attempt to enlarge our power, or are our present interests served in the international system by the power which we presently command?" "Do our relations with a neighbor require that we alter the existing balance?" or, "Is our neighbor altering the balance to our detriment, and must we, therefore, increase our power potential?"

This distinction between "power" and "power potential" is an important one in the balance of power concept. Many states have considerable *potential* power, but have little effect upon global or regional balances. Thus balance-of-power theory must take into account the *stages of power readiness*. The possession of adequate resources of power is *potential power*. When these are developed, coordinated, and supplied with the will to use power, then the state possesses *mobilized power*. And when the developed resources are applied to actual situations, the state commands *active power* (or kinetic power).

The lowest stage of readiness (potential power) ensures a state little more than a passive role in the balance of power. More powerful states are only minimally moved by the actions of the potentially powerful. Such a state, in turn, will either have to acquiesce in the prevailing norms of the international system (since it is ill-prepared to alter them), will have to tie itself to the objectives and means of a more powerful state, or will find it necessary to mobilize its power to play an active part in the balance.

Command of mobilized power, in contrast, enables the state to be a major actor. Such a status compels other contestants to assess the relativity of power, the possibility of overbearing coalitions, and the potential for sudden changes in the balance by redistribution of influence or major unilateral technological advances. The balance of power is concerned mainly with the balance of *mobilized* power.

Force—the extreme utilization of mobilized power—is used to alter the power balance drastically and rapidly. A state may wish to correct a disequilibrium by force, or to upset a power balance to the advantage of its own objectives. Perhaps the most illustrative use of active power in balance-of-power theory is the preemptive war. This is warfare in which state A anticipates attack by state B. Rather than await an orderly escalation of hostilities, A destroys B's capability before B has chance to start the fighting. A has *preempted,* and by an anticipatory attack has deprived B of altering the balance of power, and may have done so itself. Some observers have argued that Israel's purpose in attacking Arab military airfields in 1967 was preemptive. This means that Israeli intentions were not aggressive and not designed to aggrandize national territory, and that they were not intended to alter the balance in Israel's favor. Rather, it is said, Israel wanted only to strike Egypt and Syria in a selective manner so as to destroy their capability to alter the balance at a moment when Israel anticipated attacks from the Arab states.

Preventive war has similar balance-of-power connotations. This is a type of selective attack undertaken against an enemy state considerably before that state has effective military potential. Long before China was a nuclear power, for example, people throughout the West, perhaps even in the Soviet Union, openly mused on the efficacy of preventive attacks upon Chinese nuclear installations to delay its nuclear development and prolong its relative weakness. Japan's attack upon Pearl Harbor in 1941 was a different type of preventive war, conducted to deprive the United States of retaliatory strength as Japan contemplated further territorial quests in Asia and the Pacific. The only real difference between preemptive and preventive war is the time element; the effects for the balance of power are identical.

In the traditional study of international relations, it was assumed that the balance of power was determined exclusively by military relativities. More modern concepts of international relations, in contrast, recognize that relative military preparedness is not the sole determinant of the balance of power. The tendency now is to distinguish between *military power,* on the one hand, and the *overall ability* to command international influence, on the other. Thus a major component of the balance of power is *economic potential.*

Modern Japan is a case in point. Since the end of World War II, Japan has not been a significant military power. Its defense is firmly tied to American strategic policy, though in the Vietnam era that policy often offended Japan's sense of security. Despite this military inferiority, as was shown in chapter 3, Japan has resumed major power status by virtue of enormous economic revitalization. Even without military power its regional influence is growing apace, based on its bilateral economic relations and on its ability to lead Asia and the Pacific in international development programs.

Western Europe is another illustrative case. The rapidly changing technology of war has outpaced the ability of even the most industrialized Western European states to compete alone. Economically, as was demonstrated in chapter 3, it is their collective activity and production which give the European states a major world role rather than their individual efforts. Despite the continued European reliance on the trans-Atlantic security arrangement, Western Europe has achieved major-power status through its ability to compete in world trade. Thus one may go farther than to say that Western Europe plays a major role in the global power balance. One may conclude that through its economic restoration, these states acquired a role in the global balance by using their resources to force change in it.

The Middle Eastern example of forced change in the global power balance through means other than military is more recent and more striking, principally because its impact was registered in a much shorter time than in either Japan's or Western Europe's case. By determining to profit from oil in a way that their predators previously had, and by tying their oil export policy to political objectives concerning Israel, the Arab oil producing states in particular were able to force changes in the foreign policies of virtually all Western industrialized countries and Japan. While still developing industrially, their vast petrodollar reserves have substantially affected economic relations throughout the nonsocialist world. And the threat of a petroleum boycott, which their new wealth affords them, is sufficiently menacing to Japan, Western Europe, and even the United States that it is one of the most potentially fruitful nonmilitary instruments of foreign policy available anywhere. As a result, it may be concluded that this capability has forced a change in the global power balance as well as in that of the region.

Having now considered the fundamental issues of equilibrium, disequilibrium and change in balance-of-power theory, we turn to some alternative structural models.

Structural Models of Balance of Power

Although balance-of-power theory does not prescribe a preferred model of global or regional stability, it does facilitate description of the principal power configurations which have existed in the last 150 years. The theory also enables us to demonstrate graphically the power relations of major states and groups of states, whether their relation is global in interaction or limited to a region of the world.

It is cautioned at the outset that these models are of no greater value than to depict *roughly* power configurations which have existed in the past. They attempt to freeze time in the sense of describing relations in fixed position, rather than explaining the dynamic flow of relations among international actors. In this sense, these models are static; and they are as artificial as a tinker-toy model of a molecule which demonstrates the ideal configuration of its major components while ignoring the dynamic flow of subnuclear particles which either maintain or change the basic shape. The reader is asked to recall that the international system is as dynamic as such a molecule, and any attempt to reduce it to fixed form necessarily deprives it of much of its vitality. Nevertheless, since such descriptive models are typically referred to as indicators of major power configurations, they are instructive despite their static character.

1. The Nineteenth Century Balance of Power System

In illustrating different meanings of balance of power at the outset of this chapter, we used the sentence, "Britain was the crucial actor in the nineteenth-century balance of power system." What distinguished that system from the balance of power as we know it now?

Historians of the balance-of-power system (from the end of the Napoleonic Wars in 1815 until the outbreak of World War I in 1914) identify the underlying conditions. They note that it could exist only among several nation-states in a fairly well-defined territorial area. Though it was an interstate system, it was not global. The system could not have worked except among participants relatively homogeneous in political culture, who had rational means of estimating the power of one another (wealth, military potential, and so on).[2]

In retrospect, this international system seems to have been constructed on several basic assumptions. First, each state would attempt to maximize its own power for its own purposes. Second, as a consequence, as states competed for the acquisition of power and their interests (such as imperial interests) collided, there was potential for international conflict. Third, to enhance their respective power potentials, like-minded states entered into alliances, with alliance competition rather than state competition characterizing the system.

In these first three assumptions, the balance-of-power model sounds no different from any other international system. But the subsequent premises were unique. It is assumed, for example, that each participant placed a high value on equilibrium, and that in its alliance competition its objective was to achieve equilibrium rather than disequilibrium which might favor even itself. To maintain equivalence, moreover, states were willing periodically to switch alliances to adjust the balance. Adjustment, there-

[2] Edward V. Gulick, *Europe's Classical Balance of Power* (Ithaca: Cornell University Press, 1955), Chapter 1.

fore, is said to have been automatic. Figure 8–4 diagrams the process of adjustment: (A) shows an existing equilibrium which is upset (B) by the addition of a new participant or by a major technical development which adds to the weight of one coalition. In (C), equilibrium is restored by the transfer of one state from one alliance to the other.

The adjustment function and the notion of automaticity have evoked the greatest criticism. As a result, supporters have offered several other means by which the classical balance was adjusted, apparently conceding that the process is, at best, semi-automatic. The means of adjustment are said to be vigilance, alliances, intervention, mobility of action, reciprocal compensation, preservation of participants, coalitions and war. Beyond this, however, supporters have introduced the concept of "holding the balance," which calls upon a specific state to change its allegiances expressly to maintain the balance. This state is referred to as *The Balancer*.[3] The introduction of this concept means that the adjustment process is less than semi-automatic; rather, it is manual.

The concept of The Balancer is an effective modernization of this model only if The Balancer state has special characteristics. If a weak state were to take on this role, or a state that favors disequilibrium, then the function of manual balance could hardly be served. It follows that The Balancer must be an effectively powerful state, one whose strategic options enable it to have a major impact on the entire system. Moreover, it must be a state that favors equilibrium and, even more, one that demands for its own purposes that equilibrium be safeguarded. George Liska writes of The Balancer in this manner:

> His task is difficult. A balancer is expected to be partial to no single national subject of the balance-of-power system but to direct his own mobile weight in such a way as to ensure the international object of an equipoise of power. He must be both at the focus of the system and outside it; otherwise he would not be free to withdraw and engage his weight in function of the system's requirements and thus manipulate the balance. An effective balancer must be both self-restrained and quick in imposing

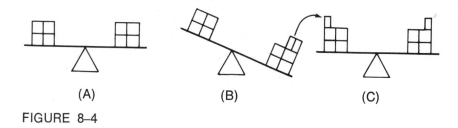

(A)   (B)   (C)

FIGURE 8–4

[3] The means of balance are derived from Gulick, *Europe's Classical Balance of Power*, Chapter 3.

vigorous restraints on others. Only then can he frustrate and thus reduce the incentive to any one nation's quest for preponderance. A sufficiently powerful balancer of this kind might check the irrational drives and the miscalculations jeopardizing the balance of power and promote the realization of its objective norm.[4]

Among historians of this model, Britain is universally looked upon as having been The Balancer, though some also identify equilibrating functions in the policies of other states. Britain's virtues as The Balancer include its geographic location (which spared it from common boundaries with other powerful European states), its apparent interest in equilibrium as the most favorable climate for its imperial policies, and its great mobility of action.

Despite the modern refinements of this theory, skepticism continues to abound. A.F.K. Organski, for instance, concludes that power is only one of the objectives of states, thus deprecating the assumption that power is the foremost national value. He also denies that nations are static and unchanging from within, insisting that through industrialization, marshalling

European Equilibrium

Lithograph by Honoré Daumier, 1867.

[4] George Liska, *International Equilibrium* (Cambridge: Harvard University Press, 1957), pp. 36–37.

of population resources, and improvements in governmental efficiency, states increase their potential power. These changes are not adjustable through the presumed mechanics of the balance of power. Third, because states are often tied to one another through economic, political or psychological bonds, the freedom to switch alliances for no other purpose than balance is uncharacteristic of history. Like other critics, Organski interprets British policy as one of self-interest, not as a self-appointed role of Balancer. In fact, he denies that *any* state in the nineteenth century preferred equilibrium to favorable disequilibrium. Finally, Organski concludes that imbalance of power is the characteristic pattern, particularly since the industrial revolution, with major states and their respective coalitions actually trying to maintain disequilibrium.[5]

Whether the classical mechanics of the balance of power model ever really operated is, therefore, in doubt. But we may accept, nevertheless, the premise that in multiparty international systems favoring equilibrium, there must be some implicit rules of behavior. These have been elucidated by Morton Kaplan, whose book *System and Process in International Relations* is a landmark study of international models, past, present, and future. Kaplan lists the "operational rules" of the nineteenth century model as follows:

1. Participants will increase their capabilities, but they will accept the responsibility to negotiate their differences rather than to fight.

2. Since increase in capabilities is the prime motive of foreign policy, states must be willing to fight, if necessary, rather than to forego further development.

3. When at war, states will be prepared to terminate fighting rather than upset the foundations of equilibrium by eliminating a participant. This is important because the model is built upon the assumption of at least five major participants.

4. Every participant, intent upon equilibrium, will contest any tendency to dominance by any state or coalition.

5. Because the system is built upon the power of states, participants must constrain tendencies toward supranational organization, or organizations that would alter the sovereign status of the system's participants.

6. Each participant must be willing to permit defeated major actors to restore their positions, and they must encourage lesser actors to achieve the status of full participants. All major parties must be treated equally as acceptable role partners.[6]

[5] A. F. K. Organski, *World Politics,* 2nd ed. (New York: Alfred A. Knopf, 1968), pp. 282–99.

[6] Morton A. Kaplan, *Systems and Process in International Relations* (New York: John Wiley and Sons, 1957), p. 23; and also Kaplan's article "Balance of Power, Bipolarity and Other Models of International Systems," *American Political Science Review* 51 (1957): 684–95, esp. 686.

These rules have a pragmatic basis: if the system is to be viable, the participating states must be viable. We will return subsequently to the question whether multipartite systems such as this or limited-bloc systems (such as bipolarity) tend toward greater stability.

2. The Tight Bipolar Balance of Power

The nineteenth century balance-of-power system involved political relationships which passed with the First World War. As a result, international stability was no longer governed by the factors which we have discussed. Other systems of power balance emerged, particularly after World War II. It is necessary, therefore, to explore the military relations of other balance of power systems to understand the contemporary distribution of power.

Although it is generally fruitless to search for the "most important events in history," World War II probably changed international politics more than any single modern occurrence. Statesmen in the postwar years were confronted with the unprecedented problems presented by atomic weaponry, and with reduction of the number of effective major powers to two, the United States and the Soviet Union. Though World War I had begun the process of restricting the number of major powers, the prostration of Western and Central Europe ensured that for the foreseeable future world politics would center upon Washington and Moscow, rather than upon London and Paris. But there was also a third critical development: the intense ideological hostility between the two principal powers, which opened an era of conflict, distrust, competition, and misperception.

These three factors together—the two-part division of power, the advent of atomic warfare, and unprecedented ideological rivalry—resulted in an international system of tight bipolarity, one in which virtually all of the world's effective power was encompassed in two competing blocs. The institutional structure was that of two formal alliance systems dominated by the Soviet Union and the United States, respectively. For diplomatic or geopolitical reasons there were a few states which did not participate (for example, Finland and Switzerland); but the fact remains that virtually all of the measurable power in international relations was commanded through one or the other of these two structures.[7]

A tight bipolar international system may be said to have existed from 1945 to 1955, a decade which saw such momentous events as the combat

---

[7] This definition is only a slight adaptation of Kaplan's, which defines tight bipolarity as a system in which "non-bloc member actors and universal actors either disappear entirely or cease to be significant." ("Balance of Power, Bipolarity and Other Models of International Systems," p. 693.) Kaplan denies, however, that a tight bipolar system has ever existed.

Soviet Union's Andrei Vishinsky at the UN (1953) accusing the U.S. and its allies of behaving like a "Master Race." American ambassador Henry Cabot Lodge and British ambassador Sir Gladwyn Jebb listen uninterestedly to the familiar invective.

Wide World Photo

use of atomic energy, the achievement of atomic capability by the Soviet Union, the establishment of NATO, SEATO, and the Warsaw Pact, the Berlin Blockade, accession to power in China by Mao Tse-tung, and the Korean War. In this era, the intense Soviet-American rivalry, particularly over Europe, resulted in the cold war exchanges of threats and competing alliances. Technically, the Warsaw Pact did not come into existence until 1954 after the NATO allies agreed to include West Germany in membership; but long prior to this formal event, the Soviet Union and Eastern Europe comprised a tacit alliance. Formal Sino-Soviet ties also existed. The American alliance structure was global (and remains so despite the collapse of SEATO after the Vietnam War), and developed as follows:

Organization of American States (The Rio Pact, or the Inter-American Treaty of Reciprocal Assistance), 1947 (twenty-two members).

North Atlantic Treaty, 1949 (fifteen members).

Security Treaty with Japan, 1951 (bilateral).

Security Treaty with Australia and New Zealand, 1951 (trilateral).

Mutual Defense Treaty with the Republic of the Philippines, 1951 (bilateral).

Mutual Defense Treaty with the Republic of (South) Korea, 1953 (bilateral).

Southeast Asia Collective Defense Treaty, 1954 (eight members).

Mutual Defense Treaty with the Republic of China (Taiwan), 1954 (bilateral).

Altogether, these treaties and the institutionalized alliances which they created encompassed some forty-four nations including the United States, with several states belonging to more than one alliance. In addition, the United States had bases agreements and status-of-forces agreements with Spain and Libya (the latter agreement no longer exists), so that the United States was involved in some level of military activity with no fewer than forty-five different governments on every continent in the world! [8] The solidarity of membership was further assisted by the alliances sponsored by London, including the Central Treaty Organization and its military prerogatives in its colonial areas, particularly in Asia and the Mediterranean (for instance, Malta). Combined, the Anglo-American alliances and the Soviet alliances involved in excess of sixty states and almost half again as many non-self-governing areas. Compare this with the 1955 membership of the United Nations, which was only seventy-six, sixteen of which were not admitted until 1955. Furthermore, of the original fifty-one signatories to the UN Charter, two—Byelorussia and the Ukraine—were not and are not sovereign states. Thus at the start of 1955, while the UN had a membership of only fifty-nine distinctly different sovereign states, the United States and Britain, on the one hand, and the Soviet Union, on the other, were formally allied with over sixty states. The universality of the alliance systems should be self-evident.

Based on this survey of alliances, we may now diagram the tight bipolar system, noting also the existence of several scattered but relatively powerless nonparticipants. Figure 8–5 demonstrates that while a tight bipolar balance of power existed from 1945 to 1955, the U.S.-oriented bloc commanded more influence when all power sources are considered. These included a superior number of allies, larger supply of resources, and the

[8] For an extraordinarily useful description of these alliances, replete with texts, maps, and comparative analysis, see the document *Collective Defense Treaties* (Washington: U.S. Government Printing Office, 1967), prepared by the Committee on Foreign Affairs of the U.S. House of Representatives.

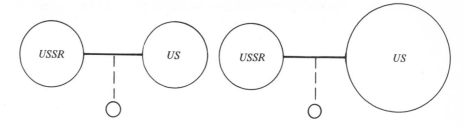

(A) Perfect Tight Bipolarity   (B) Actual Tight Bipolarity, 1945–1955

FIGURE 8–5

global character of American alliances contrasted with the regional reach of the Soviet. The point is that tight bipolarity need *not* imply equality of capability.[9]

Since power is always relative, it does not necessarily follow from lack of absolute equality that the political prerogatives of one bloc were less than those of the other in critical areas. In fact, in the tight bipolarity of 1945–1955, the disparities operated outside of Europe, beyond the sphere in which the Kremlin generally wished to compete with Washington. Thus we may say that in the tight bipolar era there existed European regional symmetry, but global asymmetry.

The operating characteristics of the tight bipolar balance of power differ markedly from those of the nineteenth century system. The basic assumption here is that international equilibrium is a second-best objective: the principal aim of governments is to belong to the dominant coalition. Furthermore, the system is built on the premise that all effective power is included in the major blocs, or poles, with the result that there is no powerful state dangling free to play the role of Balancer. Indeed, the objective of this pattern of power is to anticipate the defeat of the other coalition should it breach the frontiers of one's own members. It is for this reason, rather than mere coincidence, that the ruling American political-military strategy of this era was massive nuclear retaliation, though it is doubtful that the threat was ever taken seriously. It is far more likely that the balanced conventional strengths of the European alliances ensured stability through this era. Nevertheless, the philosophy of tight bipolarity renders massive retaliation quite logical as a strategic foundation. It is safe to say that as a result of the conditions which dictated the emergence of bipolarity, and as a con-

[9] For a study suggesting that the power distribution be described in terms of symmetry and asymmetry regardless of number of major blocs, though especially in two-bloc systems, see Wolfram F. Hanreider, "The International System: Bipolar or Multi-bloc?" *Journal of Conflict Resolution* 9: 299–308. Hanreider provides alternative diagrams for depicting perfect and actual tight bipolarity.

sequence of the strategies which it fostered, this model of international order is maximally hostile.

3. The Loose Bipolar Balance of Power

In the mid-1950's a number of fundamental changes occurred in the international system. The two superpower alliance systems began to "loosen," with internal conflicts and losses of confidence appearing in each bloc. Conflicts occurred which destroyed or weakened earlier allegiances, and the tightness of dependencies began to dissipate. In the Soviet sphere events took several paths. Eastern European dissatisfaction with Soviet control, foreshadowed a few years earlier in East Germany, climaxed with the brief Hungarian revolt of 1956. Coupled with Nikita Khrushchev's campaign to "de-Stalinize" the Soviet Union and Eastern Europe, this event resulted in increasing demands for quasi-independence among the Soviet "satellites," despite forceful suppression by Soviet troops. The politics of the Soviet sphere came increasingly to be identified as "polycentric," suggesting reduced Soviet control over the states within its orbit.

If "polycentrism" characterized Eastern Europe, only "schism" describes Sino-Soviet relations in the same era. Though not yet a major power, the Mao government, after less than a decade of controlling the Chinese mainland, found itself disaffected from Moscow and in quest of independent power status. Formal relations were broken and Soviet technicians and aid were withdrawn, leaving China to develop alone. Gone was the Korean War–inspired American theory that all Communist power and authority emanate from the Kremlin; the international Communist movement was no longer regarded as monolithic. The Soviet Union's influence in Asia was sharply curtailed, leaving Soviet-American relations that much more asymmetrical. More important, the Sino-Soviet split represented a major break in the solidarity of the Soviet world.

The American bloc began to crack also. Latin America, increasingly disenchanted with Washington's sporadic paternalism, began to consider itself a member of the Third World, despite its formal military and economic ties with the United States. Fidel Castro's accession to power through armed rebellion, followed by his conversion to Marxism, brought the first serious challenge to the ideological solidarity of the Western Hemisphere.

Western Europe presented other problems. The enormous success of the Western European economies in reconstruction led to gradual resentment of American economic domination. Charles DeGaulle's demand that Europe be "de-Americanized" threatened to dilute the potential effectiveness of the United States in facing the Soviet Union across Europe. Strategic policy in NATO led to other resentments and suspicions, with some Europeans doubting the credibility of the American nuclear umbrella, while still others feared that impetuous behavior in Washington in response to Soviet threats might unnecessarily embroil Europe in war.

Worldwide interests and associations tend to present worldwide problems, and the United States found that troubles in Latin America and Western Europe were not enough. The cornerstone of American policy in Asia, the alliance with Japan, began to show signs of decay. In the years following the Korean War (1950–1953), Japanese resentment to American security policy grew steadily, and focused upon American nuclear strategy. Disharmony rose to the point of widespread rioting on the occasion of the renegotiation of the Security Agreement in 1960. The political climate in Japan grew so menacing that the Tokyo government successfully discouraged the state visit of President Dwight D. Eisenhower. The breakdown over security matters was compounded in Japanese minds by U.S. efforts to prevent Japan from trading with China.

By 1960, then, it was clear that major shifts were occurring in the previous "tightness" of global bipolarity because of internal changes in the principal alliances. Another crucial change was taking place. Beginning in 1957, though more markedly after 1960, the number of nation-states burgeoned. In 1960, seventeen states were admitted to United Nations membership, every one of them newly independent. A world which had been revolutionary in several respects now added a new dimension—a sudden and unprecedented increase in the number of national actors. These new states, bound only by poverty, underdevelopment, and racial separation from the dominant white nations, were rigorously courted by the United States and the Soviet Union, each one seeking new adherents to its ideology. Most, however, preferred to tie themselves to neither giant but, rather, to accept assistance from either with as little political cost as possible. Thus, although they were not a solid bloc of states with coordinated behavior (except in voting patterns of economic matters at the UN), these states began to form a multistate group with potential collective impact.

Added to the polycentrism of the Soviet sphere and the beginning of decentralization among American allies, the emergence of the Third World further loosened the global polarity because it presented many "nonbloc actors." Figure 8–6 shows the resulting loose bipolarity. Diagrammatically, the differences between this and the tight bipolar model are (1) the presence of nonbloc actors and (2) splintering in the two main blocs. Yet the structure is still basically bipolar with respect to effective power relations. Only two bloc actors are portrayed as relating directly to the fulcrum. Each of the others either arises from a major bloc, or is tied to one for power purposes, though it may not be thoroughly allied.

For bloc members, the behavioral norms in tight and loose bipolar systems are essentially the same. Members are pledged to prepare to eliminate the opposing bloc, but prefer to fight small wars rather than large. Members agree to strengthen their own bloc internally, and to resolve differences by negotiation rather than open conflict. The threat of total destruction

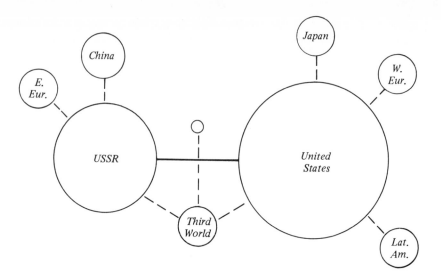

FIGURE 8–6   Loose Bipolarity, 1955–1965

leads to a tacit agreement not to provoke war between the dominant members of opposing blocs.

But for the dominant members, the Soviet Union and the United States, there is an added objective in loose bipolarity—namely, to maintain optimum tightness amid conditions that nurture fragmentation. The mechanisms for this function are like the normal rewards and punishments by which powerful states influence the less powerful: economic rewards and deprivations, offers and withdrawals of military supply beyond that needed for the state's contribution to bloc security, and so on. In extreme cases, strong states may use force as the Soviet Union did in Hungary in 1956 and the United States did in Cuba in 1961 and in the Dominican Republic in 1965. In addition, especially when alliances are institutionalized, the polar states may use the alliance structure to prolong the perception of threat by playing to the self-aggrandizing behavior of pertinent elites, such as national military commands. In this sense threat perception becomes an important aspect of dominant-member political strategy in loose bipolar systems.

The norms for nonbloc actors are considerably different. Their basic role is as a ground for peaceful competition of the major powers and blocs, each intent primarily upon gaining the adherence of the nonbloc state, but secondarily on preventing it from going over to the other side. Their conflicts must be internalized (Nigeria-Biafra), carefully circumscribed (Rhodesia and Zambia) or submitted to global institutional settlement (Congo). They must resist great-power intervention if it is likely to bring in the other major power or result in subordination.

In the normal course of events, it might be expected that loose bipolarity would give way to multipolarity, with the quasi-independent blocs becoming independent power poles. Some observers argue that such a situation now exists.[10] However, while the loosening trend has carried us out of bipolarity, it does not appear that we have yet arrived at multipolarity. Hence an interim model is necessary.

4. The Incipient Multipolar Balance of Power

This title implies that the international power system is about to be multipolar. While several international actors are beginning to form blocs of reliable behavior and while these blocs have considerable command over events in either regional or subject areas, they have not yet achieved the status of third *powers* in the sense of having global influence to determine the outcomes of events. One test of an effective third power might be the ability to determine the outcome of a direct (though not necessarily cataclysmic) confrontation between the other two major powers. Another, both more modest and more practical, might be the ability to determine the outcome of a distant event despite Soviet or American intent to achieve some other outcome(s). To what extent do some potential third powers measure up to these tests at present?

China

The Mao government used the Korean War to notify other states that it would not permit the two great powers to divide the world, and especially Asia, as they saw fit. Since then, American respect has grown for the Chinese as a result of their cautious diplomacy and because of their choice to limit strategic activities to Asia and to the Sino-Soviet border. There is little doubt that American behavior throughout the Vietnam War was restrained in part by calculations of Chinese tolerance for American control near its borders.

The Soviets have been forced to equivalent respect. The willingness of the Chinese to challenge Soviet territorial control of certain border regions, together with the growth of Chinese nuclear capability, has prompted Moscow to treat Peking with caution. This can be taken by China only as a form of Soviet containment of Chinese economic and strategic growth.

But just as China's policy is limited almost entirely to its geographic region, so too is its influence. It is no longer possible for either of the great powers to undertake an initiative in Asia, save perhaps for South Asia

---

[10] See, for example, Cecil V. Crabb, Jr., *Nations in a Multipolar World* (New York: Harper & Row, 1968).

where both have close ties with India, without cautious consideration of Chinese wishes and fears. Furthermore, at the current stage of development, the threat of Chinese nuclear strikes is regionally limited; and at present its economic power has little effect upon Asian politics which cannot be offset by Moscow, Washington, or Tokyo.

China, then, is in a peculiar position. Despite its nearly unlimited potential power and rapid advancement as a nuclear state, its capacity to determine the outcome of a direct confrontation between the Soviet Union and the United States is limited almost entirely to Asia. Furthermore, it is probable that with China's own power growing, the only area in Asia over which the two giants are likely to differ significantly—save possibly for Korea—is China. Except as a matter of self-defense, therefore, it is difficult to imagine a situation in which China might be called to play a role in a Soviet-American confrontation in Asia. China's role in the brief war between India and Pakistan showed its willingness to take part in Asian politics outside of its direct sphere, but there any Soviet-American confrontation was merely diplomatic. At present, then, within its Asian regional sphere, the likelihood of a confrontation of two major powers calling for China to play a third power role is very small.

By the same token, because China's influence at the present stage of development has but regional reach, it is improbable that it will effectively control distant events in a manner undesirable to Washington and/or Moscow. On the whole, therefore, China may be said to play a major role in its Asian tripartite relations with the United States and the Soviet Union; but given the current limitations of its capabilities and those of its preference for regional politics, China has not yet achieved the status of a third global power. Though China does not contribute affirmatively to the policy of either superpower with respect to the other, it has not yet broken the basic bipolar global structure.

Western Europe

Years have passed since the states of Western Europe were wholly dependent upon the United States. Through their economic consolidation (see chapters 3 and 12) they have struggled against American economic domination, and they have labored to compete successfully with foreign goods in Europe and throughout the world. Their declining apprehension over war has encouraged an awareness not only of Europeanness, but of pan-Europeanness, a desire for the economic and political reconciliation of all Europe as inaugurated in the Ostpolitik. This same feeling, coupled with growing resentment over American strategic supremacy on the Continent, has caused decay in the Atlantic security community, and a widespread desire for an independent security policy. Though the current rate of technological development in the United States and the Soviet Union cannot be duplicated even by the most powerful and industrialized of the

Western European partners, an independent European defense strategy is founded on the notion that with achievable capability, Europe will be able to inflict unacceptable harm on any adversary, even though unable to destroy him.

Together, the sense of economic independence and the confidence of "minimum deterrence" conceive freedom of action, particularly from the United States. Again, however, regional constraints exist. In recent years both Britain and France have sharply reduced their foreign policy commitments beyond Europe. Their armed forces are limited almost exclusively to Europe. There is no doubt that each of these states will continue to play a major global economic role, and in that sense their influence has universal ramifications. Undoubtedly, however, for the foreseeable future most of the power of these states will be focused upon regional growth and the maturation of integrated economic competition outside of Western Europe. Thus their military influence will be limited to the European region, and the lion's share of their economic energy will likewise be regionally spent. Like China, while Western Europe has earned the ability to escape subordination to bipolar politics, it has not successfully met either the extreme test or the modest test of an effective third global power.

Japan

A third country to which some look as an effective third power is Japan, whose economic stature follows only the United States and the Soviet Union. Not only has Japan risen above American domination; it has also proven its ability to compete in world markets, and is preparing to be the dominant supplier of industrial goods throughout Asia, including China.

Despite this strong position, however, Japan is extraordinarily vulnerable to external pressures, so much so that even its economic productivity suffers significant external controls. Chapter 3 detailed the susceptibility of Japan's economy to American economic policy, and its extreme exposure to the demands of the fuel-producing states. Consequently, the economic foundation of Japan's claim to third power status is a peculiar one: more than any other candidate for this global role, the greatness which Japan commands rests upon extreme dependency, for both external markets and foreign energy sources.

The security sector reveals similar weaknesses. Prohibited at present by the Atomic Energy Law from developing nuclear weapons or deploying troops outside of the home territory, and uncertain of the American security commitment at a time when the Asian power distribution is disheveled, Japan must rely on economic and political means to establish both its regional and global roles. Japan is constrained in Asia by the peculiarity of being the indigenous economic giant without nuclear capability in a region that has two underindustrialized nuclear states (China and India).

In spite of its apparent strength, then, Japan is a state struggling to adapt to the regional and global power relativities. Like Western Europe, it has escaped from the perpetual subordination of a bipolar system, but because of its dependence on others, particularly the United States and the OPEC members, it is unable to establish a self-determined third power role.

The Third World

For more than a decade many observers have claimed that the Third World is, or is about to become, an effective third power in global relations. Because of its total population, its territorial vastness, and its richness in natural resources, the potential development here is extreme. But until recently this potential has not been mobilized. Population, growing at alarming rates, has caused a decline in per capita wealth even while the GNP's of most of the Third World states have been climbing. To the burden of population has been added the new forms of dependency implanted by Western-based multinational corporations. And on very few issues, other than economic and nationalistic questions of dependency and discrimination, have the Third World states been able to work together. It has appeared that the Third World, even if considered a unitary actor, has not risen to effective third power status.

The establishment of OPEC and the events of 1973, which both enriched the fuel-producing countries and forced changes in the foreign policies of more powerful states including Japan and the United States, have forced a reassessment of the earlier conclusion. As described in chapter 5, that reappraisal begins with a division of the Third World into the resource-rich and the resource-poor, and then turns to the role of the former. Because much of the West is dependent upon OPEC, and particularly upon the Arab OPEC members, for industrial fuel, they have discovered an effective lever for dealing with those dependent states. Simultaneously, they have greatly improved their regional bargaining position. Yet their strength rests on a single asset—oil—making it vulnerable to a number of countermeasures, including alternative sources of energy, depletion of the asset and military coercion. Only if the Third World exporters of other natural resources are able to form such effective cartels can the unique instrument of oil prolong its effective leverage in world politics and be more broadly applicable among industrialized states.

The third-power aspirations of these states, therefore, are but partially and precariously fulfilled. For the moment, however, their regional influence and their impact upon the industrial growth and international economic relations in the Western world ride high.

Comment

These observations about China, Western Europe, Japan and the Third World demonstrate that while the world has outgrown the forms of subordination typical of loose bipolarity, it has not produced effective independent power centers which would usher in true multipolarity. Consequently, we conclude that the global balance of power is in a transitional phase of incipient mutipolarity, in which the secondary power centers are still more attached to the primary than the independent poles. Figure 8–7 shows this configuration.

Prior to the oil politics of 1973, it appeared that this transitional phase was part of a linear trend from loose bipolarity to a multipolar balance of power. But those events revealed the weakest among the elements on which the aspirations of Japan—and to a lesser degree Western Europe—are constructed. Japan's plea, joined by the Western European states except for France, for common diplomatic and distribution policies exposed the pre-

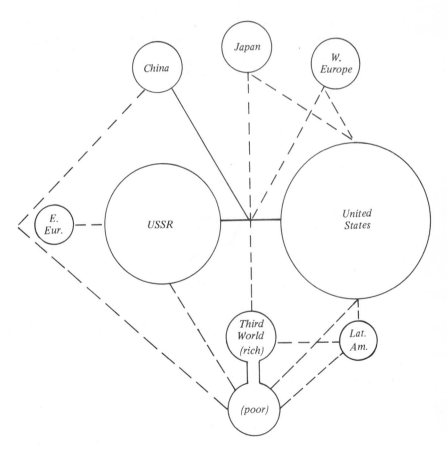

FIGURE 8–7 Incipient Global Multipolarity, 1965–present

viously hidden weaknesses of the industrial states among the incipient third-power candidates. The newly forced dependences are so vivid as to warrant the conclusion that progress toward multipolarity is arrested, with its resumption awaiting self-sufficiency in fuel among the industrialized states, and political-economic stabilization between the industrialized west and the resource-rich third world.

5. The Multipolar Balance of Power

If significant power increases should occur in the Third World, China, Western Europe, or Japan to the extent that two or more of these entities were able to challenge Soviet-American global interests, the international system could be defined as *multipolar*. Since the relative power capabilities need not be entirely equal, multipolarity might have either symmetrical or asymmetrical characteristics. The important issue is that several major power blocs would interact at virtually any place, without two-party domination. Such a system would appear as shown in Figure 8–8. As in the models previously diagrammed, the important factor here is that each of these systems is depicted as affecting the fulcrum, rather than being derived from, or dependent upon, some other power unit.

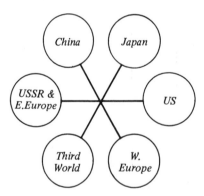

FIGURE 8–8   True Global Multipolarity, possible future

A New Balance of Power Model?

It has occasionally been suggested that multipolarity might restore the conditions of the nineteenth century balance of power. This argument has two bases. First, several independent power centers facilitate the switching of alliances and realignment of interests and power. Second, the

"Hey, sit down and start rowing – you're rocking the boat."

same feature—multiple power centers—is necessary for the appearance of a Balancer, at the service of the international system to balance the system consciously (manually). Presuming the multipolarity were approximately symmetrical, any of several power centers might serve in this capacity, and perhaps several would alternate in the role.

Because of its huge power potential, China is most probable as the next effective independent power in global politics. If it is, then great power confrontations calling for third power intervention as a Balancer take these forms:

Contestants	Balancer
China-Soviet Union	United States
United States-China	Soviet Union
U.S.-USSR	China

But there are several impediments to these relations. First, the power of each participant is so great that coalitions will necessarily overbalance. Hence the proper designation for these relations is not balance of power, but *mutual superiority* in noncoalition situations and *disequilibrium* in coalitions. Second, ideological barriers minimize the likelihood of each configuration. Third, balance-of-power theory assumes the dedication of each participant to the preservation of the others. Such devotion, whether out of strategy or sentiment, will be lacking for the foreseeable future. It follows that even the most probable form of global tripolarity is incompatible with a renewed balance of power on the nineteenth century model.

Regional Balance of Power

Throughout this discussion of balance-of-power models reference has been made to regional conditions as well as global. Although the concept has generally been applied to worldwide relations, the notion of a balance of power has critical interpretive meanings for regional conflict as well. This is true whether or not the major powers contribute significantly to the regional power equation.

Asia presents a highly complex power distribution. At the highest level, the two superpowers contribute directly because of their conflicting interests there. The Pacific Ocean, Taiwan, and South Korea are at the American nuclear frontier. At the second level, China transforms Soviet-American relations in Asia into nuclear tripolarity. Beneath that, India pursues a nuclear policy to enjoy mutual deterrence with China, but in so doing tilts the scale in its own favor against Pakistan. It is precisely because as an economic power Japan must venture into all of these relations that its military inferiority confuses its role in the overall Asian balance of power.

The balance-of-power question is less complex but equally crucial in the Middle East. There, Israel finds its tiny territory surrounded by a large coalition of hostile states, some of which are precisely those petroleum exporters who have amassed great wealth and used oil to manipulate the foreign policies of Western industrial states with respect to the regional conflict. Although the Arab-Israeli War of 1973 was brief, it was indescribably destructive. Arabs, Israelis, Americans, and Soviets were all dumbfounded by the amount of military hardware destroyed in such a short time by precision tactics. Inasmuch as both Israel and Egypt are within easy reach of nuclear technology, the regional strategic balance creeps toward one of mutual assured destruction. Quite apart from the interests and contributions of the great powers, Middle Eastern strategic relations disclose the critical importance of a regional balance of power.

Polarity and Stability: A Debate

The foregoing elucidation of past, present, and possible future power distributions produces a critical question: Is international stability better ensured by fundamentally bipolar political patterns or by multipolar balance? Each has advantages, but each also suffers from disadvantages.

One advocate of bipolarity finds four specific benefits in that system. First, with two overbearing world powers there are no peripheries from which significant conflict beyond the control of the great powers can occur. Second, the tighter the bipolarity and the more intense the inter-bloc competition, the broader the range of the subject matter over which the great powers gain preponderance and concerning which they are able to control conflict. Third, pressure is constant, and crises recur at low levels rather than in major conflict. Finally, the combination of constant pressure within blocs and the superior power of the dominant members enables the blocs to tolerate potentially disruptive change, including revolution, which might otherwise lead to widespread conflict.[12]

The disadvantages and intrinsic dangers of bipolarity have also been elucidated. One is that bipolar systems accentuate antagonism because of the reactions of the blocs to one another, leading to a degenerative aspect. There is also skepticism over the maxim that peace is best ensured by a crisis atmosphere and mutual fear. As we have previously seen, the tighter a bipolar configuration, the more tense the relations of the blocs and of their respective dominant members.[13]

Others have investigated the stabilizing potential of multipolar systems, and have concluded that the increased interaction of a multipolar model promotes stability.[14] In addition, increased interaction reduces obsession with any single one, thus enhancing the trend toward moderation. Though multipolarity cannot maintain stability interminably, it may be preferable in the shorter term.

In an empirical attempt to resolve the dispute over the stability of bipolar and multipolar systems, yet another scholar has studied the stratifica-

[12] Kenneth N. Waltz, "The Stability of a Bipolar World," *Daedelus* 93 (Summer 1964): 881–909.

[13] R. N. Rosecrance, "Bipolarity, Multipolarity, and the Future," *Journal of Conflict Resolution* 10 (1966): 315–17.

[14] Karl W. Deutsch and J. David Singer, "Multipolar Power Systems and International Stability," *World Politics* 16 (1964): 390–406.

tion and stability characteristics of twenty-one separate situations. He concludes that unipolar systems (single-nation domination), though historically rare, are the most stable. Bipolar systems, he finds, tend to produce less frequent but more prolonged wars than do multipolar. Multipolarity, in contrast, produces war among major actors more frequently and with more casualties. This argument thus leads to a choice, since neither configuration seems statistically to offer any guarantee against warfare.

> The choice between bipolar versus multipolar arrangements now seems clear. If a state or group of states is willing to accept long wars that are won by aggressor states, bipolarity provides an escape from the more war-prone character of historical multipolar subsystems. Multipolarity entails more violence, more countries at war, and more casualties; bipolarity, fewer but longer wars.[15]

Conclusion

Equivalence or Nonequivalence of Power

"What is the balance of power between the United States and the Soviet Union?" "Describe the balance of power in the Far East." "Who holds the balance of power in the cold war?" Expressions and questions of this sort are common in political discussion, and they suggest some of the ways in which the balance-of-power concept is applied to the direct relations of pairs or small groups of states. It is useful for us to think of "balance" for the moment not as a natural phenomenon, but as the familiar inanimate object. This permits us to recast the opening questions in this way: "In what position does the balance (scale) come to rest when the power of the United States is symbolically piled at one end, and that of the Soviet Union on the other?" For a tripartite situation (Sino-Soviet-American relations in Asia, for example), think of a perfectly balanced three-bulb chandelier hanging from a flexible chain. Now: "How does it hang when the power of the United States is symbolically plugged into one socket, that of the Soviet Union into a second, and that of China in the third? Does it continue to hang on a perfect level, or does it tilt in the direction of one?" It should now be evident that the expression "balance of power" in small-group interstate relations refers to a rough measure of power equivalence or nonequivalence.

Equilibrating Objectives

In the early part of this discussion on balance of power, we noted that many analysts include among its many meanings that of a policy or a set

---

[15] Michael Haas, "International Subsystems: Stability and Polarity," *American Political Science Review* 64 (1970): 98–123.

of objectives. If we assume that states are power conscious, then in their external relations they may have any one of three power objectives: (1) to maintain equality with some object-state, (2) to achieve superiority over some other state(s), or (3) to decline to keep apace of some other state(s). Again, remember that power must always be determined and measured relative to the power of someone else: Italy is more powerful than Switzerland, but less powerful than France. The power choices which a government makes with respect to its neighbors or competitors comprise its *equilibrating objectives*.

Surprisingly perhaps, some states opt not to match the power of their neighbors. Finland cannot compete with the Soviet Union and does not care to compete with Sweden. Costa Rica has virtually no military forces. And Japan, despite its image as a powerful state, maintains but a small national defense force. The Republic of China (Taiwan), however, invests a disproportionate share of its public revenue in national defense, yet could not conceivably defend itself against aggression from the mainland should it occur. In all of these cases, therefore, the potential adversaries of these countries "hold the balance" against them.

In other situations, particularly where the expectation of conflict is moderate to high, the contesting states will seek superiority, and may even abandon the traditional power balance in favor of the balance of terror variant. In contrast, where the probability of violence is perceived as low, states will seek no more than equivalence, or will arm themselves only up to the level of their alliance commitments (for instance, Canada). From the logic of these contrasting cases we may infer that in most bilateral situations, military allocations are governed by the quest for the safety of equivalence.

Balance of power, then, is an expression with many political meanings. In the global context it is useful as an analytical concept for assessing the overall power capabilities of states and coalitions, and it serves as a generic title for a host of specific power distributions. On the interstate level, in contrast, "balance of power" is a device for bilateral and small group power relativities. It also expresses the equilibrating or disequilibrating objectives of national arms policies.

The bilateral and interbloc relations of the superpowers since World War II have been so intense as to have outgrown conventional balance-of-power logic. From it has appeared the dominant contemporary variant: the balance of terror.

9

The Balance
of Terror

Think, for a moment, about the unthinkable. Imagine that you awaken in the middle of a nuclear attack. Somehow, by accident or design, nuclear war has erupted between your country and another. What would it be like?

The U.S. Atomic Energy Commission's "Nuclear Bomb Effects Computer" gives us some horrifying estimates.[1] But before it can do so, we need to set its indicators to simulate reasonable conditions. Let's say, first, that you were sleeping about four miles from the center of an important military installation, an industrial area, or a densely populated metropolis. Second, let's assume the area is a victim of a nuclear "surface blast," the bomb having detonated at ground level rather than in the atmosphere (an "air blast"). Third, to have a measure of the explosive potential of the weapon, we set the computer "yield" adjustment at one megaton, or the explosive equivalent of one million tons of TNT. That much TNT would comprise a stack reaching almost the height of the Empire State Building! One megaton is fifty times as great as the bombs used in 1945 at Hiroshima and Nagasaki (twenty kilotons each, or 20,000 tons of TNT equivalent, each kiloton having the punch of 1,000 tons of TNT).

The effects of this attack will be catastrophic. It will gouge out a crater half a mile across and 300 feet deep. Virtually everything in this area, pulverized by the blast and altered by its heat, will be engulfed in a fireball

[1] Atomic Energy Commission, *The Effects of Nuclear Weapons* (Washington, D.C.: U.S. Government Printing Office, 1962).

with a diameter of a mile and a half. The surface temperature of this fire-ball will be greater than that of the sun. A huge mushroom-shaped cloud will form, carrying up and away the particles that remain of former life and structure.

But you are four miles away. Though the effects upon you will not be quite as bad, they will be severe. Everything combustible in your area will be ignited; and things normally resistant to heat will be melted and mis-shapen. If you survive, you will be burned badly. (More than half of the people who died in the twenty-kiloton attacks upon Hiroshima and Nagasaki died of fire and heat.) If you survive skin burns, the heat of the air may destroy your lungs. Besides, the supply of oxygen in your area will have been reduced by the nearby fireblast.

Percussion effects will also be devastating. Buildings around you will crumble from the shock waves of the blast. Glass and other torn materials will catapult through the air at a speed of 200 feet per second. The misery of your burns will be compounded by injuries sustained in collisions; and your eardrums will have been shattered by violent soundwaves, and by the eighty-mile-per-hour windstorm which will have been set off by the blast. If you survive the initial dangers at four miles distance, you will be among fewer than half of your neighbors who do.

But your troubles are not over. Radiation effects are your next hazard. If you have not been severely injured by immediate irradiation, if your vital organs have not been damaged by this unique penetrating power, you will have a lengthy bout with radioactive fallout. All of the particles vaporized and sucked up into the atmosphere in the mushroom cloud will carry radioactivity. As they precipitate back to earth they will con-taminate everything in their path. Once again the air you breathe will be hazardous; your skin will be exposed once again to potentially lethal radiation; and exposed water and food supplies will carry certain death. Even if you are alive and mobile, you will be confined to your location.

We have assumed that all of this destruction has been brought on by a single one-megaton bomb. Yet in actual nuclear attack it is unlikely that a single bomb would be used or that yield would be limited to one megaton. Warheads of three and five megatons are now common in the stockpiles of the Soviet Union and the United States, and the Soviet Union is known to have tested a device of fifty-megaton yield. Altogether, the United States commands about thirty thousand deliverable megatons and the Soviet Union twenty thousand more, for a total of about fifty billion tons of TNT equivalent. On top of that, Britain, France, India and China have nuclear weapons, with Western sources estimating that China has sufficient refined radioactive materials to deploy nearly 300 warheads of twenty kilotons or more.[2] Under these circumstances, a yield of one

[2] Charles H. Murphy, "Mainland China's Evolving Nuclear Deterrent," *Bulletin of the Atomic Scientists*, January 1972, p. 29.

megaton in our imaginary attack is a conservative one. But when compared with conventional weapons, this blast exceeds all the explosives used against Germany and Japan in World War II, and equals the total of all bombing in the Vietnam War through 1972.

Furthermore, the attack on your area need not have been an isolated one. Suppose it were part of general nuclear war with some enemy seeking to destroy 50 percent of your nation's industry and 25 percent of its population. This would mean hitting several major cities in a matter of minutes, perhaps some of them with several warheads, in order to gain the advantage of instantaneous warfare. In the United States, for example, almost one-third of the total national industrial might is concentrated in the ten largest metropolitan areas, which comprise almost one-fourth of the total national population. These are, therefore, the areas of highest concentration of defense industry and trained personnel; they also house some of the major military and governmental installations. Table 9-1 details these concentrations. If the enemy prefers counter-value targeting, these areas are all vulnerable. If he chooses instead to knock out retaliatory forces (counterforce strategy), these areas may be spared.

The effect of total warfare on national survival and the human future is unmeasurable, yet subject to some disagreement. Optimistic observers such as Herman Kahn speculate that with intelligent planning, consequences could be limited to losses of not more than 25 percent of national population and recovery of gross national product within as few as ten

TABLE 9-1 American Industrial and Population Concentrations: Likely Soviet Countervalue Targets

Rank	Metropolitan Area	Population (1970)
1	New York	11,529,000
2	Los Angeles–Long Beach	7,030,000
3	Chicago	6,975,000
4	Philadelphia–N.J.	4,816,000
5	Detroit	4,196,000
6	San Francisco–Oakland	3,116,000
7	Washington–Md.–Va.	2,861,000
8	Boston	2,754,000
9	Pittsburgh	2,402,000
10	St. Louis–Ill.	2,364,000
		Total 48,043,000

Total population was 203,185,000. Therefore the ten largest metropolitan areas house about 24 percent of the total national population.

Compiled from *Pocket Data Book: USA, 1971* (Washington: U.S. Department of Commerce, Bureau of the Census, 1971, Table 14.) All figures based on the 1970 federal census.

Victims of atomic bombing, August 6, 1945, taken a few hours after the attack.

Wide World Photo

years. Scientist Linus Pauling takes quite a different view, arguing that the damage would be considerably greater and that the results for human survival are incalculable. The U.S. Department of Defense estimated in 1974 that a massive Soviet strike would result in 95–100 million American fatalities; a strike limited to missile sites and strategic submarine and bomber bases would take 5–6 million lives; and a strike limited to SAC bases or ICBM sites would result in 500 thousand to one million mortalities.[3] Such estimates are highly sensitive to assumptions about enemy

[3] Herman Kahn, *On Thermonuclear War* (Princeton: Princeton University Press, 1960); Kahn, *Thinking About the Unthinkable* (New York: Horizon, 1962), the title of which inspired the opening sentence of this chapter; Linus Pauling, *No More War!* (New York: Dodd, Mead, 1958); and James R. Schlesinger, "Briefing on Counterforce Attacks," Senate Committee on Foreign Relations Hearing, September 11, 1974.

intentions and targetting, the number of independently targetted warheads, delivery vehicle accuracy, and other variables.

The Balance of Terror

Despite these horrifying potential effects, nuclear developments, especially in the United States and the Soviet Union, have become such common parts of our lives that we seem unmoved by each new advance. Can it be that we have learned to live with the bomb? Presumably we have, though an estimate of the magnitude of the nuclear arms race and its cost may disrupt our complacency. By estimate of the United States Department of State, the United States and the Soviet Union alone spent over two trillion dollars on defense between the end of World War Two and 1972,[4] and their expenditures continue to grow at a rate of almost one hundred billion dollars per year apiece. It is now calculated by one eminent scientist that the world's total nuclear stockpile is about one million times greater than the two atomic bombs used in 1945 against Japan, and that there exist more than ten tons of TNT equivalents for every man, woman and child on earth.[5]

On what grounds are such huge expenditures and such "overkill" justified? The unanimous answer of nuclear strategists is that the nuclear arms race is not lunacy at all—that it is a carefully balanced system designed not to threaten peace, but to guarantee it. At the heart of the program is the assumption that the more potential force each adversary possesses, the less likely is it to be used in combat. The assumption that no nuclear state will launch a nuclear attack against another because of the retaliatory cost to itself is an extension of the classic *para bellum* doctrine, which offers the paradox that the best way to ensure peace is to prepare for war, while the most effective way to invite war is to trust the good intentions of others.

Among nuclear states, peace is founded upon the principle of *mutual deterrence*. Deterrence is a military potential coupled with a state of mind which, when sufficient to be a credible threat, makes it clear to a potential aggressor that the cost of his attack will be more than he is willing to bear: "Before you strike me, you had better consider that I will strike you back, and I will do more damage to you than will justify your attack upon me." Thus deterrence grows not only from the ability to attack, but from the capacity to retaliate as well. When each side is able to dissuade the

[4] U.S. Department of State, Bureau of Public Affairs, Office of Media Services, News Release of August 1, 1972.

[5] W. K. H. Panofsky, "Roots of the Strategic Arms Race: Ambiguity and Ignorance," *Bulletin of the Atomic Scientists*, June 1971, p. 15.

other from nuclear attack, a condition of *mutual deterrence* exists. The emphasis is not merely on self-defense but on capacity to equal whatever damage may be done by an attacker. Since "defense" indicates ability to repel, and since deterrence involves not repulsion but retaliation, mutual deterrence implies *equivalent offensive capability*. This system of keeping the peace by mutual threat of horrible death and destruction was dubbed by Winston Churchill the *balance of terror*. Others have referred to it, perhaps with greater irony, as *mutual superiority*.

First- and Second-Strike Capabilities

Mutual deterrence requires not only the possession of nuclear arms by two opposed parties, but also the ability of each to absorb a first strike by the other without losing the capacity to retaliate. Atomic stability depends on a belief in the mind of the potential aggressor that he will suffer retaliation at an unacceptable cost (the essence of deterrence). This means above all that a considerable portion of the defending state's strike force must survive the initial assault. If either or both parties can achieve a *first-strike capability*—a capacity to destroy the adversary's strategic arsenal by surprise attack—mutual deterrence does not exist. Stable deterrence requires that both parties possess secure *second-strike forces* capable of surviving surprise attack.

Nuclear strategists argue that it is in the interest of both parties that their adversaries have secure second-strike potential. Without it the retaliatory response, to be effective, would need to be launched before the arrival of the opponent's incoming attack forces. Intercontinental ballistic missiles travel at speeds that reduce warning times to no more than fifteen to thirty minutes. Thus, without second-strike security, a retaliatory force would need to be on hair-trigger alert during periods of political tension, and ready for instant launch. Such a time-urgent system would be prone to catastrophe in the event of misinformation or miscalculation, to the detriment of all. Stable deterrence depends on a less sensitized system that permits time to verify the existence of an attack and even to receive it before taking counteractions that are irreversible. For these reasons, the two superpowers have foresworn the development of first-strike potentials and declared their objectives to be stable and mutual second-strike deterrence.

For the American side, however, there is a contradiction between this goal of second-strike stability and the imperatives of defense in the European theatre. It is the declared policy of the United States that if NATO could not turn back a Soviet attack at the conventional weapons level, tactical and strategic nuclear forces would be used. This nuclear umbrella is the heart of the Atlantic alliance. But it implies that the United States might be in the position of making first use of strategic nuclear weapons. To reduce damage to the American homeland, and to make the threat of an American nuclear attack credible to the Soviet Union, the United States has an incentive to develop the capability to destroy the largest number of Soviet strategic forces on the ground before they can be used against U.S. targets. Thus, the logic of the NATO alliance presses Washington toward the development of a first-strike force—one declared to be defensive in intent, but one sure to be perceived in Moscow as threatening an offensive potential. The commitment to Europe poses a dilemma between the objective of second-strike stability and the requirements of a first-strike force. The United States has sought to relax the tension between these two objectives by promoting a central European military balance at the conventional weapons level adequate to stop a Communist thrust without resort to strategic nuclear weapons. But the search for a conventional military balance (discussed below) is quite difficult, and the need for a nuclear option remains.

Second-strike stability depends not only on the will to deploy strategic forces in a certain way, but also on the technical capacity to protect a retaliatory force from destruction. Up to the present, this has been achieved by the so-called *triad* of delivery vehicles: land-based ICBM's protected in underground silos; submarine missile launchers protected from detection (and therefore destruction) by thousands of miles of deep seas in which they prowl; and long-range heavy bombers kept in the air on routine alert to prevent their destruction on the ground. This triad has provided a considerable degree of security to second-strike forces.

However, a number of newly emerging technologies raise the possibility that this margin of security will be substantially reduced in the future, and even that a state may have the option if it is so disposed to develop a first-strike force able to overcome all existing defenses. The hardened silo effectively defends its missile against all but very near hits by enemy warheads, and is designed against the fairly wide circular error probabilities (CEP's) of available long-range missiles. But recent advances in micro-electronics have made possible offensive missiles with highly accurate terminal guidance, vastly reducing the CEP's and opening a new era of silo-busting options. Similarly, the margin of security of submarines and strategic bombers is eroding. The submarine is protected by the physical properties of seawater, which impede the passage of detection impulses. But advances in anti-submarine warfare technology are vastly extending the ranges over which detection is possible. Strategic bombers are likely to become vulnerable to precision-guided surface-to-air and air-to-air missiles, if radars are developed to respond to their characteristic low-level flight patterns. In general, and without overstating the point, it is fair to conclude that the new technologies will render obsolete many of the familiar means of protecting second-strike forces.

In the incessant race between offense and defense, it is predictable that new methods will develop to protect nuclear strike forces. Suggestions include superhardening, so that missile silos have extremely high levels of blast resistance; camouflage and dummies, so the enemy wastes his force on fake targets and misses the real ones; land mobile systems rather than fixed sites; electronic countermeasures to jam the sensitive guidance systems of the attacking force; high energy laser beams to destroy missiles or their warheads in flight; and, in the case of submarines, increased ranges and improved electronic warfare equipment to provide more cover against detection.

Through such means, it appears that after the next upward spiral of the arms race, we may, with careful planning and after the expenditure of many billions of dollars on both sides, arrive at a new kind of stable mutual deterrence system as good as the one we have had. Technological change will threaten, but ultimately not destroy, the security of second-strike forces that is essential to the balance of terror.

Credibility of Intent

Deterrence, as has been noted, is more than simply the possession of weapons of mass destruction. There is a reciprocal psychological factor through which the parties signal one another as to their intentions and the depth of their commitments. The possession of power is not an effective deterrent unless accompanied by will to use it in defined situations. Thus the threat of nuclear retaliation must not only be horrifying; it must also be *credible*. The probability of nuclear attack is the *product* of capability and intent: if intent equals zero, then the probability is zero.[6]

Credibility is also determined in part by the *object of conflict*. There is an obvious difference in expectation when (1) one's home territory is threatened, or (2) one's vital allies are intimidated, or (3) conflict brews over some remote areas or some remote interest. In the first case, there is little cause to doubt the credibility of deterrence. Doubt begins to spring up, however, in the second case. While the United States would surely launch a counterattack if New York City were subjected to nuclear attack, would it do likewise if the object of the first strike were a Western European city? If the United States *does* respond with nuclear weapons, does it invite an attack upon its own cities and its own defenses from the other side, after having already expended some of its deployed nuclear weapons? The European fear that the American nuclear umbrella may lack credibility for these reasons has greatly motivated the development of British and

[6] J. David Singer, "Threat Perception and National Decision-Makers," *Journal of Conflict Resolution* (1958): 90–105; also Singer, *Deterrence, Arms Control and Disarmament* (Columbus: Ohio State University Press, 1962); and Dean G. Pruitt, "Definition of the Situation as a Determinant of International Action," in Herbert C. Kelman, ed., *International Behavior* (New York: Holt, Rinehart and Winston, 1966), pp. 393–432.

French nuclear forces. In the third case of remote areas and interests, of course, nuclear deterrence has little credibility whatever.[7]

Object of conflict is closely tied to *commitment*. While there is no doubt of self-defense credibility, commitment may become obscured as the issue in question wanders farther from home. This is the case with the American pledge to defend Berlin, a small island of the Western world surrounded entirely by Eastern Germany in the Soviet world. Its size and location make it indefensible. The pledge to defend it seems to pale in the face of overbearing power from the Warsaw Pact nations. But the American pledge was boldly underscored by President Kennedy in 1961 when he declared to a cheering throng in West Berlin, in the German language, "I am a Berliner!" A few years later President Nixon told a similar audience that "All the world's free peoples are Berliners!" Some have gone so far as to suggest that even God may be a Berliner! The point is to dramatize to the Soviet Union the American commitment to defend what appears to be tactically indefensible.

But how is this commitment made credible? Among the NATO forces in West Berlin there are many thousands of Americans who, in the event of invasion, would either be killed or captured. Their deaths or detention would commit the United States to retaliatory action (not necessarily nuclear!), and the Soviets know this. Hence the commitment of the United States to the defense of a most unlikely piece of territory is made credible by the "trip wire" character of the American forces there. It is based on mutual knowledge that a Soviet attack might force the United States to do something which it does not want to do. This process of voluntarily tying one's own hands is generally called the *process of commitment* and posits this rule: credibility is assured when you deprive yourself of the option of not honoring your own threat. Among other things, this process signals to the other side that the burden is on it to prevent a clash.

This signalling process has been made most graphic by Thomas Schelling, who has proposed the game of Chicken as a model of communicating to an enemy that a situation is out of control and that you are powerless to restore control because of the depth of your commitment. He likens international conflict to two hotrodders on a deliberate collision course, each expecting the other to "chicken out." If neither does, each is the loser in a bloody conclusion. Schelling suggests a strategy in which one participant becomes conspicuously soused before the start and then, as the vehicles approach each other, the inebriated driver throws his steering wheel out of the car so as to signal to the other his inability to restore control. The burden is now on the other, because one is irrevocably committed. The major liability, of course, is that two may play at the same strategy, and instead of having one participant out of control, there may be two.

---

[7] Herman Kahn, *Thinking About the Unthinkable*, pp. 110–25 suggests three types of deterrence pertinent to three distinctly different levels of interest.

In the jargon of the nuclear era, this danger of uncontrolled escalation of commitments is called "brinkmanship," or the process of proceeding stepwise to the brink of thermonuclear war. In this process, referred to by Herman Kahn as "the rationality of irrationality," each side attempts to convince the other that its commitment is irrevocable, and that it is the other party's responsibility to defuse the situation. The irrevocability is communicated by tying it to larger values or to constituents who will not be satisfied with any other course. Language involving ideological necessity has been common in Soviet brinkmanship, especially in the Cuban missile crisis of 1962. By the same token, the specter of abandonment of allies and references to a determined Congress or electorate have accompanied American nuclear diplomacy. The danger is that if both sides play at the same tactics, issues and threats become magnified. The only full threat of bilateral nuclear confrontation—the Cuban crisis—was defused only when the Soviet Union agreed to remove its offensive missiles as a *quid pro quo* condition for an American pledge not to sponsor further invasions like that at the Bay of Pigs in 1961.

Fortunately, that crisis and all others between nuclear powers have been resolved short of the type of runaway commitment envisaged by Kahn in his image of the Doomsday Machine. This device would run on computers that could not be drawn off the course of total destruction if an adversary were to undertake any of certain selected policies; it would be capable of universal destruction. Presumably, it would be a totally credible deterrent, because it would be irreversible and would be able to compute events without human interference.

Counterforce Strategic Postures

Some strategists have argued that deterrence may operate even during a nuclear exchange. Both sides have assets of greater and lesser value, and there may be a mutual interest or a tacit understanding to limit targetting in order to minimize the loss of human life. Former U.S. Secretary of Defense Robert S. McNamara suggested in 1962 that American planners seek not only avoidance of nuclear war, but also its limitation through a *counterforce* strategy. This calls for the targeting of delivery vehicles on the *forces* of the adversary, rather than on his population, and for destruction of weapons rather than people. While we ought to maintain a strike force targetted to cities and population centers to deter attack upon our own civilian population, we should positively avoid striking cities. In this way, a level of deterrence could still operate even within a nuclear war.

Proponents of the counterforce strategy argue that any nuclear attacker realizes that his advantage comes not in killing people, but in debilitating the adversary's forces. This is an especially acute consideration in warfare which will have a duration of only hours, in which no government would be able to utilize its population for manufacturing or any other purpose.[8]

But a counterforce strategy implies the ability to destroy missiles in silos, submarines in their hidden sanctuaries, and long-range bombers on the ground or in the air. If this can be done against most or all of the enemy force, then the state with such a capability will also have achieved a preemptive first-strike potential, whether or not this capabiliy is intended. Therefore, opponents of counterforce argue, the McNamara strategy, reaffirmed by a later Secretary of Defense (James Schlesinger), is a threat to the concept of stable mutual deterrence basd in secure second-strike capabilities.

In an age of nuclear weapons, do the relative strengths of the United States and the Soviet Union in the number of missiles, bombers, and atomic warheads make any difference? Each of the superpowers has an arsenal equivalent to several tons of TNT for every living human soul. Henry Kissinger offered in 1974 the hypothesis that "when two nations are already capable of destroying each other, an upper limit exists beyond which additional weapons lose their political significance." Speaking in Moscow, he professed not to know what strategic superiority is, nor to understand its significance, nor to be able to imagine what to do with it (Press conference, July 3, 1974). Winston Churchill put it more succinctly: after a certain point, more bombs will only make the rubble bounce.

But in practice, statesmen and strategists take a different view, and regard any change in the quantitative or qualitative balance of nuclear forces as a matter for the closest scrutiny. Does a new deployment signal a change of intentions by the other side? Is there a technological breakthrough that will confer an advantage to the adversary and upset the basis of the existing balance? Is he achieving a first-strike option, or gaining a local superiority in a particular region or theatre? What political and strategic opportunities does he have under the new balance of forces, and how will our own policy alternatives be constrained? The major governments operate under the assumption that to ignore the strategic nuclear balance which underlies the panoply of relationships in the modern world system would entail great peril.

How, then, does the Soviet-American quantitative balance stand? The

[8] See, for example, Kahn, *Thinking About the Unthinkable*, p. 66, and *On Thermonuclear War*, p. 115.

"As nearly as we can translate, it says: 'We are agreed in principle on preventing the spread of nuclear weapons; however . . .' "

From *The Herblock Gallery* (Simon and Schuster, 1968).

Soviet Union is ahead in the number of missiles (2400 to 1700); the average size or "throw weight" of each missile; and the average size of the warhead measured in TNT equivalent. The total megatonnage on Soviet ICBM's and submarine launched missiles was equivalent to about 8,500 million tons of TNT in 1975, compared to less than 1,500 for the United States. Moreover, the Soviet lead on these dimensions is growing, adding to the appearance of superiority.

But on other dimensions, the superiority of the United States is evident. The Pentagon is ahead in the deployment of multiple submissile warheads (known as multiple independently targetted re-entry vehicles—MIRV's) on its strategic missiles. At the end of 1975, the U.S. could deliver up to 8,000 separate warheads, compared to less than 2,500 for the USSR. (Figure 9–1 demonstrates the developmental trend.) Moreover, the American delivery systems achieve much lower CEP's—greater accuracy—and are regarded as vastly superior against such "hard point" targets as missile silos. While the Soviet Union is believed to be capable of closing the MIRV gap in a relatively short time, the accuracy gap is expected to remain an American qualitative advantage for some years. The United States is closer to a first-strike capability, and indeed former Secretary of Defense Schlesinger announced in 1974 the United States' intention to acquire a missile force capable of destroying enemy ICBM's in their reinforced silos.

Very generally, it is said that the Soviet Union has the numbers, while the American systems are superior in performance. But there is a rather fierce debate among Western strategists regarding the acceptability of this

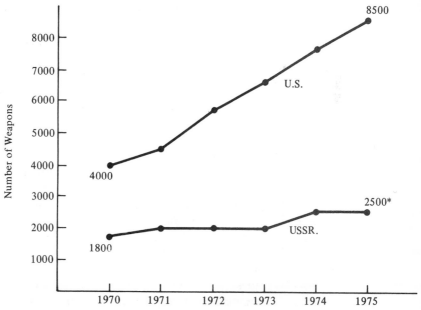

*Defense Secretary Rumsfeld projected in January 1976 that in mid-1976 the U.S. would have 8900 and the U.S.S.R. 3500. The actual mid-1976 Soviet number will probably be less than 3500.

FIGURE 9–1   U.S. and USSR Strategic Nuclear Weapons: The Trend

Source: Based on Defense Department data as collected and prepared in *The Defense Monitor,* May 1976, p. 6, by The Center for Defense Information, Washington, D.C.

state of affairs. The Soviet strategic missile inventory was only one-third the U.S. number in 1967; by 1975 it had forged ahead to a ratio of four to three. Moreover, larger missiles can carry more warheads, so when fully MIRVed, the Soviet advantage in re-entry vehicles will be still greater. Nor can the West rely on the qualitative lead in accuracy when the Soviet Union is outspending the United States on research and development. Secretary Schlesinger warned in 1973 that, "If they marry the technologies that they are now acquiring to the throw weight that they possess . . . they could develop a clear preponderance. . . ."

At the same time, the Soviet Navy has undergone a revolutionary expansion in the past decade, and now operates regularly in the Mediterranean and the Indian Ocean and at far greater reach in the Atlantic and Pacific and in the Norwegian Sea. Soviet tank production exceeds that of the U.S. by four to one, in field, medium, and heavy guns, mortars, and rocket launchers, and has an overall artillery advantage of 5,600 to 2,700. Indeed, on almost every quantitative dimension of comparison, the Communist states are far ahead of NATO in the Northern and Central European theatre.

Qualitative elements such as geographical advantage, different performance characteristics of equipment, deployment, logistics, reliability of allies, morale, training, and differences in doctrine and philosophy would have to be factored into a thorough analysis. Some of these elements favor the West. For example, the superior striking power of NATO aircraft typifies some advantages of Western equipment. Another advantage favoring NATO is much greater depth in logistical support. But other qualitative factors—including the lack of territorial depth in the NATO central sector and the failure to standardize Western equipment for "interoperability"—favor the Pact.

Overall, the Western side has had some success in emphasizing quality of equipment to offset quantity. Yet, the conventional forces of NATO in Central and Northern Europe are inferior to those of the Communist bloc. This is widely recognized in the West, though there is some confidence that the *costs* of war have been made so dear that even victory would be unacceptably costly to an aggressor. Moreover, the conventional military balance must be related to the possible use of tactical atomic weapons and to the risks of escalation to strategic nuclear war.

Tactical nuclear weapons are designed for use against targets within the battlefield area or directly connected with the maneuver of combatant forces, as distinguished from *strategic* nuclear weapons designed against targets within the interior of the enemy's homeland. Ordinarily, the distinction also connotes several orders of magnitude difference in yield. Strategic weapons produce the very large effects identified in the popular imagination with nuclear warfare, while tactical weapons have yields akin to the explosive power of the largest conventional weapons.

NATO has some 7,000 tactical nuclear warheads, compared to about

3,500 for the Communist bloc. In the event that an attack by the Warsaw Pact could not be repelled by the conventional forces of NATO, a controlled escalation to tactical nuclear weapons is a strategic option for the West. This threat is believed to create an overall balance that will make military aggression appear quite unattractive.

The use of small nuclear weapons within a given theatre would also present incalculable risks of escalation to global nuclear war. Once the psychological step has been taken of moving from the upper end of the conventional range of choices to the lower end of the nuclear range, the combatants are on a new escalation ladder. The gradations between steps on the nuclear ladder are fine, and there is no clear and highly visible threshold between the "tactical" end of the ladder and the "strategic." Thus, the tendency to escalate might be irresistible once tactical weapons were employed. An aggressor's computation of military advantages would have to relate the conventional balance to the possibility of tactical atomic war, and the latter to the danger of escalation to total war. It is reasonable to conclude from this analysis that the defenses of Western Europe are formidable, even if the comparison of tanks and combat aircraft appears to favor the Warsaw Pact states.

There is considerable disagreement within the Atlantic alliance on how much emphasis to place on each of the three components of NATO strategy. The United States favors a posture of flexible response, and seeks a balance at the conventional level that will minimize the likelihood of escalation to tactical or strategic nuclear war. However, conventional formations are extremely expensive to maintain, and domestic political constraints within many of the NATO states make the establishment of standing armies on a scale comparable to the Communist states quite difficult or impossible in peacetime. Indeed, public and congressional opinion within the United States appear to be moving toward a substantial reduction of U.S. forces still stationed in Western Europe thirty years after the end of the world war. At the same time, some of the European states are wearying of the burden, and are tempted to rely more heavily on strategic deterrence based on U.S. and European nuclear forces. There is a periodic cycle of pressures and counterpressures as the various NATO partners attempt to redistribute the burdens of the alliance to reduce their own costs while calling upon others to contribute more to the pool of conventional forces.

The tactical option has some advocates, particularly in the United States, as a form of deployment with lower operating and maintenance costs: defense on the cheap. But some European states on whose territories the weapons would be used are understandably less enthusiastic about this option. Thus, there is pressure on the United States to commit itself to emphasis on strategic deterrence directly against the Soviet Union, rather than on large scale conventional or tactical nuclear warfare on the territory of the European allies. Conversely, the United States seeks to minimize reliance on strategic nuclear weapons, and pressures its NATO partners to spend more on conventional defense to create a regional military balance that will deter aggression.

The Spread of Nuclear Weapons

This constant tug of war between the United States and its NATO allies has convinced some Europeans that the time may come when the American security guarantee will become conditional, and that in any case European defense should be in European hands. This has led, in turn, to demands for an independent continental strategic deterrent, or for independent national strike forces. Britain and France have long since gone nuclear, each using a combination of arguments in justification: self-reliance, uncertainty of American commitment, technological pride, retention of great power status, and needs of their own foreign policies (such as British problems in the Middle East and French difficulties in North Africa and Southeast Asia). By the time France formally entered the club (1960), most of its foreign commitments had abated. France's justification was built upon Gaullist distrust of the American umbrella and the power gained by Washington through control of NATO's deterrent. Hence the French set out through their *force de frappe* (nuclear strike force) to present their own finite deterrent. French strategists conceded that they could not match the might of the Soviet Union alone, but they reasoned that they could make the costs of war prohibitive to any potential aggressor. Retaliation need not equal the damage done by a Soviet first strike so long as the Kremlin recognized French ability to inflict unacceptable losses. France's decision to bear the cost of atomic research and development was thus dictated more by political motives than by military necessity.

Nuclear spread did not stop with Europe, and China became the fifth member of the nuclear club in 1964. China's motives were much the same as those of the Europeans: lack of access to a superpower ally, prestige, self-reliance, technological machismo, the pursuit of a world role, and so on. But the urgency of atomic development was probably much greater in the Chinese case. The People's Republic is the only state known to have been threatened explicitly with nuclear attack in the postwar era—specifically by the United States during the Korean War. Moreover, the reliability of China's superpower ally has appeared increasingly to be not merely conditional, but possibly nonexistent. Indeed, many observers believe that the Soviet Union is now more directly threatening to China than the United States, and that China's deterrent is oriented more to defense against Soviet attack than to fears of the Western threat.

At least two other states are widely believed to possess nuclear explosives suitable to military use: India and Israel. India tested a device in

1974 that it insistently described as a "peaceful nuclear explosive" to be used for massive civilian projects. But the distinction between a peaceful explosive and a warlike one depends only on where the owner chooses to detonate, and not on any innate difference in the devices themselves. Thus, India is regarded as the sixth member of the nuclear club.

Israel has repeatedly denied possessing atomic weapons, and has pledged that it will not be the first to introduce them in the Middle East (though the Israeli foreign minister has also said that "We will not be the second either.") But Israel's Arab neighbors and many other careful observers have arrived at the conclusion that it already has a nuclear arsenal. Israel has the capability to go nuclear; it lives under a constant state of seige; and the temptation might well be irresistible for a Jewish government, with a living memory of the results of defenselessness during the Hitler era, to buy a "last resort" deterrent in the event that conventional defense fails. Egypt has now declared its intention to give a high priority to the advancement of nuclear science and industry, and other Arab states, including Libya, are known to be seeking a military nuclear capability.

Nor does the list of potential atomic powers stop here. At least twenty-five additional states have the technological base and the economic capability to develop atomic weapons and in some cases to deploy fairly large-size forces. Notable in this list for the sensitivity of their international positions are East and West Germany, Japan, South Africa, South Korea, Taiwan, and several East European allies of the USSR. Examples of states in less sensitive positions include Argentina, Brazil, Mexico, Australia, Canada, and virtually all the West European states.

The decision in each case whether to go nuclear will depend on strategic, economic, and political issues too complex to detail for all twenty-five states. But a few cases are worthy of mention. Pakistan will have a fairly strong incentive to act now that its traditional adversary, India, has a rudimentary nuclear capability. Taiwan may be tempted to develop a self-reliant defense against China if it fears that the security umbrella provided by the United States until now may no longer be reliable as the U.S. improves its relations with the mainland. Similarly, South Korea may feel itself unable to continue relying upon the American guarantee, and even Japan, restrained in the past by a deep aversion to atomic weapons, may change its view. Other states with less compelling security needs could be tempted by the advantages of prestige, influence, and self-reliance that are believed to attach to nuclear status. Iran is embarked on a civilian nuclear development program of breathtaking proportions, and it will be only a small step from this to atomic weapons if Iran decides to add these to its energetic military procurements.

If so many states have the option, one may safely predict that at least a few will go nuclear. What will be the effects on regional and global stability, especially as atomic weapons are introduced in high tension areas? Will it be possible to reproduce the mechanisms of the delicate balance of terror in regional minibalances between hostile neighbors such as Egypt and Israel, India and Pakistan, North and South Korea, and China and Taiwan? If so, then proliferation may contribute to regional stabilization—*if* these governments can adapt themselves to the model of rational planning, caution, and ideological moderation that are appropriate to the atomic age. Also, will it be possible to reproduce in inexpensive and relatively primitive nuclear systems the technological conditions for secure, second-strike forces? Distances are shorter in regional conflicts, which means less warning time, greater accuracy, and increased opportunities for surprise attack. There will be many technical problems in hardening a second-strike force to absorb the impact of a first-strike and to survive for retaliation. If second-strike security cannot be attained, then regional systems will be on hair-trigger alert, producing temptations to preempt and incalculable dangers of uncontrolled crisis escalation.

Most scholars and statesmen prefer a world in which the management of nuclear power is kept in as few hands as possible. Controlling the spread of nuclear weapons has been an agreed goal of most of the leading powers. Efforts to stem proliferation of these weapons reached their height in the Non-Proliferation Treaty (NPT), which entered into force in 1970. In this treaty, the nuclear members pledge not to transfer to nonnuclear states any form of nuclear explosive, and not to assist in its development. Likewise, the nonnuclear members agree not to accept such weapons or assistance. But like virtually all treaties, signature is wholly voluntary, and compliance with the terms is left to self-restraint. Furthermore, Article X provides that any state may withdraw from the treaty's obligations upon three-month notification by merely informing the other parties and the United Nations Security Council. The notification must be accompanied by a statement of the "extraordinary events it regards as having jeopardized its supreme interests."

Although ninety-six governments had ratified the NPT by mid-1976, it does not enjoy universal popularity. Nonnuclear states have often objected that the treaty is a luxury of the nuclear states, designed to freeze the international distribution for maintenance of special superpower privileges. Others have been reluctant to enter into the treaty without guarantees of deterrence assistance from one or another of the nuclear powers. We have already seen that such guarantees are without practical benefit, since the level of commitment embodied in them leaves much slack in credibility.[9]

The nonnuclear states have not been alone in their objections. Among those who enjoy nuclear status, both China and France have vigorously opposed membership in the NPT. Each argues that it is a Soviet-American device to subordinate others, and to profit from their unique ability to offer and withdraw the nuclear umbrella. France especially insists that the

---

[9] Joseph I. Coffey, "Nuclear Guarantees and Nonproliferation," *International Organization* 25 (1971): 836–44.

possession of even minimal nuclear capability is a political and strategic equalizer.[10] China adds the view that nuclear status promotes the decay of imperialism, and is therefore a progressive international trend. The opponents of the NPT are not necessarily reckless strategists, since their arguments are intended not to destabilize the international system, but to challenge the political superiority of a few nuclear states. While the United States pledges its aid against "nuclear blackmail," France, China, and India refuse in turn to be "blackmailed" by the United States and the Soviet Union.

The NPT is a fragile concensus. It excludes three nuclear states and most states within reach of combat nuclear capacity. But the threat of the destabilization implicit in nuclear proliferation is scarcely historical. If escalation and proliferation are the two characteristics of the arms race which are most to be feared, let us now explore some of the other liabilities.

Other Hazards of the Nuclear Arms Race

Popular literature has, throughout the nuclear era, given much attention to the possibility of *unintended* nuclear war ignited by accident, human error, nervous impulse, or unauthorized behavior. Occasionally, these horrors have been brought to life by close scrapes with nuclear disaster, or of perceived disaster. On some occasions errant signals have indicated the possibility of incoming missiles over the North Pole to the United States. Soviet behavior in Germany, especially in the Berlin air corridors, has sometimes raised fears of nuclear war out of sheer nervousness. The alternative of "surgical strikes" on Soviet missile encampments in Cuba in 1962 might have brought Soviet nuclear response. And the use of tactical weapons, and even low-yield strategic nuclear weapons, has been advocated by the American political right in both the Korean and Vietnam wars.

A vivid example of the possibility of accidental nuclear warfare occurred when a nuclear-bomb-laden American stratofortress crashed off the Spanish coast in the mid-1960's. Though its cargo did not detonate, two bombs were temporarily lost, one on land and one in shallow waters. With nuclear bombs in the air at all times, and with knowledge that reconnaissance craft have been shot down in the Pacific and the Caribbean, do such incidents suggest that misunderstandings and coincidental happenings in international crises could touch off holocaust?

American strategists are convinced that the risk of Soviet-American nuclear war through *technical* accident is negligible. The risk may be in-

[10] Raymond Aron, "The Spread of Nuclear Weapons," *Atlantic Monthly*, January 1965.

creased, however, by proliferation of "cheap" thermonuclear systems in the hands of states with inferior scientific development whose economies force dangerous shortcuts in safeguard systems. While the giants invest heavily in careful electronic and mechanical shielding devices that make unintended detonation quite unlikely, similar protective devices may be either technically or economically beyond the reach of smaller states. It is believed that the bombs of the big powers are less accident-prone than those of small future atomic powers might be.

American strategists are also confident that an accidental detonation would be unlikely to ignite a world conflagration. The superpowers depend upon careful systems of bureaucratic checks and controls designed in part for exactly such a contingency. The maintenance of secure second-strike capabilities permits methodical inquiry rather than impulsive reaction. Here again, smaller powers, lacking protected capabilities and intricate verification devices, might be forced to react more hastily. Even the Soviet-American "Hotline," instituted after the Cuban missile crisis, is available for the respective heads of government to communicate their intentions during conflict. The hope was that accident might not be taken as open hostility, and that a single firing might not burgeon into global destruction.

Despite human faith in science, strategists continue to acknowledge the tiny possibility of accidental nuclear launchings. For that reason Moscow and Washington have joined in an Agreement on Measures to Reduce the Risk of Outbreak of Nuclear War between them. Effective in 1971, this bilateral treaty calls upon the parties "to notify each other immediately in the event of an accidental, unauthorized or any other unexplained incident involving a possible detonation of a nuclear weapon which could create a risk of outbreak of nuclear war." They agree in such cases to take measures to render the weapons harmless. They also pledge to communicate with one another upon sighting unidentified incoming vehicles, and to notify one another in advance of missile tests which will extend beyond home territory in the direction of the other. To ease such communications, they entered into executive agreement to update the Hotline by adding communications links through two or more telecommunications satellites.

Another popular fear is the *Dr. Strangelove* concept, or the idea of a perverse individual who, for reasons known only to himself, uses military position to make an unauthorized attack on the enemy. Even the most careful psychological testing and training cannot, of course, guarantee that an anti-Communist paranoiac on the American side or an overzealous Soviet anti-imperialist cannot somehow gain access to the buttons and take matters into his own hands. As a safeguard against this remote possibility, the superpowers have installed elaborate *multiple control* systems, which require the coordinated acts of two or more persons at separate centers of decision to unshield nuclear weapons. No one knows who operates the other button to the same weapon. In this way, unauthorized use of weapons of mass destruction would require a conspiracy of people who do not know one another's identities. Short of all-out conspiracy achievable probably only through *coup* of the entire armed forces, the two-key system prevents unauthorized firings.

Still another danger is that of *catalytic war*, or unwanted war between superpowers provoked by a calculating third party. This concept arose in popular literature in the early days of the atomic race, especially from the book (and later movie) *On the Beach*, in which a nervous third party prompted nuclear war between two superpowers. In the days of American massive retaliation policy, many Americans feared that a nervous European decision-maker might deliberately provoke war with the Soviet Union and force the United States to demonstrate the credibility of its defense doctrine. All in all, however, the vast increase in destructive potential makes it unlikely that any third party would provoke a war from which no nation could escape entirely.

These dangers of accidental, catalytic war, as well as war through psychological derangement, do not unsettle most nuclear strategists. They continue to contend that if the structural relationship between the nuclear adversaries is based on secure second-strike deterrence, the stable foundations of nuclear diplomacy can withstand most extraneous shocks.[11] Their principal concern is that unilateral technological achievement might threaten the stable balance, returning advantage to the offense and inviting first strike. If this should occur, then the nuclear race and its attending psychological factors return to a hair-trigger status.

Chemical and Biological Warfare

Beyond nuclear weapons, missiles, infantry and artillery, arms designers have created a variety of weapons less well known but equally horrifying. One of these is *chemical warfare*, which consists of several methods of using chemical agents to poison, burn, blind, expose, and otherwise incapacitate enemy troops.

Chemical warfare has a long, and often colorful, history. First known use was by Solon of Athens, who defeated the army of Kirrha in 600 B.C. by throwing bundles of hellibore roots into the enemy's water supply. While the enemy attempted to contend with the resulting diarrhea, Athenian troops marched in for the conquest. Other ancient uses involved leaving poisoned wine in evacuated camps, tossing venomous snakes into

---

[11] See, for example, Herman Kahn, "The Arms Race and Some of Its Hazards," in Richard A. Falk and Saul Mendlovitz, eds., *Toward A Theory of War Prevention*, vol. I in the series *Strategy of World Order* (New York: The World Law Fund, 1966).

enemy ships, and the use of poison for arrows and wells. Fire was used by Sparta as early as 429 B.C. in a mixture of pitch and sulphur used to ignite enemy cities. "Greekfire," first used in 350 A.D., acted as a primitive flame-thrower by spurting burning liquid from a siphon. Smoke has been used since early times to seclude troop movements and naval maneuvers.

Chemicals have played a role in twentieth century wars, too. Tear gas grenades were introduced by France during World War I, and Germany responded by the full-scale use of lethal chlorine gas (contemplated, but not used, by Union troops during the American Civil War). The United States fielded a Gas Regiment in World War I, which launched as many as 2000 cannisters in a single battle. In 1936 mustard gas was dropped from Italian planes onto Abyssinian troops in the conquest of Ethiopia, causing incapacitating burns to bare feet. Only a year later, Japan used toxic gases against Chinese troops. During World War II, in the battle against Japan, the United States advanced modern incendiary warfare with *napalm*—a soap-thickened petroleum, capable of igniting human torches which cannot be extinguished. In the Vietnam War, American troops experimented with induced forest firestorms using the same principle.

Though toxic gases were not used during World War II, German researchers happened upon discovery of the deadly "nerve gases," which cause paralysis of the motor nervous system. Through captured documents, the United States acquired the secret of *sarin*, while the Soviets seized a *tabun* plant. Either of these gases is lethal to a full-size man even if only a drop penetrates his skin. Contact causes instant nausea, vomiting, diarrhea, convulsions, respiratory paralysis, and death in a few moments. These agents are most effective in local warfare for population attrition. Like other gases, their battlefield use is limited by the liabilities of wind-shift and self-affliction.

A new category of chemical methods is called the "incapacitating agents," designed to cause *temporary* paralysis, blindness, dizziness, and narcosis. They are not lethal. The *psychochemicals* are a special category which have incapacitating *mental* effects such as paranoia, confusion, delirium, hallucinations, disorientation, giddiness, or maniacal behavior. These can seriously alter an army's fighting capacity, its will, its speed of movement, its reaction time, and other variables of ground warfare. General William M. Creasy, former chief chemical officer of the U.S. Army, suggests that the future of warfare may lie in the psychochemicals.

The actual future of chemical agents for combat purposes is still under debate. While there is strong sentiment for their categorical elimination, there are others who consider incapacitation preferable to slaughter. Proponents of their prohibition insist that the greatest danger is from the thought-controlling potentiality of the psychochemicals, opening new and incalculable opportunities for tyranny. But fire, incapacitating agents, and defoliants have become so important to modern land armies that they are unlikely to be given up, especially when, with nuclear arms limitations, conventional arms are being restored to first priority. The flexibility, mobility, and visibility of flame, defoliants and "incaps" are likely to give them the stature of machine guns, especially in guerrilla and counter-guerrilla warfare. They are not apt to vanish from the conventional arsenals of major powers.[12]

Biological warfare has horrors of its own. Often called *germ warfare*, it utilizes infectious agents. It is the deliberate inducement of disease, either by spreading bacteria or viral microbes, or by using their organic toxins. Though efforts have been undertaken sporadically since 1925 to outlaw these methods, not until 1972 was a multilateral treaty signed by states to that effect. Again, however, compliance is left to self-restraint and the possibility of requesting investigation by the UN Security Council of alleged violations. Moreover, the Convention on the Prohibition of the Development, Production and Stockpiling of Bacteriological (Bacterial) and Toxin Weapons and Their Destruction, permits any state to withdraw from its obligations by three-month notification accompanied by a statement of the jeopardy to national interests which motivates the withdrawal. The same treaty defers chemical elimination to a future "objective," and stipulates only that outlawing biological weapons may also be a step toward prohibition of chemical weapons. At present the United States is destroying much of its chemical and biological arsenal, while troops of the Warsaw Pact are being equipped to fight in a poisoned environment. Their training and exercises include simulation of such an environment.

Other Developments

The focus upon developments in the nuclear field ought not to obscure other parallel advances in the conventional arsenals. The Vietnam War, like all others, has improved human ability to destroy. The United States, for example, applied electronic science to conventional war, especially for automated air warfare. Other innovations included weather modification to disrupt movement of enemy troops and goods, and "smart bombs," which are able to seek out specific targets and aim themselves by reciprocating signals. Fragmentation bombs were used to inject painful fishhooks into the skin so as to demoralize troops and strain the enemy's medical

[12] United States Senate, Subcommittee on Disarmament, *CBR Warfare* (Washington, 1960); *Chemical Warfare of Special Significance to Civil Defense*, Civil Defense Technical Bulletin, TB-11-28; J. Leiberman, "Psychochemicals as Weapons," *Bulletin of the Atomic Scientists*, January 1962; "Biological and Chemical Warfare: An International Symposium," *Bulletin of the Atomic Scientists*, January 1960; Marcel Fetizon and Michel Magat, "The Toxic Arsenal," in Nigel Howard, ed., *Unless Peace Comes* (New York: Viking, 1968).

facilities. Bomb targeting devices were developed that detected humans in the dark of night, thus depriving the North Vietnamese of the cover of darkness and the fighting lull of wartime nights.

The prospects for future arms seem limitless. Nuclear weapons may be miniaturized for movement by saboteurs as plastic bombs are now used. Robot tanks will have multiple tactical uses, as will "kamikaze" bombers on "suicide" missions. Some writers envisage the use of anthropomorphic robots on the ground within this century to replace shock troops, and possibly even two-sided robot warfare. The robot may be the soldier of the future.

In addition, greater efforts at weather modification may have a role in future tactical warfare, both to slow the enemy through natural disaster and bad visibility, and to facilitate one's own tactics by clearing techniques. Growing seismological understanding suggests that eventually it will also be possible to induce earthquakes in some regions.

Underwater and outer space zones will become more important. Undersea operations are ideal because the physical properties of salt water impede the passage of detection impulses. If downward-pointing anti-aircraft devices are circulated in space, the role of supra-atmospheric space may increase. Control of interplanetary space may determine control of airspace, even national airspace. Despite the fact that the United States and the Soviet Union have entered into treaties prohibiting the orbiting of nuclear devices in space (1967) and the placement of such weapons in or on the ocean floor beyond a twelve-mile national limit (1972), the military importance of both sea and space is steadily increasing, and is likely to continue to do so.[13]

War, Peace, and the Arms Race

Thermonuclear war, deterrence, brinkmanship, ABM, MIRV, tactical nuclear weapons, committal strategy, counterforce, nuclear proliferation, finite deterrence, accidental war, catalytic war, incendiary weapons, nerve gas, incapacitating agents, psychochemicals, robot warfare—to many people, all this sounds like Dr. Strangelove's inventory of madness. To the ordinary person, these preparations add up to *less* security rather than more. What chance of peace is there when every nation of the world is armed to the teeth, when a dozen different arms races of differing proportions are conducted simultaneously, when the best of science is turned to killing? Many people share Kant's view in *Perpetual Peace* that standing armies and arms races are inextricably linked to war, and that high levels of armament *guarantee* war rather than ensure against it.

But to statesmen, nuclear strategists, and students of war this belief

[13] For a scientific forecast of future weapons, see Nigel Howard, ed. *Unless Peace Comes.*

that men fight because they have arms reverses history. Nations arm because they have conflicts with other states: it is these conflicts over mutually exclusive goals that cause war, not the maintenance of arms. The cold war caused the arms race, since the incompatibility of potential objectives of the United States and the Soviet Union requires military preparedness. Only stable competition in arms prevents existing conflicts from erupting into war.

This conclusion does not, however, deny the wastefulness of arms races as measured both in economic cost and in nonproductive absorption of resources. National strength is a nearly universal valve, easily sold to frightened populations. In addition, professional military elites want the most modern equipment available, in some cases, if only for personal or service aggrandizement. As a result, a generous share of national resources is given by most countries to national defense, ranging from a low of less than 1 percent in Iceland, to a high of over 20 percent of gross national product in Israel, Egypt, and North Korea. These figures exclude many costs such as veterans' benefits and pensions. All told, the world devotes over 7 percent of total annual production to military expenditures.

Contrasted with critical social indicators, these amounts loom even larger. While most of the Southern hemisphere seeks to modernize, and while most of the industrialized world searches for remedies to problems created by technology, the world's governments go on spending billions of dollars per year more on military expenditures then upon such things as public health, foreign economic assistance, and international peacekeeping. In 1974, world expenditures on education exceeded the cost of the arms race by a slight margin, but for only the first time. Figure 9–2 shows the comparison for 1974.

To be sure, the bulk of this is expended by a few states: the United States, the Soviet Union, Britain, France, West Germany, Israel, Egypt, Italy, East Germany, Poland, Czechoslovakia, and China. But it is not merely the total number of dollars which is striking; for in addition, it is revealing that as a fraction of total wealth produced, *every* region of the world invests more on military preparedness than in public health, and only in Latin America and Africa is more spent on public education than on the military. The conclusion is startling, but hardly new: while the world goes on spending some 300 billion dollars per year on its war-making potential (or war-preventing potential), basic needs such as nutrition, shelter, clothing, health care, and educational development go unmet in many places, including parts of the world's most developed economies. Armaments comprise the world's biggest business.

The human cost of this proliferation of arms is staggering. A single modern jet fighter, such as the F-14, costs as much as a community hospital. A single second-generation nuclear submarine (ULMS) costs the equivalent of 500 schools. One modern nuclear-powered aircraft carrier equals four years' budget of the United Nations! American ABMs, if de-

In 1974 only education, by a narrow margin, took more public revenue than arms programs. Public spending for the health care of 4 billion people was 60 percent of military spending. World economic aid was under 6 percent, international peacekeeping outlays far less than 1 percent of military expenditures.

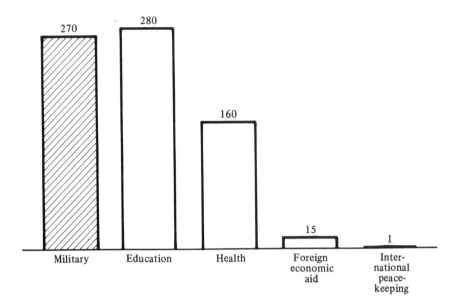

FIGURE 9–2   World Public Expenditures, 1974 billion dollars

Source: World Military and Social Expenditures, 1976, copyright © by Ruth Leger Sivard (Leesburg, Virginia: WMSE Publications, 1976), p. 12. Published by the Institute for World Order.

ployed in the numbers originally planned, would equal the cost of 2½ million small houses. These costs are increasingly unacceptable in industrialized economies with constant growth in public revenue; but they are wholly unbearable in the poor countries which, ironically, are now increasing their military budgets the most rapidly.[14]

Arms Control and Disarmament

Should arms races be controlled? If so, how? The answers to these questions may be critical to the human future. With respect to the nuclear race, have we reached the point of diminishing returns? At this point, each new increment of power is not only vastly more expensive than its

[14] Data on military expenditures are compiled in the Center for International Programs and Comparative Studies, State University of New York at Albany, *Data on the Human Crisis* (Albany, 1972), and in the Center for Integrative Studies, School of Advanced Technology, State University of New York at Binghamton, *World Facts and Trends* (Binghamton, 1971).

predecessor, but buys relatively less security than previous developments. If so, what is the sense of undergoing the expense and the potential destabilization generated by further enlargement of nuclear stockpiles and development of more sophisticated vehicles? Does the respectability of membership in the nuclear club portend proliferation despite treaties to the contrary? Does the temptation among nonnuclear powers to enter into the club because of lingering regional disputes (for example, the Middle East) raise the prospect of future nuclear blackmail and, with it, increased regional instability? In short, does the continuation of arms races, and the modern strategic arms race in particular, absorb more human and material resources than is now justified? Do arms contests prevent or delay peaceful transformation of the international system?

There is scarcely a student of public affairs who does not fault the logic of arms races on one or more of these bases. For those who find such competition important enough to exceed even treatment of social problems, the fear of nuclear proliferation is a major concern. Others lament the massive expenditures for small incremental gains in security which postpone correction of social inequities. Still others fear that the price of nonproliferation may be increased nuclear protection of many states by a few states; and to ensure credibility of these defenses, there may be a greater impetus to brinkmanship. To reduce arms, a particular party must first build more in order to have negotiating advantages, though this increase itself may delay political agreement until the other party catches up, thus sparking yet another turn in the upward spiral. However, regardless of what position one may take on the value of arms and their costs relative to other needs, arms control and disarmament is on everyone's mind save, perhaps, a few unthinking profiteers.

The expressions *arms control* and *disarmament* are so habitually linked (as in the title of the U.S. Arms Control and Disarmament Agency) that the distinctions between them have been obscured. *Disarmament* connotes abolition of arms. This is distinguished from *arms limitation* which implies reduction of arms. *Arms control*, as contrasted with both, may be interpreted either narrowly or broadly. In the narrower sense, arms control refers to "restraint internationally exercised upon armaments policy, whether in respect to the level of armaments, their character, deployment or use." [15] Viewed in broader perspective, arms control may be understood to reach all the way down to social values and economic allocation, as reflected in propaganda and political campaigning upon the need for arms, and the common warning of economic disaster if the nation were to depart from its industrial "war footing."

A few examples may illuminate these distinctions. *Disarmament*, as distinct from arms limitation, is difficult to illustrate, since governments

---

[15] Hedley Bull, *Control of the Arms Race*, 2nd ed. (New York: Praeger, 1965), p. vii.

have not agreed to eliminate their arsenals. In postwar situations, vanquished nations have been disarmed as a requirement of surrender. Germany was "permanently" disarmed after World War I, and the intention was to limit German industrial potential so that it might not again become a threat to world peace. Again in 1945, both Germany and Japan were disarmed. In both cases, however, the act was a consequence of coercion, and was not arranged mutually through the normal bargaining procedure. Since World War II, there have been occasional exchanges of suggestions for "complete and general disarmament" (CGD), but the complex hostilities of the era have prevented these suggestions from advancing beyond propaganda stages.

Arms control in its broad sense is more easily exemplified in political debate than in diplomatic arrangements. The American presidential election of 1972 provided an excellent opportunity to view clashes in social values as they are reflected in the arms race. President Nixon advocated *increased* arms strength despite both the strictures of the SALT agreements and the demand for reordered priorities. Senator George McGovern, on the other hand, proposed significant unilateral arms *reductions* on the grounds that (1) existing stockpiles are unnecessarily large, (2) excesses of armaments threaten international stability, and (3) new generations of weapons defer treatment of social problems with minimal additional security. The temperature was raised by an economic issue: much of the so-called "middle-class unemployment," particularly among persons previously engaged in weapons development and the aerospace industry, was attributable to controls already decided upon. Appeals for rekindling the war-making aspects of the economy were welcomed by many. Ultimately, arms control in its full meaning concerns motivation, domestic politics, the externalization of individual perceptions, and the social and economic uses which are made of the war-preparing industries.

Arms control in its narrower sense of restraint on weapons policy is illustrated with relative ease, though this does not mean that arms control agreements have been abundant. The *Antarctic Treaty* (1959) controls the deployment of nuclear weapons to this barren region. Latin America has been a nuclear-free zone. (The Rapacki Plan of 1957, though never implemented, would have prohibited deployment of nuclear weapons in central Europe.) The *Hotline Agreement* tries to control impulsive armed reactions by facilitating communications which may prevent tragic and irretrievable miscalculations. The nuclear *Nonproliferation Treaty* lends control to the nuclear arms race by limiting the number of participants. And both the *Seabed Treaty* and that forbidding the stationing of nuclear weapons in interplanetary space prevent use of nonnational territory for nuclear deployment.

The SALT agreements of 1972 provide additional controls. In the Treaty on Anti-Ballistic Missile systems, the United States and the USSR pledged to restrict their ABM deployments to two sites each, one at the respective national capitals and the other one not less than 800 miles away. Only the latter may be placed in relation to ICBM silos so as to protect a second-strike encampment. At each of these sites, the number of interceptors, radar installations, and launchers is specifically restricted. By prescribing ceilings, the treaty contributes to controls. Its only arms reduction clause calls for dismantling of additional ABM sites already under construction.

An accompanying executive agreement (a formal commitment made by the president but not needing the approval of the Senate), called the Interim Agreement on Limitation of Offensive Arms, contains similar provisions. It is designed to control the upward spiral by placing ceilings upon ICBM deployments and on submarine-based missiles. The controls are entirely *quantitative*, pertaining only to numbers of weapons. There are no *qualitative* limitations: the agreement permits replacement and modernization. This agreement does not represent a victory for arms reduction, since no weapon has been dismantled, no nuclear submarine has been moth-balled, and no missile silo has been vacated.

Achievement of modest bilateral quantitative controls suggests that the nuclear arms race may take either of two subsequent turns: (1) qualitative controls or (2) *arms limitation* through actual reduction. In the conventional field, the United States and USSR began exploratory talks in 1972 toward eventual "mutual balanced reduction" of forces in Europe. Though the weapon and troop levels may be reduced, the *ratio* of strength will probably be preserved at current levels.

Proportional reduction of nuclear weapons is far more complex. The variety of weaponry, the distances over which warheads can be delivered, the inaccessibility of some weapons to detection and surveillance—these problems and more vastly complicate mutual reduction. To make matters worse, neither side is eager to enter into negotiations while substantially ahead. Thus parity seems to be the ideal negotiating posture, but it probably has never existed. The result has been to approach nuclear arms limitation item by item, or on the basis of direct trade-offs. It was formerly believed, for example, that the United States might decline to deploy ABMs if the Soviets would not proceed with MIRV. As timing and strategies dashed hopes for such an agreement, each party proceeded to deploy both ABMs and MIRVs. The SALT I agreements are the result.

It is apparent that arms control and arms limitation, while directed toward the same ends, operate from quite different vantage points. Arms *control* measures are designed either to freeze an existing situation or to anticipate future relative strengths and to prescribe ceilings. In contrast, arms *limitation* measures are designed to reduce existing levels toward disarmament.

Despite these differences, however, there are certain technical and substantive similarities between arms control and arms limitation which may be compared as follows:

Arms Limitation	*Arms Control*
1.	Preventive communication
2.	Weapons-free zones
3. Reduction ratio	Production ratio
4. Post-reduction ceiling	Future production ceiling
5. Arms production moratorium	Arms production moratorium
6. Qualitative reduction	Future qualitative limit
7. Quantitative reduction	Future quantitative limit
8. Disarmament	....

Since items (1) and (2) have previously been introduced, we may proceed directly to item (3).

Reduction ratio implies mutual dismantling of existing potential to a lower absolute level. *Production ratios* place limits on future construction and deployment without reducing existing material. Hence a SALT agreement which restricts deployment of additional missiles or which limits the number of ABM encampments is an arms control agreement. But an agreement such as the famous naval ratios of the Washington Treaty on the Limitation of Naval Armaments (1922), is an arms *reduction* agreement. These fixed ratios were achieved only after the parties dismantled portions of their existing navies, discontinued ship-building already in process, and scrapped plans for additional naval construction. It was agreed that after the initial reductions, a fixed ratio of 1:1 would be maintained between the U.S. and Britain, and that for each five units of naval power which these states had, Japan would have three and Italy and France would have one and three-quarters each. Hence the ratios were expressed as 5:5:3:1.75:1.75.

The same treaty illustrates *post-reduction ceilings*. Not only were the parties limited in naval power relative to one another; their absolute strength was also limited by treaty specification on numbers of certain classes of ships. Naval competition was thus regulated both absolutely (ceilings) and relatively (ratios). The arms control counterpart to post-reduction ceilings is production ceilings (also deployment ceilings), which restrict arms policy beyond the immediate condition. The SALT I agreements exemplify this condition.

The concept of *arms production moratorium*, or "holiday," is one which calls for the cessation of further research, development, testing and/or deployment for a specified time. Such agreements are rare. The League of Nations called for such a holiday in 1921, unsuccessfully. President Herbert Hoover hoped through the League of Nations' World Disarmament Conference of 1933 to achieve such a moratorium, but by the time the conference opened, Sino-Japanese fighting was widespread and World War II in Asia had begun. An informal Soviet-American testing moratorium did occur in 1959–60. When abruptly terminated by the Soviet

Union in 1961, it was followed by two years of unprecedented numbers of explosions by each of the parties. In 1961, the Soviet Union tested more devices than ever before in a single year, only to break that record the following year. For its part, in 1961 the United States detonated more nuclear devices than in any single year before or since.[16]

Qualitative reduction and *quantitative reduction* refer, respectively, to the reduction of quality and destructibility of weapons and to reduction of numbers of weapons. Any agreement that reduces the absolute number of weapons is an instrument of quantitative reduction, such as the first phase of the Washington Treaty of 1922. In contrast, a treaty that reduces the quality of military potential is an instrument of qualitative reduction. That same Washington Treaty contained such elements, prescribing reductions in the firepower potential carried by certain classes of ships. The text is replete with references to numbers of guns of specified caliber. The counterparts in arms control are agreements to restrict future numbers of weapons and future quality of weapons, by prescribing ceilings and by limiting replacement and modernization. While ceilings are not uncommon (for instance, SALT I), treaties of future qualitative limitation are rare, since governments are not able adequately to predict future weapons quality.

There is yet another aspect of arms control which we have not considered, namely, control not upon arms policy itself, but upon the use of force in international relations. In Article 2, paragraph 4, of the United Nations Charter, for example, the member states agree to "refrain in their international relations from the threat or use of force against the territorial integrity or political independence of any state, or in any other manner inconsistent with the purposes of the United Nations." Governments have sometimes circumvented this prohibition by arguing that the fundamental purpose of the UN is to maintain international peace, and that states are obligated to use their power through regional organizations ("selective security") to fulfill this purpose.

But by far the most elaborate plan for renouncing force as an instrument of national policy occurred in the General Pact for the Renunciation of War (the Kellogg-Briand Pact) in 1928. This was to supplement the League of Nations' encouragement of general disarmament. But the pact left to each state the sovereign prerogative of determining the needs and conditions of self-defense. Given the range of interpretations permitted by this privilege, and given the tendency to claim self-defense, the Kellogg-Briand Pact was doomed from the start.

Even though governments might enter into arms control or arms limita-

---

[16] For a comparative study of number and frequency of tests, see Martin L. Perl, "SALT and Its Illusions," *Bulletin of the Atomic Scientists*, December 1971, p. 7, with a revealing diagram on p. 12.

tion agreements in good faith, the need to *verify* compliance with such agreements is a paramount problem. If obligations are carried out by only one state, the other state's opportunity for blackmail is extreme. Generally this is thought of as a problem unique to the nuclear era, but it is not. Unilateral failure in conventional reduction might produce such instability as to tempt the stronger. There is considerable likelihood that the threat here is greater than in noncompliance with nuclear control or reduction agreements, since both the United States and the USSR have sufficient deterrent capability to tolerate even sizable imbalances in strategic potential. But if the two should arrange an agreement on mutual and balanced (conventional) force reductions for Europe, and only one party were to comply, the danger of war through temptation of the stronger might be increased.

On the nuclear side, however, the problem of verification is much more difficult. Ships, tanks, troops, air bases, and so on, are more accessible to counting than are strategic submarines and hardened missile sites. In addition, even though exposed delivery vehicles may be counted with some accuracy, the problem of counting warheads and estimating their megatonnage remains. How many missiles does a submarine carry? How many warheads does each bear? What is their total explosive potential? Similar problems arise with respect to hardened missiles.

Diplomats and scientists have shared the problem of perfecting verification systems. Early in the atomic age, the United States and the Soviet Union exchanged ideas for detecting atomic tests. These included on-site

Death Leads the Charge

The Logic of Power

inspection plans involving neutral personnel, and the use of "black boxes," or seismographic stations, which could be monitored for explosions and estimates of yield. Other plans included "open skies," in which the nuclear states would permit one another to enter national airspace for photoreconnaisance flights. None of these proposals ever materialized.

Modern technology has resolved much of the verification problem. The participants in the nuclear arms race have tracked one another's missile firings, and have been able to estimate rocket thrust. From this each has been able to estimate the amount of nuclear power capable of being delivered by specific missile systems. The United States knows, for example, that the successful testing and deployment of the giant SS-9 rocket by the Soviet Union represented MIRV potential. By the same token, the Soviet Union knows the lift potential of the Minuteman II and the Poseidon II. Furthermore, by orbiting reconnaisance satellites, each party is able to monitor the construction of missile sites, and to determine satisfactorily the number of missiles poised for firing. ABMs are easily detectable from above because of the huge radar complexes which they require. About the only important thing technology is unable to determine is the momentary location of nuclear submarines.

The role of the spy has been overly romanticized. In the early days of the nuclear race, undercover agents working the scientific centers of the United States and the Soviet Union were credited (or discredited, depending on one's position) with accelerating the race by providing critical information about the adversary's strategic developments. To a large extent, this role has been superseded by the technological monitoring systems now in use. But the undercover agent still plays a role in information flow, since laboratories still can be monitored only by people, and longrange plans are not detectable from space. Likewise, while information gained from photoreconnaissance may suggest changes in strategy or political plans, these can be verified only through human contact. The role of the agent now, therefore, is altered by technology but not eliminated; he/she is still the critical link on the subjects of future strategies, planned deployment patterns, and both internal and external political maneuvering. In days gone by, the agent's main question was "What does the enemy have?" Today, this being known through other means, his main questions are "What is he planning to develop? How is he developing it? How does he plan to deploy?" In addition, the agent still monitors political objectives and plans. Hence, though the role is altered, governments are still sensitive to the type of situation which arose in 1958 when Nikita Khrushchev was introduced to CIA Director Allen Dulles in a White House reception line and remarked, "Oh, how do you do? I read your reports!" Lacking diplomatic arrangements for on-site inspection, espionage will continue both as an instrument of verification and as a tool for gaining information about the strategic and political futures.

But just what is it, technically, that verification seeks? There are four general objectives of verification. First, each party wishes to be satisfied of the other's compliance with immediate obligations of the treaty, such as dismantling, termination of site construction, or closing of bases. Second, each party needs to know that the other is not undertaking to replace what has been removed. Third, each wants satisfaction that the other has not merely moved certain instruments to other places and concealed them from surveillance. Finally, each wants demonstrated assurance that remaining forces *are* what they are said to be. Therefore, verification of four objectives must be achieved: *initial obligation, nonreplacement, nonconcealment,* and *remainders.*[17]

The problem of *enforcement* of arms control and arms limitation agreements is even more difficult politically than that of verification. If two states agree to limit their arms and only one complies, then it is difficult for the weaker to enforce the agreement against the stronger. Ideally, therefore, enforcement ought to be left to some neutral agent which has both the political capability to enforce agreements and the military wherewithal. Yet imagine states giving over to some other party or institution authority greater than their own, and military power superior to their own even though they are capable of creating more and better! To expect the United States and the Soviet Union to vest in the UN, for example, both the political power to order sanctions against a great power, and independent nuclear capability, is now politically naïve. Hence international arms agreements have traditionally left to states the privilege of "national means of enforcement." Often implicit in reluctance to negotiate reduction of arms is the argument that such reduction would minimize ability to enforce compliance against a treaty partner which violates its obligations.

Since every arms race is tied to a political context, arms reduction and political thaw are interdependent. Where favorable political chance is lacking, most progress toward arms reduction is dictated by cost factors. In 1899, Czar Nicholas of Russia convened the First Hague Conference not to negotiate a new political order for Europe, but because he felt economically incapable of competing in arms development with Germany. Likewise, the American "return to normalcy" after World War I was motivated largely by budgetary fatigue, coupled with the desire to retreat from power politics. The SALT I agreements arose from mutual Soviet-American desire to control the costs of yet another spiral in the race between offensive and defensive missiles.

Other motives exist, such as avoiding nuclear-related hazards. The Limited Nuclear Test Ban Treaty (1963) is a case in point. This was adopted not to desensitize the nuclear race, but to reduce the dangers of radioactive fallout. Prohibitions on chemical and biological warfare hardly

[17] Hedley Bull, *The Control of the Arms Race*, p. xix.

affect the tone of intergovernmental relations, but they may spare civilian populations some of the potential horrors of war. Expansion (or dum-dum) bullets were outlawed at the start of the century because of their effects upon humans, not because their absence would enhance the political climate. The Nuclear Non-Proliferation Treaty was sponsored by Washington and Moscow not because it would improve their own relations or reduce the prospects of war between them, but to limit the potential fallout by restricting nuclear development to a few states, and to guarantee the maintenance of at least one aspect of the international power distribution: a small membership in the nuclear club.

The modest progress thus far made toward arms control arises only partly because the possession of arms threatens international stability. In fact, the two principal competitors take the opposite view, namely, that mutual deterrence is the guardian of international peace and security. It may be concluded that the overall impetus of arms control efforts in the modern world is not to *end* the balance of terror, but to stabilize it at acceptable cost and risk. The goal is not peace through disarmament; it is peace through controlled, but precarious, mutual deterrence.

National Perceptions of the Balance of Terror

The American Perception

The popular outlook upon the balance of terror in the United States is sharply divided. Those who object to American participation insist that the arms race is unjustifiably costly, both absolutely and in relation to other needs. Each new generation of arms is more expensive than is justified by the minimal gains in security; and each new upward spiral may accentuate insecurity. Furthermore, the critics ask, are official assessments of need built on misperceptions? Do the emnities which characterized the cold war still rule world politics? Are our legitimate interests so vitally challenged that we must go to such exorbitant extremes to preserve them? Critics farther to the left wonder if such levels of arms are not maintained simply to safeguard less legitimate interests.

The official view is markedly different. It holds that in addition to the need for strategic balance, military threats to our interests are ever present. American foreign interests are targets of China and the Soviet Union, which seek to divide the Western allies, undermine confidence in American leadership and the American economy, and to seize territories and governments not vigorously defended by the United States. Only the defense of Berlin and the resolute interventions in the Korean and Vietnam wars taught these foes that Washington will not tolerate encroachments on its interests. Establishment of the North Atlantic Treaty Organization, the Truman Doctrine (determination to prevent the spread of Soviet influence), and incorporation of Japan and West Germany in our defense alliances were the types of actions which signaled to the Kremlin our intent to resist challenge to our interests.

But there was another lesson as well. Soviet threats dramatized the need not only for intense political relations and institution-building among our allies, but for impressive arming. Only by being able to signal the Soviet Union, with credible threat, that the use of their arms would bring about massive retaliation, could we free our allies from impediments to the founding or restoration of democratic political institutions. Arms policy was coupled with the "export of democracy," and provided the umbrella under which we could "help others to help themselves." If the Soviet Union proceeded to greater threat with improved weapons, then we had to improve ours. Each new Soviet development demanded American response: the Soviet Union was responsible for fueling the strategic arms race, through its combined political threats and strategic capability.

The villainous interpretation of Soviet intentions abated only slightly with the death of Joseph Stalin, the Soviet policy of peaceful coexistence, and the de-Stalinization campaign of Nikita Khrushchev. But the tone did change. With the exception of rare direct confrontations (such as the Cuban Missile Crisis), the Soviet-American arms race began to yield to the need for rational policies of stable deterrence. The lessening of political tension did not result, however, in bilateral willingness to reduce stockpiles. Before such events could take place, a new factor arose: the prospect of China, with its immense potential power, as a nuclear state in emnity with *both* Washington and Moscow. The U.S. was finally obliged to acknowledge that there does not exist a Communist monolith, that the threats of Moscow and of Peking are politically and strategically distinct. But in the presence of a third hostile member, how do two states reduce their arms?

The American government found itself caught in a bind. While Washington was intent upon improved relations with Moscow and less costly strategic policy, Moscow perceived new threats from China, necessitating a two-front strategy. The Soviet need for stable deterrence with the United States and a separate military potential toward China is a problem with which Washington can sympathize, but which its defense policies cannot tolerate. Regardless of presumed targets, the total amount of Soviet destructive capability is increased by this dual targeting. Could missiles aimed to Asia be conveniently retargeted? Could mobile marine rocketry be dispatched to sites within range of American foreign interests on the pretense of being deterrents to Chinese policy? Could strategic defense against China be a cover for potential nuclear blackmail against American allies such as Japan and South Korea? What of American interests in Southeast Asia and the Pacific?

In the absence of answers to these and other critical questions, the redoubling of Soviet defenses could not be taken without response. Despite their occasionally favorable political effects upon Soviet-American diplomacy, Sino-Soviet differences meant new efforts for American strategy. In consequence, the SALT agreements dealt only with deployment in defense of solidified spheres of influence, particularly home territories, the entire Western hemisphere and all of Europe. But they did not limit potential developments relating to the great political question mark: the area of the world in which the struggle for spheres is a *trilateral* one. Here the principal villain is China and its uncertain nuclear future. The need for the Soviet Union to prepare for this serves only as a secondary irritant.

The Perceptions of America's Major Allies

Caught between the need for security and the desire to liberate themselves from American domination, Washington's principal allies have an ambivalent outlook on the balance of terror. Yet there are considerable differences in their attitudes, owing particularly to their geographic locations, the external imperatives which guide their foreign policies, and the coincidence of their interests with those of the United States.

Japan. For twenty years, Japan was paradoxically one of the most involved states in the global balance of terror and one of the least involved. It was intensely interested in the balance because of its location, within easy flying distance of the three Asian preoccupations of its American ally: Korea, China, and Vietnam. For over twenty years Japan served as a major staging base for American strategy throughout Asia, and as a principal deployment site for American military activity and materiel. Yet because of this relationship, Japan itself was not a major participant in the global balance, entrusting its defense to the United States and maintaining a low annual defense appropriation. Despite the anxieties of location and possible embroilment in American wars, Japan for the most part profited from the Soviet-American arms race and from global bipolarity.

More recently, however, the Japanese outlook has shifted. American withdrawal from mainland Asia, together with the uncertainty of the Nixon Doctrine, has kindled a sharp internal debate concerning the future of Japan's defense. While opting thus far for a nonnuclear course, the Japanese government has already embarked on a three-fold increase in defense expenditures. While its relations with both China and the Soviet Union have lent stability to Japan's Asian policy, assertive reestablishment of regional economic supremacy may upset contemporary tranquility. Demand for natural resources and India's new nuclear capability further destabilize the Japanese outlook, as do the growing uncertainty of the American nuclear umbrella and the Nixon Doctrine. Japan's future perception of the global and regional balances of terror will evolve with the stability of Asia and with Tokyo's vital economic and territorial interests. Available technology is equal to either a nuclear or a nonnuclear choice.

Western Europe. Proximity to the Warsaw Pact nations, the degree of American security and economic domination, and progressive reestablishment of Western Europe as a vital world center all contribute to the maturation of the attitude concerning the global balance of terror. Through the years following the Second World War, American responses to what Europe perceived as Soviet military threat were a welcome instrument of stabilization, one which permitted the gradual resurgence of economic activity and the integration of Western Europe. But now the Europeans are cold-war weary, resistant to additional increases in defense expenditures, and simultaneously desirous of more American security and less American interference. They recognize that the two are incompatible. Unlike many areas of the world, however, Europe does not consider the global arms race to have been particularly wasteful. It has achieved European security without substantial reduction in European expenditures on economic objectives, for the United States has borne the largest burden. Indeed, in the European view, by having done so the United States has enjoyed unequaled scientific, industrial, and technological advances which have contributed to the means by which American manufacturers and the American defense establishment perpetuate Europe's dependence upon the United States. Thus it is less over the fear of Soviet invasion than the growing resistence to American penetration that the European perspective is formulated.

There is also some division of opinion among the members of the European Community themselves concerning the balance of terror. France, in particular, wishes to proceed at virtually any cost to provide for a European defense force independent of the United States. Germany, the economic and conventional forces fulcrum of the Community, demands American nuclear protection. Britain and the other Community members are in such economic condition as to require that Washington bear as much of the cost of Europe's defense as can be arranged. It is only as the U.S. demands redistribution of the costs of NATO that most of Western Europe perceives the expense of Western defense, and thus of hemispheric defense arrangements which stress costly conventional capabilities as against minimal strategic deterrence. It is likely that if the demand for independence from the United States continues to mount, the choice will be forced upon Europe to forsake costly conventional strategies and join the balance of terror in full by proliferating dangerous but less expensive (in the long run) instruments of minimal strategic deterrence.

Canada. In contrast to Japan and Western Europe, Canada has been relatively removed from the balance of terror. Though it participated in the Korean War and has been a member of NATO, it has avoided major military commitments and has chosen instead to be an important part of United Nations peacekeeping efforts. While maintaining a small but relatively modern defense force, Canada has avoided the nuclear option and has chosen to divert into economic development funds which might normally have gone to defense.

In part the Canadian position is a fortuitous result of proximity to the United States. Even if we disregard for the moment Ottawa's efforts to maintain friendly relations with Moscow and its relatively early recognition of China, it remains true that the closeness of Canada to the United States, and particularly to its industrial heartland, has lent a strategic immunity to Canadian policy. But this proximity is a double-edge sword. For like Western Europe, Canada has felt the penetrating effects of American industries, and of the technological and industrial superiority which the balance of terror has enabled American manufacturers to develop. Thus while Canada has remained aloof from the balance of terror as an active participant, it has quietly deplored its wastefulness and with increasing vigor resisted its domestic economic consequences. In particular, the wastefulness which the balance of terror imposes upon North American natural resources now threatens to force upon Canada a continental allocation policy, one which will further erode national sovereignty. To Canada, then, while the balance of terror may have produced coincidental security, it has resulted in economic relations with its continental neighbor which have been injurious to national self-esteem and integrity. Thus while intact territorially, Canada perceives itself to have been a casualty of the balance of terror through indirect and continental economic means.

The Soviet Perception

Far from accepting the role as antagonist in world politics and in the strategic arms race, the Kremlin seeks to defend its island of socialism from capitalist encirclement. Bolstering their traditional fears of exposed borders, the Soviets have experienced overt attempts by Japan and the West to bring down their power. Japanese and American landings in Siberia at the close of World War I, shortly after the Bolshevik Revolution of 1917, were historic signals of the need to maintain rigorous defense against the capitalist industrialized states. More recently, American efforts after World War II to influence Soviet policy in Eastern Europe through atomic monopoly have accentuated the need for vigilance. NATO in particular, and the string of anti-Soviet alliances in general, added further to the need. Incorporation of West Germany into NATO in apparent violation of the Potsdam Agreement of 1945 was the ultimate sign of American intentions of maintaining anti-Soviet tension throughout Europe; the Kremlin responded by forming the Warsaw Pact. Soviet arms policy, far from being the cause of the balance of terror, is a response to the capitalist (specifically American) political and strategic threats.

The new Soviet concern with Chinese growth compounds matters. These two powers, previously tied in ideological and political bonds, now vie for legitimate leadership of the socialist world. The Chinese cannot be true Marxist-Leninists because of the peasant base of the revolution. Instead, they are conservative Stalinists bent upon division of Marxism and upon anti-Soviet sponsorship of the Third World. Ever since the estrangement in 1956, the growth of Chinese power has been a threat to the Soviet Union. Violent border clashes, combined with Chinese entry into the nuclear club, have enlivened previously dormant fears. The two Communist giants are now enemies, as Moscow sees it, because of Chinese adherence to old Stalinist ways, the ideological perversions of Maoism, and the military attempts of the Chinese to force settlement of old territorial questions.

The prospect of a modern Chinese nuclear force menaces the Kremlin. Hence the need to conduct two simultaneous arms policies, one for Soviet-American strategic stability, and one for superiority over China. The failure of the United States to perceive this dual need properly is the real remaining strategic issue of Soviet-American diplomacy. It indicates Washington's intention to maintain Asian instability by promoting Sino-Soviet tension. Meanwhile, what will the United States do elsewhere if the Soviet Union lets down its guard? What threat might NATO and the United States present if the Kremlin must concentrate its strength in Asia? For as long as the Chinese strategic future remains uncertain and the United States is able to exploit Sino-Soviet differences, the Soviet Union must maintain its dual arms policy. Moscow is victimized by two power struggles, and must be prepared to deal with the relative threats of two antagonists.

The Chinese Perception

The Century of Humiliation and the growth of power under Mao Tse-tung shape the Chinese view of the balance of terror. Hemmed in by the Soviet Union to the north and America and its allies to the west and south, China has experienced a modern history of containment. The achievement of nuclear combat potential has been the sole means by which Peking has been able to demand that Washington and Moscow take account of it.

If political advantage is a product of equality in arms, China must compete to gain full political potential in the international system. Only in this way can China achieve its ultimate aim of preventing the Soviet Union and the United States from carving the world into two giant hegemonies.

But there are other objectives in the Chinese quest for full participation in the balance of terror. In addition to wanting to escape from nuclear blackmail, Peking fears the restoration of Japanese military power, especially if it should become nuclear. Sino-Japanese rivalry has been one of history's most bitter. At the end of the last century Japan defeated China in war, and propelled itself far ahead of China in modernization. China took advantage of this during World War I. From 1931 to 1945 the two were embattled again. American occupation of Japan was the first real Chinese reprieve from the Japanese threat, but the respite terminated with the American decision during the Korean War to establish Japan as the prime Asian link in the American Pacific security program. The establishment of a formal treaty of alliance in 1951 signaled the fusion of the Japanese and American threats to the Maoist government, which had come to power on the mainland only in the last month of 1949.

By the late 1960's, the close identification of these two enemies began to divide. The return of Japan to full economic competition with the United States brought jealous and recriminative actions from Washington. The Nixon Doctrine—a plan for the post-Vietnam years for decreased American participation in the territorial defense of allies—threatened deterioration in Japanese-American security policy. Leftist political groups in Japan demanded increased independence from Washington, even if that should mean constitutional change (the current constitution renounces the development of combat nuclear potential) and development of nuclear forces. The threat of a Japanese nuclear potential separate from that of the United States is one to which China must react.

The final motive is China's desired leadership of the Third World. Knowing that the less developed countries wish to break the bipolarity of world politics, China has set its sights on championship of this group. Sharing with them a history of imperialism, of forced racial inferiority, of territorial exploitation and involuntary constraint, China plays a natural role. In addition, sharing the problems of underdevelopment, but having enormous productive potential because of population reserves, China sees itself as the future industrial center of the Third World. But to achieve that status it must be able to safeguard prospective partners from Soviet or American overtures and threats, from neoimperialism and from their attempts at co-optation. All of this requires the ability to offer a credible nuclear force, both to attract partners through the status of nuclear membership and to make serious threats of coercion.

The Third World Perception

Faced with the costly and difficult problems of modernization in a world in which the rich get richer and poor get poorer, the Third World nations deplore the unproductive squandering of natural, human, and economic resources. The balance of terror fits especially into this vision, inasmuch as it has absorbed over three trillion dollars during the past quarter century.

But it is not merely the cost of the strategic arms race which is objectionable. Added to it is the unjustifiable vigor with which the United States and the Soviet Union deny their economic capability to assist the fledgling governments, or even to aid old and trusted, though impoverished, friends. But the Third World has been a casualty of the nuclear era in yet

Every Twenty-five years?

Source: Catalog of the Garland Library of War and Peace. This cartoon appeared in an unknown American newspaper, September 11, 1939.

a second way. At the height of the cold war, when both the United States and the Soviet Union sought the allegiance of newly independent nations, their aid programs were considerably larger than at the present time. Since then, the strategic race has stabilized and the expensive quest for friends among the ideologically uncommitted nations has become less competitive. As a result, development assistance from the superpowers has diminished, and the two wealthiest and most powerful governments have only reluctantly participated in enlarged multinational aid programs through international institutions.

Conclusion

With or without arms races the world will continue, for as long as the nation-state remains the dominant actor, to face problems of power, competition, and potential conflict. Disparities of wealth, ideological distrust, conflicts of interests, confrontation of objectives, perceptions and misperceptions—these and other aspects of international relations will continue to ensure that states will apply their power in pursuit of their interests and of their needs. And, regrettably, they will also continue to ensure that humans will expend their scientific genius and their technological achievement as much to destructive purposes as to the betterment of the human condition.

10

Twelve Causes
of War

One of the most pressing matters in the field of international relations is the cause of war. Why are international political controversies so often violent? The pages of international history are saturated with blood; and the moralist may fairly ask why people condone in war behavior that they would not tolerate in peace. Is war an international disease of the human social system, a collective insanity, a malfunction like falling down the stairs? Is it the product of conspiratorial behavior by certain interests and groups? Or is war a rational and functional, if horrible, component of the international system? In this chapter, we shall review twelve theories of the causes of war that have emerged from the growing field of conflict and peace research.

War is one of the most carefully studied human activities, and literally tens of thousands of books and tracts have been written about it. Many universities have established research centers and teaching programs focused on conflict and violence, and several major journals are devoted exclusively to the subject (*Journal of Conflict Resolution,* U.S.; *Journal of Peace Research,* Norway; *Peace Research Reviews,* Canada). Findings by conflict researchers in various disciplines are exchanged at dozens of national and international conferences annually. Peace research has by now generated many scientific findings and spawned several distinct schools of thought. The theories of the causes of war that we will review in this chapter represent some of the most important propositions and findings that have emerged in this burgeoning field.

Scientific research on war is based on a critical assumption: *that there*

TABLE 10–1   Twelve Theories of the Causes of War

1. Power asymmetries.
2. Nationalism, separatism, and irredentism.
3. International social Darwinism.
4. Communications failure and mutual misperception.
5. Runaway and uncontrolled arms races.
6. The promotion of internal integration through external conflict.
7. Instinctual aggression, cultural propensities to violence, and war/peace cycles.
8. Economic and scientific stimulation.
9. The military-industrial complex.
10. Relative deprivation.
11. Population limitation.
12. Conflict resolution.

are patterns and regularities in conflict behavior that can be identified systematically. If this assumption is not true—that is, if war behavior is random, idiosyncratic or unique from case to case—then research of this kind will be unproductive. But historians and statesmen tend to agree with the conflict researchers that orderly principles *do* underlie the complexities of warlike behavior. It follows that war is a serious question for social inquiry.

In reviewing the twelve principal causes of war listed in Table 10–1, we define war as *the organized conduct of major armed hostilities between social groups and nations.* This definition enables us to consider internationally significant civil wars as well as international conflict, the distinction between the two having been eroded in recent years. Varying length of discussion of the individual causes should not be interpreted as implying greater or less importance.[1]

1. Power Asymmetries

The condition most feared among governments as a cause of war is the *power asymmetry*—that is, an unfavorable tilt in the distribution of power. There is widespread conviction that, whatever other impetuses to war may be present, a careful equilibration of power between antagonists will tend to prevent war, while a disequilibrium will invite aggression. The maintenance of international peace therefore requires that technological and other gains on each of two sides be matched and kept relatively even. A

---

[1] For a penetrating analysis of several key theories, see Kenneth Waltz, *Man, the State, and War* (New York: Columbia University Press, 1965); also, Quincy Wright's classic, *The Study of War* (Chicago: The University of Chicago Press, 1965), 2nd ed.; and Karl von Clausewitz, *On War* (Washington: Infantry Journal Press, 1950), reprint.

"vacuum" of power, such as that created by unilateral disarmament, destabilizes international relations and encourages military ventures. Proponents of this *realpolitik* believe that occasions and issues for conflict always exist, and that the immediate cause of warfare is usually a failure to balance power symmetrically.

In conflicts in which one side seeks a major redistribution of values while the other wishes to preserve the status quo—that is, when there is a clear distinction between the offense and the defense—peace may be preserved by a certain kind of asymmetry. An advantage to the *defensive* party will more reliably deter aggression than a close balance. Conversely, an overbalance in favor of the *offensive* party will make war more likely. Thus, in the clear offense/defense case, peace is more nearly ensured by superiority of the nonrevolutionary antagonist. For example, Winston Churchill argued in his "iron curtain" speech at Fulton, Missouri, in March of 1946, that Soviet aggression would be stopped only by Western military *superiority:* " . . . the old doctrine of a balance of power is unsound. We cannot afford, if we can help it, to work on narrow margins, offering temptations to a trial of strength." However, power asymmetries are inherently dangerous and tend to produce aggressive policies even when the favored state was previously peace loving and defensive.

Asymmetries mean not only different levels of industrial capacity, population, and other physical elements of war potential (see preceding three chapters), but also more variable and volatile political elements. Of special importance is the ability to attract and retain *allies* willing to pool resources for mutual security. Only two states in the modern world, the United States and the USSR, are able to act alone in most contingencies, and even for them there are many political and strategic advantages in joint action. For lesser powers, it is vitally important to cement alliances to prevent asymmetries. For example, Israel depends on the United States while Syria relies on the USSR.

Another important factor is *will*. Even very good capabilities and solid alliances can result in asymmetries if a party declines to fight. Conversely, a state with limited resources and support may be able to prevent asymmetry by showing a resolute determination to utilize its capacities fully. To prevent power asymmetries, it is not necessary that all possible pairs of states be balanced perfectly, but only that potential aggressors know in advance that the costs of overcoming resistance will outweigh the benefits. Thus, the asymmetry of power is one cause of war that can be controlled.

2. Nationalism, Separatism, and Irredentism

Nationalism and nationalist movements are the second cause of war. Nationalism is a collective group identity that passionately binds diverse individuals into "a people." The nation becomes the highest affiliation and obligation of the individual, and it is in terms of the national *"we*-group" that personal identity is formed: "I am a Canadian." From Hitler's celebration of the *Folk* to DeGaulle's near-mystic belief in the French, the most powerful elements of the political spectrum seem to agree that the ethnic nation is the highest form of identity.

This curious and compelling identification with one group tends to produce conflicts with others. A 1969 research team enumerated 160 disputes having a significant likelihood of resulting in large-scale violence within fifteen years. This large inventory fell broadly into the following classifications:

1. *Nationalist* conflicts, including disputes between ethnic, racial, religious, and linguistic identity groups perceiving themselves as "peoples."
2. *Class* conflicts, including issues of economic exploitation.
3. *Other* conflicts not characterized primarily by clashes between identity groups or classes.

Significantly, nationalist and ethnic conflict accounted for about 70 *percent of the cases*, while class and other conflicts divided the balance. Indeed, nationalism appears to be a potent factor in the causal chain to war, accounting for more bloodshed than any other cause.[2]

In recent years, the main link between nationalism and war has been the survival of separate identities among populations whose geographical distribution differs from the international boundary lines. "Peoples" who do not have "countries" tend to feel an infringement of basic human rights in a world of *"nation*-states." Populations submerged in other peoples' countries (Lithuanians), populations divided among two or more countries (Kurds), and populations denied the control of the governments of their own countries (black Rhodesians and South Africans), tend to rebel against these denials. But territorial and political rearrangements often cannot be achieved without armed conflict between the deprived groups and other interests. Thus, the link between nationalism and war today operates most importantly through militant territorial and political demands organized around certain principles of ethnic, linguistic, religious, and racial *we*-group identities.

Two key forms of nationalist militancy predominate in modern war: the *separatist* form and the *irredentist* form. In the separatist form, a nationalist group attempts to secede from an existing state to form a new

---

[2] Steven Rosen, ed., *A Survey of World Conflicts* (Pittsburgh, Pa.: University of Pittsburgh Center for International Studies Preliminary Paper, March 1969).

The Separatist Model	The Irredentist Model
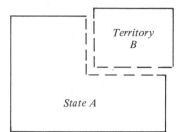	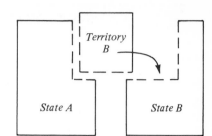
Territory B secedes from state A to form new state B.	*State B claims territory B from state A.*

FIGURE 10–1

one. In the irredentist form, an existing state lays claim to a territory and population group presently subsumed within another state. These forms are illustrated in Figure 10–1.

Separatism and War

Most of the world's approximately 145 nation-states incorporate substantial minority populations. Even after prolonged periods of apparent assimilation among other groups, many minorities continue to think of themselves as separate and distinct. (See Table 10–2). This feeling of distinctness becomes a *separatist movement* when a formal demand is made for territorial secession to form a state, or, short of this extreme, for a considerable measure of internal autonomy from control by the existing political order. These separatist demands usually are resisted by the incumbent authorities because of the perceived threat to the state's political and territorial integrity. In this way, conflicts over separatist demands become common causes of war.

Minority movements take on added significance for the study of international relations when *outside powers* intervene. Often, one comes to the aid of the threatened government, while another lends its support to the restive minority. The various factions in the internal dispute become clients of outside sponsors motivated by their own interests. Foreign intervention is particularly important when a neighboring state allows its territory to be used as a sanctuary and staging area for guerrilla forays and political organization by the dissident population. This is seen by the threatened government as subversion and tends to lead to intergovernmental conflict.

TABLE 10-2   Some Separatist and Autonomist Movements

A. Recent wars of secession
  1. Nigeria: struggle by Ibos for a separate Biafra; unsuccessful
  2. Pakistan: secession of East Pakistan to form Bangladesh; successful
  3. Sudan: black secessionists vs. Arab state; unsuccessful
  4. Chad: Arab secessionists vs. black state; unsuccessful
  5. Iraq: Kurds; unsuccessful
  6. Ethiopia: Arabs of Eritrea, supported by Arab states; unsuccessful
  7. Oman: Dhofar region; unsuccessful

B. Other separatist movements
  1. Spain: Basques; Catalans
  2. Yugoslavia: Croatians; Albanians
  3. Uganda: Bugandans
  4. India: Sikhs
  5. Puerto Rico: Independista movement
  6. France: Brittany; potentially Basques
  7. United Kingdom: Ulster Catholics; Welsh; Scots
  8. Indonesia: minorities in Moluccas, Sumatra, Celebes
  9. Russia: Latvians; Estonians; Lithuanians; Ukranians
  10. Sri Lanka: Tamils
  11. Switzerland: Jura
  12. Canada: French of Quebec
  13. China: Sinkiang; Tibet
  14. Burma: Karens; Kachins; Shans; Chins; Mons; Arkanese
  15. Pakistan: Baluchis
  16. South Africa: Namibia (Southwest Africa)

C. Multiple secession movements
  1. Kurds from Iraq, Iran, Turkey, and USSR
  2. Bakongos from Zaïre, Congo, Cabinda, and Angola

D. Strained federations
  1. Lebanon: Moslems vs. Christians
  2. Yugoslavia: Serbs, Croatians, and others
  3. Guyana: Blacks, East Indians, and others
  4. Ghana: northern vs. coastal tribes
  5. Czechoslovakia: Slav minority
  6. Mauritius: Hindu, Creole, Moslem
  7. Surinam: Creole, East Indian, Japanese
  8. Rwanda and Burundi: Wa-Tutsi vs. Bahutu
  9. Belgium: Flems and Walloons
  10. India: many minorities

Irredentism and War

Nationalist and ethnic disputes have still greater significance for international relations in their *irredentist* form. Virtually all the world's populated land surfaces are by now identified with the delineated territory of particular nation-states. But in many cases the historic demarkation of boundaries (mainly through war and conquest) ignored "natural" lines of division between different peoples. Thus, *political* lines often are not congruent with *ethnogeographic* regions, and in many places one "people" straddles a border between two states. Irredentism is the struggle of such a people for reunification,[3] and the *irredenta* is a territory regarded as lost or stolen in which a portion of the ethnic nation resides.

The irredentist territorial claim normally evokes resistance from the state, which would be reduced in the event of its success. This state often can base its own claim on historic ties and treaties regarded as legally binding. There is a fog of claims and counterclaims, and the stirring patriotic call of one side is a threat to the other. Even the most barren piece of territory is regarded as a sacred part of the national patrimony, and seldom does a border move a hundred yards in any direction in the modern world without the spilling of human blood.

Four kinds of resistance to irredentist claims are significant: (1) where another state would lose territory; (2) where another state would cease to exist as an independent entity; (3) where the claim would reunify two halves with different political ideologies (such as the two Koreas); and (4) where another population in the territory comprising the irredenta fears it would become a disadvantaged minority in the event of reunification. The last case is illustrated by the Protestants of Northern Ireland and the Turks of Cyprus, who would be vulnerable in the event of reunification of their regions with the Irish Republic and Greece, respectively. In all four cases, somebody stands to lose if the irredentist movement wins.

Issues in Separatist and Irredentist Conflicts

Economic consequences. Although territorial issues of separatism and irredentism begin as ethnic questions, they also entail profound economic and natural resource issues. When Hitler seized the Sudetenland from Czechoslovakia in the name of the 3 million Sudeten Germans, he also seized 70 percent of Czechoslovakia's iron and steel, 86 percent of its

---

[3] The term referred originally to the late nineteenth century struggle of Italian patriots to redeem or reincorporate into Italy certain neighboring territories having a predominantly Italian population. As the term is used here, the impetus for reunification can come from the separated population (irredenta), the main body, or both.

Yassir Arafat, head of the Palestine Liberation Organization (PLO), addressing the General Assembly of the UN in November 1974, on the question of Palestine (the U.S. and Israel objected to the PLO's participation in the discussions).

Courtesy United Nations / T. Chen

chemicals, and 70 percent of its electrical generating capacity. Similarly, British support for the self-determination movement in Kuwait and Brunei is related to their oil wealth. Belgian support for the Katanga secession attempt in the Congo was keyed to the copper deposits of that region. The secession of Biafra would have taken from Nigeria not just the Ibo people, but also much of the national resource base and industrial capacity. Thus, nationalist disputes are also international economic issues.

The moral dilemma. Aside from economic issues, separatist and irredentist movements pose a moral dilemma for the international system. National self-determination is a cardinal value, and many concerned observers support struggling peoples seeking their own places in the sun. But the immense complexity of ethnogeography means that the world cannot possibly accommodate each splinter group with its own territory. All African states, for example, include members of tribes that straddle international borders. If each national group were given its own country, thousands of economically nonviable units would result. The fifty states of Africa, with a total population less than half that of India, already are too fragmented. When the Ibos sought secession from Nigeria, they were supported by only a few outside states (notably, Tanzania, Zambia, Gabon, and Ivory Coast), despite the moral appeal of their position. Pan-Africanists hold that the real future of the continent is in regional amalgamation and federation—not further "Balkanization." In addition, wholesale border revisions probably could not be achieved without an unacceptable amount of conflict and warfare among interested states.

Colonial boundaries. Many frustrated minorities blame their problems on past imperialism. Borders violate ethnic lines primarily because they reflect the points at which advancing armies stopped, or where "deals" between big powers were reached. They rarely reflect "natural" lines of human settlement. In many underdeveloped regions, precolonial societies simply did not have officially drawn boundaries. When the Europeans came, they drew lines that seemed administratively, economically, and politically convenient in Paris, London, Lisbon, and Brussels, but which often ignored tribal and ethnic lines in the subject countries. Unified peoples were splintered, and incompatible tribes and groups often were lumped together. Part of this was not chance but was calculated to divide and conquer the subjugated peoples. Thus, many peoples have permanent problems as a consequence of past colonialism.

Unresolved and unresolvable irredentist and separatist issues are threats to the territorial interests of many nations. (See Table 10–3). Nationalist conflicts may be latent and seemingly forgotten for prolonged periods, suddenly to emerge with renewed vigor as group identity reawakens. Recollections of lost territory tend to simmer beneath the political surface, and it is a simple matter for a jingoist leader or a demagogue such as Hitler to stir them up and ride to power a nationalist tide. A latent irredentist or separatist feeling is a potent chemical reaction waiting for the right catalyst and is always, therefore, a potential cause of war.

TABLE 10–3   Some Irredentist Movements

A. Claims to whole states:
1. Tibet was reincorporated by China.
2. Togo has been claimed by Ghana on grounds of Ewe reunification.
3. Mauritania is regarded by some as part of Morocco.
4. French Somaliland (now Afar-Issa or Djibouti) has been claimed by Somalia.
5. Israel is regarded by Arab nationalists as a land stolen from the Arab nation.
6. Kuwait has been claimed by Iraq.
7. Gambia was carved artificially out of Senegal by the colonial power.
8. Cyprus is regarded as part of Greece by Greek Cypriotes.
9. Taiwan is claimed as part of China.

B. Divided states with different political orientations:
1. North and South Korea.
2. East and West Germany.
3. The two Yemens.
4. The two Vietnams, now undergoing reunification.

C. Claims to parts of states:
1. United Kingdom is threatened by IRA demands that Northern Ireland (Ulster) be reunited with Ireland.
2. Algeria is threatened by Moroccan claims in Spanish Sahara, rich in phosphates, and Tindouf, rich in oil.
3. India is threatened by Pakistan's claim to Kashmir.
4. Kenya is threatened by Somali nationalist claims to the Northern Frontier District.
5. Guyana faces territorial claims by Venezuela and Surinam.
6. Italy has negotiated territorial claims by Austria and Yugoslavia.
7. China has extensive claims against the Soviet Union, Mongolia, and other states.
8. Malaysia has resisted Indonesian and Philippine claims to Sabah.
9. Germany, under Hitler, laid claim to regions of Czechoslovakia, Poland, and Austria on grounds of Aryan reunification.

3. International Social Darwinism

The third theory of war is a philosophy that may be called *international social Darwinism*. This is the belief that societies, like biological species, evolve and advance through competition resulting in the survival of the fittest and the elimination of the weak. The social Darwinist sees the war of each against all as a cruel necessity for the progressive advancement of civilization. International relations is, in this perspective, the arena of combat between whole peoples where the global destiny of humanity is determined. The role of war is to pass the reins of power from the weak and decaying to the strong and dynamic.

In recent years, this philosophy has most often been associated with *fascism*. In advancing war as a positive aspect of fascism, Benito Mussolini declared:

> Fascism sees the imperialistic spirit—i.e., in the tendency of nations to expand—a manifestation of their vitality. In the opposite tendency, which would limit their interests to the home country, it sees a symptom of decadence.[4]

Moreover,

> Fascism above all does not believe either in the possibility or utility of universal peace. It therefore rejects the pacifism which masks surrender and cowardice.
> War alone brings all human energies to their highest tension and sets a seal of nobility on the peoples who have the virtue to face it. . . .[5]

Carried to its logical conclusion in nazism, the fascist philosophy views societies as biological entities united by blood ties. Two principles link nazism with war: the principle of *race* and the principle of *territory* (*Lebensraum*). Nazism, according to Adolph Hitler, "by no means believes in equality of the races, but along with their difference it recognizes their higher or lesser value. . . . Thus, in principle, it serves the basic aristocratic ideas of Nature." Moreover, because population expands but living space (*Lebensraum*) is limited, races must compete for territory.

> Nature knows no political boundaries. First she puts living creatures on this globe and watches the free play of forces. She then confers the master's right on her favorite child, the strongest. . . .[6]

The higher races must not agree "in their pacifistic blindness to renounce new acquisitions of soil" or they will leave mastery of the world to "the culturally inferior but more brutal and more natural peoples." Hitler was deeply suspicious of international law and diplomacy—"a cozy mutual swindling match"—and frankly set out "to promote the victory of the better and stronger, and demand the subordination of the inferior and weaker in accordance with the eternal will that dominates this universe."

[4] Quoted in S. William Halperin, *Mussolini and Italian Fascism* (Princeton: Van Nostrand, 1964), p. 152.
[5] Benito Mussolini, quoted in Reo M. Christensen, Alan S. Engel, Dan N. Jacobs, Mostafa Rejai, and Herbert Walter, *Ideologies and Modern Politics* (New York: Dodd, Mead, 1971), p. 70.
[6] Adolph Hitler, *Mein Kampf* (Boston: Houghton Mifflin, 1943), pp. 134–57.

Adolph Hitler addressing crowd. His nationalistic and maniacal rantings contributed much to the German war fever from 1933 to 1945. (This photo is from a privately published book of Hitler's taken from Hitler's own library by an American soldier after Germany's defeat.)

As these passages suggest, international social Darwinism glorifies conflict and focuses on incompatibilities among groups. It offers an appealing and simplistic account of history, providing a perfect rationalization for aggression. And, of course, it raises many questions for social theory.

Is race the basic human unit, or only a biological accident that is pro-moted and distorted by corrupt politics? Is competition the "basic law of nature," or are the most important human achievements attained mainly by cooperation and mutual effort? Do nations in fact face a shortage of "living space," or are the most densely populated nations (for example, Japan) often the most prosperous? (It is interesting here that of the esti-mated 25 million square miles of arable land in the world, only about one-sixth (4 million) is under cultivation.) Are people pressing outward from overcrowded population centers, or is the trend toward urbanization and concentration increasing and rural population declining? Is the creative height of civilization reached in war, or in peace?

We cannot answer all these questions here, but they are worthy of the most serious attention. While the fascist and nazi movements are now nearly dead, the philosophy of international social Darwinism is alive and well.

4. Communications Failure

Another cause of war treated extensively in the conflict literature is the theory of *communications failure*. Nations perceive each other through ideological lenses and with stereotypical images,[7] as we showed in discuss-ing the cold war conflicts. These perceptual distortions result in selective reception of messages and signals and in mutual misperception of inten-tions.[8] For example, potentially threatening message content may be more salient or perceptually prominent than cooperative or conciliatory state-ments of another government. *The listener hears what he expects to hear,* as in the theory of cognitive dissonance: The images that nations have of each other not only fail to match the realities they are supposed to repre-sent, but these images are also highly resistant to change—even when evi-dence and experience contradict fixed expectations. (See chapter 6 for a more detailed treatment of this process.) Communications failure and exaggerated fear contribute to escalatory processes by multiplying the con-sequences of international tensions.

[7] See, for example, H. C. J. Duijker and N. H. Frijda, *National Character and National Stereotypes* (Amsterdam: North Holland Publishing, 1960), and O. Kline-berg, *Tensions Affecting International Understanding* (New York: Social Science Re-search Council, 1950), Bulletin 62.

[8] See Anatol Rapoport, "Perceiving the Cold War," in Roger Fisher, ed., *Inter-national Conflict and Behavioral Science* (New York: Basic Books, 1964); also Ken-neth Boulding, *The Image* (Ann Arbor, Mich.: University of Michigan Press, 1956); and Karl W. Deutsch and Richard L. Merritt, "Effects of Events on National and International Images," in Herbert Kelman, ed., *International Political Behavior* (New York: Holt, Rinehart and Winston, 1965).

5. Arms Races

Another theory links the outbreak of war to *runaway arms races* that become unstable and uncontrolled. Here, hostile nations lock into a cycle of mutual fear (a process called *hostility reaction formation*), in which each side believes itself to be threatened by the other. The defensive preparations of one are taken as evidence of offensive intentions by the other, who then arms in response. Each seeks a margin of superiority, leading to qualitative and quantitative competition in armaments and organized forces. The assumption that such arms races tend to erupt into active conflict after a certain critical point in the reaction process is passed was the basis of a pioneering mathematical study of war.[9]

Many thoughtful people on the liberal end of the American political spectrum agree that excessive military preparations and armaments accumulation are a cause of war. On the other side, conservatives tend to favor the adage, *"Si vis pacem, para bellum"* (if you want peace, prepare for war). Do armaments cause wars or prevent them? Norman Cousins once invented a completely imaginary computer study of all the arms races in history to determine whether arms races were a cause of war or a guarantee of peace. This supposed study "found" that since 650 B.C., there had been 1,956 arms races, of which only 16 did not end in war, and that most of the exceptional cases ended in economic collapse.[10]

More authentic studies have been much more equivocal and ambiguous in their findings. In the best-known study, Samuel P. Huntington found that arms races may be *either* a prelude to war or a substitute for war, depending on other conditions.[11] Even if a significant *correlation* were discovered between arms races and the outbreak of war, it could not be inferred that the former *caused* the latter. It is plausible that profound political disputes cause both arms races *and* wars, so correlation in this case would not prove causation. A might correlate with B because both are caused by C.

Arms races, like communication failures, are seldom the root cause of conflict. The decision to maintain extremely high military expenditure most often reflects a prior condition of discord and conflict with an opponent. Arms races and exaggerated fears may inflame an existing conflict, but seldom create one that does not otherwise exist.

[9] Lewis Richardson, *Arms and Insecurity* (Pittsburgh: Boxwood, 1960).

[10] See Norman Cousins, *In Place of Folly* (New York: Harper & Row, 1961); also, Brownlee Hayden, *The Great Statistics of War Hoax* (Santa Monica, Calif.: Rand Corporation, 1962).

[11] Samuel P. Huntington, "Arms Races: Prerequisites and Results," in Robert J. Art and Kenneth N. Waltz, eds., *The Use of Force* (Boston: Little, Brown, 1971), pp. 365–401.

6. Internal Cohesion Through External Conflict

Another theory sees war as the product of policies designed to promote *internal* group cohesion through the unifying effects of *outside* conflict—the process of drawing together to face a common enemy. Bismarck's calculated provocation of three external wars from 1866 to 1871 to integrate the German states is the classic example of wars fought purposely. Secretary of State William Henry Seward's fruitless proposal to President Lincoln that the United States precipitate international warfare to reunite the nation and to avoid civil war exemplifies the same tactic. There exists an extensive literature which demonstrates the relationship of external conflict to internal cohesion at all levels of social interaction.[12] In international relations the implication of this theory is that resort to international warfare may be preferable to internal dissolution.

Despite the apparent weight of this theory, however, most scientific studies conclude quite differently. If internal conflict tended to be externalized in foreign wars, it is hypothesized that there should be a statistical relationship between the frequency of internal and external conflict. But in the most careful quantitative research, no clear and consistent relationship has been found.[13]

Among the scientific studies, only one has substantiated the theory that the quest for domestic cohesion is a cause of war, and that one finds only a slight relation.[14] Whatever may be the merits of these conflicting findings, it must be conceded that most studies have *not* found the relationship that was predicted between internal unity and external conflict.

---

[12] Anthony de Reuck and Julie Knight, *Conflict in Society* (Boston: Little, Brown, 1966), p. 32; D. Kahn-Freund, "Intergroup Conflicts and Their Settlement," *British Journal of Sociology* 5 (1954): 201; Georg Simmel, *Conflict and the Web of Group Affiliations* (Glencoe, Ill.: The Free Press, 1955); Lewis Coser, *The Functions of Social Conflict* (Glencoe, Ill.: The Free Press, 1957), pp. 104–6 and 92–93. For a thorough review and synthesis of the literature up to about 1959, see Robert North, Howard Koch, Jr., and Dina Zinnes, "The Integrative Functions of Conflict," *Journal of Conflict Resolution* 3 (September 1960): 355–74.

[13] Rudolph Rummell, "Testing Some Possible Predictors of Conflict Behavior Within and Between Nations," *Peace Research Society (International) Papers* 3 (1963): 17; Rudolph Rummel, "The Relationship Between National Attributes and Foreign Conflict Behavior," in J. David Singer, ed., *Quantitative International Politics* (New York: The Free Press of Glencoe, 1968): Michael Haas, "Social Change and National Aggressiveness, 1900–1960," in Singer, p. 213; Raymond Tanter, "Dimensions of Conflict Behavior Within and Between Nations, 1958–1960; *Journal of Conflict Resolution* 10, no. 1 (March 1966): 46; and Samuel P. Huntington, "Patterns of Violence in World Politics," in Huntington, ed., *Changing Patterns of Military Politics* (New York: The Free Press of Glencoe, 1962), pp. 40–41.

[14] Jonathan Wilkenfeld, "Domestic and Foreign Conflict Behavior of Nations," *Journal of Peace Research* 1 (1968): 55–59.

7. Instinctual Aggression

One of the most popular theories of war among laymen is the idea of an *instinct of aggression*—the blood lust that is depicted in so many lurid movies and magazines. In the aggression theory, the root of war is seen as a vestigial instinct of pugnacity or bellicosity that has survived from our animal roots. Many observers have concluded that people *like* to fight, and that at least in part, international conflict has its basis in male competitiveness *(machismo)* and even direct sadism. The outbreak of war is traced to biological proclivities and to individual and collective psychopathology.[15]

It is quite evident that people enjoy violence; otherwise television and the movies would not be so full of it. But there is much controversy concerning the relationship between aggressive impulses and the decision to go to war. One major study of twenty-five wars found that the decision to go to war was "in no case . . . precipitated by emotional tensions, sentimentality, crowd behavior, or other irrational motivations." [16] As organizations become more bureaucratic, controls are put on personal impulsiveness and deviance; studies have found that decisions made by groups are more likely to approximate "rational" choices than decisions in similar situations by individuals.[17]

On the other side, several theorists view aggression as a dominant impulse which is triggered by political disputes that provide the necessary rationalization for violence. As Albert Einstein said, "Man has within him a lust for hatred and destruction. . . . It is a comparatively easy task to call this into play and raise it to the level of a collective psychosis." [18] Ber-

[15] William McDougall, "The Instinct of Pugnacity," in Leon Bramson and George Goethals, *War: Studies from Psychology, Sociology and Anthropology* (New York: Basic Books, 1964), pp. 33–44; Edward Glover, *War, Sadism, and Pacifism* (London: Allen and Unwin, 1933). See, for example, the work of psychologist Elton McNeil: "Psychology and Aggression," *Journal of Conflict Resolution* 3, no. 3 (September 1959): 195–293; "Personal Hostility and International Aggression," *Journal of Conflict Resolution* 5, no. 3 (September 1961): 279–90; "The Nature of Aggression," in McNeil, ed., *The Nature of Human Conflict* (Englewood Cliffs, N.J.: Prentice-Hall, Inc., 1965), pp. 14–44.

[16] Theodore Abel, "The Element of Decision in the Pattern of War," *American Sociological Review* 6 (1941): 855.

[17] See O. G. Brim, ed., *Personality and Decision Processes* (Stanford, Calif.: Stanford University Press, 1962). For an important view on the other side, see Harold Lasswell, *Psychopathology and Politics*, 2nd ed., (New York: Viking, 1960). Lasswell found a tendency for psychopathological individuals to go into public life out of proportion to their numbers in a group, displacing and rationalizing private disturbances in terms of the "public interest." For a review of literature on this question, see Brent Rutherford, "Psychopathology, Decision-Making, and Political Involvement," *Journal of Conflict Resolution* 10, no. 4 (December 1966): 387–407.

[18] From a letter to Sigmund Freud in James Strachey, ed., *The Standard Edition of the Complete Psychological Works of Sigmund Freud* (London: Hogarth, 1964), vol. 22, pp. 199–202.

trand Russell claimed that "War is accepted by men . . . with a readiness, an acquiescence in untrue and inadequate reasons. . . ." [19] Naturally, this opinion is more convincing to those who reject the official rationale but must account for the persistence of their opponents in adhering to it.

Systematic studies distinguish between "realistic" and "nonrealistic" conflicts.[20] In a *realistic* conflict, the cause of struggle is rational disagreement over goals. In a *nonrealistic* conflict, the immediate issues are merely a pretext for fighting, and the real purpose of the combatants is violence itself. When we have both an instinct of combativeness *and* a disagreement over political issues, we have a chicken and egg problem of deciding which is the *real* cause. Are the political issues only *rationalizations* to justify violence and to permit the relaxation of normal inhibitions against bloodshed that are applied unless "reasons of state" are involved? Or is it the reverse —that leaders facing *realistic* disagreements with opponents take advantage of the aggressiveness of their followers to arouse a spirit of national struggle? Is aggressiveness a *cause* of war or only a *consequence* of it?

No final answer to this question has emerged from conflict research, but it is a reliable maxim that the aggressive urge is important only insofar as it is translated into ideology. Sheer blood lust plays a relatively minor role, but aggressive and demanding definitions of the political situation are commonly behind warlike disputes. If the aggressive urge distorts perceptions and magnifies perceived threats (cold war, for instance), it is a causal contributor to war. Thus, serious researchers tend to reject the crudest forms of the aggression theory, but to accept the more complex and subtle formulation.

If an aggressive instinct is the cause of war, what is the cure? Some theorists have argued that the solution to the problem of aggression is not to attempt to eradicate the instinct, but to channel it into constructive forms. Freud believed that if the aggressive urge were not released in socially functional expression, it would turn inward as a death force and destroy the individual.[21] Even Gandhi, the apostle of nonviolence, said that he would rather "risk violence a thousand times than [risk] the emasculation of a whole race." [22] The classic advocate of this view was philosopher William James, who argued in 1912 that a warless world with "no scorn, no hardness, no valor any more" would be "a cattleyard of a planet." War elicits from men and women the highest ideals of self-sacrifice and personal striving for excellence. The goal according to James, should not be to eliminate the aggressive urge, but to develop a "moral equivalent of

[19] Bertrand Russell, *Why Men Fight* (New York: Bonibooks, 1930), pp. 5–6.

[20] Lewis Coser, *The Functions of Social Conflict* (New York: The Free Press of Glencoe, 1957).

[21] Reply to Einstein in Strachey, ed., *Complete Works of Sigmund Freud*, pp. 209–11.

[22] See Norman Bose, ed., *Selections from Gandhi* (Ahmedabad, India: Navajivan Publishing House, 1957), pp. 159–63.

war" as an alternative constructive outlet for the same capacities. He proposed a cooperative struggle to tame nature for human betterment, with workers organized in paramilitary units.[23]

There is now a substantial research literature on the nature and function of the aggressive urge and its relation to political violence. Much of it focuses on animal behavior for clues to human aggression. In the best known of these reports, Konrad Lorenz examines the logic and functions of aggression in a variety of animal species. He finds that aggression is useful in many ways: for self-defense and protection of the young; for forcing territorial spacing over the available food area, preventing depletion in one location; or for mate selection through male rivalry, leading to the upward evolution of the species. He then asks, What keeps aggressive behavior within tolerable and useful limits and prevents it from destroying the species altogether?

This question leads him to his key finding: that a second, previously unknown factor exists alongside the aggressive urge. This is a built-in inhibition *against* the use of violence, which is present in every species whenever aggression occurs. The inhibition is biologically triggered when the victim of an attack gives an appropriate signal of submission; the exact signal is different for each species. Most important, the *strength* of the inhibition in each species is *proportional* to the innate "lethality" of the species—the stronger the natural weapons of the species, the firmer the inhibition. The supposedly vicious wolf, for example, is quite incapable of continuing an attack on another wolf once the victim signals submission by exposing a vulnerable section of its neck. The dove, on the other hand, supposedly as peaceful as the wolf is warlike, is actually quite vicious. Having poor equipment for aggression, it has little inhibition against aggression and has been known to pluck apart another dove ruthlessly over a forty-eight-hour period of torment, disregarding signals of submission.

Lorenz extends this theory to an explanation of human aggression. He reasons that man lacks teeth, claws, poison, and other natural weapons of great power. Hence, the corresponding level of his inhibition is relatively moderate, but he has used his brain to develop artificial weapons which greatly enhance his lethality. His programmed inhibitions are exceeded by his unprogrammed potential for destruction, and he is able to release his aggression with relatively little restraint. Aerial bombardment, long-range artillery, and other remote control weapons interfere with the passing of signals that would restrain the attacker. Thus, man, according to Lorenz,

[23] See *The Moral Equivalent of War* (Cabot, Vt.: International Voluntary Service, 1960); reprinted from James, *Memories and Studies* (London: Longmans, 1912). Elsewhere, Seymour Melman proposes to replace the arms race with a "peace race"; see *The Peace Race* (New York: Ballantine, 1961).

has upset nature's balanced design, and the aggressive urge threatens to destroy us.[24]

If aggression, in fact, does underlie violent political ideologies, political controls on the outbreak of wars will be difficult to institute. Some have proposed that candidates for national leadership in all countries be subjected to psychiatric examination. Utopian thought in the science fiction literature has even raised the possibility of hostility-suppressing drugs being given routinely to heads of state to control their pugilistic drives. Another idea is to change the psychological environment of international conferences to remind statesmen of the potential consequences of their acts. One creative suggestion is to place a child maimed in war in the middle of the conference table, and to have the windows of the conference room open onto a playground. Still another idea is to keep the families of national leaders in rival capitals as hostages against bombardment and surprise attack. These measures would strengthen the weak inhibitions postulated by Lorenz.

Unfortunately, these colorful if macabre suggestions overlook the subtle process by which aggressive drives are translated into depersonalized *ideologies*. Once this translation is made, national policy becomes a matter of high principle, and controls on purely personal impulses are quite beside the point. If the national belief system itself incorporates a biological tendency into a highly rationalized form, biological and psychological solutions will be less important than *political* controls (such as the balance of power) that check aggressive policies. While the problem of war may have in part a biological cause, the solution must be political.

Cultural Differences and Aggression

Are some countries and cultures more aggressive than others? Many historians and social scientists have attempted to match degrees of aggressiveness with different national characters. Germany, for example, has been identified as a country with a cultural background particularly conducive to authoritarianism and the use of force as reflected in prevailing child-rearing practices, the martial quality of German music, and other cultural attributes.

Nineteen hundred years ago Tacitus gave this classic account of the German propensity to war:

> Many noble youths, if the land of their birth is stagnating in a protracted peace, deliberately seek out other tribes, where some war is afoot. The Germans have no taste for peace; renown is easier won among perils, and you cannot maintain a large body of companions except by violence and

[24] Konrad Lorenz, *On Aggression* (New York: Harcourt Brace Jovanovich, 1966); see also Robert Ardry, *The Territorial Imperative* (New York: Atheneum, 1966).

war. . . . You will find it harder to persuade a German to plough the land and to await its annual produce with patience than to challenge a foe and earn the prize of wounds. . . . When not engaged in warfare, they spend some little time in hunting, but more in idling, abandoned to sleep and gluttony. All the heroes and grim warriors dawdle their time away, while the care of the house, hearth, and fields is left to the women, old men and weaklings of the family. The warriors themselves lose their edge. They are so strangely inconsistent. They love indolence but they hate peace.[25]

This opinion accords with the views of many observers of German behavior during the present century.

But is there a scientific basis for the opinion that different cultures have varying propensities to political violence? Careful studies disagree on the answer. Some relate various cultural attributes to the occurrence of aggressive behavior, taking the frequency of violence as an indicator of the cultural propensity for war.[26] But others doubt that the frequency of violence and war is attributable to culture. A more important factor may be the number of common borders that a country shares with other nations. This is the theory of "geographical opportunity"—the more borders, the more war.[27] Another factor unrelated to aggression is the territorial distribution of ethnic groups. As we have seen, multi-ethnic countries have more opportunity for conflict than homogeneous populations. Against these and other factors, purely cultural variations in aggressiveness may be a weak explanation for warlike behavior. At least one study concludes that there is no good evidence for a cultural propensity to aggressiveness:

> . . . although culture patterns may be fruitfully compared in terms of their ways of handling and expressing hostility/aggression, it is essentially meaningless to describe one culture as more or less hostile/aggressive than another in any absolute terms, since no external criterion exists that is not in some sense arbitrary.[28]

In general, one may say that the present evidence for cultural propensities to aggressiveness (in the sense of warlike violence) is inconclusive.

War-Peace Cycles

Another strand of aggression research is the search for *cycles* of violent behavior. Does the amount of violence in human society ebb and flow in

---

[25] Tacitus, *On Britain and Germany* (Baltimore: Penguin, 1948), pp. 112–13.

[26] For example, Tom Broch and Johan Galtung, "Belligerence Among the Primitives," *Journal of Peace Research* (1966): 33–45; and Quincy Wright, *The Study of War*, Appendices 9, 10, and 20.

[27] James Paul Wesley, "Frequency of Wars and Geographical Opportunity," *Journal of Conflict Resolution* 4 (December 1962): 387–89.

[28] R. T. Green and G. Santori, "A Cross Cultural Study of Hostility and Aggression," *Journal of Peace Research* 1 (1969): 22.

patterns? Is there a "war curve"? Such research is generally based on the aggression view of war, but sometimes the aggression theory is left implicit.

Early quantitative research into this matter varied in conclusions, with some researchers rejecting the cycle theory, some demurring from it though finding some trends, and others accepting the theory.[29] Most recent studies point more conclusively toward validating the war-cycle theory. One finds a trend of an upswing in the level of violence about every twenty-five years, with a twenty-year cycle prior to 1680 and thirty years the apparent cycle after that. Denton and Phillips hypothesize that the observed cycle of war is caused by patterns in social psychology. After a war, memories of suffering are vivid and further fighting is avoided. As time passes, unpleasant memories fade or are repressed, and "the themes employed in the descriptions of the last great war shift from 'horror'-dominant to 'glory'-dominant." War is then romanticized again until, Denton and Phillips imply, a new opportunity arises to satisfy violent needs. There is a parallel rotation of decision-makers every twenty to twenty-five years, and the new leaders, it would appear, need to have their "own" war. Denton and Phillips assume that "the opportunities for employing violence are always present." [30]

With these exceptions, most researchers have not found a uniform pattern in the temporal spacing of wars. There does not appear to be a reliable war-peace cycle. This suggests that aggressive war is not a simple instinctual need, since instinctual desires, by nature, require periodic satisfaction. The frequency of wars is not primarily a function of culture or time, but of political conflicts. War cannot be understood apart from politics.

8. Economic and Scientific Stimulation

Another theory of war concerns its economic functions. War has promoted the acceleration of scientific discovery, technical innovation, and industrial development. It might be said that a major "external economy" of war is this great industrial spinoff. Sluggish economies may be stimulated by the creation of "artificial demand": ". . . the attacks that have since the time of Samuel's criticism of King Saul been leveled against military expenditures as waste may well have concealed or misunderstood the point that

[29] See, respectively, Pitrim Sorokin, *Social and Cultural Dynamics* (New York: Bedminster, 1962), vol. III, p. 357; Lewis Richardson, *Statistics of Deadly Quarrels* (Pittsburgh: Boxwood, 1960), pp. 137–41; and J. E. Moyal, "The Distribution of Wars in Time," *Journal of the Royal Statistical Society* 112 (1949): 446–58.

[30] Frank Denton and Warren Phillips, "Some Patterns in the History of Violence," *Journal of Conflict Resolution* 1, no. 2 (June 1968): 193. A similar conclusion positing fifty-year cycles is found in Oswald Spengler, *Decline of the West* (New York: Alfred A. Knopf, 1926), vol. I, pp. 109–10.

some kinds of waste may have a larger social utility." [31] There is little doubt, for example, that the Great Depression of the 1930's ended for America only with the onset of the Second World War. Military demands put Americans back to work and primed the pump of economic recovery. Today, with economic pump-priming managed principally through manipulation of the public sector, military spending is a crucial factor in most industrialized nation-states.

Again, empirical studies challenge the intuitive logic. Some argue that, on the whole, the economy would prosper with substantial cuts in defense spending. However, some industries would feel harsh effects, while the gainers would profit only slightly.[32] Supporters of military spending are therefore better organized than opponents.

Nevertheless, even if high levels of military *spending* can be shown to be good for the corporate economy, it does not follow that *war* is good for business. Major wars tend to produce side-effects such as inflation, the tightening of credit, and the interruption of international trade and financial flows—all of which harm the largest corporations. The New York stock exchange averages *declined* in response to escalation in Vietnam and Cambodia and recovered their losses only with the deescalation of the war.[33] Even firms specializing in the production of military hardware did not flourish during the Vietnam years. U.S. defense profits ran at substantially higher rates during 1961–64 than during 1965–72. Thus, we are led to the paradoxical conclusion that defense *spending* might be good for the capitalist economy, but *war* definitely is not. Perhaps the perfect combination from a profit viewpoint is a prolonged state of controlled international tensions (such as the cold war) with high military spending but without the actual outbreak of war.

[31] Arthur Waskow, *Toward the Unarmed Forces of the United States* (Washington: Institute for Policy Studies, 1966), p. 9. Also, David Bazelon, "The Politics of the Paper Economy," *Commentary* (November 1962): 409, and Michael Reich, "Military Spending and the U.S. Economy," in Steven Rosen, ed., *Testing the Theory of the Military-Industrial Complex* (Lexington, Mass.: D. C. Heath, 1973), pp. 85–6. See also John Nef, *War and Human Progress* (Cambridge: Harvard University Press, 1950).

[32] Stanley Lieberson, "An Empirical Study of Military-Industrial Linkages," in Rosen, ed., *Testing the Theory of the Military-Industrial Complex.* For more general issues, see especially Robert G. Kokat, "Some Implications of the Economic Impact of Disarmament on the Structure of American Industry," in U.S. Congress, Joint Economic Committee, *Economic Effects of Vietnam Spending* (Washington, D.C., 1967); Wassily Leontief, Alison Morgan, Karen Polenske, David Simpson, and Edward Tower, "The Economic Impact of an Arms Cut," in Wassily Leontief, ed., *Input-Output Economics* (New York: Oxford University Press, 1966). See also Emile Benoit and Kenneth Boulding, eds., *Disarmament and the Economy* (New York: Harper & Row, 1963).

[33] See Betty Hanson and Bruce Russett, "Testing Some Economic Interpretations of American Intervention," in Rosen, ed., *Testing the Theory of the Military-Industrial Complex.*

Even if warlike policies were clearly and unambiguously favorable to business, it would not automatically follow that governments would act in these interests. Eugene Staley found in 1935 that financial and industrial elites had played a relatively secondary role in the expansionist policies of the imperialist states. Investors supported governments interested in expansion for other reasons, but the political elite "used" the business groups, rather than the reverse.[34] In another study, Lewis Richardson found that economic causes figured directly in less than a third of wars from 1820 to 1949, and that they have been more important in small wars than in large wars.[35] The results in studies like these often depend on the way that the question is posed and the measures that are used for key variables.

---

9. Military-Industrial Complexes

One issue of special interest in the debate over causes of war is that of military-industrial complexes. Powerful domestic groups within the major states who have vested interests in military spending and international tension use their influence to promote antagonistic relations between nations, according to this theory. These domestic groups which comprise the military-industrial complex include (1) the professional soldiers, (2) managers and, in the capitalist states, owners of industries deeply engaged in military supply, (3) high government officials whose careers and interests are tied to military expenditure, and (4) legislators whose districts benefit from defense projects.

These core members of the military-industrial complex are supported by associated and lesser groups such as the the veterans and military service associations, labor unions tied to the defense industry, and scientists and engineers who do defense-related research. These groups occupy powerful positions in the political structures of the major states, and they exercise their influence in a coordinated and mutually supportive way to maintain optimal levels of war preparation and to direct national security policy. According to proponents of this theory, the influence of the military-industrial complex exceeds that of any opposing coalitions or interests.

This complex rationalizes high levels of military spending with an ideology of conflict, such as the mythology of the cold war. This ideology may be a deliberately manufactured deception to mislead the public, or it may

[34] Eugene Staley, *War and the Private Investor* (Garden City, N.Y.: Doubleday, 1935). See also Kenneth Boulding and Tapan Mukerjee, eds., *Economic Imperialism* (Ann Arbor, Mich.: University of Michigan Press, 1962), and Steven Rosen and James Kurth, eds., *Testing the Theory of Economic Imperialism* (Lexington, Mass.: D. C. Heath, Lexington Books, 1974).

[35] Richardson, *Statistics of Deadly Quarrels*. Contrast John Bakeless, *The Economic Causes of Modern War* (London: Yard, 1921).

be a militaristic false consciousness that arises spontaneously with high military spending. Whether or not the complex is a conscious conspiracy, it requires an ideology of international conflict to guarantee its position within the political and economic structure of the society. To the *conventional theorist*, arms races are caused by realistic conflicts and a cycle of mutual fear betwen opposing states. To the *military-industrial complex theorists*, the external threat is merely a necessary projection for the self-aggrandizing activities of domestic military-industrial complexes.

In the classic formulation of C. Wright Mills, this theory applies to both capitalist and socialist states.[36] In the latter, the professional military combines with managers of state defense industries and with related functionaries within the Communist party apparatus and the ministries and bureaucracies. There is a natural and effective alliance of interests between Soviet heavy industry, the armed forces, and the conservative wing of the Party, forged upon "their understanding of the interdependency that exists between security, heavy industry, and ideological orthodoxy." Without it, harm would befall the career interests and social positions of both the professional military elite and some of the most highly paid civilian personnel in the country. Thus, despite state ownership of productive facilities, the USSR also has a military-industrial complex interested in the continuation of international conflict.[37]

The theory of the military-industrial complex is far from faultless. It fails to account for the decline in the percentage of national production devoted to defense in both the United States and the USSR. The U.S. defense budget in constant dollars (that is, discounted for inflation) declined by 1973 to a level comparable to the 1950's. Several congressional battles over military procurement bills have resulted in the loss of entire weapons systems sought by the military services. These losses have been reflected in the decay of profits. At one time, several major aerospace firms faced bankruptcy. Rather than exceeding profits in the nondefense commercial economy, defense earnings were in fact substantially lower than comparable nondefense work from 1965–1972. In many ways, the defense sector shows signs of decline and weakness rather than the omnipotence attributed to it by the military-industrial theorists, at least in the United States (which alone accounts for over 40 percent of world military expenditures). A similar process is believed to be underway in the Soviet Union.

Even if the defense sector were expanding rather than shrinking, other doubts of the critics would apply. The theory of the military-industrial complex assumes that political behavior is motivated essentially by private

---

[36] C. Wright Mills, *The Causes of World War III* (New York: Ballantine, 1958) and *The Power Elite* (New York: Oxford University Press, 1956).

[37] Vernon Aspaturian, "The Soviet Military-Industrial Complex: Does It Exist?" in Rosen, *Testing the Theory of the Military-Industrial Complex.*

interest rather than public good or "national interest." At the core of the theory, critics charge, is a crude and simplistic economic determinism. Careful studies of international events generally find a much more complex pattern of motivation behind national policies. Particularly in warlike conflicts, where the highest values of life and death and national survival are at issue, behavior tends to be guided by principled conviction rather than crude self-interest.

The theory of the military-industrial complex gains plausibility if ideology is considered alongside self-interest and conflict behavior. Behavior may be determined by convictions, but where do these come from? Perhaps self-interest sets the frame for broader values and perceptions. If so, military-industrial dependency might produce a conflict-filled world view.

This analysis is similar to the view we took earlier of the relationship between the aggressive instinct and warlike behavior. War decisions are guided by rational calculations, but the conscious values and perceptions themselves may conceal an underlying aggressiveness. Similarly, values and perceptions may sublimate private interests into the supposed national interest. Social scientists are only now beginning to inquire where political ideologies, convictions, and beliefs come from. More research on this question will be needed before we can arrive at a definitive analysis of the role of the military-industrial complex and the aggressive instinct.

---

10. Relative Deprivation

The concept of relative deprivation is especially useful in describing the origins of internal wars. It holds that political rebellion and insurrection are most likely when people feel that they are receiving less than their due. To achieve greater benefits or to relieve the frustration of denial, groups may turn to aggression and political violence.[38]

This differs from mere common sense in one important respect: the objective or absolute conditions of poverty and oppression do not lead directly to rebellion, but rather the subjective or psychological response to these conditions is determinate. Studies of rebellion and revolution, to illustrate, find that violence most often occurs when conditions are begin-

[38] See especially Ted Gurr, *Why Men Rebel* (Princeton, N.J.: Princeton University Press, 1970). Also, Crane Brinton, *The Anatomy of Revolution* (New York: Vintage, 1965), and James Davies, "Toward a Theory of Revolution," *American Sociological Review* 27 no. 1 (February 1962). See also Peter A. Lupsha, "Explanation of Political Violence: Some Psychological Theories Versus Indignation," *Politics and Society* 2, no. 1 (Fall 1971); John Dollard, Leonard Doob, and Neal E. Miller, *Frustration and Aggression* (New Haven: Yale University Press, 1939); and Ivo and Rosalind Frierabend, "Aggressive Behavior Within Politics, 1948–62," *Journal of Conflict Resolution* 10, no. 3 (September 1966): 249–71.

ning to improve rather than when they are at their worst point. The beginnings of improvement after a long period of deprivation trigger a "revolution of rising expectations." Hopes rise more rapidly than realities, and an "aspiration gap" results, as shown in Figure 10–2. Careful statistical studies have found that violence has tended to increase during the transitional period from traditional to modern society, as predicted by the theory of relative deprivation. Figure 10–3 shows the general relationship between violence and level of economic development.

Since 1945, civil wars have been more frequent in the developing world than in already developed states. While there were more than *sixty wars* of varying magnitude in the Third World between 1945 and 1972, some quite substantial, the developed countries experienced only sporadic incidents of riot-scale violence on their own territories. In Korea, Vietnam, Nigeria, Bangladesh, Indonesia, Colombia, Algeria, Cambodia, Laos, Zaïre, Angola, Mozambique, Guinea-Bissau, Chad, China, Sudan, Yemen, and India, the dead numbered in the tens and hundreds of thousands and even in the millions. But in the highly publicized violent events in the developed countries, the dead have numbered "only" in the tens of hundreds: in the United States (the black revolution), Northern Ireland, French Canada, Belgium, Portugal, and Czechoslovakia. As an explanation for this disparity between rates of violence in developed and less-developed countries, the theory of relative deprivation and the aspiration gap is attractive.

However, several objections arise. Rich countries have engaged in many hostile confrontations *outside* their own borders, usually on the territory

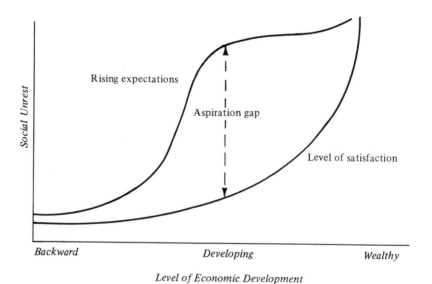

FIGURE 10–2   Level of Economic Development: The Aspiration Gap

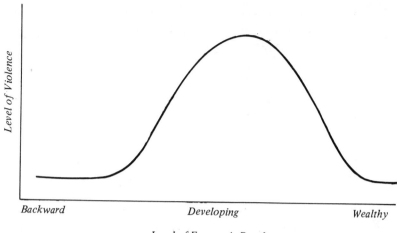

FIGURE 10–3   Economic Improvement and Rebellion

of dependent client states in the Third World. This *displacement of violence* to the developing countries may be a privilege conferred by the unequal distribution of influence in the international system. Also, Marxist critics have argued that there is an essential unity in the global revolutionary movement, and that even revolutions in remote parts of the world are challenges to the worldwide system of imperialism. Today's struggles occur in the periphery rather than in the center because of the relatively weaker hold of the imperialists in outlying regions. The overbalance of violence in the developing nations is, in the Marxist view, a transient historical phenomenon from which causal inferences cannot be too hastily drawn.

Another objection to this theory of political violence concerns the separation of physical bloodshed from other forms of abuse. The isolation of "violence" as the dependent variable in many studies ignores the fact that physical conflict exists on a continuum with other forms of harm, such as systematic oppression, imprisonment, and political denial. Such "institutional violence" can be quite as painful as physical abuse, and it can continue over much longer periods of time. Singling out rebellious violence alone as a social disease ignores the everyday suffering of millions of people and may result in false theories and vacuous remedies.

11. Population Limitation

One of the precursors of Hitler's theory of *Lebensraum* is the theory of population expansion and war suggested by Sir Thomas Malthus. In his *Essay on the Principle of Population* (1798), Malthus argued that there is an innate tendency for population to expand geometrically while food resources expand only arithmetically. Thus, "the power of population is infinitely greater than the power in the earth to produce subsistence for man." Since population must be proportioned to food supply, there must be controls on population growth. One of these is war.

This theory of war as a control on surplus population growth still remains attractive to laymen, though not to conflict researchers. The rate of global population expansion is much greater now than in Malthus' time. Indeed, more people have lived on the earth since 1900 than in the sum of

The Last War

A drawing by W. A. Dwiggins from October, 1914.

human history before that date! And this number is expected to double and redouble in the next 100 years. Some observers, echoing Malthus, predict cataclysmic wars and famines in the future to dispose of surplus population.

This theory, however, does not accord with the facts. Wars have in general taken very few lives when measured as a percentage of populations, even when the deaths have been in the millions. Only the most exceptional wars have taken more than 5 percent of the populations of the warring parties; more than half of all wars end with battle losses under one half of 1 percent (see Figure 10–4). Even during World War II, the loss rate did not significantly depress populations. The losses of the North and South Vietnamese, staggering as they have been, were lower than the birth rate, so the population continued to climb.[39] These figures do not accord with the Malthusian view of war as a significant population-limiting device. In addition, the technology of the Green Revolution now promises to multiply the capacity of the earth to produce food geometrically—finally putting to rest the theory of Malthus. Unless, of course, we include nuclear war in the analysis; but an atomic cataclysm would destroy arable land as well as population.

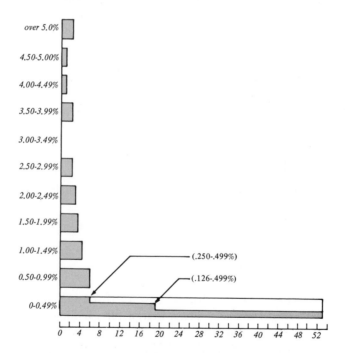

FIGURE 10–4 Percentage Population Lost in Battle Deaths in Major International Wars

[39] See Steven Rosen, "War Power and the Willingness to Suffer," in Bruce Russett, ed., *Peace, War, and Numbers* (Beverly Hills, Calif.: Sage Publications, 1972).

12. Conflict Resolution

We have saved for last the most general and comprehensive theory: war as a device for *conflict resolution*. In the general theory, conflict exists when two or more groups make mutually exclusive claims to the same resources or positions, and war is a means of allocating scarce values to resolve the conflict. War, in this view, is a rational *instrument* of decision, and war policies are decided by a logical computation of costs and benefits.

The claim of rationality is controversial. Conflicts can be decided by arbitration, elections, courts and tribunals, administrative decisions, direct negotiation and compromise—even the flip of a coin. How is it rational to spill blood when nonviolent means are available?

The answer lies in the importance of the issues typically involved in warlike disputes. Every nation or movement has a few "core" values which cannot be compromised and many "shell" values that it would also like to satisfy but which are not vital. Secondary interests can be compromised with an opponent, but leadership is obligated to defend core values by all available means—including, if necessary, violent defense. War is the *ultima ratio*—the last resort. In the words of Walter Lippmann, war is "the way in which the great human decisions are made."[40]

In recent years, the image of the armed forces and military policy has been depreciated in the United States and other countries, partly as a consequence of the unpopular Vietnam War. At the same time, most people reject absolute pacifism and retain a belief in the "just war." For example, on May 24, 1969, the World Council of Churches resolved that, "All else failing, the church and churches would support resistance movements, including revolutions, aimed at elimination of political or economic tyranny which makes racism possible." While most people value nonviolence, they evidently value other things even more and are willing to pay the exorbitant price of human lives in their pursuit of core value objects.

Conclusion

Many of the theories that we have reviewed imply that the cause of war can be found in conspiracies, irrationality, hidden motives, and the influence of certain elites. One is attracted to the conclusion that calm and thoughtful people who are not involved in the munitions industry or the military high command, and who are not particularly aggressive or greedy

---

[40] Walter Lippmann, "The Political Equivalent of War," *Atlantic Monthly*, August 1928, pp. 181–87.

or sinister, and who neither hate the "enemy" unreasonably nor misunderstand them, and who detest the idea of war as a waste of life and treasure do not make wars, but are led or duped into them.

But most wars involve very real incompatibilities between the basic moral objectives of the two sides, and it is historical fact that ordinarily the population of each side deliberately and without any element of crowd irrationality supports the carefully formulated policy of the leadership. In his zeal to eradicate war, the political scientist cannot ignore the nonconspiratorial and quite rational processes in social life that turn the peace loving into warriors. It is the behavior of these people that is at the core of the theory of war as a rational instrument of conflict resolution.

Part Three

THE LOGIC OF
WORLD ORDER

11

International Law
and Organization

Part Two dealt with specific power configurations among states and with the mechanisms of international stability and change. The thesis was that international relations consists of the pursuit of interests by states, often in an environment of conflict, with each state driven by its own perceptions, fears, and expectations. The purpose of this chapter is to explore the possibilities for restraining the external behavior of states. Rather than leave the future of international relations to force and counterforce, does the international system contain remedies for anarchical behavior?

It is not merely that we live in a nuclear age that makes this a critical question. Since power is a relative concept (powerful with respect to what?), the ability of one people to destroy another almost instantly is only a *comparatively* greater threat to the survival of states than other means of exercising power. For as long as states have been able to threaten one another with enslavement, their relations have always confronted the same choices. Whenever states are unwilling to exercise self-restraint (*autolimitation*), there have been but two alternatives for securing international stability: holding the future of other states in ransom by threat of superior force, or submitting to collective means for making decisions and for enforcing compliance. The present chapter deals with the latter of these alternatives by exploring two specific methods which have been tried in practice, and upon which contemporary research concentrates: international law and international organization. How do these processes promote a more stable world order?

317

In a well-ordered domestic society, there is a complex legal system with specific organs for making, adjudicating, and enforcing laws. The state has authority to call individuals to account for their behavior relative to the law. Laws are made in their behalf, they can be called to court against their will, and legal regulations are enforced whether an individual likes them or not.

The international system is not so well ordered. Since only the nation-state is sovereign, it is not subject to the decisions of external institutions in the way citizens are to the institutions of their society. No legislative body exists above the state, no international court has the capacity to compel its behavior, and there are few organs to execute international regulations. If the parallel between the domestic legal system and the legal attributes of the international system is lacking, just what *is* international law? If it is not by nature a formal system of regulations made by a supreme legislature, judged by supreme courts and enforced by a supreme executive agency, what is it?

No student need feel alone in his or her doubt and skepticism about the existence or the nature of international law. It is a matter about which scholars and governments have been debating for centuries. The debate among scholars is in the realm of *jurisprudence* (science of law), within which countless interpretations have been offered. It will be useful to look into two theoretical interpretations which differ vastly. These two extremes are called *positivism* and *neorealism*.

Positivism

Positivist theory is based on an analogy between domestic law, with its rules and institutions, and the international setting. It understands the law to be a *system of rules* (norms) which specify rights and obligations that govern the external behavior of states. Positivist theory holds law to have a *consensual basis*—that is, states become subject to rules only by voluntary consent. These two concepts are summarized in an opinion of the Permanent Court of International Justice, to which France and Turkey voluntarily submitted *The Lotus Case* for decision in 1927.

> International law governs relations between independent States. *The rules of law binding upon States therefore emanate from their own free will* as expressed in conventions [treaties] or by usages generally accepted as expressing principles of law and established in order to regulate the relations between these co-existing independent communities or with a view to the achievement of common aims. *Restrictions upon the independence of States cannot therefore be presumed.*[1]

[1] PCIJ Series A, no. 10. The emphasis has been added to illuminate the twin positivist principles of *rule orientation* and *consent*.

The progressive development of an international legal order depends, accordingly, upon convincing governments that their relations are best protected by mutually-arranged norms with which they will comply consistently and voluntarily.

Neorealism

Far down the theoretical spectrum is the neorealist school. This interpretation denies that rules are at the center of a legal order, and argues instead that policy and values are the foci. This theory is said, therefore, to be *policy-oriented* and *value-oriented.* Since international relations are in constant change, regulatory law must be a process of decision-making in which all states and international agencies participate, with the content of the law changing at every moment. There are no fixed rules which can be relied upon tomorrow as they are today. Thus international law is not a system of rules, but a constitutive process of authoritative decision. The law is what the policies of the contributors make it, and it is imposed in the world by power of the actors in accordance with the values which they wish the law to promote and defend. When major actors dispute the outcomes of the constitutive process, or when they disagree on the values to be promoted, then international law is identified with the foreign policy of that state whose value objectives most nearly approximate the pursuit of human dignity. The highly subjective standard is a product of the cold war.[2]

The political uses to which these two theories can be put by governments are as different as the doctrines themselves. If a government accepts the positivist definition, it will presumably regulate its behavior by existing treaties and other agreements, and it will expect other governments to regulate their actions by formal norms as well. In this way governments will be able to predict one another's actions, and will have solid grounds on which to question one another's motives. Compliance or noncompliance with formal agreements communicates the intentions of governments.

If, however, a government prefers the neorealist interpretation of inter-

[2] For statements of the neorealist theory, see Harold D. Lasswell and Myres S. McDougal, "Jurisprudence in Policy-Oriented Perspective," *Florida Law Journal* 19 (1967): 486–513; Myres S. McDougal, "The Comparative Study of Law for Policy Purposes: Value Clarification as an Instrument of Democratic World Order," *Yale Law Journal* 61 (1952): 915–46; and Myres S. McDougal, "International Law, Power and Policy," *Recueil des Cours* 82 (The Hague Academy of International Law) (1953): 133–259; and Harold D. Lasswell, Myres S. McDougal and W. Michael Reisman, "The World Constitutive Process of Authoritative Decision," *Journal of Legal Education* 19 (1967): 253–300 and 403–37, in two parts.

For critiques, see particularly Stanley V. Anderson, "A Critique of Myres S. McDougal's Doctrine of Interpretation by Major Purposes," *American Journal of International Law* 57 (1963): 378–83; Rosalyn Higgins, "Policy and Impartiality: The Uneasy Relation in International Law," *International Organization* 23 (1969): 914–931; and Wesley L. Gould and Michael Barkun, *International Law and the Social Sciences* (Princeton: Princeton University Press, 1970), p. 197.

national law, it will shun the reliability of formal agreements and justify its behavior on the claim that its value objectives are superior to those of its adversary, that its foreign policies more nearly approximate the goals of human dignity than do those of someone else. In this way declarations of foreign policy become international law. One neorealist author, for example, argues that the Truman Doctrine "has gradually evolved . . . into a kind of common law of international order, a prudent rule of reciprocal safety."[3] The Doctrine was uttered in 1947 as a unilateral policy of the United States under which the growth of international communism would be stemmed. It was an instrument of *containment* undertaken by the United States against the Soviet Union.

No government accepts either view of the law exclusively. In fact, for most powerful states, the choice of legal interpretations depends on the facts at hand. A safe rule of thumb emerges: governments will seek to maximize their rights (neorealist interpretation) and minimize their obligations (positivism); but they will attempt to minimize their adversaries' rights (positivism) and maximize their adversaries' obligations (neorealism). When governments have genuine concerns for legal interaction, they will speak as positivists; but when they have politicized concerns for the law they will come forth as neorealists.

The Sources of International Law

Think again about the analogy to domestic law. Rules arise from constitutions, formal legislation, custom, and the decisions of formally constituted courts. Such institutionalization exists in the international system to a far less authoritative degree. From where, then, do the norms of international law come? What are its sources?

The authoritative statement of the sources of international law is found in Article 38 of the Statute of the International Court of Justice, the permanent judicial organ of the United Nations. The Statute lists the sources as (1) international conventions (treaties) in force between parties, (2) international customary rules, (3) general principles of international law, and (4) such subsidiary sources as prior judicial decisions and the writings of the highly qualified publicists.

Treaties, bilateral and multilateral, are the most logical primary source. Whether a convention be one of *codification* (merely formalizing in codes practices already accepted through custom) or of a *legislative* character (creating new rights and obligations), it represents the maximum explicit

---

[3] Eugene V. Rostow, *Law, Power and the Pursuit of Peace* (Lincoln, Nebr.: The University of Nebraska Press, 1968), p. 43. Also published in paperback edition by Frederick A. Praeger.

consent of the signatories. Much of the business of twentieth century inter-governmental organizations has been the codification of existing principles and customs. Hence only in the present age has the bulk of international law come to be treaty law.

Custom, until recently the largest component of positive law, is the practice of states. It is generally held that usage grows into an international legal norm when it has been repeated over a period of time by several states, when they have generally acquiesced in such behavior by one another, and when governments begin to act in certain ways out of a sense of legal obligation. In this manner most of the international laws of the high seas originated, as did the laws of diplomatic and consular privileges and immunities, and the rules governing neutrality and international commerce, to mention only a few.

General principles of international law are less clearly defined, partly because it is difficult to demonstrate widespread acceptance, and partly because the distinction between a firm principle and a customary rule is an obscure one. Nevertheless, there are general principles which can be readily identified. Many of the amenities of international relations are general principles which arise out of the theory of sovereignty. Other general principles emerge from the necessity for sovereign equality, including the

The International Court of Justice at The Hague hears oral arguments pertaining to territorial rights in Spanish Sahara, 1975.

Courtesy United Nations / ICJ

principle of legal equality and the expectation of fair treatment of one another's nationals.

Subsidiary sources are still less specific, and merit last place among the sources of international law. In judicial tests of legal rules, the rules themselves must undergo interpretation. The business of courts is to interpret the law and to apply it. In international adjudication, rules may be interpreted by national courts, standing international tribunals, panels established to deal with specific problems, or by the International Court of Justice (ICJ). In most national systems, courts are bound by the rule of *stare decisis*, meaning that what the court has previously decided *is* the law, and is precedent binding upon courts. International tribunals generally subscribe to the same principle, and the decisions of such courts contain references to former cases just as the decisions of American courts do in domestic cases. The International Court of Justice, however, while availing itself of its prior decisions and of those of other courts, does not feel itself so firmly bound by precedent. Unlike other tribunals, the ICJ may interpret the legal significance of declarations and resolutions of the political organs of the United Nations. This is especially the case in its advisory jurisdiction, which enables the ICJ, upon request from the UN organs, to render "constitutional" interpretations which may have political effects upon member states.

Viewed from a Great Power standpoint, the most significant example of this action was embodied in the advisory opinion, *Certain Expenses of the United Nations* (1962).[4] Because the Soviet Union and other governments had refused to pay their apportioned shares of financing UN peacekeeping operations in the Middle East and in the Congo, the General Assembly requested clarification of its authority under the Charter to bill members for such expenses against their will. The Court dealt with the legitimacy of the operations themselves, rendering a "constitutional" interpretation on the limits of UN authority. It favored an expansive view. Out of this controversial decision, an argument has arisen that the Charter contains implied powers of UN organs over and above the explicit ones.[5] The contrary view holds that the most effective contribution which the ICJ might make to the progressive development of international law is through the cautious use of advisory jurisdiction—that the Court might thus earn and attract the trust of states, which might then be more willing to submit to it their bilateral disputes.[6] Whichever of these positions may carry the greater hope of eventual judicial contributions to a more stable international order is for the moment less important than that the *Expenses* case reveals the potential political impact of international judicial activity.

[4] International Court of Justice, advisory opinion of July 20, 1962, found in *ICJ Reports*, 1962, pp. 151–80.

[5] Rahmattullah Khan, *Implied Powers of the United Nations* (Bombay: Vikas Publications, 1970).

[6] Leo Gross, "The International Court of Justice and the United Nations," *Recueil des Cours* 120 (The Hague Academy of International Law) (1967): 313–30.

How is international law enforced without international government or police? Merely to posit the existence of a body of international law is not to claim that the international system is capable of legal regulation. We must demonstrate the extent of states' willingness to *comply* with legal norms. What, then, is the compelling force of international law, and by what mechanisms is it presumably enforced? Is international law "law, properly so called," or is it merely "positive international morality" which lacks the enforceability necessary to make it law?[7]

Any form of law has as its incentives a variety of *normative, utilitarian,* and *coercive* sanctions. While an individual may drive his automobile lawfully because he fears the consequences of wrongdoing (fear of coercive sanction), he may do so as a matter of personal safety (utilitarian sanction) or as a contribution to orderly social coexistence (normative sanction). Likewise among states, compliance with rules of law is rather consistent, and is grounded in normative and utilitarian motives. Governments *do* generally regard reciprocal behavior as mutually beneficial, and are often sensitive to international pressures. They wish to avoid reprisals and embarrassing declarations and resolutions brought on by untoward behavior, except when perceived needs exceed the risk of external criticism. Furthermore, states rarely enter into formal international agreements unless they intend to benefit, and unless they intend to comply with them. Nor do they acquiesce in custom over the long run without anticipating benefits. Accordingly, it is not at all extraordinary that states should normally comply with their voluntary obligations.

Coercive sanction takes over where all else fails. Indeed, the necessity for coercion occurs only when a state departs from its normal pattern of behavior under existing rules, when a behavior pattern is devoid of legal restraint, or when a state does not participate in what is considered by other nations to be law. All of this is just another way of saying that when a state is not party to formal normative or utilitarian sanctions generally applicable, its behavior with respect to others may be controllable only through the threat of coercion.

Coercive theories of law abound, especially of international law. John Austin argued vigorously that norms are not *legal* norms unless they are capable of coercive enforcement by some political entity juridically superior

---

[7] This is the classic distinction made by the English positivist John Austin. For American expressions and discussions of the argument, see particularly Westel W. Willoughby, *Fundamental Concepts of Public Law* (New York: Macmillan and Co., 1924), p. 224 ff., and "The Legal Nature of International Law," *American Journal of International Law* 2 (1908): 357–65; and Hans Kelsen, "The Pure Theory of Law and Analytical Jurisprudence," *Harvard Law Review* 55 (1941): 44–70.

to the actor. Hence, unless international law is enforceable by some power above the sovereign state, it is not really law. Hans Kelsen, founder of the Pure Theory of Law, goes so far as to define law in terms of its enforceability: Only if violation of a norm elicits a coercive response can that norm be interpreted as a legal rule.[8] It is the *response* that defines the character of a norm rather than the mere content. *Law* is a statement of coercibility.[9]

Among the coercive measures that states utilize is a vast array of forceful and nonforceful acts. Nonforceful acts are referred to as *retorsions, which are reciprocal punitive acts,* and often referred to as nonforceful *acts of retaliation.* If one state should take steps to restrict the imports of another, the victimized state may respond by freezing the assets of the first state held in the banks of the second. In general, such acts are proportionate, so that escalation might be averted.

Retaliatory acts which are responses to forceful violations and which themselves involve actions that would otherwise be considered illegal, are called *reprisals.* Because such acts involve use of military matériel, it is difficult to measure and to maintain proportion. Yet it is normally held that reprisals ought to be equivalent to the original violation. Familiar acts of reprisal in recent history include the American bombing raids of North Vietnam as a response to the alleged attacks upon American destroyers in the Tonkin Gulf in the summer of 1964, and Israeli air strikes on guerrilla sites after Arab governments failed to prevent terrorist activitists.

The ultimate sanction in international relations is *war.* War is a political instrument, undertaken not always to destroy, but to deprive the target state of the ability, and of the will, to undertake further violations of normal behavior. The threat of war, then, may deter states from aberrant behavior; and the use of war as a response to prior actions is punitive. But in either case, the major intention of a state undertaking responsive warfare is to force *political* submission.

Traditionally, responses to illegal behavior have been left to aggrieved states. Indeed, international law includes a doctrine of *self-help*, which permits each state to launch punitive responses to illegal or other noxious acts. But while the doctrine of self-help (a by-product of absolute sovereignty) tries to provide international politics with formal and legal means for sanction, it is apparent that abuses or excesses actually contribute to international anarchy. Primarily for this reason, twentieth century interna-

---

[8] See Hans Kelsen, "The Pure Theory of Law and Analytical Jurisprudence," p. 58; "The Pure Theory of Law," *Law Quarterly Review* 50 (1934): 474–98: 485 ff.; and *General Theory of Law and State* (Cambridge: Harvard University Press, 1949), pp. 51–58.

[9] The coercive theory of law is not, however, universally accepted. For major exceptions, see Gerhart Niemeyer, *Law Without Force: The Function of Politics in International Law* (Princeton: Princeton University Press, 1941) and Michael Barkun, *Law Without Sanctions: Order in Primitive Societies and the World Community* (New Haven: Yale University Press, 1968).

tional organizations have striven to replace unilateral sanctions by *collective sanctions*.[10] This process was begun by the League of Nations Covenant (Article 11), which inscribed the principle that "Any war or threat of war . . . is hereby declared a matter of concern to the whole League. . . ." This concern was manifested through Article 16:

> Should any Member of the League resort to war . . . it shall *ipso facto* be deemed to have committed an act of war against all other Members of the League, which hereby undertake immediately to subject it to the severance of all trade or financial relations, the prohibition of all intercourse between the nationals of the Covenant-breaking State and the State, and the prevention of all financial, commercial or personal intercourse between the nationals of the Covenant-breaking State and the nationals of any other State, whether a Member of the League or not.

The Covenant further authorized the Council to recommend to states what military forces they should contribute for the implementation of Article 16.

These principles of the League of Nations were greatly expanded by the Charter of the United Nations. Chapter VII of the Charter, entitled "Action with Respect to Threats to the Peace, Breaches of the Peace, and Acts of Aggression," authorizes the Security Council to determine the existence of a threat to international stability and to recommend either peaceful measures for its resolution or coercive acts short of force. Ultimately, however, in Article 42, the Security Council is authorized to call upon states to use armed force in behalf of the organization.

> Should the Security Council consider that measures provided for in Article 41 would be inadequate or have proved inadequate, it may take such action by air, sea, or land forces as may be necessary to maintain or restore international peace and security. Such action may include demonstrations, blockade, and other operations by air, sea, or land forces of Members of the United Nations.

This principle of "all against one"—the entire world against the aggressor— is termed *collective security*. This differs both from self-help, which is a doctrine of unilateral action, and from collective self-defense, which is an alliance arrangement by which a few states agree that an attack upon one shall be considered an attack upon all.

Since the United Nations is not a government and must depend upon states for military forces, much of Chapter VII is devoted to the means by which such forces are to be placed at the disposal of the Security Council. Since the Military Staff Committee has been wholly unable to create a stand-by force, the ability of the Security Council to act still rests upon

---

[10] For a systematic study of Security Council responses to unilateral reprisals, especially in the Middle East, see Derek Bowett, "Reprisals Involving Resource to Armed Force," *American Journal of International Law* 66 (1972): 1–36.

states' willingness to be the Council's agents. To this end, Article 48 provides that:

> The action required to carry out the decisions of the Security Council for the maintenance of international peace and security shall be taken by all the Members of the United Nations or by some of them, as the Security Council may determine.

Despite the apparent limitlessness of Security Council authority on enforcement action, the Council has never undertaken an act of enforcement within the full meaning of the expression and of the Charter's provisions. Demands for action have been highly politicized, and have failed to achieve the concurrence of a majority of the Security Council members—including the permanent members, which are the United States, the Soviet Union, Britain, France and China (until 1971 the last of these having been represented by an envoy of the government of the Republic of China on Taiwan). Among the great impediments to Security Council action is that in creating the United Nations, the Great Powers sought to prevent action against their own interests by including in the Charter the principle of Great Power unanimity. Article 27 requires that matters of substance be decided by a majority of nine of the fifteen members "including the concurring votes of the permanent members." Only in the case of the United Nations response to the invasion of South Korea in 1950 has the Security Council been able to transcend its internal politics to vote enforcement; but since the Soviet delegation did not participate in the decision (because of their boycott after UN refusal to seat the Peking representative), it cannot be said that collective security was invoked within the full meaning of the Charter even in the Korean situation.

Enforcement measures are not the sole means of United Nations sanction. Other methods involve diplomatic intervention, economic sanctions, and peace-keeping operations. In the thirty-years of the United Nations, over one hundred disputes have been submitted for collective consideration. While none has resulted in enforcement except for the peculiar Korean decision, troops have been dispatched in a dozen cases for truce observation purposes or for interposition between combatants. In the same time period, there have been thirty-five cases which have *not* been submitted for UN consideration.[11]

In its economic sanctions, the UN has followed in the path of the League of Nations, which undertook economic sanctions against Italy in 1935–36 for its attack upon Ethiopia. In the UN period, the most celebrated sanctions have been those voted against China by the General Assembly in 1951 as a result of Chinese intervention in the Korean War, and the 1967 decision of the Security Council to isolate Southern Rhodesia for

[11] Ernst B. Haas, Robert L. Butterworth and Joseph S. Nye, "Conflict Management by International Organizations," (a learning module) (Morristown, N.J.: General Learning Press, 1973).

Early Post-War View of the United Nations

Source: Philip Dorf, *Visualized World History* (New York: Oxford Books, 1952). Copyright © 1952 by Oxford Book Co., a division of William H. Sadlier, Inc. Reprinted by permission.

its policy of racial separation following its unilateral declaration of independence from Britain.

As in other cases of economic sanctions, effectiveness in the Rhodesian situation was limited by the twin problems of (1) achieving universal participation and (2) the resistance of national elites to external coercion, especially when the issue was one of prominent internal concern. With respect to universal participation, even states usually sympathetic to Britain's policy demonstrated weak compliance.[12] The United States, for example, by executive order, imposed restraints upon imports originating in Rhodesia,

Provided, however, that the prohibition against dealing in commodities

[12] Report of the Committee Established in Pursuance of Resolution 352 (1968) of May 29, 1968 (New York: UN Publications S/8954, dated December 30, 1968); also, Johan Galtung, "On the Effects of Economic Sanctions, with Examples from the Case of Rhodesia," *World Politics* 19, no. 3 (April 1967): 378–416; Frederick Hoffmann, "The Functions of Economic Sanctions," *Journal of Peace Research*, no. 2 (1967); 140–60; and Ronald Segal, ed., *Sanctions Against South Africa* (London: Penguin, 1964).

or products exported from Southern Rhodesia shall not apply to any such commodities or products which, prior to the date of this Order, had been lawfully imported into the United States.[13]

As a matter of international interest, the United States sought formally to implement the Security Council sanctions. But as a matter of self-interest, the U.S. government demurred from full implementation by interpreting the sanctions to affect only commodities in which trade had not customarily occurred between the two nations. The reason was that Southern Rhodesia is a prime supplier of chromium to the United States, and continued flow of this resource is necessary for production of steel alloys needed in, among other things, military hardware.

This decentralization of international sanctions remains one of the major weaknesses of international politics. While international bodies sometimes make *decisions* in the implementation of sanctions, member states must implement them. The states are the importers and exporters in the international system. It is they that command industrial economies and the passage of goods across national boundaries. Just as Joseph Stalin once remarked that the Pope has no divisions, so too does the United Nation have no troops of its own, no industries that produce the coveted commodities which, if withheld, might alter the external or internal policies of states. The UN has no chromium deposits to withhold from the United States. Furthermore, the United Nations is wholly dependent upon its members for operating funds, and whatever decisional authority its members give it, its ability to take action depends not only upon decision, but upon means. Without the support, the wealth, and the material assistance of national governments, the United Nations is incapable of effective implementation of sanctions. The resistance of governments to proposals that would give the UN an independent treasury is motivated principally by the desire to retain control over sanctioning processes in international politics.

In the absence of a reliable system of collective sanctions, individual and group sanctions must be accepted as legitimate within current international law. Until the states can achieve their demands through collective actions, governments and their close allies will invoke coercive self-help. As a result, the imposition of individual sanctions is abundantly common.

Some cases in which sanctions are threatened see no actual implementation. The United States, for example, did not impose measures upon those Latin American states which nationalized privately-owned American property, despite legislation that authorizes the president to discontinue aid in the absence of adequate compensation.

A most interesting possibility of sanctions between major powers has

---

[13] United States Department of State Release no. 176, July 29, 1968; in *U.S. Department of State Bulletin* 59 (1968): 199, and as reprinted in *American Journal of International Law* 63 (1969): 128–30 in the section entitled "Contemporary Practice of the United States Relating to International Law."

been raised by the Soviet refusal to permit Jews to emigrate, and later the Soviet consent to do so only after payment of an exorbitant "education tax." This became an issue of public debate when hopes for expanded Soviet-American trade brightened (1972–74). Several interest groups demanded withholding agreement until after relaxation of Moscow's emigration policy. These pressures were expressed in the Jackson-Brock Amendment, which imposed restraints upon American trade with the Soviet Union until the latter recognized the open right to emigrate.

Other acts of unilateral sanction may also be noted. In the fall of 1975, after the United States suffered several embarrassing defeats at the United Nations, including the majority declaration equating Zionism with racism, it became American policy to threaten with economic sanction those of its friends who contributed to the continuing embarrassment. In another instance, as potential recipient of sanctions, the United States was informed by Britain and France early in 1976 that if it refused limited landing rights in American airports to the supersonic transport plane Concorde, they would initiate economic sanctions against the U.S.

The frequent resort to individual sanctions leads some to conclude that international law is incapable of restraining states. Yet we know beyond doubt that much of the conduct of states *is* regulated, and that it is regulated by legal means. We know, for example, that the law of the high seas is highly developed though laden with modern complications; that diplomatic and consular personnel may rely upon foreign governments for specified treatment; that there exist developed principles for international exchange of fugitives through extradition; and that a host of relatively nonpolitical functions is regulated by international conventions. We know equally well, however, that the power relations of governments are but sparsely regulated, and even then imperfectly. The General Pact for the Renunciation of War (The Kellogg-Briand Pact, 1928) was considered inapplicable in cases of self-defense, and each state retained the right to determine the conditions and needs of its defense. Article 51 of the UN Charter continues to permit "individual or collective self-defense" prior to Security Council assumption of responsibility. By the same token, neither France nor China has entered into the Nuclear Non-Proliferation Treaty nor is either likely to do so until after having achieved its desired level of deterrent capability. And while the United States, the Soviet Union and Britain have foresworn nuclear testing at sea and in the atmosphere, they have reserved the right to continue nuclear competition by underground testing.

The Effectiveness of International Law

If we are to conclude that international law provides effective restraints upon states, then we must demonstrate not merely the existence of legal principles, but also the willingness of states to comply with them. Compliance is a function of several factors, among them: (1) the subject matter that law seeks to regulate; (2) changes in the motives and needs of governments; (3) the ability of states to violate the law without serious threat of sanctions; and (4) the importance of the outcome of an event. So while we are concerned here with international *law*, each of these elements is subjected to the *political* judgment of the state. The decision as to whether one will be "law-abiding" is a decision for the state's political apparatus. A state's compliance with legal obligations is a function of (1) the degree to which issues are politicized and (2) the state's ability to behave in a lawless manner without serious threat of adverse consequences.

International law consists of norms of varying political levels. On some subjects states readily recognize the utility of collective regulation, especially where the subject matter is relatively mechanical and depoliticized. This level of law, referred to as *the law of reciprocity*, is a network of treaties and customs through which governments acknowledge reciprocal benefit. Compliance with these norms is predictable.

As the subject matter of the law becomes more politicized, however, states are less willing to enter into formal regulation, or to do so only with loopholes for escape from apparent constraints. In this area, called *the law of community*, governments are generally less willing to sacrifice their sovereign liberties. In a revolutionary international system, in which change is rapid and direction unclear, the integrity of the law of community is weak, and compliance with its often flaccid norms is correspondingly uncertain.

The law of the political framework resides above these other two levels, and consists of the legal norms governing the ultimate power relations of states. This is the most politicized level of international relations; hence, pertinent law is extremely primitive. Those legal norms that do exist suffer from all of the political machinations which one might expect. States have taken care to see that their behavior is only minimally constrained; the few international legal norms they have created always provide avenues of escape. The Great Power veto in the UN Security Council is a case in point.[14]

If law attempts to depoliticize international relations, then what may exist today in one of these levels of law, may tomorrow reside in another. International conditions may change, or domestic politics may alter a government's willingness to depoliticize an external issue. Thus the predictability of compliance may be determined not merely by the level of the subject matter, but by a state's determination to affect certain outcomes of international events. Compliance, then, and the overall effectiveness of positive international law, may be viewed as a horizontal problem as well as a vertical one, and may be represented as shown in Figure 11–1. Behind these indicators of compliance are social and political motives. It is the intent of this

[14] Stanley Hoffmann, "International Systems and International Law," *World Politics* 14 (1961): 205–37.

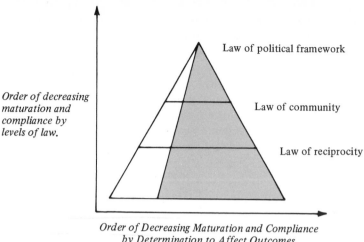

Order of decreasing maturation and compliance by levels of law.

Law of political framework

Law of community

Law of reciprocity

Order of Decreasing Maturation and Compliance by Determination to Affect Outcomes.

FIGURE 11–1   Levels of Compliance and Political Salience

book to demonstrate that the socio-political motivation is attributable primarily to the respective perceptions which the major actors hold of the international system. Therefore, to understand more fully the effectiveness of international law, it is necessary to turn to the views those actors hold of it.

The American View of International Law

The view which the United States takes of international law stems from America's European origins and from the fact that the United States is heir to the central political position previously held by Great Britain. The United States is a by-product of Western European culture and civilization, and is the first offspring of the British Empire. Despite the revolutionary separation from Britain, in its legal traditions and international outlook the United States behaves as the progeny of Europe.

International law evolved in a Eurocentric world, its norms originally serving the reciprocal convenience of European monarchs. But as the trade of the European states became global, and as European empires swelled, the European view of international law became imprinted upon much of the inhabited world. Law came to protect and serve *capitalist* economic interests; the doctrine of noninterference in the policies of other states was used in part to foster imperialism; the law of the seas facilitated the commercial and military shipping of the richest and most powerful. Many of these laws were oblivious—and occasionally hostile—to the interests of competing economic systems and to colonized populations. Yet they enjoyed a high degree of integrity, since they had the political protection of the states whose interests they served. Thus the United States, reared in the cultural, economic, and legalistic traditions of Britain and Europe, inherited dominance of a Euro-American world prior to World War II in which existing international law was much to its advantage. In the interwar period the United States took a major role in expanding this legal system along the same lines, seeking, for example, to sponsor a vast network of treaties for peaceful settlement of international disputes. It also participated in the functional activities of the League of Nations, and sought international economic regulation through bilateral and limited multilateral pacts.

The postwar world presented different conditions as the Euro-American domination of international politics began to dissolve. The security of the Western-oriented concepts of international law fell under stern challenge. The breakup of colonial empires strained legal norms, as did the rapid proliferation of new states. The bellicose unwillingness of the Soviet government to comply with formal norms threatened American interests throughout the world. Soviet refusal to permit self-determination in the countries of Eastern Europe, the brutal absorption of Latvia, Lithuania, and Estonia, the Soviet-inspired Czechoslovakian *coup-d'état* in 1948, the launching of the Korean War, guerrilla fighting in Greece, Turkey, and Iran—all these events and more underscored the law-breaking character of Soviet foreign objectives.

Besides codifying customary law to formalize the international legal order, the United States turned to the UN as a focal point of international political and ideological struggles. It relied upon the General Assembly to pass quasi-legislation designed to foster peaceful change. At the time of the Korean War (1950) it utilized the Security Council in calling for defense of the aggrieved South Koreans. The refusal of the Soviet Union to participate in this collective deliberation gave further testimony to the Kremlin's refusal to cooperate in the legal order. The military intervention of China accentuated the law-breaking character of international communism, but the General Assembly joined with the United States in labeling China an aggressor and retaliating with economic sanctions.

But the revolutionary international system in the years following World War II was not always receptive to the positivist concept of international law. Soviet and Chinese behavior often threatened global norms, and often made compliance with them quite dangerous for the United States. As new forms of politics appeared, they escaped from positivist regulation. Finally the United States was forced by Soviet policies to adopt neorealistic attitudes toward the law. Hence the Truman Doctrine occurred outside the UN, and the occupation of Japan was replaced by a close Japanese-American security arrangement for the Far East. Whenever possible, then, Washington pursued a policy of enhancing the positivist approach to international law; but whenever Soviet foreign policy prevented this, the United States was forced to resort to the broader standards of neorealism.

The View of America's Major Allies

Because of the cold war, rapid rates of industrialization and the westernization of the Japanese economy after World War II, Washington's principal allies have had similar attitudes toward positive international law in all three categories: community, reciprocity, and the political context. Indeed, because of their social and economic origins, the United States and Canada derived much of their perception of international law from Europe. Japan, earlier a victim of such a legal order, after 1950 came to enjoy its fruits, and thus adopted a Western sympathetic attitude.

Recent events have forced changes in the attitudes of these industrialized states, however. The burgeoning resource scarcity in Europe and Japan, in particular, has resulted in a call for new systems of allocation; but more specifically, it has given rise to new attitudes concerning economic coercion. While industrial states have always appreciated the coercive capability of resource boycott, they have only recently felt the negative effects of such boycotts themselves. Now, though they hardly share with the resource-rich Third World the same objectives concerning international economic law, they are prepared at last to clarify economic rights and duties on a reciprocal basis. Thus necessity has forced upon them a reassessment of the economic portion of the law of community. Canada, itself richly endowed in natural resources, is driven to the same sense of reciprocal adjustment not out of fear of boycott, but out of sympathy for the Third World's sovereign compromises in asymmetrical economic relations, a sympathy engendered by Canada's own asymmetrical relation to the American economy.

The Soviet View of International Law

In contrast to the United States, the Soviet Union gained major power status in a world fundamentally hostile to its political, ideological, and economic principles. Its view of international law arose from the writings of Karl Marx, who had seen the state as an instrument through which one class oppresses others. To Marxist jurists, law is the formal instrument of such oppression. They looked upon the law of nations, therefore, as a body of rules and principles through which powerful classes in several societies undertake jointly to promote class exploitation in the international system. International law, like all other law, is of class origins.

Yet Soviet leaders have always found reason to cooperate with prevailing international law. Their principal justification was the Stalinst premise that the withering away of states must await the universal socialist revolution; and, meanwhile, Soviet politics is partly motivated by the horror of capitalist encirclement. It is necessary to participate at least minimally in capitalist international law to survive this encirclement. In later years, after Nikita Khrushchev introduced his notion of peaceful coexistence, it became the fashion of Soviet international legal science to promote cooperation with the institutions of interstate law as a means to achieve peaceful coexistence.

Although it is officially denied by Soviet spokesmen, the contemporary view, for practical purposes, is founded upon the notion that three bodies of international law exist concurrently. The first is that body of law which regulates the class interests of the capitalist nations. The second pertains to the relations between the capitalist and socialist worlds. Finally, they posit a totally separate body of Communist-bloc law.

The second category is the law of peaceful coexistence. Here the Soviets understand there to exist a body of rules and principles which govern diplomatic and economic relations between East and West. While they take a positivistic view of its content, they nevertheless insist upon distinguishing between textbook law and political reality. While they opt for treaties, particularly bilateral treaties, as the source of choice, they nevertheless hold that politically outmoded rules have lost the quality of law. Probably because of their political minority status in international organizations, they are more sensitive than the United States to political controls of international law.

Intra-bloc law is another area in which Soviet outlooks appear more forthright than those of the United States. While the United States purports to respect the self-determination of its friends and allies, it has not always demurred from commanding domestic politics abroad. Recent examples are the American manipulation of the government of South Vietnam especially from the mid-1950's to the mid-1960's, and American intervention in the Dominican Republic in 1965. In broader terms, the Monroe Doctrine was more a doctrine of unilateral intervention than a doctrine of hemispheric self-determination.

Soviet policy, at least recently, has been more forthright in its treatment of intra-bloc law. The climax occurred in the invasion and occupation of Czechoslovakia in the summer of 1968 by troops of the Soviet Union and of its Warsaw Pact allies. The legal rationale for this act, called the Brezhnev Doctrine, holds that among socialist states, sovereign liberties are subordinate to the needs of all the states collectively. Hence the Czech government is free to establish internal policy, but not to the detriment of the overall interests of socialist states. Presumably, the Brezhnev Doctrine is as much a part of the international law of the socialist states as the Monroe Doctrine and its remnants have been of inter-American relations. In addition, while Marxist theory requires that nonsocialist law be of *class* origins, that of the group members is based upon collective social need as centrally determined.[15]

[15] For recent interpretations of the Soviet science of international law, see especially Kazimierz Grzybowski, *Soviet Public International Law* (Leyden: A. W. Sijthoff, 1970). Good Western commentaries may be found in James L. Hildebrand, *Soviet International Law* (Buffalo, N.Y.: William S. Hein and Co., Inc., 1969); Edward

To summarize briefly, Soviet jurists understand general international law to be rules and principles which govern the relations of socioeconomically different states, based upon the necessity of peaceful coexistence. Socialist international law, however, which regulates the relations of the socialist countries, emerges from the principle of socialist internationalism, a doctrine which goes directly to the heart of sovereign theory. According to G.I. Tunkin, at present the most authoritative spokesman among Soviet jurists, this new principle is "the result of the application of the principle of proletarian internationalism to relations between states of the socialist type."[16]

The Chinese View of International Law

Though the Chinese share with the Soviet Union the notion of the class origins of international law, they face the additional problem of having been a major victim of Western treaty law. During the Century of Humiliation, China was subjected to treaty relations based on Western power superiority and the ability of other states to imperialize its territory and its commerce. More recent events, such as exclusion of the People's Republic of China from the Japanese Peace Treaty (1951), have accentuated the Chinese alienation from prevailing international legal norms. Although all Chinese governments of the present century have deplored the "unequal treaties" and have shared the determination to repossess territory granted to other states, none has coupled these determinations with other diplomatic grievances more vigorously than the present government.[17] It looks upon Western-oriented international law as vacuous humanistic platitudes designed to attract China's support and participation on Western grounds. The concept of President Wilson's Fourteen Points as the gospel of World War I and the Atlantic Charter of World War II with its stress upon fundamental freedoms, seem to the Chinese to have been withdrawn in time of peace, and the actual destiny of China cynically given over to other "legal" agreements. Most vexations among these is the Soviet-American

---

McWhinney, *"Peaceful Coexistence" and Soviet-Western International Law* (Leyden: A. W. Sijthoff, 1964); and Bernard A. Ramundo, *Peaceful Coexistence: International Law in the Building of Communism* (Baltimore: The Johns Hopkins Press, 1967). A useful collection of papers by authors of several nationalities appears in Hans W. Baade, ed., *The Soviet Impact on International Law* (Dobbs Ferry, N.Y.: Oceana Publications, Inc., 1965).

[16] As quoted in Chris Osakwe, "Socialist International Law Revisited," *American Journal of International Law* 66 (1972): 596–600, at 598.

[17] For a general treatment of the unequal treaties, see William L. Tung, *China and the Foreign Powers: The Impact of and Reaction to Unequal Treaties* (Dobbs Ferry, N.Y.: Oceana, 1970).

Yalta protocol (1945), which enlisted Soviet military assistance against Japan at the cost of Chinese political and territorial integrity.[18]

The contemporary Chinese view of international law, then, is shaped by three factors: (1) the historical perception that Western-oriented law has aided Western growth at the expense of China, and that the Soviet Union increasingly benefits from the same; (2) that international law has class origins which make it a peculiar instrument of transnational class struggle through economic oppression and intervention; and (3) that as an industrializing socialist state, China's sympathies on the restraints and licenses of law lie more with the Third World nations than with the Soviet Union.

Unlike the highly industrialized states whose interests are worldwide, China's growth phase dictates that its interests be regional and, for the most part, defensive. Except for attempts to repossess former territories lost under duress, and except for its intervention in Korea when its borders seemed threatened, modern China has not behaved as an aggressive or expansionist state. China's interest is not so much in expanding its rights as in attempting to restrict the rights, and formalize the obligations, of other major powers who have interests in Asia. Thus China argues for the sanctity of treaties, though it acknowledges membership in few. As its fundamental statement on international law, it has accepted the content of a Sino-Indian declaration of 1954, which encompasses the five Primary Principles of Peaceful Coexistence:

1. mutual respect for sovereignty and territorial integrity
2. mutual nonaggression
3. mutual noninterference in internal affairs
4. sovereign equality and mutual advantage (or benefit)
5. peaceful coexistence

(Unlike the Soviet formulation enunciated by Khrushchev in 1961, "peaceful coexistence" in Chinese terms does not mean peaceful *competition*.)

Although most of these principles do not depart substantially from the classical notions of Western international law, the Chinese formulation stresses mutual advantage more than others do. Imbued with an historical sense of inequality in treaty relations, the Chinese argue that unless a treaty exists for mutual benefit, it is not binding regardless of the apparent formalities of consent. Although many Western scholars and statesmen subscribe to the principle *rebus sic stantibus* (inapplicable treaties cease to carry obligations), Chinese jurists tend to argue explicitly that treaties need not be renegotiated or formally terminated if their obligations were im-

---

[18] Ishwer C. Ojha, *Chinese Foreign Policy in an Age of Tradition: The Diplomacy of Cultural Despair* (Boston: Beacon Press, 1969), particularly Chapter III, "China and the Western World Order."

perialistically imposed. It is held, rather, that in these cases the victim state may simply renounce obligations.[19] Despite ideological origins similar to the Soviet Union, the Chinese view of international law is tempered more by history and policy imperatives than by ideology.[20]

The Third World View of International Law

The Third World nations share China's perception of having been victimized by the Western international order, and view much of its legal content as designed to facilitate Euro-American growth at their expense. New states of revolutionary birth sympathize, furthermore, with the Chinese view that the law of nations still is pitted against their interests. But even old Third World states, and those which became independent through peaceful means and with formal preparation for self-government under UN surveillance, have found that much existing international law is inimical to their needs and politics.

The element of succession which distresses these states most is *devolution*. Upon achieving independence, many states have found themselves left with debts and commitments which they are expected to honor. Certain obligations have devolved upon new governments, some informally and others through the formal device of the *inheritance agreement*. Some of these may be bilateral obligations easily renegotiated into modified arrangements called *novations*. In other cases, however, the other partner may be unwilling to change the agreement. Here the new state is likely to adopt the Chinese view that, conditions having changed, the obligation no longer holds. Some new states have taken up the *clean slate doctrine*, which insists on the nullity of all prearrangements.

Multilateral treaties present a more complex problem, since renegotiation with multiple partners is more difficult. The pressure to accept responsibility may be heightened by the former controlling capital in behalf of third parties. Furthermore, upon entry into international organizations the new state assumes oblgations in the creation of which it did not participate.

---

[19] Hungdah Chiu, *The People's Republic of China and the Law of Treaties* (Cambridge: Harvard University Press, 1972), especially Chapter VI, "Suspension and Termination of Treaties."

[20] James Chieh Hsiung, *Law and Policy in China's Foreign Relations: A Study of Attitudes and Practices* (New York: Columbia University Press, 1972). For general studies of the Chinese attitude not previously cited, see Hungdah Chiu, "Communist China's Attitude Toward International Law," *American Journal of International Law* 60 (1966): 245–67; Jerome Alan Cohen, "China's Attitude Toward International Law—and Our Own," *Proceedings of the American Society of International Law* (1967), p. 108–16; Luke T. Lee, "Treaty Relations of the People's Republic of China: A Study of Compliance," *University of Pennsylvania Law Review* 111 (1967): 271; and Suzanne Ogden, "Sovereignty and International Law: The Perspective of the People's Republic of China," *New York University Journal of International Law and Politics* 7 (1974): 1–32.

Certain unwanted restraints may have to be undertaken as the price of membership benefits.

Customary law creates larger problems, too. The Third World countries are expected to partake virtually without consent; and it is here that they find themselves most disadvantaged by the legal rules and principles created by, and in the interests of, the more powerful states. This is especially true in the economic sphere, where the desperate need for investment capital and favorable terms of trade may be held in ransom by externally imposed trade principles, liquidity agreements, and tariff regulations.[21] In this regard, the Third World has combined efforts to develop a more advantageous structure of positive international law designed to overcome some of the collective economic strength of the industrialized states. Their principal mechanism has been the creation of the United Nations Conference on Trade and Development (UNCTAD), and its use to press their common needs upon the wealthier countries in the United Nations. More recently, the voting majority which the Third World has achieved at the UN has enabled it to pass the Declaration of the Establishment of a New International Economic Order and its companion Programme for Action, as well as the Charter of Economic Rights and Duties of States. It is now clear that the efforts of the underindustrialized world toward the establishment of an international legal order will turn principally upon effective law for economic self-determination. Accordingly, it will applaud the efforts of both the Organization for Economic Cooperation and Development and the United Nations Task Force on Multinational Corporations to conclude codes of conduct for international business, with the hope of reducing by law some of the neoimperialistic patterns justified under existing Western-oriented international law. So too will it welcome the recent efforts of the International Criminal Law Commission to define international economic crimes, and the concurrent work of the Foundation for the Establishment of an International Criminal Court to found a Commission of Inquiry to hear allegations of violation of new international economic law.

To the Third World, and especially to its newly independent members, the main objection to international law combines the notion of sovereignty with the philosophical understanding of self-determination. The achievement of independence illuminates a bold fact of international life—that in the face of disparate power, sovereignty is an abstraction; while formal self-determination may have been achieved, it does not confer all the latitudes of an economically powerful state. The destiny of the state is in large measure determined from without, both because it is expected to comply with certain established rules, and because relations with more powerful states and corporations may limit economic and political prerogatives. In

[21] An exhaustive study of the problems of succession is found in D. P. O'Connell, *State Succession in Municipal Law and International Law*, two volumes (Cambridge: Cambridge University Press, 1967).

place of formal colonialism, the economically less developed states find that international law provides few, if any, defenses against the *neoimperialistic* trend by which the developed states encroach upon their economies.[22]

Conclusion

The diverse outlooks toward contemporary international law have occurred because four fundamental bases of the Western legal order no longer enjoy universal validity. First, it is no longer accepted that there is a fundamental distinction between law, on the one hand, and ideology and politics on the other. Second, there has been a breakdown in the practical distinction between war and peace, and the mere conviction of the desirability of peace. Third, our revolutionary international system does not accept the sanctity of the coexistence of independent, territorially discrete states. And finally, it is no longer universally held that governments are able to undertake mutually-binding obligations through consent and voluntary compliance.[23] These premises have deteriorated primarily because we live in a multicultural world which the West no longer dominates.

The future of international law, however, is not bleak. Though multiculturism will continue to mark the international system, there is encouraging evidence that material interdependence, especially among states of equivalent power, fosters the growth of positive legal principles. In addition, as friendships and enmities change, some bilateral law may cease to be observed among new enemies; but new law may arise among new friends who have new-found mutual interests. In the meanwhile, some multilateral law may have developed. Finally, research suggests that the social effects of industrialization are universal, and that they result in intersocietal tolerances which did not exist during periods of disparate economic capability.[24] On social, political and economic grounds, therefore, international law is intrinsic to transformation and modernization of the international system, even though the "law of the political context" has remained primitive so far.

International Organization

In the discussion of international law, we noted that the development of an effective legal order is impeded by the lack of authoritative international institutions. Since 1648, and especially since 1815, statesmen have sought to remedy this defect by creating a network of international agencies for

[22] For self-determination aspects of the outlook upon international law, see Hann Bokor-Szego, *New States and International Law* (Budapest: Akademiai Kaido, 1970).

[23] Adda B. Bozeman, *The Future of Law in a Multicultural World* (Princeton: Princeton University Press, 1971), pp. 35–48 and 180–86.

[24] Edward L. Morse, "The Transformation of Foreign Policies: Modernization, Interdependence, and Externalization," *World Politics* 22 (1970): 371–92.

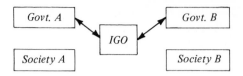

FIGURE 11–2   Intergovernmental Organizations (IGO's)

international decision-making. While there is little expectation that these will replace nation-states as principal actors, there is considerable evidence that their presence contributes to settlement of disputes, prevents the occurrence of disputes, and facilitates decision-making on a broad spectrum of problems.

But the notion of collective decision-making may carry an over-zealous implication. International institutions are authorized only in rare cases to impose their decisions upon members. *Inter*national organizations conduct their business among states, and do not reside above them. *Supra*national organizations, in contrast, of which there are few, have authority above the state and are capable of compelling it within carefully defined limits. International organizations, as presently constituted, do not pretend to supplant the nation-state or its authority over internal or external policies.

In a world of hostilities and power politics, students of international relations have traditionally focused upon public international organizations (also called *intergovernmental organizations* or IGO's). Their status with relation to states is described in Figure 11–2.

Recently, on the heels of communications and travel revolutions, and recognizing that business and other interests often transcend international boundaries, attention has been directed to private international organizations (also called *nongovernmental organizations*, or NGO's). These facilitate transactions by means other than governments, and they are the vehicles of transnational participation. Because governments become involved in their business only indirectly or secondarily, and because their principal subjects are individuals and organized social groups, they show a different picture (see Figure 11–3). While the IGO is a government-to-government institution, the NGO deals people-to-people. They are, respectively, intergovernmental and intersocietal.

The total number of international organizations is so vast as to require some systematic way of separating the parts from the whole; the distinction

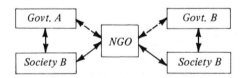

FIGURE 11–3   Nongovernmental Organizations (NGO's)

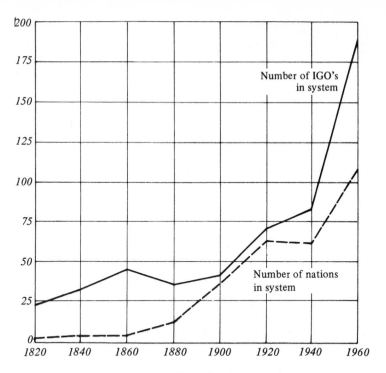

FIGURE 11–4   Number of Nations and IGO's in System in Successive Periods, 1815–1964

Source: Michael Wallace and J. David Singer, "International Organization in the Global System, 1815–1964: A Quantitative Description," 24 *International Organization* (1970): 277. Reprinted by permission of University of Wisconsin Press.

between NGO and IGO is only the beginning. (Figure 11–4 depicts the growth of each category.) In 1969, there existed no fewer than 2471 international institutions, of which 229 were IGO's and the remainder NGO's. But even among the IGO's the variety of content and intent is so wide that further subdivision is needed. That the North Atlantic Treaty Organization and the International Court of Justice are both IGO's ought not to imply that they have very much in common except that each has several member governments! The following typology (breakdown of types) suggests some of the important classifications and provides familiar examples:

I. Global Organizations
   A. Multi-purpose (United Nations)
   B. Single purpose or functional
      1. Economic (Economic and Social Council)
      2. Security (Security Council)

3. Anti-Imperial (Trusteeship Council)
4. Nutrition (Food and Agricultural Organization)
5. Transportation—sea (International Maritime Consultative Organization), air (International Civil Aviation Organization)
6. Communications—mail (International Postal Organization), telegraph (International Telegraphic Organization)
7. Judicial (International Court of Justice)

II. Sub-Global Organizations
  A. Intra-bloc organizations
    1. Economic (International Monetary Fund)
    2. Security (North Atlantic Treaty Organization)
  B. Regional Organizations
    1. Economic (European Economic Community)
    2. Security (Organization of American States: Rio Pact Aspects)
    3. Sociocultural and economic (Organization of American States: Bogotá Pact Aspects)
  C. Integrating Organizations
    1. Economic (European Coal and Steel Community)
    2. Judicial (European Court of Human Rights)

Whatever form an IGO may take, states enter into it because of anticipated benefits. But in determining the effectiveness of such institutions from a collective viewpoint, it is not mere service to governments that matters. There are three critical measurements of organizational ability to draw states into collective policies and, therefore, to overcome the potentially anarchical characteristics of the nation-state system.

Association or Disassociation?

The first of these is the *associating* or *disassociating* character of the organization. Does the activity of membership tend to draw states closer together, or does it accentuate their differences and drive them farther from collective decision-making? Does parliamentary diplomacy facilitate the discovery of workable common denominators, or does it magnify the differences among states? Does it help to remove the clouded images that states hold of one another, or does it further distort them? [25] From global perspective, even associating organizations have a paradoxical component: the more associating they may be with respect to members, the more disassociating they may be in relation to outside states. The North Atlantic Treaty Organization is a case in point. Though it intends to be associating among the members, its existence maintains the disassociation of Europe.

[25] Bruce Russett, *International Regions and the International System* (Chicago: Rand McNally and Company, 1967).

But it exemplifies also a second phenomenon: as the necessities of the cold war have abated, and as Europe has embarked upon other paths of association, NATO has come to have internal *disassociating* effects.

Contribution to Future Improvements

The second test of organizational effectiveness is its contribution to change in the international system. While institutions are often imprisoned by the will and power of their members (which, as sovereign states, safeguard their supreme decision-making capability), they may make independent contributions to world politics, often by helping members to clarify obscured possibilities in their relations. But they may also contribute through a more complex mechanism. Dag Hammarskjold, second Secretary-General of the United Nations, visualized two distinctly different models of UN effectiveness. The organization might be either a "static conference machinery" or a "dynamic instrument of governments" for introducing a new world order. Far from prescribing a supranational role, Mr. Hammarskjold hoped only that a politically immune international civil service, together with quasi-legislative competence of the deliberative body, might help states overcome their immediate and narrow interests.[26] The extent to which an international organization is able to emulate the second model may be taken as one of the criteria of its effectiveness in stabilizing the international system.

Constraints on Member States

The third criterion is closely related. It is taken for granted (1) that states enter IGO's in anticipation of benefits to their individual interests and (2) that institutions become the instruments of their members' foreign policies. Under these circumstances, are such institutions ever capable of bringing restraint upon states' behavior? True, they serve definite purposes for specific governments; but in the long run, are they able to constrain governmental behavior?

Since our concern is with the global system, it is necessary to assess by these three standards the effectiveness of global IGO's. In the next chapter we consider integrating organizations and NGO's.

The United Nations System

The United Nations consists of six permanent organs, and a vast array of specialized agencies, conferences, funds and commissions. Table 11–2 categorizes some of these. Each body has different objectives and capa-

[26] Dag Hammarskjold, "Two Differing Concepts of United Nations Assayed," *United Nations Review* 8, no. 9 (September 1961): 12–17.

TABLE 11–2   United Nations System

Permanent Organs	Specialized Agencies	Conferences, Funds, Programmes, Commissions
General Assembly	World Health Organization	United Nations Conference on Trade and Development
Security Council	Food and Agricultural Organization	
Trusteeship Council	Intergovernmental Maritime Consultative Organization	United Nation's Children's Fund
Economic and Social Council	International Civil Aviation Organization	United Nations Special Fund
Secretariat	Universal Postal Union	Action Programme on International Environment
International Court of Justice	International Telecommunications Union	Action-Programme on Establishment of a New International Economic Order
	World Meteorological Organization	
	International Labor Organization	United Nations Development Programme
	United Nations Educational, Scientific and Cultural Organization (UNESCO)	International Law Commission
	International Atomic Energy Commission	International Refugee Organization
	International Bank for Reconstruction and Development	High Commission on Human Rights
	International Monetary Fund	
	International Intellectual Properties Organization	

bilities. As a result, each relates differently to the sovereignty of the state, and each has a different potential impact upon the international system and change therein.

The General Assembly

If modern IGO's attempt to emulate the American doctrine of separation of powers, then the General Assembly may be said to be the legislative branch of the UN system. Yet such a claim does not hold up much beyond form. The work of the Assembly is done through *parliamentary diplomacy*, a principle which combines the techniques of legislation and negotiation.[27] Yet while the General Assembly has broad competence to consider virtually any subject so long as it does not intrude upon the domestic jurisdiction of states, it has little authority to make binding decisions. Except for final decision-making authority on certain matters internal to the organization (budget, membership, temporary members of the Security Council), its conclusions are expressed in three forms, none of which is decisive.

Declaration. The first of these is the *declaration*, which is a pronouncement of principle. Such pronouncements do not have binding capacity, though they may result in subsequent treaties and may have customary or moral impact. One of the declarations of the General Assembly which has been most celebrated but least observed is the famous Universal Declaration of Human Rights (1948). Its principles have found their way into several constitutions, and it has become the substance of two international covenants on human rights. But the declaration itself lacks the force of law, despite adoption without a dissenting vote. By declaration, the General Assembly cannot render binding international law, though its activities may precede usage and later customary law. Since law-making is a highly political process, states are not generally willing to subordinate their sovereign controls to the General Assembly.

Resolution. The General Assembly's second decision-making instrument is the *resolution,* around which there swirls a controversy. Is it or is it not a source of international law binding upon states? If a resolution encompasses a previously accepted law, then the resolution does little more than illuminate existing law. But what is the effect of a resolution that imposes some new standard? Presumably, until many states acquiesce, law cannot be said to have been generated.[28]

But may it not be that *policy* has been implemented through the subsequent actions of states? If a resolution is of a recommendatory nature, calling upon states to act as agents of the General Assembly, then perhaps the General Assembly has transcended the will of some states in bringing about collectively determined policy. The *recommendatory resolution*, then, may not be legally binding, yet its execution by eager states may nevertheless place the imprimatur of the General Assembly upon their policy.[29] This distinction between legally binding norms and nonbinding

[27] Philip C. Jessup, "Parliamentary Diplomacy," *Recueil des Cours* 89 (The Hague Academy of International Law) (1956): 181–320.

[28] Leo Gross, "The United Nations and the Role of Law," *International Organization* 19 (1965): 537–61, especially 555–58.

[29] Jorge Castaneda, *Legal Effects of United Nations Resolutions* (New York: Columbia University Press, 1969).

norms engenders the notion of quasi-legislative competence of the General Assembly.[30]

But all of this assumes the willingness of states to act in behalf of the organ, usually indicating prior intention to act. As a result, the recommendatory resolution may have less of a policy-making function than a *legitimizing* function—one of the major activities of the United Nations.[31]

Convention. The third mechanism by which the General Assembly expresses its decisions is the *convention,* or multilateral treaty. Although we have previously noted the primacy of the treaty as a source of international law, the treaty-making power of the General Assembly is more qualified. In fact, the expression "United Nations treaty" has two meanings. The first refers to treaties signed by a state and by an organ of the UN, such as the General Assembly. These treaties, envisioned by the Charter, concern relations not between states, but between a state and the IGO. As a rule, these do little to alter the behavior of the state with respect to other states, though there are exceptions. When, in 1956, the Egyptian government agreed with the United Nations to permit the dispatch of peacekeeping troops to Egyptian soil, that agreement resulted in a major temporary change in the area's political events.[32]

The more common meaning of "United Nations treaty" concerns conventions generally applicable among members. Such treaties are debated on the floor of the Assembly and then put to votes. With passage, the treaty is carried back to member governments for domestic ratification. Ultimate decision-making, therefore, lies not with the membership collectively, but with individual governments. No government is bound until it has given formal constitutional assent, or until the treaty is formally in effect, conditions of which are determined by the treaty itself. Thus, despite the favorable position which treaties hold as sources of international law, treaties arranged by the General Assembly represent minimal concession to collective decision-making; and the process is not so centralized as the title indicates.[33]

It seems, then, that General Assembly decision-making authority lends little to situations affecting the interests of states. Yet history shows that

[30] For example, Richard A. Falk, "On the Quasi-Legislative Competence of the General Assembly," *American Journal of International Law* 60 (1966): 782–91.

[31] Inis L. Claude, "Collective Legitimization as a Political Function of the United Nations," *International Organization* 20 (1966): 367–79. This article does not deal specifically with the General Assembly.

[32] Rosalyn Higgins, *The Development of International Law Through the Political Organs of the United Nations* (London: Oxford University Press, 1963), especially Part V, "The Laws of Treaties: United Nations Practice."

[33] For a comprehensive treatment, see Henry H. Han, *International Legislation by the United Nations* (New York: Exposition Press, 1971).

majority voting has on some occasions bypassed the immobility of member governments. The first major case, one born out of the Korean War, was the Uniting for Peace Resolution, which sought to enlarge the Assembly's security role. The return of the Soviet delegation to the Security Council after a long absence stymied American ability to use that body to legitimize its war policy. Washington sought through this resolution to give the Assembly emergency capability, including the authority to call upon states to act in behalf of the membership in repelling armed aggression. The Soviet Union denounced the move as a subversion of the Council and of the special powers and privileges inscribed in the veto. Yet in practice, the Soviet Union has not consistently condemned the resolution. In the Middle East fighting of 1956, the disaffected Communist state Yugoslavia proposed placing the item on the Assembly's agenda; and when war resumed in 1967, the Soviet delegate did the same. Although the General Assembly has not discovered magical solutions to international conflict, the growth of its authority (to the consternation of at least one major power) has created a forum other than the veto-prone Security Council for collective consideration of matters affecting the peace of all.

A much more innovative role was played by the General Assembly, on the initiation by the Secretary-General, in 1956. Because of their participation in Middle East combat, Britain and France had immobilized the Security Council. When the issue was shifted to the General Assembly, it was suggested that Britain and France remove their forces in favor of a United Nations presence. The result was an Assembly mandate to Secretary-General Hammarskjold to formulate the principles of a new system which came to be known as "peace-keeping"—a *specific way* of keeping peace. The idea was not to enforce a political objective of one party against that of another, but to interpose a lightly armed force between belligerents to gain time for diplomacy. This was, then, preventive deployment of troops made available to the Assembly by states. Not only was its concept a departure from UN standards; its implementation was, also. Most remarkably, the membership accepted Hammarskjold's idea that the great powers be excluded from the action, on the ground that their presence would tend to expand, rather than to contract, the scope of conflict.

The Soviet Union's reaction to this step was the predictable one: The General Assembly had exceeded its powers and once again eroded the exclusive authority of the Security Council to take action on security matters. Furthermore, though the same principles were invoked by the Security Council in the handling of the Congo crisis of 1960, the Soviet Union objected to the Western-oriented manner in which the Secretary-General executed his mandate. Hence, by 1962 the Soviet Union, along with France and other governments, refused to pay their apportioned shares of the operations. They objected to the General Assembly's role in the Emergency Force for the Middle East, and they protested the Secretary-General's handling of the Congo operation. The financial crisis followed and, as we have seen, was only partially resolved by the International Court of Justice in the *Certain Expenses Case.*

It is widely agreed today that, except in matters directly affecting the Great Powers, peace-keeping has come to replace the original concept of collective security, though the Soviet Union and the United States are still at odds over the General Assembly's role.[34] Despite Great Power disagreement, the General Assembly created in 1965 a United Nations Special Committee on Peacekeeping Operations (the Committee of Thirty-three). As the only forum in which Washington and Moscow have directly traded ideas on peace-keeping, the hopes of this committee have run high. Its immediate aim is to arrange standby agreements with governments. Already, Canada, Norway, Iceland, Sweden, and Denmark have planned such contingents.[35]

The future of peace-keeping is far from determined, yet the fact remains that through its own initiative, over the objection of a major power, and with the help of a controversial advisory opinion of the ICJ, the General Assembly *has* contributed a new security concept. Even if it comes to rest exclusively in the hands of the Security Council, peace-keeping incontrovertibly came from the General Assembly. In this important matter, the Assembly was able to add to the international system, to transcend the will of many of the states, and not only to bring restraint upon parties in the Middle East and in the Congo, but to defuse the interests of the United States and the Soviet Union in intervening. Keeping in mind that this mechanism originated from a resolution of the General Assembly, measure the tone of this statement of a distinguished scholar of international organization:

> Perhaps the most significant development in the thinking of scholars and statesmen about international organization in the postwar period has been their gradual emancipation from the collective security fixation, their breaking out of the intellectual rut in which it was taken for granted that the suppression of aggression was so crucial a function of general international organizations that if this function could not be exercised, the only issue worth thinking about was how to make its exercise possible. Dag Hammarskjold gave dramatic and forceful expression to the new and less constricted approach to international organization when he put the question of how the United Nations could contribute directly to keeping the peace when it could not enforce the peace and answered the question

[34] Lincoln Bloomfield, "The United States, the Soviet Union, and the Prospects for Peacekeeping," *International Organization* 24 (1970): 548–65.

[35] Larry L. Fabian, *Soldiers Without Enemies* (Washington: The Brookings Institution, 1971), especially chapters V–VIII. For another general discussion of the future, see Arthur M. Cox, *Prospects for Peacekeeping* (Washington: The Brookings Institution, 1967).

by formulating the theory of preventive diplomacy, now generally known as peacekeeping.[36]

Clearly, one oak does not constitute a forest; demonstration of the General Assembly's overall effect upon the international system cannot hang upon one or two dramatic incidents. Yet there is reason to believe that its effectiveness is more frequent than the conventional wisdom admits. One study, which attempts to correlate effectiveness of action with the willingness of states to comply with Assembly resolutions, concludes that in twenty-nine resolutions concerning international political situations between 1946 and 1962, effectiveness of action reached 87 percent among those resolutions complied with by states. Where compliance has *not* been forthcoming, the level of effectiveness has been a scant 21 percent. It also substantiates that in matters dealing with threats to the peace, breaches of the peace are acts of aggression, the level of compliance and effectiveness is higher than in less dangerous and nonmilitary situations.[37] But these data pertain only to compliance with, and effectiveness of, General Assembly resolutions, which often deal only with parts of disputes. To this extent, and except for specified situations, the General Assembly shares with other international agencies failure to stop war situations, as detailed in the empirical data of yet another study.[38]

This discussion of the General Assembly's role has been confined to matters of international peace and security. But given the broad competence of the body, it is unjustifiable to write off its successes on social and economic issues. These, however, are left to later discussion of functional activities.

The Security Council

In comparison with the General Assembly, the Security Council of the UN is both more complex and more simple. It is more complex because it is the forum not only of general world politics, but of Great Power politics more intensively than is the General Assembly, with the result that clashes of opinion tend more deeply to wound the international system. Complexity is added by the type of subject matter with which the Council deals. Yet it is less complex because it has fewer methods by which to conduct its business, and because the veto power of the permanent members is able to prevent effective decision-making. Even more than in the General Assembly,

[36] Inis L. Claude, "The United Nations, the United States, and the Maintenance of Peace," *International Organization* 23 (1969): 621–36, p. 631.

[37] Gabriella Rosner Lande, "An Inquiry into the Successes and Failures of the United Nations General Assembly," in Leon Gordenker, ed., *The United Nations in International Politics* (Princeton: Princeton University Press, 1971), pp. 106–29.

[38] J. David Singer and Michael Wallace, "Preservation of Peace, 1816–1964: Some Bivariate Relationships," *International Organization* 24 (1970): 520–47.

the Security Council suffers from the inability to pass meaningful resolutions—a problem which logically precedes that of seeking compliance and effective implementation.

The Security Council grew out of the so-called "grand design" or "grand alliance" of World War II, from the hope that wartime Soviet-Western cooperation might endure in the postwar years, and that together they (with the help of China) might accept the responsibility for maintaining peace. The idea thrived on wartime necessity, itself a "strange alliance," considering the ideological disparities, suspicions, and mutual antipathies of the Kremlin and the West. But these suspicions, coupled with the historic American fear of being unwillingly dragged into foreign warfare, are expressed in a complex voting formula in the Council. This provides that, on matters of substance, decisions of the Council shall be made by a majority of nine votes "including the concurring votes of the permanent members." This final phrase is the veto power. (Abstentions are not counted as negative votes. A controversy has raged over the meaning of absences, since it was during the Soviet absence in June and July 1950, that American Korean War policy was legitimized by the Council.[39])

The main impediment to effective Security Council action is Great Power dominance. Though the Council is composed of fifteen members, only five of them are permanent members and have the veto power. The result is that while decision-making is relatively centralized for ten members, the ability of any single permanent member to prevent action means that ultimately the Security Council is highly decentralized. It is true that if all five permanent members abstain and nine of the others constitute a majority, then a decision can be reached. But what is the likely effectiveness of Security Council resolutions in which the Great Powers take no part? Is there an obligation to comply? As in the Assembly, the making of formal norms by majority voting can be deceptive; unless states are willing to put their power behind decisions, no effective impact upon the international system will occur.[40]

Even the membership of the Security Council fails to reflect international political reality. True, the belated seating in 1971 of the delegation from the China Mainland erased a long-standing gross misrepresentation. But the changing global power distribution complicates the situation in other ways. West Germany, one of the most powerful economic competitors in the world, is probably permanently denied membership on the

[39] For starkly contrasted interpretations of this matter, see the works of a positivist and of a neorealist, respectively: Leo Gross, "Voting in the Security Council: Abstention from Voting and Absence from Meetings," Yale Law Journal 60 (1951): 210–57; and Myres S. McDougal and Richard N. Gardner, "The Veto and the Charter: An Interpretation for Survival," Yale Law Journal 60 (1951): 258–92.

[40] Leo Gross, "Voting in the Security Council: Abstention in the Post-1965 Amendment Phase and its Impact Upon Article 25 of the Charter," American Journal of International Law 62 (1968): 315–34.

Security Council because of Germany's division. Likewise Japan, now restored to full power except for its nonnuclear status, and beginning to work out its relations with the Soviet Union and China as it rejects American paternalism, may eventually seek a permanent seat on the Security Council.

But the expansion of Security Council membership would not of itself generate greater effectiveness. In fact, the opposite is more probable: The more the Council reflects conflicting policies and outlooks, the less likely it is to achieve its objectives. Indeed, granting the veto power to more states by Charter amendment would decrease the likelihood of Security Council effectiveness. It is regrettable but nonetheless true that despite the "grand design," the major powers consciously created such a situation by insisting upon veto power.

Again, however, all is not hopeless, though Security Council performance has been less than fully encouraging. While it has occasionally achieved peaceful settlement of incipient crises, it has instituted enforcement measures in the sole case of the Korean War; and since the Soviet delegation took no part in those decisions, it must be concluded that the Council's actions in that case constituted legitimization rather than collective security. Now, however, as attention turns from collective security toward peace-keeping, the Security Council may find a less politically-charged method by which to exercise its responsibility. Logically, the Security Council is the proper organ for the uses of peace-keeping, though politically it is a most difficult forum from which to get action.

The logical argument stems from the historical anticipation that the Great Powers should make the critical decisions regarding international peace and security. Yet politically, the hope of their electing enforcement procedures against their own interests is unrealistic. Because peace-keeping is intended to be *preventative* rather than enforcing, *neutral* rather than carrying the stamp of great power, and *impartial* rather than serving the will of one party against another, it is not so inimical to the interests of Great Powers as is collective security. War (and the implementation of collective security *is* war) is intended to erase political alternatives. Peace-keeping is intended only to prevent warfare while political wrangling proceeds.

Although the Congo operation (1960–64) is an unsatisfactory test of Security Council peace-keeping because of Soviet objections to its implementation, it appears that this may become the method of choice. Council utilization of this method is preferable to Assembly use for two reasons. First, a decision by the Council obviates the charge of organizational violation of authority. Second, because of its authorization to intrude upon domestic jurisdiction when operating under Chapter VII of the Charter, the Council may in some cases be able to exercise peace-keeping without host consent to deploy troops to its territory.

Even in the hands of the Security Council, however, peace-keeping has severe limitations. Foremost among these is that it can be used only in very special circumstances. First, there must be a relative equivalence of power among the local forces, since the UN can usefully interpose a force only if neither party can gain a quick military advantage. Second, unless the Security Council is willing to use its special privileges under Chapter VII to bypass host-state rejection of forces, it is able to operate only with the consent of one or more of the local disputants. Finally, either the General Assembly or the Security Council must be able politically to agree on the mandate and organization of the emergency force. This is a lengthy catalogue of politically sensitive conditions, and it cannot be expected that many local disputes will fit them. Only under special and peculiar circumstances will the political and military conditions permit a United Nations peace-keeping role.[41]

The International Court of Justice

The World Court enjoys a dual role in the international system. It is at once the "constitutional court" of the UN and the court of international law among states. The first of these roles has been discussed previously, along with its potential impact on organizational authority.

The judicial model upon which domestic systems operate includes the concept of *compulsory jurisdiction*. This means that courts determine their jurisdiction according to law, and that the subjects of the legal system are bound to appear when called. Individuals in the United States can be summoned before courts; corporations can be sued against their will; and governmental officials can be enjoined from certain acts. But in international law, such authority does not exist. When the Statute of the Permanent Court of International Justice was drafted in 1921, the Committee of Jurists recognized both the desirability and the political impracticability of compulsory jurisdiction. They knew that inclusion of this concept in the Statute would dissuade states from membership. They sought, therefore, to create an interim arrangement, by which states could accept limited compulsory jurisdiction with respect to certain matters, with or without reservation, and on condition of reciprocity. These conditions, comprising the Optional Clause, have not achieved the hope of a growing acceptance of compulsory jurisdiction.

A second problem with respect to the ICJ is *compliance*. It is commonly thought that states ignore or violate the Court's decisions. In fact, however,

---

[41] James Stegenga, "United Nations Peace-Keeping: Patterns and Prospects," in Robert Wood, ed., *The Process of International Organization* (New York: Random House, 1971), pp. 299–316. For a study of proposed methods of overcoming both national and international barriers to peace-keeping, see Indar Jit Rikhye, Michael Harbottle and Bjørn Egge, *The Thin Blue Line: International Peacekeeping and Its Future* (New Haven: Yale University Press, 1974).

this is not so. A high degree of compliance exists for two reasons. First, the ICJ is capable of rendering either *declaratory* or *executory* judgments. In declaratory judgments, it declares itself on a point of law, and may in effect advise states as to their rights, or may limit behavior by clarification of existing law. These judgments are not intended to favor one state over another in a specific issue; and neither contestant need make restitution to another. Executory judgments are quite a different matter. These arise when the Court finds for one contestant rather than for another, and orders one to undertake remedial or compensatory action. It is these judgments about which so much misinformation has circulated, leading to the impression that states have rarely carried out judicial awards made against them. In fact, however, such cases are exceptional.

The second reason is closely akin to an argument used in earlier discussion of states' compliance with treaties. Since, in the absence of compulsory jurisdiction, use of the Court is almost wholly voluntary, it stands to reason that a government will not make the political decision to seek a judicial settlement without having assessed possible outcomes, and without having accepted the obligation to carry out an award in case of an adverse decision.

What remedies exist when states refuse compliance? As the traditional standards of sanctions suggest, a judicial award gives a state an *actionable right*. This may be exercised through general IGO's, functional organizations, or regional organizations. Conceivably, even the Security Council might be called upon to enforce compliance, as provided by Article 94 of the UN Charter. Such actions, however, may serve merely to *repoliticize* a dispute previously *depoliticized* by having been taken to the Court in the first place. The other alternative is to rely upon self-help, with all its potential anarchical and escalatory effects.

Social, Economic, and Humanitarian Functions

In addition to the specific functions of the three permanent organs thus far discussed, the United Nations engages in a host of activities through its other agencies. Of these, the most conspicuous are human rights and refugee programs, and economic programs, supported in part by the voluntary contributions of governments, in which aid is given to less developed countries on the basis of need.

One area which merits specific mention here, however, is the progress toward self-government of formerly colonized peoples. The UN shares with the League of Nations formal commitment to the self-determination of national peoples, largely on the ground that competitive imperialism is a cause of war. To deal with this problem, the League created a system of *Mandates* by which established states undertook formally to prepare colonized peoples for self-government in the League's behalf. The UN has provided a dual system, consisting of a Trusteeship System and a Declaration Regarding Non-Self-Governing Territories.

The Trusteeship System was arranged (Chapters XII and XIII of the Charter) for international surveillance of progress toward self-government. To colonized peoples, the Trusteeship was a desirable mechanism, for it included formal terminal dates and the promise of international pressure to enforce major power compliance with the terms of the agreement. But to the major states, Trusteeship agreements involve too much obligation and exposure. As a result, Trusteeship has not been the main route to independence.

But out of this gap between plan and performance emerged one of the great success stories of UN history. In Chapter XI of the Charter, the framers had arranged a Declaration Regarding Non-Self-Governing Territories. Though it was initially assumed merely to inscribe principles rather than legal obligations, this became the prime peaceful mechanism through which sovereign status has been achieved in the postwar era. The focal point of this development has been the evolution of Article 73(e). Here UN members who control non-self-governing territories accept as a "sacred trust" the responsibility to achieve well-being for the inhabitants, and in pursuit of this goal they consent:

> to transmit regularly to the Secretary-General for information purposes, subject to such limitation as security and constitutional considerations may require, statistical and other information of a technical nature relating to economic, social and educational conditions in the territories for which they are respectively responsible.

By evolution, this hope has been transformed into an obligation. Article 73(e) became a source of international scrutiny (it would be excessive to say "surveillance"). It shares significant responsibility for the huge increase in the total number of states and in the membership of the UN, of which approximately half the members are newly independent.

To a large extent, these newly emancipated peoples make up the Third World; and for the United Nations, they have created huge problems. While sovereign equality enables them to control much decision-making in the General Assembly and elsewhere, and while these states are the recipients of much of the total treasury of the UN system, their dollar contribution is small. Yet it has been shown that relative to gross national product, and in comparison to national expenditures on armaments, the two poorest categories of states have had better UN financial records than the two richest.[42] In the political realm these states together present other problems. Foremost among them is the "ministate problem"—the difficulty of equal voting when many of these states are very small, ranging even below 100,000 inhabitants.

[42] Edward T. Rowe, "Financial Support for the United Nations: The Evolution of Member Contributions, 1946–1969," *International Organization* 26 (1972): 619–57.

Evaluation of United Nations Performance

As finally drafted in 1945, the preamble of the Charter declares the establishment of "an international organization to be known as the United Nations." The members consciously rejected suggestions that the word "government" be substituted for "organization." Thus despite the occasionally high-sounding terms of the Charter, observers would be mistaken to expect the UN to exercise governmental authority. Composite performance must be evaluated with this understanding.

The United Nations is not a political system acting in a vacuum; nor does it operate *above* the international system. Its effectiveness depends on the quality of world politics and the degree of community among members. In a revolutionary system, community is at best fictitious, with the United Nations representing victories for legal authorization but only modest advances in political impact. While it presents a picture of utmost institutionalization, all of its structure contributes only intermittently to change in the international order. As the international system moderates, especially in the post-Vietnam era and in the trend toward political multipolarity, the sense of community may become stronger, and more progress may be made toward collective decision-making.[43]

Just as the international system undergoes change, so too does the United Nations, and with change in the UN national attitudes about its effectiveness may alter. In American public opinion, for example, the United Nations has declined in popularity in recent years, principally because the UN has not consistently endorsed or legitimized American foreign policy. Disapproval has occurred partly because of the character of American overseas operations, and partly because the UN has seen a fundamental change in its membership, resulting in an "automatic majority" for the Third World members and with it a new policy orientation.

When the UN was founded in 1945 it had fifty-one members, each of which was represented in the General Assembly. By 1975 the total membership was 138. Virtually all of the states admitted after 1956 were newly independent states. Before 1957, the membership of the Assembly was such that the United States could count on being in the majority on virtually every issue. But the new membership deprived the United States of that certainty. Not willing to align themselves with American foreign policy and not willing to be taken into the vituperative politics of Soviet-American relations, these new states have taken a highly independent course. Sometimes neutral to American objectives and sometimes critical, the attitudes of the Assembly have eroded American confidence in the UN,

---

[43] Stanley Hoffmann, "An Evaluation of the United Nations," *Ohio Law Review* 22 (1961): 474–94, and by the same author, "International Organization and the International System," *International Organization* 24 (1970): 389–413.

and the new voting patterns rarely support American policy. This has been especially true on matters of the international economy and on the Middle East. On each of these the U.S. has suffered major diplomatic setbacks at the hands of the "automatic majority."

Changing voting patterns in the UN have had even more profound effects. The Third World voting majority has seen to it that the advancement of industrialization is the UN's first concern. But within that goal there has taken root a Third World ideology, sympathetic to neither the Soviet Union nor the United States. Instead, it is an ideology of independent leftism, scornful of industrial states but covetous of industrialization. To the West it is ill-conceived and petulant; to the Soviet Union it is useful as a constraint on American control of UN decision-making. But in any event, it has diverted the UN, and particularly the General Assembly, from its old obsessions with security as an East-West problem. The UN is now more typically a forum for the war of wits and dollars between the industrial North and the maturing South.

Organic Growth and Humanitarian World Politics

In addition to changes in political patterns at the UN brought on by the maturation of the Third World, events of the age have also refocused the concerns of the world organization. In the past decade the world has undergone the crisis of recognizing that humanity is imperiled by its own excesses, that the catastrophes which one may safely predict will result not from natural forces, but from people's overzealous efforts to conquer those forces. In the search for a better life we have contaminated our biosphere, polluted our environment and offended all our senses. Through the battles against disease, old age, and premature death, we have created a global population boom which now threatens to exceed food supplies even as nonreplaceable resources are consumed at an increasing pace. These three crises—ecocide, excess population, and agricultural limitation—have forced a reassessment of the trend toward undifferentiated growth, and have called forth an attempt at balanced, planned development the world over. This latter concept, often labeled organic growth, has found itself at the center of the UN's new concern for humanistic world politics.[44] They are treated in the final chapter as issues of future world order.

---

[44] Mihajlo Mesarovic and Eduard Pestel, *Mankind at the Turning Point* (New York: New American Library, 1974). This is The Second Report to the Club of Rome, in which the authors report computerized projections about the human condition, and reflect on the consequences of delaying action toward resolving the principal human crises. The references to "undifferentiated" and "organic" growth are biological analogies, the former representing growth for the sake of growth (as cells dividing without changes of function) and the latter coordinated growth (as cells dividing into organized units for interdependent activity).

Can the United Nations Keep Peace?

Few questions in international relations are so frequently asked. The ability of the UN to safeguard international stability rests on three issues: (1) the fostering of peace, (2) the making of peace, and (3) the keeping of peace. Can it improve international perceptions so that the impulse to war will be less frequent? When conflict does occur, can the UN rise above some of the political muddle and restore order? And once a conflict has been extinguished, can the UN provide a consistent influence to maintain the peaceful status quo?

Among these questions, the most immediate is whether the UN can stop fighting already in progress. The peace-keeping concept has been the most promising contribution of the UN in the security field thus far. Designed during the Suez crisis of 1956 and executed by the General Assembly in the Middle East from 1956–1967, peace-keeping has occurred in three other extensive operations: the Congo (1960–64), Cyprus (1964–1974), and again in the Middle East (1973 to the present). Each of these operations was voted by the Security Council. A brief history of each will help to illustrate the limited potential of the method.[45]

Egypt

Although Egypt expected the United States to finance construction of the Aswan High Dam, Secretary of State John Foster Dulles announced in 1956 that Washington would not do so. In disgust over this announcement, Colonel Gamel Abdul Nasser, Egyptian chief of state, seized the Suez Canal, despite a treaty by which it was internationally owned. This seizure affected Israeli imports, threatened the flow of Middle Eastern oil, upset the British, and infuriated the French, who were beset by problems in Algeria. Jointly, these three nations tried to drive Egyptian troops away from the Suez region and reestablish control.

At the United Nations, Britain and France prevented the Security Council from assuming responsibility for order, voting against everything from censure to action. In the voting, a most unusual thing occurred: the United States and the Soviet Union voted together against two of Washington's most prestigious allies! This American reaction ought not to have surprised its friends, since President Eisenhower had warned that he would not support their operations. Yet not until faced with the American vote did the British will begin to subside. France was more deeply committed, but British

---

[45] For a synopsis of all UN interventions and peace observer groups, see Larry L. Fabian, *Soldiers Without Enemies* (Washington: The Brookings Institution, 1971), pp. 261–68. An exhaustive treatment of military, logistical, and budgetary details is found in David Wainhouse, *International Peacekeeping at the Crossroads* (Baltimore: The Johns Hopkins University Press, 1973).

second thoughts sent Paris scurrying for an alternative policy. Thus when the issue arrived in the General Assembly, the stumbling block was not a superpower confrontation, but the embarrassment of second-ranking powers who by then were amenable to collective decision. The atmosphere was receptive to the new principles of peace-keeping, which resulted in the stationing in Egypt of a multinational interventionary force from 1956 to 1967.

The Congo

The situation in the Congo in 1960 was wholly different. There, stability had been upset by the secession of Katanga Province, with a resulting civil war. In the view of third parties, widespread fighting in the Congo was a threat to the stability of the entire African continent, especially in the small and struggling new states below the Sahara. But the Congolese situation did not rival the Middle East or Cyprus in the interests of the Soviet Union or the United States, with the result that major power demands were not a barrier to effective management. Thus partly liberated from the normal constraints upon its politics, the Security Council was able to adapt the peace-keeping principles used by the General Assembly in the Middle East. Though there were serious (and at one point almost disastrous) Soviet-American differences over execution of the principles, the convergence of their interests in settlement permitted the Security Council to restore stability by dispatch of a peace-keeping force from 1960 to 1964.

Cyprus

Cyprus was still a different problem. A small insular state in the eastern Mediterranean, its domestic politics suffered from a power struggle between the majority Greek population (about 80 percent) and the smaller Turkish population. As far back as 1931 there had been moves by the Greek population to merge Cyprus with Greece. In the years immediately prior to independence in 1960, there was sporadic violence. Fed up with responsibility and under pressure to divest itself of colonial holdings, Britain agreed to the formation of a Republic of Cyprus in 1960, with guarantees that the president would be elected by Greek Cypriots and the vice president by Turkish Cypriots. The former were also to hold 70 percent control of the national legislature.

But independence was only a palliative for the social and ethnic problems of the tiny republic. By 1963 Turkish Cypriots were charging the Greek majority with denial of rights. Open hostilities began. Amidst crisis, in March 1964, the Security Council voted a peace-keeping operation, which it still maintains, despite seizure by Turkey of much of Cyprus in a brief war in 1974.

Again, the objectives of the great powers are a critical consideration in the successful utilization of peace-keeping principles. Since both Greece and Turkey are formal allies of the United States, Washington saw the crisis as a threat of intra-alliance warfare. Though Britain had retained two small military posts on the island, it wished to have collective responsibility lest anyone accuse the British government of resort to imperial tactics. France, by then extricated from both Algeria and Indochina, was receptive to any plan for stability in the Mediterranean. And the Soviet Union, though always ready to profit from disruption among the Western security allies, wanted peace in the Mediterranean. Most particularly, Moscow wished to court the favor of Turkey, since Turkey controls the Bosporous and the Dardanelles through which Soviet ships must move from the Black Sea to the Mediterranean. With plans for a major naval build-up, the stability of Turkish foreign policy was critical to Moscow. The conditions were optimal for interventionary peace-keeping.

The Middle East, 1973

The resumption of war in the Middle East in 1973 threatened once again to plunge that area into catastrophe. This time, the interests of the United States and the Soviet Union were more directly touched, with the U.S. strongly in support of Israel and at the threshold of a major petroleum crisis, and the USSR newly determined to support its Arab friends and to maintain a naval balance in the Mediterranean. A Soviet threat to intervene militarily in the fighting, reported to the American people without detail as "a brutal note," resulted in a temporary worldwide alert of American forces, including mobilization of some reserve units. In withdrawal from potential superpower crisis, the Soviet Union proposed a joint Soviet-American peace-keeping operation for the region—a proposal vigorously rejected by Washington on the traditional ground that such an operation would threaten larger crisis. As an alternative, the Security Council agreed to establish a multimember peace-keeping force consisting of the troops of lesser powers, to be commanded by a Finnish general. The initial troop contingents were ferried to the area from Cyprus. The command assumed the functions of interposition, administration of prisoner repatriation, exchange of check-points, and logistical facilitation of truce talks in the desert.

The Council's decision to establish this force signaled the growth of a Soviet-American concensus on the utility and political acceptability of peace-keeping as a means of regional security. This promising characteristic was partly offset by Chinese refusal to take part. Though the force was established without a negative vote, the Chinese were recorded as "not participating." They repeated their view that such operations are instruments by which the two largest powers use the UN as a tool for perpetuating their control of world events and regional conflicts. That China did not veto the proposal, however, restores expectation that the major powers may now have come to accept peace-keeping as the most appropriate means of maintaining regional stability. The Security Council's willingness and poli-

"Somebody else has been down in this same hole."

Source: LePelley in *The Christian Science Monitor.* Copyright © 1973 TCSPS.

tical ability to reaffirm the mandate of UN functions both in the Sinai (where American diplomacy had arranged for Egypt-Israeli agreement) and for the Golan Heights (where no Syrian-Israeli agreement applies) adds encouragement to peace-keeping as a means of ensuring regional tranquility.

These brief histories of the largest and most important of the peace-keeping operations illustrate the limitations on peace-keeping. If the Soviet

Union is successful in restricting use of this method to the Security Council (as it wishes to), then it will face the same potential fate that has destroyed collective security—namely, the difficulty of achieving Great Power unanimity. The type of operation and the depth of commitment which it entails are entirely different from those involved in collective security; hence, the superpowers need not think so much of the security implications as of the political implications of peace-keeping. On the other hand, if the General Assembly should attempt again to institute peace-keeping after the financial crisis spawned by the Middle East and Congo operations, it will run the risk of Soviet challange, of another financial crisis, and of institutional destruction.

The future of peace-keeping is tied to the Security Council, and to the willingness of the major powers to use neutral forces of interposition in situations in which their conflicting interests are not involved (Congo), marginally involved (Middle East), or embarrassingly involved (Cyprus). Great power unanimity is still the key to effective execution; but the peace-keeping involves a sufficiently lower commitment that it may prove more effective than collective security. We understand, of course, that peace-keeping will no more regulate the bilateral relations of the permanent members of the Security Council than collective security has.

The impact of the United Nations is measured by its performance in five major issue areas of world politics. The first measure is its contribution to regulating power relationships. Second is its effect in arranging agreements among major powers. The third issue is its usefulness as an instrument of partisan interests, and the extent to which it controls them. Fourth, is its effectiveness at creating norms and legitimizing policies. The final measure is its contribution to the long-term viability of nation-states.[46] In the foregoing discussion we have explored each of these criteria and offered information for assessment. We turn next to the views that the major international actors take of international organization.

The American View of International Organization

The American record of participation in international institutions has been spotty. To avoid involvement in European war after 1918, the United States Senate rejected American membership in the League of Nations in a fascinating and tragic struggle with President Woodrow Wilson, who had created the League concept. Despite nonparticipation in the League's

[46] Oran R. Young, "The United Nations and the International System," *International Organization* 22 (1968): 909–22, especially pages 903–4. See also by the same author a later version of the same article in Leon Gordenker, ed., *The United Nations in International Politics* (Princeton: Princeton University Press, 1971), pp. 10–59.

political activities, the United States was an active contributor to its functional activities. Most American policy between the world wars, however, was conducted with little regard for the League. Furthermore, despite the efforts of the European states to enlist the United States in the Permanent Court of International Justice, reaching as far as willingness to alter the statute and to limit the advisory jurisdiction of the Court if the United States should wish, Washington steadfastly declined membership.

Relations between Washington and the United Nations system have been quite another story. Finally convinced during World War II that global international organization and collective security were indispensable to future world stability, the United States played a leading role in the creation of the UN. Virtually throughout the war, planning groups—at first quite secret—worked on drafts of the Charter. Even the major political parties declared their support for a renewed outlook upon international organization. In September, 1943, the House of Representatives resolved, with the Senate concurring,

> . . . That the Congress hereby expresses itself as favoring the creation of appropriate international machinery with power adequate to establish and to maintain a just and lasting peace, among the nations of the world, and as favoring participation by the United States therein through its constitutional processes.[47]

Not to be outdone in its influence upon the foreign-policy process, the Senate resolved two months later:

> . . . That the United States, acting through its constitutional processes, join with free and sovereign nations in the establishment and maintenance of international authority with power to prevent aggression and to preserve the peace of the world.
>
> That the Senate recognizes the necessity of there being established at the earliest practicable date a general international organization, based on the principle of sovereign equality of all peace-loving states, and open to membership by all such states, large and small, for the maintenance of international peace and security.[48]

American interest in establishing the United Nations was portrayed most vividly by its sponsorship of the Dumbarton Oaks Conference in May 1944, at which delegates of the United States, the Soviet Union, Britain, and France studied draft proposals for the UN Charter. Finally, after an

[47] House Concurrent Resolution No. 25, 78th Congress, first session; sponsored by Congressman J. William Fulbright of Arkansas, passed by the House September 21, 1943. *Congressional Record*, vol. 89, p. 7729. As reprinted and footnoted in Ruhl J. Bartlett, ed., *The Record of American Diplomacy*, 4th ed. enlarged (New York: Alfred A. Knopf, 1964), p. 675.

[48] Senate Resolution No. 192, as amended, 78th Congress, first Session, vol. 89, p. 9222, November 5, 1943. This resolution was offered by Senator Tom Connally of Texas, and is generally referred to as the Connally Resolution.

additional year of diplomatic exchanges, including a Great Power agreement at the Yalta Conference (February 1945) on the veto provision, the United States hosted the San Francisco Conference (June 1945) for the formal signing of the Charter.[49]

American interest evolved from two directions. First, there were those, believers in the Grand Design of continued Soviet-Anglo-American cooperation, who anticipated Great Power enforcement of the peace and who looked upon the veto in the Security Council as insurance against unwilling involvement in war. But there were others, second, who more realistically assessed the postwar situation. Why, they asked, ought we to expect that the Soviet Union will not return to its prewar attacks upon capitalism and on the West? The other side of this question, which plagues revisionist scholars of the cold war, was this: since the postwar bipolarity is likely to necessitate a *Pax Americana*, why not create international machinery through which American foreign policy toward the Soviet world can be pursued with collective legitimacy? Depending upon one's historical outlook, therefore, the American interest in the UN originated either from naive expectations of Soviet-American cooperation in power politics or from the American intent to establish global institutions for facilitating American foreign relations.

It stands to reason that in an American-dominated world, Washington would seek consistently to enlarge the UN's authority insofar as such increases helped American policy. This explains the American approval of the ICJ's interpretation of the UN's legal status in the *Reparations Case*, in which the UN was held to be a subject of international law with certain characteristics resembling those of states, and having implied powers to fulfill specified functions and responsibilities. It also illuminates American sponsorship of the Uniting for Peace Resolution, which created a recourse in security matters in the General Assembly, free from Soviet veto. The American reaction was similar to the ICJ's advisory opinion in the *Certain Expenses Case*, which rejected the Soviet argument that security measures which circumvent the special prerogatives of the Security Council are illegal.

In organizing the economic sector, the United States also played a leading role. It hosted the Bretton Woods Conference in 1944, out of which arose the International Monetary Fund (IMF) and the International Bank for Reconstruction and Development (IBRD). Washington rejected the founding of the International Trade Organization in 1948,

[49] For a comprehensive study of the American role in the founding of the UN, and of the various political and diplomatic forces which shaped that role, see Robert A. Divine, *Second Chance: The Triumph of Internationalism in the United States During World War II* (New York: Atheneum, 1967). See also Ruth B. Russell (with the assistance of Jeannette E. Muther), *A History of the United Nations Charter* (Washington: The Brookings Institution, 1958). Miss Russell was a staff member of the Leo Pasvolsky Committee, which prepared the American draft proposal.

which would have limited the exercise of unilateral restraints to trade. The General Agreement on Tariffs and Trade (GATT), now with permanent institutional structure, has adopted much of this function.

This Western economic structure was created in an era in which the United States was undisputed king among the trading partners. It was the most productive and largest exporter; it enjoyed the most favorable balance of trade (income from exports greatly exceeding cost of imports); and the American dollar was not only in great demand overseas, but was virtually the standard medium of international exchange.

Recently the American position has deteriorated. Inflation has reduced export potential; Western Europe and Japan have regained productivity and favorable trade and payments balances; the European Community has enough combined strength to spurn the American dollar and to compete with American manufactures. All of these contributed to a reversal of the American balance of trade in 1971, when imports exceeded exports for the first time in sixty years. Furthermore, the export of capital has brought on disastrously high balance-of-payments deficits.

Looked at from abroad, American reactions to these problems have been retaliatory. Western Europeans in particular feel that after years of attempts to persuade Germany, Japan, France, and other countries to alter their currency values in relation to the dollar, the United States in 1971 undertook vigorous changes which either frankly or marginally violated international economic rules. The imposition of a 10 percent surcharge on all imports—a unilateral act designed to reduce the imports which were throwing the trade balance into deficit—was clearly a violation of the GATT. Furthermore, only months later Washington forced wholesale changes in the world's currency valuations by informing other governments of the changes which the United States would expect in return for an American devaluation. All of this was done without formal adherence to the rules of the IMF.

Washington's interpretation of these events differs. The official view is that, because of its postwar economic superiority and Europe's need for special trade conditions, the United States has voluntarily endured trade discrimination. Now, however, having through its foreign assistance programs restored Europe's economic vitality, and having encouraged the European Community to establish still further trade restraints disadvantageous to the U.S., the American competitive position has been eroded to the point at which Washington must demand international trade equality. The official view holds that the United States started from a weak position and is bargaining back to equality.

On other economic fronts, the record of the United States is unsurpassed. No government contributes more to the economic programs of the UN than does the United States (although relative to its total wealth American contributions are not great). Overall, however, the United States bears about 40 percent of the total burden of financing UN programs.

Thus, it has resisted proliferation of UN programs, having worked assiduously to prevent the founding of the Special United Nations Fund for Economic Development (SUNFED) and having shown little if any early enthusiasm for the UN Conference on Trade and Development (UNCTAD). The motive for this resistance is as follows: such changes in institutional structure do not contribute to American interests, but turn the collective voting strength of the less developed nations into a bloc intent upon availing itself of American wealth.

The General Assembly's decision of 1972 to reduce the American share of the *apportioned* budget (as contrasted with total budget, which includes voluntary contributions) from 31.5 percent to 25 percent, at American request, ought not to be interpreted as acquiescence in a reprisal based on declining American confidence. The request was made as part of the Nixon administration's general distaste for UN activities and as a domestic budget-cutting measure. While the organization needs American money, the proposal was acceptable to the Assembly mainly because payment of one-third of the apportioned budget symbolizes American domination. Immediately after the Assembly's decision, the Soviet delegation announced that it would reserve the right to request reduction in its apportioned share as well.

But just as the members of the United Nations do not want their organization dominated by the United States, so too does Washington look with disfavor upon the current trend in which the Third World uses the UN as a forum for global anti-Americanism. Throughout 1975 in particular, the string of American embarrassments over economic questions and over policy with respect to Israel and the Palestine Liberation Organization

"Then it's unanimous . . . we deplore the senseless deaths of the three Arab terrorists."

Reprinted with permission of Chicago Tribune–New York News Syndicate, Inc.

resulted in outspoken counterattacks by Ambassador Daniel Patrick Moynihan. Washington made clear its dissatisfaction with the United Nations as an instrument of global diplomacy. Whereas Washington once used the UN in the battle against the Eastern (Communist) world, it is now being used against the United States by the Southern (underindustrialized) world. American governmental and popular reactions to this reversal add up to hostility to the UN and declining willingness to fund its programs.

A dangerous paradox emerges. If the UN system reflects an American-dominated world order, and if the United States is its largest financial supporter, and if the UN is an important element in international progress, American dissatisfaction with the UN may either destroy the organization's role, or drive the United States farther from support of the UN and from willing participation in collective decision-making. If the United Nations lacks the authority to compel the United States, and if the United States is unable to manipulate the membership to its policy needs, the disaffection between Washington and the UN may destroy the organization's role in a changing world.

The Views of America's Major Allies

Because in general they have shared the cold war preoccupations of the United States, the major American allies have held views of international organization similar to those of the United States. There have been, however, some outstanding exceptions.

The Japanese position has been anomolous. Having been one of the wartime enemies against which the UN was founded, Japan was excluded from the UN by the terms of its Charter. It was nearly a decade before East-West agreement permitted the seating of a Japanese delegation. Since then, Tokyo has served as a loyal American ally at New York, though its role has been a quiet one. It has not wanted to serve American interests to the detriment of normal relations with the USSR, and it has not wanted its American ties to make more difficult the problem of working out effective relations with both China and Taiwan. Probably for these reasons, Japan has disavowed any intention of requesting a permanent place on the Security Council, even though its accession to great power status (in all but the military sense) might otherwise justify such a claim. Finally, recent events in the Middle East, including the politically inspired petroleum crisis to which Japan is uniquely susceptible, has caused a departure from American policy as Japan has been forced out of economic necessity to sympathize more with the demands of the resource-rich Third World. These departures result less from disaffection with the United States than from gleaming regional and economic realities.

The Western European attitude, too, is much like that of the United

States, though there are marked differences. During the peak of the cold war trans-Atlantic objectives were identical, so Western Europe clung to the anti-Soviet successes of the United States at the UN. European dissatisfaction with the extent of Washington's commitment to Asia during the Korean War, and American criticism of Britain and France over the Suez venture of 1956, were the only substantial exceptions to coincidental attitudes about use of the UN.

But in the dynamics of world politics, the Western European partners have begun to move away from the United Nations, and away from some of the positions that the United States holds there. Most importantly, the progress of European regionalism has both altered the focus of Europe's organizational attention from the global to the regional, and created the strength with which to pursue policies independently of Washington. On global issues, such as petroleum, the Europeans prefer a policy of industrial states consortium; and on the political issues of the Middle East which threaten the steady flow of oil they have abandoned such major American concessions to Israel as excluding from UN debate representatives of the Palestine Liberation Organization.

The Canadian attitude is genuinely unique among Washington's principal allies. Having for the first ten postwar years gotten caught in the flow of Soviet-American events at the UN, including participation in the Korean War, Ottawa's independence began to show in 1956. It was Ambassador (later Prime Minister) Lester Pearson who conceived the idea which Dag Hammarskjold later developed into peace-keeping, and Canada has since been one of the prime contributors to interventionary peace-keeping. It also served a brief and unhappy term as part of an international (non-UN) truce observer team in Vietnam.

On economic matters the Canadian position is also a unique one. Resource rich but industrially dominated, it is subject to all the fluctuations of American demand and American business. In a peculiar sense, then, Canada is an industrialized state which confronts many of the problems that are typically those of the Third World. On issues of the New International Economic Order, therefore, Canada is defensive where the United States is assertive, and often assertive when the United States is defensive. The role which the United Nations plays in Canadian foreign policy, accordingly, is increasingly different from that which it plays in American policy. Consequently, the attitude which Canadians hold toward international organization is gradually diverging from that of the southern neighbors.

The Soviet View of International Organization

The Soviet view differs spectacularly from those of the United States and its principal allies. All of the latter take a Western view of matters of organization, as of law, pertaining to the world confrontation between communist and socialist states, on the one hand, and non-communist and capitalist states on the other. Because of its sharply divergent perspective on these matters, the Soviet political attitude differs vastly.

The Kremlin sees international organization as an instrument of Western, and particularly American, policy designed to weaken the Soviet Union and to enhance capitalistic imperialism. Traditionally, then, its approach to the UN system has been defensive. Because of the composition of the organs, the Soviets have been able to pursue few if any major policies through the UN; they hope at best to prevent American instrusions in their interests. If they have outdone the American delegations in maximizing the propaganda potentiality of the UN organs, it is only because the make-up of the organs makes a negative approach to collective diplomacy necessary.

Several focal points have emerged in Soviet outlooks. The first was opposition to the Uniting for Peace Resolution on the ground that it subverts the prerogatives of the Great Powers in the very founding spirit. Second, the ICJ's advisory opinion in the *Certain Expenses Case* further infuriated the Soviet Union on the ground that it illegally expands the authority of the General Assembly at the expense of major power domination in security matters. A third major bone of contention has been the principles of *peace-keeping*, toward which the Soviets have taken the view that the *Security Council* must control the issue to preserve the Great Power authority. Connected to the issue of peace-keeping finance is the Soviet complaint that the Secretary-General managed the Congo operation in a pro-Western manner.

It would be a grave error to argue that, as the membership has become less sympathetic to American foreign policy, it has become more oriented to the Soviet Union. Although voting patterns in the 1960's gave greater strength to Soviet positions, it was not because increasing numbers of states were adhering to the Soviet line. Yet the Kremlin took a more patient view of the UN during the latter half of the 1960's. Attacks upon the organization were both less frequent and less vehement; and aside from refusal to pay for peace-keeping operations, Soviet willingness to fund the UN improved. Although it is a passive policy, the increasing failure of the organization to support American policy must have raised Moscow's spirits and its view of happenings on the East River.

Because of the long-standing conflict between Moscow and Peking, the seating of the Chinese delegation at the UN was not a victory for the Soviet Union—as it would have been in 1950 or 1955. Indeed, it is likely that the presence of the Peking delegation will set back the Soviet outlook on the UN. It is the avowed intent of the Peking delegation to champion the cause of the Third World; and in the long run this will mean renewed losses of votes in the Soviet column. The enlightened power picture of the UN, with the seating of the Chinese, will probably have a detrimental effect upon Soviet interest.

Aside from the political organs and the economic programs of the UN, the Soviet Union is not an active participant in the UN system. It has never agreed to submit a dispute to the ICJ. Because of its different economic system, it has refused to participate in the institutions of Western imperialism. Neither it nor its allies takes part in the GATT. It was not until November 1972, that Rumania became the first Soviet ally to enter the IMF and the IBRD.

Overall, although the Soviet view has been one of disaffection from the United Nations, there have been only a few issues which have threatened the existence of the organization because of that disaffection. The future is not likely to change. The Soviet Union will gain little new support in the UN, and with the presence of China and its special objectives, some recent apparent support may actually be lost. But being alone at New York is not new to the Soviet Union, and the depth of Soviet dissatisfaction is not likely to bring much change to the UN's role in the international system.

The Chinese View of International Organization

Among the major powers, Mao's China is the youngest. Its development toward full status has been retarded by the United States and the Soviet Union. American resistance was facilitated by the United Nations, through which Washington conducted a consistent anti-Peking policy from 1949 until the General Assembly session of Fall, 1971. It follows that Peking shares the Soviet view of the United Nations as the handmaiden of American foreign policy and of Western imperialism. More specifically, the UN is the forum through which the ruse was perpetuated that the nationalist government on Taiwan is the real representative of the Chinese people, while over 800 million Chinese people on the Asian mainland were ignored.

The Korean War is also at the center of Peking's vision of the UN. In the hands of pro-American majorities, the General Assembly labeled China an aggressor despite obvious threats to its borders, and despite the urgings of General Douglas MacArthur that the Western allies in Korea attack Chinese targets. The UN, moreover, submitted to American pressures to vote an economic boycott against China. The continued refusal to seat the Peking delegation was the largest single source of China's sense of isolation from world politics, and was interpreted in China as an extension of the Century of Humiliation. Its embarrassment was further heightened by the comparative diplomatic positions of the two Chinas prior to the seating of Peking. By that time, sixty-six states had recognized the People's Republic, of which sixty still had active diplomatic relations.

Of these, fifty-five were UN members. Meanwhile, sixty-one states had formally recognized the Taiwan government and fifty-nine had active diplomatic relations, of which fifty-six were UN members.[50]

When finally seated at the UN, the Peking delegation was notably restrained. It insisted before arriving that it would take no part until remnants of nationalist representation had been expunged from *all* UN agencies except the IMF and the IBRD, in which Peking has no interest. Its only other uncompromised position was refusal to pay for maintenance of military cemeteries in South Korea! Otherwise it announced, quietly but resolutely, that it recognized its duty to pay a larger share of UN expenses than the weaker nationalist government had, and volunteered to increase its contribution from 4 percent of the budget to 7 percent over a five-year period.

On other fronts the Chinese introduction to the UN was less quiescent. The major event which followed upon its seating was the Pakistan civil war and fighting between India and Pakistan, out of which Bangladesh was born. In this conflict China—ever hostile to India—sided with Pakistan, and found itself in the unfamiliar position of being aligned with the United States against the interests of the Soviet Union. When Bangladesh subsequently applied for admission to the UN, China took its inaugural opportunity to exercise the veto in the Security Council. Bangladesh was not admitted.

China's second chance to promote its policy and propaganda through the UN came at the global UN Conference on the Human Environment at Stockholm, June 1972. There the Chinese delegation sought to condemn the United States for the use of defoliants in the Vietnam War. It also declined participation in certain declarations of the conference for their failure to call for the complete elimination of nuclear weapons.

But it ought not be assumed that the Chinese use the UN strictly as a forum in which to take on the United States. Things are not good in China's relations with the Soviet Union, either, and Chinese speeches at New York are abundantly candid on this. Mao Tse-tung has contended ever since the Sino-Soviet rift began that Washington and Moscow are bent upon dividing the world into two giant hegemonies. It is his utmost objective to prevent this by carving out his own regional sphere of influence. Although the Chinese have not actually charged the Soviets with using the UN system to further this hegemonial aim, they have made it plain that they intend to use the UN to prevent it.

Not all Chinese policy at the UN is limited to countering the policies of the other great powers. On the positive side, China has taken representa-

---

[50] Summarized from Byron S. J. Weng, *Peking's UN Policy* (New York: Praeger, 1972), appendexes B1–3, pp. 232–35.

tion at the UN as a way of promoting China's long-standing aim of championing the less developed countries, an aim originally articulated at the Bandung Conference in 1955. This is not merely an opportunistic policy, as it is often viewed from the West. The Chinese share many of the economic problems of the Third World. They also feel that they have been driven into a position of inferiority and that their achievement of national self-fulfillment is tied to the nonwhite nations, regardless of politics or ideologies, more than to the industrialized world or to other Marxist societies.

The Third World View of International Organization

Although the cold war has left the impression that all international conflict is arranged along east-west lines, it is the feeling of the less developed states that the focus of world politics is really north-south. The bulk of the world's industrial power is in the northern hemisphere, while most of the southern half of the globe languishes in poverty. As a result, the less developed states have a mixed view of the UN system. On the one hand, they see it as the special preserve of the major powers, one through which the latter have promoted economic domination and resisted adequate development programs. Yet, on the other hand, much of the Third World enjoys national independence principally because of the UN's activities in promoting self-government; and they see in the UN agencies hope for relatively depoliticized programs of aid, trade, and technical assistance. Thus while the ideologically uncommitted states play an active and often vocal role in higher politics, their principal energies in the UN are reserved for the organs and agencies which serve their development needs.

The Third World's relations with these agencies are not entirely smooth. Since the funds for these programs come from the industrialized states, attempts to control the politics of assistance are never far off. The developed states, insisting upon maximum efficiency in the expenditure of funds, impose difficult criteria. They insist upon preinvestment development, designed to mature the nonvisible aspects of an economy so that larger and more productive projects can follow with maximum probable success. The LDC's view this sequence with impatience. Likewise, the LDC's, in their long-range planning, seek commitment of funds from plan to completion, while the lending agencies generally prefer to fund in stages and to require successful completion of each stage before releasing money for the next. More recently, the lending institutions have required consideration of ecological hazards in development projects. This requirement the LDC's view with disdain, since in their quest for rapid development they view environmental protection as a luxury appropriate only to developed economies. All impediments to accelerated development are viewed by the Third World as attempts to retard the pace of economic sovereignty in the southern hemisphere, and as methods of collective neoimperialism. Nevertheless, acquisition of funds through the UN system is less costly, both economically and politically, than attaining them directly from other governments.

The need second to capital is *trade concessions*. The Third World has a difficult time trading in a world dominated by enormous economies in which trade regulations serve industrial states. To counter this situation, the Third World pressed for the establishment of the United Nations Conference on Trade and Development (UNCTAD), which provides a collective voice in confronting the GATT for more advantageous terms of trade with industrial countries. Specifically, UNCTAD seeks to press upon the GATT a unified program of preferential trading conditions. As we have seen, in 1974 and 1975 the underindustrialized states succeeded in focusing the attention of two Special Sessions of the General Assembly on economic problems, and achieved passage of the Charter of Economic Rights and Duties of States and the Declaration on the Establishment of a New International Economic Order, together with a Programme of Action.

Technical assistance is the third principal area of need. The UN's contribution began in 1949 with the founding of the Expanded Program of Technical Assistance (EPTA). Technical assistance continues to be provided through the Technical Assistance Board (TAB), the United Nations Industrial Development Organization (UNIDO), and appropriate offices of such functional agencies as the Food and Agricultural Association (FAO) and the World Health Organization (WHO). Administrative personnel are offered to governments through the OPEX program (Operational and Executive Services), which locates administrative talent and places it on loan to Third World governments.

To meet the combined needs of the LDC's with respect to aid, trade, and technical assistance, the United Nations General Assembly designated the 1960's the "development decade," and combined the Special Fund, the TAB, and the EPTA into the United Nations Development Program (UNDP). The aim was to achieve 5 percent per year economic growth among the LDC's, and to raise foreign assistance to a level of 1 percent of the annual gross national products of the industrialized states. During this period, however, unilateral nonmilitary aid did not increase substantially, and the UN's own programs were only a little more successful than they had been. The modest successes of the UNDP did, however, restore hope for collective advancement, and the 1970's were designated the "second development decade." UNDP II was launched.

In all of these undertakings, the Third World nations are engaged in the difficult process of turning the United Nations to a goal which in practice has taken a decidedly secondary role to the Great Power struggle. Now as the world recedes farther from bipolarity, the hope is kindled that the UN may turn to saving "succeeding generations from the scourge of war" by employing "international machinery for the promotion of the economic and social advancement of all peoples," as envisaged in the Preamble to the Charter. Patient and long-suffering, the LDC's look to the UN system to lift them above exploitation by the Great Powers and to carry them over the seemingly implacable barriers of neoimperialism.

EURO AN COMMON MARKET

12

Beyond

the Nation-State

Centuries of study of the nation-state system have raised doubt as to whether governments can preserve international peace and stability. International law and organization have assisted, but neither has ensured lasting international harmony. What, then, are the alternatives to the nation-state system? What new political contexts might be framed through which familiar international transactions might continue, but in which peace might be a closer prospect?

At present, attention is focused upon two possible alternatives: international integration and transnational participation, the subjects of this chapter. Will political history reach beyond the nation-state?

International Integration

International integration is the process by which a *supranational* condition is achieved, in which larger political units conduct the business now carried out by national governments. Defined succinctly, it is:

> the process whereby political actors in several distinct national settings are persuaded to shift their loyalties, expectations, and political activities toward a new and larger center, whose institutions possess or demand jurisdiction over the pre-existing national states.[1]

[1] Ernst B. Haas, *The Uniting of Europe: Political, Social and Economic Forces 1950–57* (Stanford, Calif.: Stanford University Press, 1958), p. 16.

375

Unlike international organization, which establishes institutional machinery *among* states, international *integration* provides decision-making machinery *above* the nation-state—institutions capable of making obligatory decisions in behalf of national governments. It is the merger of separate authorities and jurisdictions, usually in a well defined geographic region, into a larger unit, a higher unity, and a single polity.

Integration and the Functional Model

Integration by any means is a long and arduous process. Although some observers have predicted integration through federation, most hold that integration is a testing process tied to compiled successes. This *functional model* of integration rejects rapid constitutional consolidation and looks instead to progress in specific *sectors*. The functionalist view holds that even compatible societies cannot simultaneously integrate all public functions. Collectivization may be based on economics, on politics, or on security. Gradual and parallel progress in several sectors may converge into general, cross-sectoral integration. Without this convergence, integration is "encapsulated," or isolated, having no carry-over effects in other sectors.[2]

1. The Sectors of Integration

What functions have been given over to the integrative process? What purposes, normally served by national governments, have been entrusted to higher political levels? The answers to these questions lie in the different *sectors of integration.*

Economics

Historically, the sector most frequently integrated has been the *economic sector*. The most familiar integrative organizations are "common markets," in which the member states consolidate all or part of their economic activi-

---

[2] For a study of the distinction between the federationist and the functionalist approaches, see particularly David Mitrany, "The Prospect of Integration: Federal or Functional?", *Journal of Common Market Studies* 4 (December 1965). A useful study of the multivariate nature of integration is found in Leon N. Lindberg, "Political Integration as a Multidimensional Phenomenon Requiring Multivariate Measurement," *International Organization* 24 (1970): 649–731. The neofunctionalists hold that federation can ultimately occur upon a well-established and solid functionalist base. See for example Joseph S. Nye, "Comparing Common Markets: A Revised Neo-Functionalist Model," *International Organization* 24 (1970): 796–835.

The European Council during recess in meeting at Luxembourg, 1976.

ties. The European Economic Community (EEC), the Central American Common Market (CACM), the Latin American Free Trade Association (LAFTA), and the European Free Trade Association (EFTA) are among the most familiar.

The function of a common market is to raise economic potential through policy consolidation. Two particular instruments are used. First, the member states eliminate barriers to trade among themselves, so that goods flow freely in trade among them. Second, they agree to confront outside states with a single economic policy. Their economic policies concerning non-member states are not only coordinated, but are identical and mutually enforced.

Because economic interaction is highly complex, it is necessary to consider economic subsectors. In the European experience, for example, progress toward a full free trade area has progressed at different rates and with vastly different amounts of enthusiasm in the industrial and agricultural subsectors. Although it has not been easy, principles for industrial free trade areas were more readily achieved than those for agriculture. In addition, Britain's entry into the Common Market was delayed not only by French politics (in its first serious attempt to gain entry, in 1963, President deGaulle vetoed British membership), but by British fears of the impact upon its agricultural subsector. Upon entry in 1973, Britain expected inflation in food prices, but anticipated that gains in industrial trade would favorably affect its balance of payments (increase exports over imports), and would stabilize the British economy.

Another subsectoral distinction separates production from producer. Though we generally think of economy as production of goods and services, we must remember that goods and services are produced by people. Thus there are important labor aspects to a free trade area—standardization of wages in industries, community agreement on fair labor practices, free flow of labor across national boundaries, and agreement on pension and unemployment benefits.

In addition to labor and produce, another aspect of economic integration is the availability of capital, without which efficient, coordinated growth cannot occur. If this means borrowing from abroad, then one state (even perhaps an outside state) may dominate growth by controlling both capital and decisions about capital utilization. Creation of a common medium of exchange among participating central banks facilitates payments. Western European integration achieved this milestone in 1971 with the establishment of the E-note (£), which is exchangeable only among the member treasuries.

Social Considerations

The second major sector is the *social sector*. While it may be technically feasible to integrate economies, ultimate integration requires mutual toleration and common social and political values. Social integration means transforming national preferences into loyalty to the larger political community. Supranational attitudes must evolve.

There is considerable evidence that such a process is now occurring in Europe. Studies reveal that the degree of "Europeanness" among nationals of various European states—the degree to which people sense themselves part of a larger political community—is growing steadily. They also demonstrate variations among age groups, with younger people generally more favorably disposed toward supranational attitudes.[3] Furthermore, available data suggest that the growth of supranational consciousness is accompanied by outward-looking attitudes, meaning that a uniting Europe is seen not only as a political community for self-service, but as a stabilizing force in the international system.[4]

---

[3] See, for example, Ronald Inglehart, "Public Opinion and Regional Integration," *International Organization* 24 (1970): 764–95 and "The Silent Revolution in Europe: Intergenerational Change in Post-Industrial Societies," *American Political Review* 65 (1971): 991–1017.

[4] Ronald Inglehart, "The New Europeans: Inward or Outward Looking?" *International Organization* 24 (1970): 129–39.

Politics

A third sector of concern to integration theory is the *political* sector, though it is not neatly distinguished from other sectors. Societies are replete with bonds of patriotism, loyalty, historical mythology, and sense of national difference. *Political* integration refers, therefore, to the relatively narrow concept of integration of basic political institutions—with transfer of sovereignty over *external* policy to common international institutions. It aims not to eliminate national governments, but to alter their control over specific functions. These changes may affect internal matters of the state, such as fiscal policy or production policy. In integration short of full federation, there is no pretense to transfer of full sovereignty over internal matters.

Despite this limited expectation, political integration is more difficult to achieve than is economic integration, chiefly because economic integration is expected to strengthen the national economy, thus encouraging dual loyalty between nation and larger community. Political integration, in contrast, directly affects the state's sovereignty over decision-making with respect to its nationals. Its institutional effects are more visible, and the assault upon nationalism is more nearly frontal. The state is reduced in stature. Only where this is regarded as a desirable objective has the concept of political integration caught on.

There exists a variety of interpretations of the relationships among political integration, social integration and general governmental cooperation.[5] Some hold that social predisposition is the critical measure of integration potential. Others insist that the creation of institutions among generally sympathetic states will create the social conditions necessary for political integration.[6] Empirical studies now indicate, however, that improvements in intergovernmental relations must precede *both* institution-building and changes in societal attitudes.[7] Western European integration illustrates this point.

It was apparent by the mid-1960's that political unification of Europe required a revival of internationalism in France. Always conscious of French historical and cultural uniqueness, President Charles deGaulle's view of European organization was pragmatic: how much can France profit from integration without sacrificing national identity? Toward the end of his long public career, President deGaulle confided to Christopher Soames, British Ambassador to France, that he anticipated as an ideal "a looser form of free trade area with arrangements by each country to exchange

[5] See, for example, the discussion of Karl W. Deutsch's "sociocausal paradigm" in the section of this chapter entitled "Background for integration."

[6] This is the original functionalist model, propounded especially by David Mitrany in *A Working Peace System* (Chicago: Quadrangle Books, 1966).

[7] See Barry B. Hughes and John E. Schwarz, "Dimensions of Political Integration and the Experience of the European Community," *International Studies Quarterly* 16 (1972): 263–94.

agricultural produce, and a small inner council of a European political association consisting of France, Britain, Germany, and Italy." Broad political integration was not part of Gaullist politics, and both the entry of Britain into the EEC and French governmental receptivity to political unity awaited the passage of the Gaullist era.[8]

The forthcoming entry of Britain along with Denmark and Ireland in 1973 set the stage for a forward-looking summit conference in October 1972, at which ministers from the three incoming states participated. There a general agreement was signed calling for a phased schedule of political unity by 1980. Details of the unity were to be culminated in the first phase, scheduled to end in 1975. The departure of deGaulle, the enlightened attitude of his successor, the willingness of the British Conservative government to withstand the attacks of the Labour opposition in entering the EC—these and other events converged to give new life to the spirit of political supranationalism among the Nine.[9] By January 1976, major strides had been achieved. The Tindemans Report on progressive integration was published; a formal agreement had been made for direct election of the European Parliament in 1978 (as contrasted to assignment of members from the respective national parliaments); and the members had intentionally presented a common front at the United Nations on the economic matters considered at the Special Session.[10] In addition, within the Community new political alliances had formed, and on matters of deliberation there had developed a tendency for cross-national parties and interest groups to discuss policy on the basis of shared interests rather than to resort to the more primitive device of national caucuses.[11]

With respect to the European experience:

> The European Community as already functioning is reaching out towards the status of an economic super-power, but it is still far from being a super-power in the full sense since the constituent countries refuse to merge their political and defense structures. It has been said that the

[8] The words are those of British Foreign and Commonwealth Secretary, Michael Stewart, as he reported the deGaulle-Soames conversation to Parliament in February 1969, as described by Hugh Corbet, "Role of the Free Trade Area," in Hugh Corbet and David Robertson, eds., *Europe's Free Trade Area Experiment* (Oxford: Pergamon Press, 1970), pp. 1–42, at pp. 29–30.

[9] Studies of deGaulle's attitudes toward the European future, and of the European Communities in particular, are many. For a succinct and lively discussion of the topic, see Walter Laqueur, *The Rebirth of Europe* (New York: Holt, Rinehart and Winston, 1970), especially pp. 328–36. For a general study of the political union question from the Fouchet Plan through 1967, see Susanne J. Bodenheimer, "The 'Political Union' Debate in Europe: A Case Study in Intergovernmental Diplomacy," *International Organization* 21 (1967): 24–54.

[10] *Christian Science Monitor*, December 31, 1975, p. 13. See also Robert R. Bowie, "Program for a Federal Europe," *Christian Science Monitor*, February 4, 1976, p. 27.

[11] *New York Times*, February 9, 1976, pp. 1 and 18.

theory of the Community is based upon a recognition of the economic importance of the political frontier and of the political importance of the economic frontier, and these two aspects of a nation's life have to be in unison if they are to be meaningful. Economic integration is the basis of political integration, and it is even now in process of removing national sovereignty not by direct frontal assault but by steady erosion at the foundations.[12]

But the formal impact of economic integration on politics is far from automatic; it takes conscious effort and institutional preparation. In the case of Western Europe, the first formal nurturing of the carryover was the Fouchet Plan of 1961 (Fouchet was the French Ambassador to Denmark). This plan called for a preparatory committee to sit in Paris and to operate on the principle of unanimity. Though the committee did convene, the smaller European members were skeptical of French motives, and refused to proceed further with plans for political unity until after the entry of Britain into the EEC as a counterweight to French power.[13]

Security

The fourth major sector in integration is the *security sector*. Integration may follow from existing alliances, but it implies considerably more than mere alliance. Generally, an alliance is a political instrument through which the dominant member gains political access to the decision-making processes of the lesser members, in return for which the weaker states are guaranteed strategic assistance. Integration calls upon all members, whatever their relative power potentials, to contribute to decision-making at all levels of planning, deployment, and command.

Integrated alliances are rare. Despite the frequency of alliances since the Concert of Europe (1815), governments have generally resisted giving total strategic control to common institutions. The Warsaw Pact—the military alliance of the Soviet Union and its Eastern European allies—is about as integrated as an alliance can be. The Soviet Union, through its political control and economic supremacy, regulates the power and the respective roles of the other allies, thus virtually dictating policy. The North Atlantic Treaty Organization (NATO) has more collective decision-making, though in nuclear affairs Washington has consistently clung to unilateral control. Much of the recent history of NATO diplomacy has revolved around at-

---

[12] Geoffrey Parker, *An Economic Geography of the Common Market* (New York: Praeger, 1968), p. 133 in a chapter entitled "The Logic of Unity." Parker's reference in this passage is to U. Kitzinger, *The Challenge of the Common Market*, 4th ed. (1964).

[13] For a brief discussion of this plan, see Werner Feld, *The European Common Market and the World* (Englewood Cliffs, N.J.: Prentice-Hall, 1967), especially pp. 52–55.

tempts by the Western European members to break down this American position. While troops and conventional war materials have been integrated to a considerable extent, fully integrated decision-making does not yet exist.[14]

These observations lead to preliminary conclusions. First, considering the importance of strategic policy to national survival and to powerful national elites, security integration has to follow political integration. The mere creation of alliances does not ensure integrated policy-making, integrated commands, or integrated allocation of resources. Second, given the same political realities, moves toward security integration occur only in time of crisis. They are the result not of political and social preferences, but of immediate vital need.

2. The Momentum of Integration

What causes integrating energy to continue to gain? If the impetus exists for sector integration at all, what forces permit it to surpass mere organization and to enter into supranationalism? And what are the prospects that success in one sector will "catch on" in others?

Each of these questions is answered by a single word, though neither connotes a simple process. Sector integration, once begun, gains steam by *feedback*. This is analogous to gravity: a falling object gains velocity. In like manner, if a snowball rolls down a sharp decline, it gains mass. Put simply, integration theory posits that if a formal process of sectoral interaction is *allowed free forward propulsion*, it will gain in intensity by strengthening itself.

The analogy is, of course, oversimplified. Social phenomena are obstructed from free forward propulsion, as wind alters the free downward fall of an object or as friction reduces the energy of a rolling snowball. Social scientists have as their laboratory only political systems, and the data invariably show the feedback process to be halting and sporadic. The ideal condition is continuous, growing, and mutually perceived success, and equal sharing by all the participants in the continuing benefits. Generally, these inside conditions must be accompanied by external inducements. The impetus to advancement must, on the whole, exceed occasional setbacks.

What of the second question: what forces carry the energy of integration from one sector to another? The answer is found in the *spillover* phenomenon, in which integrative successes in one sector awaken integrating

[14] For an extensive treatment of the NATO experience, see Francis A. Beer, *Integration and Disintegration in NATO: Processes of Alliance Cohesion and Prospects for Atlantic Community* (Columbus: Ohio State University Press, 1969).

objectives in another. The integrative energy from one sector spills over to another. But once spillover has occurred, there is no assurance that feedbacks within the new sector will keep pace with the first, or that one spillover will produce the next.

Thus far we have considered four basic issues of the integrative process: (1) the distinction between organization and integration (or internationalism and supranationalism), (2) the notion of sector differentiation, and (3) the concepts of feedback, and (4) spillover. Behind these concepts is an array of social and political conditions which determine the start of the process, as well as its pace, progress, and end products.

---

3. Goals of Integration

Since integration is a conscious process, nations and governments must have explicit motives for seeking it. This is especially so since self-preservation is one of the major aims of statehood and of governmental activity. What expectations are sufficiently intense to motivate governments toward integration?

Economic Potential

Historically, the largest single motive has been the desire to *maximize economic potential*. In the presence of a few giant economies, smaller states have been unable to keep pace with competition. Whether they be underdeveloped states or old industrial states, the hope of restoring full competition may be a call to integration.

After World War II the Western European states rebuilt their industries only to discover that once great national economies were lost in the American shadow. The economy of the Western world had become asymmetrical, with the United States commanding the greatest produce for export, the largest and most technically developed labor force and the most innovative entrepreneurial skill. For reconstructed Western Europe to compete, it was necessary to merge national economies. Though this meant hardships for agriculture, six governments agreed in 1957 to establish the European Economic Community (the Common Market), with an elaborate plan for integrating trade among themselves, and for a common trade policy with respect to nonmembers.

Table 12–1 demonstrates the combined economic potential of the EEC members in comparison with the capabilities of the United States, the Soviet Union, and Japan as of 1969, fully three years prior to British, Irish, and Danish membership (1973). As these figures indicate, except in production of energy and gross national product, the Six surpassed the productivity of the United States; and they trailed the Soviet Union only in energy

TABLE 12–1 Some Leading Economic Indicators, 1969

	EEC	U.S.	USSR	Japan
Steel Production (million metric tons)	137	128	110	82
Motor Vehicle Production (million)	11	10	1	5
Primary Energy Production (million tons coal equivalent)	506	2020	1050	76
Imports ($ billion)	50	36	n.a.	15
Merchant Fleet (million tons)	77	19	n.a.	27
Industry as Contributor to GDP (%)	46	37	n.a.	39
GNP ($ billion)	564	948	490	167
Population (million)	256	210	250	102

Source: Uwe Kitzinger, "Problems of a European Political Economy," in Steven Joshua Warnecke, ed., *The European Community in the 1970's* (New York: Praeger, 1972), p. 41. Reprinted by permission.

production. By consolidating their economic activities the Common Market members comprised the second largest industrial producer in the world even before growth to nine.

While the organizations of economic integration in Western Europe and the Western Hemisphere are fully voluntary, we have also seen examples of forced or coerced economic integration. Best known and most highly developed among these is the Council for Mutual Economic Assistance (CMEA), formerly known as COMECON. Through this organization the economic resources of the Soviet Union and Eastern Europe are coordinated and allocated.[15]

Political Potential

A second major motive for integration is the desire *to maximize political potential*. With rare exception, small and politically powerless states have had little impact upon the international system. They found this as especially damaging in the bipolarity which followed World War II. Small states have felt either left out of, or victimized by, a world of two massive power centers. Some view integration as the route to reestablishing a multipolar world in which their diplomacy may achieve better results. Repeated attempts at integration by Egypt and Syria have been motivated principally by the desire to coordinate their common enmity with Israel, and to pre-

[15] Andrajez Korbonski, "Theory and Practice of Regional Integration: The Case of COMECON," *International Organization* 24 (1970): 942–77.

sent a single front in their dealings with the Soviet Union over warmaking potential and war-peace diplomacy in their region.

Conflict Resolution

A third impetus to integration is the desire *to resolve potential conflict* among territorial neighbors. If there is nascent conflict among states forced by geography to be interdependent, integration of vital sectors of their interaction may outweigh the existing sources of strife.

The most notable instance of such motivation was the founding in 1951 of the European Coal and Steel Community by the same six states which founded the EEC a few years later. Though the ECSC was the first implementation of a long-range plan for European economic integration, it was addressed more immediately to a specific problem: the age-old Franco-German rivalry over coal and steel resources. At a press conference in 1950, French Foreign Minister Robert Schuman declared that:

> The gathering of the nations of Europe requires the elimination of the age-old opposition of France and Germany. The first concern in any action undertaken must be these two countries.
>
> With this aim in view, the French Government proposes to take action immediately on one limited but decisive point. The French Government proposes to place Franco-German production of coal and steel under a common "high authority," within the framework of an organization open to the participation of the other countries of Europe.

The Schuman Declaration, previously approved by the French Council of Ministers, resulted in the ECSC. Most important, however, is the specific intent which Schuman emphasized—the interdependence of European economic integration with elimination of this historic cause of war.

How effectively does progress toward supranationalism *actually* diminish conflict among the participants? While integration does not eliminate strife, it does reduce its frequency. Denying that this proves a causal link, one scholar contends that "when combined with awareness and concern on the part of Central American elites about the relationship between economic integration and violent conflict, it does provide some useful evidence for the existence of the probable relationship. . . ." [16]

But not all students of integration are persuaded that organizations reduce the likelihood of war among members. Using five measurements of integration (common institutional membership, proximity, economic interdependence, sociocultural similarity and similarity of UN voting behavior), for example, another scholar has reviewed the history of conflict among

---

[16] Joseph S. Nye, *Peace in Parts: Integration and Conflict in Regional Organization* (Boston: Little, Brown, 1971), p. 120.

forty-one pairs of states. He found that "All five of these conditions may be necessary to prevent war between states . . . , but not even all five together are sufficient to do so." The greater the interdependence among nations, the more sensitive their salience becomes, and the greater their prospects of conflict.[17] Unfortunately, the closest neighbors may have the largest number of chances to fight—and may do so *despite* their interdependence. Thus the desire to resolve conflict is not invariably an adequate cause for integration. Even in such circumstances the loads (duties, expectations and so on) placed upon integrative processes may exceed the stabilizing capabilities of organization.

Even though Western Europe now exemplifies a high degree of integration, conflict has not disappeared. Raymond Aron, French political scientist, has warned that Europe is a place and an idea, but it is not a unity. Still another European has written a Ten Commandments for "The Nine," the first of which is, "*Do not confuse Europe with Uniformity. Europe is not uniform and attempts to make it so will be rightly resented and resisted.*" [18]

Scholars have adopted the same tone. Noting that community is built upon a growing sense of cooperation, we are reminded that:

> The members of the Community do not confront each other only or chiefly as diplomatic gladiators; they encounter each other at almost every level of organized society through constant interaction in the joint policymaking contexts of officials, parliamentarians, interest group leaders, businessmen, farmers, and trade unionists. Conflicts of interest and purpose are inevitable. *There is no paradox between the progress of economic integration in the Community and sharpening political disagreement*; indeed, the success of economic integration can be a cause of political disagreement. The member states are engaged in the enterprise for widely different reasons, and their actions have been supported or instigated by elites seeking their own particular goals. Therefore, conflicts would seem endemic as the results of joint activity come to be felt and as the pro-integration consensus shifts.[19]

Progress aside, integration is a dynamic process. Goals change, roles shift, new leaders and elites emerge, old influences wane and new ones burst onto the scene. Integration may thus proceed in a regional system of constant conflict. Indeed, since progress toward supranationalism creates stresses of its own, the process may have *negative* effects upon the overall relations of members. Reason dictates that while the resolution of regional conflicts

[17] Bruce M. Russett, *International Regions and the International System* (Chicago: Rand McNally and Company, 1967), Chapter 12, "Conflict and Integration," especially pages 198–201.

[18] John Pinder, "Ten Commandments for 'The Nine,'" *European Community* 161 (December 1972): 18–19.

[19] Leon N. Lindberg, "Decision Making and Integration in the European Community," *International Organization* 19 (1965): 80. The emphasis has been added.

may be one of the expectations of integrating members, the very process itself may be the cause of strife.[20]

---

4. Background Conditions for Integration

Alone, common expectations about regional future are not sufficient to promote integration. Certain preconditions must be satisfied, though subconsciously for the most part.

Social Assimilation

To some observers, the foremost precondition of regional integration is *social causation*, resulting in a so-called *sociocausal paradigm of integration*.[21] Focusing upon transnational attitudes, this posits that social assimilation is a precondition of integration. Critics of this concept reject the assumed necessity of social assimilation. Nevertheless, most observers agree that minimal social prerequisites do exist, and that among them are mutual tolerance of cultures, common identity of foreign policy goals, and generally cordial contacts of governments and respective nationals.

Value Sharing

A second precondition is *value sharing*, especially among elites. In the economic sector, for example, unless the elites of participating states share common values, such as capitalism or socialism, or free market as contrasted with central controls and subsidies, they will expend little energy toward integration, and little pressure will be exerted upon governments. Again, this is a sociopolitical condition.

Mutual Benefit

Expectation of mutual benefit is the third precondition. Since states will enter into a process which fundamentally alters national prerogatives only with sufficient incentives, states must be able to predict that benefits will

[20] Leon N. Lindberg, "Integration as a Source of Stress on the European Community System," *International Organization* 20 (1966): 233–65.

[21] See particularly the classic study by Deutsch et al., *Political Community and the North Atlantic Area* (Princeton: Princeton University Press, 1957). See also Deutsch's several contributions to Philip E. Jacob and James V. Tascano, eds., *The Integration of Political Communities* (Philadelphia: J. B. Lippincott and Co., 1964), including "Communication Theory and Political Integration," "Transaction Flows as Indicators of Political Cohesion," and "Integration and the Social System: Implications of Functional Analysis."

For an evaluation and critique of the sociocausal paradigm, see William E. Fisher, "An Analysis of the Deutsch Sociocausal Paradigm of Political Integration," *International Organization* 23 (1969): 254–90.

accrue from the process. Some states may expect to profit in one sector, while others seek advancement in another. Remember, however, that the integrative process involves not only international politics, but intense domestic bargaining as well.[22] While a government may be willing to sacrifice major industrial gains to achieve agricultural integration, the industrial elites may resist. Thus, their expectation of benefit is just as important as aggregate national expectations.[23]

Congenial Past Relations

A fourth precondition is experiential: *a history of frequent pacific transactions*. This acknowledges the functionalist precept that nothing succeeds like success itself; and it posits that elites, nations, and governments are unlikely to integrate without already operating cordiality.

Importance of Integration Itself

Closely related to this is the fifth criterion—namely, *the salience of transactions*. If interests are remotely related, integration is unlikely, but if participants recognize the importance of activities in other countries, impetus for integration may awaken. The prospects for integration in these cases are governed by "the law of inverse salience," which holds that the growth of integration is inversely related to the political importance of the subject matter. Another functionalist proposition, this argues that since integration proceeds only with prior progress, it is seen first in matters which are politically expendable. Only through feedbacks and spillovers does the process begin in politically sensitive areas.[24]

Low Relative Costs

Since there are bound to be costs as well as benefits, another precondition must be the *anticipation of low costs relative to benefits*, measured eco-

[22] Stuart R. Scheingold, "Domestic and International Consequences of Regional Integration," *International Organization* 24 (1970): 978–1002; and Robert J. Lieber, "Interest Groups and Political Integration: British Entry into Europe," *American Political Science Review* 66 (1972): 53–67.

[23] Karl W. Deutsch has been in the forefront of scholarship investigating the impact of elites. For major studies see particularly these of his works: "Integration and Arms Control in the European Political Environment: A Summary Report," *American Political Science Review* 60 (1966): 354–65; *Arms Control and the Atlantic Alliance* (New York: John Wiley & Sons, 1967); and with coauthors, *France, Germany and the Western Alliance: A Study of Elite Attitudes on European Integration and World Politics* (New York: Charles Scribner's Sons, 1967). Also see Robert Weissberg, "Nationalism, Integration, and French and German Elites," *International Organization* 23 (1969): 337–47.

[24] Nye, *Peace in Parts: Integration and Conflict in Regional Organization*, pp. 23–24.

nomically, socially, or nationalistically. Likewise, while they will probably be assessed principally with respect to domestic policy, a prospective participant may wish to predict the effects upon other foreign policies, or upon other regions. Britain's delayed entry into Europe stemmed partly from the potential effects upon the British agricultural sector, on its relations with the British Commonwealth members, and on its "special relationship" with the United States.

External Influences

The last issue raises what generally has been an underestimated precondition of integration: *external influences*. Virtually every integration movement can be attributed in part to external stimuli. In Western Europe, for example, painstaking progress toward strategic (military) integration would not have occurred without a threat of war from the East; and with the waning of the cold war that movement might by now have stopped, had it not been for the interest in Europe's own nuclear deterrent that American dominance of NATO has generated. The European members of NATO have undergone two different "generations" of thought about their security problems since World War II, one conditioned by external threats posed by the Soviet Union, and a second by U.S. policy.[25]

Economic integration, too, may have external stimuli. The threat of American domination of European economies after the Marshall Plan unquestionably increased the cries for economic consolidation. Also, the desire to coordinate trade policy with respect to the U.S. contributed to the establishment of the Central American Common Market and the Latin American Free Trade Association. External conditions may even have spillover effects.[26] For example, while French military policies during the 1950's in Algeria and Indochina may have contributed to the French defeat of the European Defense Community (EDC), they also helped to change the older notion of forceful maintenance of an overseas empire and inspired new demands that the deGaulle government turn the national resources and energies inward to Europe.[27]

[25] David Owen, *The Politics of Defense* (New York: Taplinger, 1972) and François Duchene, "A New European Defense Community," *Foreign Affairs* 50 (October 1971): 69–82. Both writers are European. See also chapter 3 of this book.

[26] Literature on external preconditions to integration is not abundant. For a seminal inquiry, see Karl Kaiser, "The Interaction of Regional Subsystems: Some Preliminary Notes on Recurrent Patterns and the Role of the Superpowers," *World Politics* 21 (1968–69): 84–107.

For a comprehensive study of the interactions between Washington and the European capitals which resulted in integration movements, see Ernst H. van der Beugel, *From Marshall Plan to Atlantic Partnership* (New York: American Elsevier Publishing Company, Inc., 1966).

[27] This outline of preconditions of integration is intended not as construction of a new model, but as an eclectic review drawing upon prior studies. Among those works

5. Maintaining the Momentum of Integration

Starting along the integrative path and continued progress toward the goal of supranationalism are quite separate issues. Hence, in addition to certain preconditions which permit the process to begin, certain combinations of "process factors" must be present to govern steady progress.

Functional Satisfaction

First among these is *functional satisfaction*; that is, recognition by pertinent elites and officials of the degree to which integrated policy is serving their interests. This recognition promotes feedback, thus fueling greater sectoral integration and encouraging spillover.

Increased Pacific Transactions

A second process factor is an *increased frequency of pacific transactions*. The rate and number of transactions are measures of mutual reliance, revealing governmental willingness to compromise sovereignty in specific sectors. Since increasing interdependence is indispensable, the rate of transactions is a critical measure of progress. Yet one recent study has cautioned against overvaluing transactions as a causal factor in the growth of integration; increased transactions are more a reflection of integration than a cause.[28] Yet it is probable that satisfaction in these contacts, originally an effect of integration, now encourages additional contacts, and is thus a major determinant of sectoral feedback.

Regulation

Gradually, the transactions of integrating sectors must become institutionalized. Informal regulation cannot continuously serve the objective of formal integration. A third major process condition is the *proliferation of*

---

which have been drawn upon, the most important are Haas, *The Uniting of Europe: Political, Social and Economic Forces, 1950–57*, a classic study on the subject of regional integration; Amitai Etzioni, *Political Unification* (New York: Holt, Rinehart and Winston, 1965); Ernst B. Haas and Philippe C. Schmitter, "Economics and Differential Patterns of Political Integration: Projections about Unity in Latin America," *International Organization* 18 (1964): 705–37; Bruce M. Russett, *International Regions and the International System*; Philippe C. Schmitter, "A Revised Theory of Regional Integration," *International Organization* 24 (1970): 836–68; Joseph S. Nye, "Patterns and Catalysts in Regional Integration," *International Organization* 19 (1965): 870–84.

[28] Donald J. Puchala, "International Transactions and Regional Integration," *International Organization* 24 (1970): 732–63.

institutions with sufficient authority to regulate. Ultimately, these institutions must assume the national governments' normal legislative and executive prerogatives. Complete transfer of such authority from national governments to common institutions is the final stage of the integrating process; and with its completion a supranational community may be said to exist. At present, the maximum progress toward complete integration of a subsector is represented in the High Authority of the European Coal and Steel Community (ECSC), which has been authorized by its members to exercise sovereign authority over the allocation of the pertinent resources.

The achievement of full multisectoral supranationalism requires establishment of sufficient institutional machinery to govern the community. This means development of legislative, executive, and judicial institutions, each vested with full authority in its realm. At present, one of the most interesting developments in Western Europe is the drive, inspired principally by Great Britain, to wrest legislative control from the Council of Ministers of the European Communities and to invest full legislative authority in the European Parliament. Eventually, it is hoped by advocates of ultimate federation of Europe, this body will be a true multinational legislature.

Bureaucracy

The institutionalization of a political process involves the *generation of a bureaucracy*, specially trained to manage sectoral activities. Since a high degree of technical competence is needed in addition to administrative skills, these bureaucracies are customarily referred to as *technocracies*. But not only do the technocrats manage the day-to-day affairs; they must also coordinate the expectations of elites, soothe the sensitivities of governments, and make the unremitting case for further development. They are not only technical experts and intergovernmental managers; they are also the guardians of the integrative process.

Community Jurisprudence

Another, though less visible, process condition is the development of a *community jurisprudence*, a commonly recognized body of law which governs legal relations of the respective states. If governments or corporations of different states become involved in legal problems, it is not productive in an integrating community to rely upon the judicial practices of one state or another. Furthermore, if a community institution and a state have a legal disagreement, the development of a body of law and of community courts is eventually necessary in the development of supranational politics. The Court of Justice of the European Communities serves this need, and has already developed a large body of case law governing the relations of the communities, the member states and individual technocrats.

Increased Decisions

Increased transactions, formation of institutions and technocracies, and the establishment of a common core of jurisprudence all point to the next process condition: *increased decisional output*. It cannot be said that integration is under way merely because of institutional appearances; rather, measurable and reliable decisions, upon which governments and pertinent elites willingly depend and with which they comply consistently, are indispensable. Institutions can have no productive effect upon national elites unless they are able to command the external transactions of those elites. Only through actual decisions does the institution become the authoritative vehicle of an international process.

Mass Attitudes

All of the foregoing process factors imply increased relations and communications among elites. But in addition, the process of integration requires that mass political and social attitudes also be nurtured. Thus, a seventh important process factor is the *development of mutual mass attitudes*. Though progress toward integration may build upon elite pressures, governments are not likely to sacrifice national prerogatives or to respond to narrow demands for supranationality until appropriate attitudes have rooted among their electorates. This development must take place in most or all of the participating nations. In this way, mutual expectations are regularly communicated across national boundaries, the benefits of continued progress become more familiar to individuals, and nationalistic attitudes begin to recede.[29] British entry into the Community was paradoxical in this regard, since polls showed in 1973 that the population did *not* favor membership. It was thus expected that while Britain's membership might eventually accelerate integration, there would be a lag time during which British elite and popular attitudes would catch up with those on the continent.[30] In fact, it was not until 1975 that a British referendum demon-

[29] A pioneering effort to measure the impact on individual reward structure of internationalization of business enterprise in Europe (specifically Germany) is found in Bernard Mennis and Karl P. Sauvant, "Describing and Explaining Support for Regional Integration: An Investigation of German Business Elite Attitudes toward the European Community," *International Organization* 29 (1975): 972–995.

[30] For a study of mass opinion as well as elite opinion with respect to European integrative progress, see Donald J. Puchala, "The Common Market and Political Federation in Western European Public Opinion," *International Studies Quarterly* 14 (1970): 32–59.

strated decisively the public desire for full membership in the European Community.

External Factors

External factors of either of two types may influence the integrative process. First, they may be external events which absorb the energies of one of the participants in community. These events may prevent full and earnest participation or in some cases accentuate regional preferences. French foreign policy provides examples of both phenomena. Before the Gaullist era, French participation in European integration was impeded by preoccupation with problems in North Africa and Indochina. But for a decade commencing in the mid-1950's, President deGaulle turned these problems around and directed energies inward. Those years witnessed the most vigorous steps toward European supranationalism. Thus integration may depend on external events in which one of the community members is vitally engaged. These are "member-centered" external events.

Other external events are not member-centered, but may nevertheless have major impacts upon the integrative process. The foreign policies (potentially even domestic policies) of other nations may touch upon one or more of the members of a growing community with either integrative effects or disintegrative effects. The unpopularity among Europeans of American policy in Southeast Asia undoubtedly heightened the sense of Europeanness and correspondingly diminished the psychological bonds with Washington. Except in the security sector (NATO), then, the Vietnam War (as a nonmember-centered external factor) had integrative effects upon Europe. Warsaw Pact occupation of Czechoslovakia in 1968, a resort to long invisible Soviet politics, was an event of similar meaning to Western Europe.

A most instructive nonmember-centered external event occurred in 1962 with telling effect upon European economic integration. Already concerned about future competition from Europe, American merchants sought long-term relief from tariff barriers. As a result, the Kennedy administration sought and secured from Congress discretionary authority to negotiate substantial reciprocal tariff reductions. The Trade Expansion Act of 1962 authorized executive discretion for a period of five years, during which major changes in American trade policy might be negotiated.

The EEC members entered into the subsequent negotiations called the Kennedy Round with full awareness of the American intent to safeguard industrial exports against future competition. This awareness sparked renewed activity in the EEC toward eliminating internal restraints to trade, and resulted particularly in resolution of many of the thorny agricultural problems which had previously retarded progress toward a full free trade arrangement.

These negotiations, together with growing American direct investment in Europe designed to "get behind" the tariff barriers, comprised a clear signal to EEC members that major industrial competitors feared the successful culmination of the free trade area, and provided added incentives for conscious development. Resentment over this form of exploitation also sparked European attacks upon the American balance-of-payments deficit, accentuated European criticism of American policy in Vietnam, gave credence to President deGaulle's efforts "to de-Americanize Europe," and generally raised the level of Europe-consciousness. Hence there were significant social and political spillovers.

Transfer of Loyalty

The final process condition is really the measure of all of the others: the *transfer of loyalty* gradually from national community values, objectives and institutions. It means the adoption by national majorities of far-reaching supranationalist attitudes. As this itself is a functional requisite, such a development does not occur except through individual recognition of the profitability of integration. Nor will it occur in several nations unless there is sufficient communication by which societies can measure attitudinal progress in neighboring lands. Social communication is thus vital to the transfer of loyalties.[31]

The loyalty transfer process is one of continuing socialization in which positive value communication substantiates the need for community-oriented attitudes. Several studies have concluded that Europeans look less and less to national governments for critical decisions and increasingly to community institutions. Socialization data point almost incontrovertibly to further integration in economic, social, and political sectors in Western Europe.[32] Public opinion polls in 1962, for example, showed overwhelming preference for unification and widespread expectation that it would occur within ten or fifteen years, as revealed in Tables 12–2 and 12–3. Furthermore, responses to questions pertaining to internal matters of the Euro-

---

[31] For a study of the impact of international events upon the loyalty problem, see John Herz, *International Politics in the Atomic Age* (New York: Columbia University Press, 1959). The foremost study of communications in nationalist and supranationalist attitudes is Karl W. Deutsch, *Nationalism and Social Communication*.

[32] Leon N. Lindberg and Stuart A. Scheingold, *Europe's Would-Be Polity: Patterns of Change in the European Community* (Englewood Cliffs, N.J.: Prentice-Hall, 1970), especially Chapters 8 and 9; Carl J. Friedrich, *Europe: An Emergent Nation?* (New York: Harper & Row, 1969); Deutsch et al., "Integration and Arms Control in the European Political Environment," p. 355.

For summary socialization data pertaining to transfer of loyalties, see particularly Ronald Inglehart, "An End to European Integration?" 61 *American Political Science Review* (1967): 91–105. The paper is framed as a response to the article by Deutsch et al., Ibid. Also, Puchala, "The Common Market and Political Federation in Western European Public Opinion."

TABLE 12–2 Are You For or Against the Efforts for European Unification?

	For	Against	No Answer
Belgium	65%	5%	30%
France	72	8	20
Germany	81	4	15
Italy	60	4	36
Luxembourg	27	5	68
The Netherlands	87	4	9

Source: *Communauté Europeenne* (December, 1962), as reprinted in W. Hartley Clark, *The Politics of the Common Market*, pp. 111–12, © 1967, reproduced by permission of Prentice-Hall, Englewood Cliffs, New Jersey.

pean Communities showed huge favorability of integrated policy (Table 12–4). More recently, a survey of French attitudes has been conducted (within three weeks of British entry in 1973). On questions of direct election of the European Parliament, the evolution of a formal Community government and Community supremacy in such critical areas as defense, diplomacy economics, and nuclear and space development, the number of respondents who preferred Community-oriented solutions consistently exceeded those who favored state-oriented policy, though approximately one-third of respondents gave no opinions.[33] Repeatedly, therefore, socialization data have underscored public preference for, and acceptance of, regional integration to the extent of spillover from the economic to the political sector.

TABLE 12–3 When Will Europe Unite?

	Belgium	France	Germany	Italy	Luxembourg	The Netherlands
Never	9%	11%	17%	9%	6%	18%
In several generations	9	12	4	3	10	11
In 20 to 30 years	14	14	10	8	18	23
In 10 to 15 years	20	14	16	9	12	21
In the next 10 years	23	21	26	10	14	15
No answer	25	28	27	61	20	12
Total	100	100	100	100	100	100

Source: *Communauté Europeenne* (December, 1962), as reprinted in W. Hartley Clark, *The Politics of the Common Market*, pp. 111–12.

[33] *Le Figaro*, February 27, 1973, as reproduced in Ernest H. Preeg, *Economic Blocs and U.S. Foreign Policy* (Washington: National Planning Association, 1974), p. 109.

TABLE 12–4   Are You For or Against the Following Measures?

| | Average percentage for all six countries, weighted according to size of country | |
	For	Against
Elimination of tariffs in Europe	81	6
Free circulation of workers in Europe	68	16
Equating of diplomas given by schools in Europe	72	4
A common foreign policy for Europe	60	9
Common administration of scientific research in Europe	75	3
A common farm policy	69	8
Common standards of social welfare throughout Europe	77	4
Subsidizing development of poor areas of Europe	49	28
Subsidizing African development	35	40

Source: *Communauté Europeenne*, as reprinted in W. Hartley Clark, *The Politics of the Common Market*, p. 113.

With the conclusion of this discussion of sectors, objectives, preconditions and process conditions of integration, we are now ready to summarize the critical issues of the supranational quest. (See Table 12–5.)

An Evaluation of Integration

In this examination of integration, we assume that supranationalism is healthy and that it is to be encouraged and lauded. But if integration occurs, then its impact upon people and upon international order is worth exploring.

First consider the effects of integration upon the subjects of an integrated community. Although it is conventionally presumed that these persons will, for the most part, profit from integration, some observers raise the negative aspects. Integration may very well raise standards of living, indices of production, and so on, but what will life be like? Does supranationalism necessarily make the individual's life more pleasant?

Although this question defies definitive response at the present time,

TABLE 12–5 Summary of Integration Factors

Integration Sectors	Momentum	Objectives	Preconditions	Process Conditions
Economic Social Political Security	Feedback (intrasector) Spillover (intersector)	Maximize economic potential Maximize political potential Regional conflict resolution	Social assimilation Elite value sharing Expectation of mutual benefits History of pacific transactions Favorable ratio of costs to benefits External influences	Functional satisfaction Increased frequency of transactions Institution-building Technocracy-building Community jurisprudence Growing decisional output Mass attitude assimilation External Factors a. member-centered b. nonmember-centered Transfer of Loyalty

perhaps healthy skepticism is appropriate. The consolidation of economics and politics does, to be sure, have the effect of eliminating competition and some differences among participants, but it creates a new form of political community. Is this new form merely an enlarged nation-state? Is there anything fundamentally different an integrated community and a large nation-state that is multilingual and culturally and socially heterogeneous?

These are not merely abstract questions. In their concerns with mass anxiety, crises of identity, break-up of the nuclear family, lack of pride in work, and the "generation gap," social observers today have begun to explore the social and psychological consequences of mass industrialization. They have turned their sights upon the issue of whether there are ill effects from the modern philosophy of the huge industrial state: "There's more of it where that came from!" Does integration for purposes of successful international economic competition rush a society blindly toward these effects? Does it hasten the alienation of men and women from the politics, institutions, and lip-service ideals of mass society?

Another concern is with the antidemocratic effects of centralization and bureaucratization. As policy becomes less the result of public participation and more a consequence of administrative pragmatism, does a society relinquish to functional technocracies its grip of its own destiny?" What is the likelihood that increased reliance on technocracy will degenerate into new forms of oligarchy? Are there major divergences between the values, needs, and expectations of technocrats, on the one hand, and those of society on the other? What is the future of the political role of nonelite social sectors?

These and other "quality-of-life" questions have led to a call for a normative critique of integration theory and for research into the social consequences of regional supranationalism. To be socially tolerable in the long run, life in supranational communities must be preferable and superior to life in contemporary nation-states. Otherwise, the achievement of higher political community may merely be a new organizational stage in the destruction of societies.[34]

The view from outside raises equally troubling questions. Even if one accepts the intragroup benefits of integration, what are the effects upon *inter*group relations. Do the consolidated policies of like-minded states *necessarily* contribute to international order, or do they merely accentuate the effects of the nation-state? What are the prospects that European economic integration will lead to trade warfare even with the United States if European production and trade volumes should have long-term detrimental effects upon the American economy, its exports, and its balance of payments? Perhaps we have already been introduced to this possibility in the unilateral policies of Washington in 1971 and 1972 when unilateral increases in tariff were attached to imports from all industrial countries, and the United States forced reconsideration of the international monetary system. If regional integration tends to have associating characteristics among its members, its external policy may have a disassociating effect on overall international stability.

The potential for global disassociation is especially apparent in security communities, which exist as the result of previously identified enemies. Because the enmities exist before the security arrangements, disassociation is a product of earlier political relations. Yet like all other institutions in society, security institutions tend to become self-sustaining. The elites which manage them continue to have interests, and their operations may

[34] These questions have been broached in a most incisive manner in John W. Sloan and Harry R. Targ, "Beyond the European Nation-State: A Normative Critique," *Polity* 3 (Summer, 1971): 501–520.

depend upon perpetuating the initial causes. In security communities, the original cause is *threat*; and the perpetuation of security institutions may thus depend upon successful threat perception and the ability to convince populations and appropriating agencies of the continuing character of potential crisis. Should this occur—if persons propagandize and even romanticize crisis-potential for institutional or personal aggrandizement—then institutions may prolong crises, contributing to the disassociating effects carried by the original antipathy. Institutionalized alliances always bear this danger; and since integrated institutions magnify the political potential of elites, supranational security communities may impede global stability.

There may also be a dangerous aspect to the connection between supranational institutions and domestic institutions. Since successful integrative trends require close cooperation between regional technocrats and domestic leaders, they may learn to use one another and one another's services for personal purposes. Thus the command officers of an integrated military community may gain inordinate access to legislative politics, to the great detriment of domestic policy. Strong and semisecretive national-regional competition among interacting elites may hasten the erosion of the beneficial aspects of national life.

Despite the dangers implicit in integration from both domestic and international perspectives, at present the prevailing attitude is that regional integrative trends are healthy, productive, and promising of a brighter future for national peoples and for global stability. Indeed, one French student of Community affairs has gone so far as to write that "Europe as a whole could well become the first example in history of a major centre of the balance of power becoming in the era of its decline not a colonised victim but the examplar of a new stage in political civilisation."[35] But two others have entered an incisive condition: that "the Community's capacity to act constructively in the world depends in the last resort on its success in establishing within its boundaries a more united and more just society."[36] It is safe to conclude that the application of integration to any region will encounter a similar variety of predictions.

The American Perception of Integration

Having maximized its own political, social, and economic potentialities through federative integration and having undergone a bloody Civil War to preserve union, it is natural for the United States to favor integration.

[35] François Duchêne, "The European Community and the Uncertainties of Interdependence," in Max Kohnstamm and Wolfgang Hager, eds., *A Nation Writ Large?: Foreign Policy Problems before the European Community* (New York: John Wiley and Sons, 1973), pp. 1–21, at p. 19.

[36] Max Kohnstamm and Wolfgang Hager, in "Conclusion" to *A Nation Writ Large?*, p. 256.

Indeed, at the close of World War II the United States not only encouraged but also paid about $15 billion to reconstruct Europe through the Marshall Plan (European Recovery Program). From the start the United States assumed that the Western European participants would plan together a forerunner to the economic integration which the United States intended to encourage. Taking cues from Winston Churchill, Jean Monnet and others, Americans such as Secretary of State George C. Marshall, William L. Clayton, and Christian Herter joined from this side of the Atlantic in constructing the foundations for a United States of Europe.

The dramatic recovery of Western Europe depended in large measure on America's assistance and willingness to undergo a decade or more of disadvantageous trade principles so that Europe might speed its reconstruction. Although the principles of the international monetary system and of free world trade were dictated principally by the United States, they benefited Western Europe even more. They opened wide American markets to European produce; and they protected the infant European industries from American competition. Now that the EC has matured, time has come to restructure the system, for the United States ought no longer be asked to bear the burdens of trade and monetary disadvantages. For economic purposes, a U.S.E. (United States of Europe) now exists, and its competitive ability has surpassed the American concessions to its maturation. That the EC not have disassociating effects in the Western hemisphere, the rules of the road must be changed. Negotiations for the new codes of economic behavior between Europe and the Americas commenced at the close of 1971, precipitated largely by justified American insistence and partly by European responses to Washington's unilateral policies in the two preceding years.

Other than in Europe, the United States continues to encourage economic integration, though successful *industrial* competition which might alter American attitudes has not arisen from any other integrated region.

On the matter of political integration, the United States takes a somewhat dimmer view. Even in Europe, Washington's view is ambivalent about political supranationalism, which would deprive Washington of the ability to negotiate with European capitals individually on certain matters, and would remove the traditional rite of playing one power off against another. Preservation of the American role in the larger trans-Atlantic community thus dictates a cautious approach to European political integration.

The Perceptions of America's Major Allies

As the world's prime promoters of integration, the attitude of America's Western European allies is in the record of their experience. But what of Japan and Canada?

The Japanese view is not entirely clear, though logic would seem to construct a negative attitude. In the first place, just as the United States had retaliated against Japanese economic success, so too has it against the resurgence of Europe. But since the target of such actions is rarely specified, any Western-oriented industrial producer is likely to feel the brunt of American protection. Secondly, Japan's exports are industrial and Europe is a large industrial market. The efficiency of European industry, together with the common barriers to trade raised against external competitors, reduces the probable sales of Japanese goods in Western Europe. And third, because of Japan's huge balance-of-payments deficit to the oil-producing states, it desperately needs to compile surpluses by its industrial trade to places like Europe. Though it cannot be said that Japan is hostile to European integration, it appears that integrative success is detrimental to the distribution of Japan's industrial exports.

In its own region of the world, Japan is actively promoting development both through public assistance (largely through the Asian Development Bank) and through private capital flows, but its interest is not now in integration. Instead, Japan is attempting to construct industrial markets, particularly in places rich in natural resources.

Canada's view of integration is typically restrained. Itself a federal state, integrative experience is understood by custom. Yet the British entry into the European Community placed economic strains on Canada which, as a member of the British Commonwealth, had previously enjoyed a free-trade relation with Britain and had particularly profited as an agricultural supplier. British entry not only removed those advantages, but presented the added strain of making industrial trade more difficult at precisely the point when Canada was undergoing a major phase of industrial development. Even in 1973, nevertheless (the year of British entry), Canada's balance-of-trade surplus with respect to Britain continued to rise. But it will be a few years before Britain must comply fully with the common tariff policy of the Community, suggesting that the Canadian payments surplus may be tentative. Since Canada suffers a substantial deficit with respect to the world at large, it is probable that the European Community will eventually present costly barriers to Canada's industrial trade.

The Soviet Perception of Integration

The forced integration of the Soviet regions in the civil war which followed the Bolshevik Revolution, succeeded by years of intense "Russification" of the non-Russian peoples of the Soviet Union, speaks vividly for the Soviet tendency to favor integration, at least among its friends and allies. Post–World War II incorporation of Eastern Europe in a related economic supranationalism directed from Moscow, as capital of the Socialist Commonwealth, accentuates this view. But as for integration in the West, the Kremlin's view is mixed, and has changed with progression from the cold war to the era of peaceful coexistence.

Initially, the Soviet Union saw American interest in the integration of Europe not as a move toward economic stabilization, but as part of the effort to subject the Soviet Union and Eastern Europe to capitalist encirclement. In the wake of World War II and the division of Europe, the United States sought to isolate the East politically and economically by strengthening Western Europe as a huge economic colony and political puppet of American interests. In a view increasingly shared by Western Europeans, the Soviets see American economic restoration as a way not to creases through the EC, the Soviets look upon the effects as salutary to American economy overseas. And in a view increasingly shared by American revisionist historians, the Kremlin sees economic restoration principally as a step toward preventing the kinds of economic and social conditions which might have made Marxism an attractive doctrine to Western Europeans. American motives were, therefore, either imperialistic or ideological, or perhaps both.

The integrative trends in Europe have been both more peaceful and more successful than those of Eastern Europe, a contrast which is a source of embarrassment to the Soviet Union. Yet as economic integration increases through the EC, the Soviets look upon the effects as salutary to their objectives. Western European economic strength decreases dependence upon the United States. This facilitates pan-European trade without involvement with American capital. It also may diminish the general harmony of trans-Atlantic relations, giving Europeans more independence in their policies, especially toward the Communist world.

But to the Soviets, Western European integration has one characteristic that is especially important. The Kremlin is aware of the partial incompatibility of European integration, on the one hand, and security dependence upon the United States through NATO, on the other.[37] Like many Western observers, they acknowledge that NATO has had disintegrating effects upon the European members. If integration is to proceed, Washington's domination of NATO must be minimized. The spin-off effects of integration upon the American security role in Europe are thus negative as viewed from Washington, but positive from the vantage point of the Kremlin.

At present, therefore, the Soviet Union favors Western European integration because it tends to reduce the American role in Europe, principally in the security sector, but in the economic as well. If the aim of Soviet foreign policy is to divide the Western allies, then European progress that causes any division from the United States—particularly that reduces Amer-

---

[37] Otto Pick, "Atlantic Defense and the Integration of Europe," *Atlantic Community Quarterly* 10 (Summer, 1972): 174–84.

ican dominance—is to be encouraged. Hence the fundamental paradox of the Soviet perception: while the Soviets use coerced integration to keep Soviet allies in line on political, economic, and security matters, they expect voluntary integration in Western Europe to *divide* the Western alliance, reducing the United States as a European actor.

The Chinese Perception of Integration

In Peking, regional integration is seen through the lenses of both an emerging superpower and a huge underdeveloped country. As a major power, China's principal objective is to prevent the United States and the Soviet Union from dividing the world into two giant camps. Thus any reduction of the Soviet role in Eastern Europe is useful; and any political trends that diminish American dominance in Western Europe are likewise desirable. Such developments dilute superpower politics, and reduce the gap which China must fill to reach full major-power status.

As an underdeveloped country, China strives for multipolarity and encourages competition among major blocs that will further reduce superpower control. While China itself intends to be a power pole in a future multipolar world, it looks to other centers to achieve the same end. Western Europe, with its enormous economic potential and its ability to generate a nuclear deterrent free of American strategy, is one of the critical areas in the future global power distribution.

Pragmatic considerations also govern the Chinese perception. Faced with the huge problem of industrializing rapidly, China's trading needs are large. And although Japan is a natural target for trade, a long history of Sino-Japanese antipathy, coupled with the humiliation of Japan's close relations with the United States during the years in which the U.S. isolated China, mitigate against full reliance on Japan. Industrial trade with Western Europe, as productive as Japan and as much in need of China's raw materials, is an available alternative. And, paradoxically, with the vacuum left by American withdrawal from Southeast Asia, China expects to benefit from any strong Western coalition which will divert the attention of the Soviet Union from the Asian theater, even if pan-European stability enables the Soviets to station more divisions along the Chinese border.[38]

As to China's view of integration elsewhere, its policy is not yet clear. While integrated economies in Asia and the Pacific would both accelerate development and reduce foreign interference, such trends would rely heavily

---

[38] See also Alain Bouc, "Peking Now Wants a United Europe," *Atlantic Community Quarterly* 10 (Summer, 1972): 167–73. Briefly considered in Robert S. Elegant, "China, the U.S., and Soviet Expansionism," *Commentary* 61 (1976): 39–46.

upon Japanese capital, goods, and political superiority. This is unacceptable to China. Hence while somewhat reticent on the subject, China for specific political reasons does not look favorably upon integration in its own geographic region.

The Third World Perception of Integration

Although there is considerable regional organizational activity in the Third World, progress toward integration is beset by a peculiar dilemma. The governments are confronted simultaneously by a need for rapid development and by the careful nurturing of nationalist spirits required by modernization. While integration of the economic sectors might increase the pace of modernization, the other edge of the sword of nationalism prevents such progress. In the older regions of Central and South America the dilemma has been bridged, with the resulting Central American Common Market, the Latin American Free Trade Association, and the Andean Pact. But in the newly independent areas, only the East African Common Market (EACM) has achieved much integrative progress. The merger of Tanganyika and Zanzibar into Tanzania has had little external effect, and the Arab states have not successfully integrated either politically or economically. While the Asian and Pacific Council (ASPAC) and the Association for Southeast Asia (ASA) may eventually embark upon supranational trends, they have made no measurable progress to date.

Yet Western Europe continues to be the focus of forward-looking Third World statesmen, both as a model of economic promise and as a symbol of the passing of bipolarity and of superpower imperialism. Some Third World states, particularly former colonial possessions of France, enjoy the status of associate membership in the EEC. This status is controversial, for while the associate member is accorded tariff concessions among the EEC members, it must also award such preferences to other members. This latter condition in some cases offsets the benefits of associate membership, payments balances, and infant industries.

There is one aspect of the European Community which is of undeniable benefit to the Third World. In recent years the members of the community, acting in a coordinated but nonintegrated way, have become major providers of development funds. By 1970, the total foreign assistance offered by the Six exceeded the annual foreign aid budget of the United States for the first time. Generally, however, such lending is limited to associate members and to former colonial possessions of the members. Thus it is enjoyed only selectively by the Third World.

On balance, however, integration is a common goal of the Third World, though the necessity for nationalism both impedes progress and ensures that, for the foreseeable future, supranationalist progress will be limited to the economic sector.

Transnational Participation

Every structure of world order which we have thus far considered presumes as its central feature the nation-state, intergovernmental organization or the integration of states into higher political units. Sovereignty, power, and official diplomacy lie at the heart of each of these systems. All of them are considered to be "state-centric" models of world order. Yet every traveler, every student of other cultures, every devotee of the creative arts and every businessperson is aware that many transactions of the international system do not involve governments alone, and that much that happens across international boundaries is removed from sovereignty and intergovernmental negotiations. Despite the omnipresence of governments and official regulations, many international transactions occur on a people-to-people basis, or between one government and the corporations of another state. This process, referred to as *transnational participation*, has recently become the focus of new forms of research and observation in international relations.

Transnational interaction is defined as "the movement of tangible or intangible items across state boundaries when at least one actor is not an agent of a government or an intergovernmental organization."[39] It may be contact between two or more nongovernmental actors, or between one official actor and one or more private actors. The nongovernmental participants may be corporations, social organizations, interest groups, political parties, elite structures, or formally instituted organizations designed to facilitate private relations. An agreement between an oil company and a foreign government falls in this category, as does contact between the International Red Cross and the government of Cuba. An International Youth Conference, involving no governments, is also transnational.[40]

[39] Joseph S. Nye, Jr. and Robert O. Keohane, "Transnational Relations and World Politics: An Introduction," *International Organization* 25 (1971): 329–49, esp. 332. This section borrows extensively from this article.

[40] The summer 1971 edition of *International Organization* (vol. 25, no. 3) is devoted to the subject "Transnational Relations and World Politics," under the editorship of Robert O. Keohane and Joseph S. Nye, Jr. Among its many papers it considers the Ford Foundation, the Roman Catholic Church, airlines flying international routes, labor unions, and scientific societies as transnational actors. Though these papers are not specifically cited here, the reader is alerted to this edition of the journal as the best single source of papers on theory and illustrative studies of the transitional phenomenon.

Goals of Transnational Participation

While these forms of international contact have always occurred, their importance has traditionally been minimized because of state domination of the global system. Now it is acknowledged, however, that such contacts contribute to the quality of coexistence, either directly (by improving perceptions and tolerances) or indirectly (by affecting intergovernmental relations). With increasing private contact, ubiquitous international trade and social communication, transnational participation can no longer be overlooked as a major aspect of international stability or of integration.

There are six kinds of prospective impact of these interactions. First, transnational contact is assumed to promote *changes in attitude* among the actors. Contact may break down perceptions, erase social and cultural barriers, enlighten outlooks, and dissipate animosities. In general, such attitudinal changes may help to transform the international system by raising levels of tolerance among peoples, especially elites.

The second identifiable impact is the *promotion of international pluralism*. More and more linkages will be developed bewteen domestic political processes and the international system. More interests will come to be involved in decision-making; more national elites will gain contact with their counterparts abroad; and more services will be provided for more people.

The creation of new avenues of *dependence and interdependence* is the third expectation. Transnational contact illuminates mutual needs, and in the long run it may obviate some causes of intersocietal conflict. In addition, reliance will be built upon other societies, upon their productivity, and upon their unique forms of creativity. In this manner, transnational contact may assist in "denationalizing" the energies of national peoples, thus taking governments out of the spotlight at the center of international transactions.[41]

Fourth, increases in transnationalism may create beneficial side effects for those parts of the international system which remain state centered. Specifically, stabilization of relations among peoples, with increasing intersocietal dependence, may enlarge the peaceful contacts of governments, and actually create for them *new avenues of influence*. A dramatic and unusual example of this impact was President Richard Nixon's trip to the People's Republic of China in 1972, a trip which was made possible in American public opinion by the prior amicable visit of a table tennis team. Following the president's sojourn, informal contact was utilized further to break down long-standing barriers by exchanges of scientists, physicians, and surgeons. This feature of transnationalism has led one observer to describe the pro-

---

[41] These first three features of transnationalism are especially well illustrated in the study of Robert C. Angell, *Peace on the March: Transnational Participation* (New York: Van Nostrand Reinhold, 1969).

cess as "transactions which bypass the institutions of government but strongly affect their margin of maneuver." [42]

Fifth, transnational participation, when institutionalized, may create new influential *autonomous or quasi-autonomous actors* in the international system. Among these are scores of nongovernmental organizations (NGO's) and informal institutional arrangements through which transnational interactions are regulated. The International Red Cross is the best known such actor, one which not only conducts its own relief operations, but to which governments frequently turn to arrange official contacts. Another important NGO is the International Chamber of Commerce, which has already contributed to international stability and amicable exchange by formulating norms of international business relations.[43]

This fifth possible effect of transnationalism is the *gradual institutionalization of intersocietal transactions*, which may become the private counterpart of functional international organizations. While public single-purpose organizations go about formulating international norms in their respective fields, transnational groups may proceed to develop the norms of their own relations. Furthermore, the national elites which direct functional organizations will be identical in some instances to those which regulate transnational contact. Such a process would maximize the linkages between national and international decision-making processes.[44]

Types of Transnational Participation

Having noted the functional characteristic of transnational research, we may now classify and exemplify types of transnational participation. Most informal among them are the *sociocultural* activities, of which there are thousands annually. Most common is individual travel, which has some cumulative effect upon international attitudes. Other sociocultural activities of significance are international visits of symphony orchestras, touring exhibits, lecture series, touring dance companies, and so on. International athletic events, particularly the Olympics, the Pan-American Games, and the Soviet-American games, also are in this category.

Political transnational activity is another. The earliest events were the International Peace Congresses of the nineteenth century, which met to formulate treaties for world peace. These were returned to national societies and national governments, with the Congress members serving as interest groups. At present, the World Peace Through Law movement does much the same thing. Other political transnationalism involves the inter-

[42] Karl Kaiser, "Transnational Politics: Toward a Theory of Multinational Politics," *International Organization* 24 (1971): 790–817, at p. 790.

[43] Percy E. Corbett, *From International to World Law* (Bethlehem, Pa.: Lehigh University Department of International Relations, research monograph no. 1, 1969).

[44] The functional character of transnationalism is also stressed by Karl Kaiser, "Toward a Theory of Multinational Politics," p. 803.

national communications and meetings of some political parties, such as the Socialist parties of Western Europe, National Communist Parties and the several National Liberation Fronts. International Youth Conferences sponsored periodically by the United Nations and other organizations are also examples of political transnationalism, since they present and discuss the political attitudes of young people from different lands.

By far the most important transnational activities are in the *economic* realm. Though many aspects of the international political economy are conducted by governments, and while most are regulated by official norms, much of the modern international economy is privately regulated. At present, the transnational actor with the greatest power to affect national economies and the flow of international transactions is the *transnational (or multinational) corporation* (TNC). Its center of operations is in one country, but it has subsidiaries in several others which have major effects upon international economics and upon the host economies. At present there are over 4000 corporations whose tentacles reach out in this manner, many of them American. In 1975, of the twenty largest corporations in the world (this excludes, of course, the state-owned enterprises of socialist states) thirteen were American; and of the largest fifty, twenty-four were American. In addition, of the largest 300 such corporations in the world *excluding* those which are American-based, twenty-six were wholly-owned subsidiaries of American firms. Table 12–6 lists the top twenty companies, their countries of origin and their annual sales volumes. There are few countries in the world which have gross national products as large as the annual sales of Exxon! And in 1972, when the domestic and overseas operations of ITT came under fire, the Solicitor General of the United States remarked that the company was so big that it was beyond the laws even of the United States!

Looked at from the viewpoint of a host government, the power of these corporations is equally great. An anecdote may suffice to illustrate. The British Ford subsidiary manufactures approximately 650,000 automobiles per year, slightly fewer than the Belgian and German subsidiaries. In 1971, when corporation president Henry Ford II arrived in Britain during a strike, he warned that unless the British economy presented less threat to productivity, Ford would consider closing its British operations and expanding productivity on the Continent. Though labor reacted with a "we're-not-afraid" attitude, Mr. Ford was generally "treated more like a visiting head of state than an ordinary industrialist."[45] The story illustrates the immense power held by these corporations.

What about the relations of the transnational company to the parent

---

[45] As related in Christopher Tugendhat, "Transnational Enterprise: Tying Down Gulliver," *Atlantic Community Quarterly* 9 (1971–72); 499–508, esp. 499–500.

TABLE 12–6   Major Transnational Corporations, 1975

Company	Base	World Sales ($US Billions)
Exxon	US	42.1
Royal Dutch/Shell Group	Brit/Neth.	33.4
General Motors	US	31.6
Ford Motor	US	23.6
Texaco	US	23.3
Mobile Oil	US	18.9
British Petroleum	Brit.	18.3
Standard Oil, Calif.	US	17.2
National Iranian Oil	Iran	16.8
Gulf Oil	US	16.5
Unilever	Brit.	13.7
General Electric	US	13.4
IBM	US	12.7
ITT	US	11.1
Chrysler	US	11.0
Philips' Gloeilampenfabrieken	Neth.	9.4
U.S. Steel	US	9.2
Standard Oil, Indiana	US	9.1
Cie Française des Pétroles	France	8.9
Nippon Steel	Japan	8.8

Source: Adapted from Fortune, August, 1975, p. 163.

government—that is, the government of the state in which the corporation is based? American-owned TNC's produced abroad goods amounting to three times total annual American exports, and these companies were growing at an average rate twice that of the world's most vigorous national economies. By the year 2000, it is estimated the transnationals will produce upwards of one half of the total gross *world* product.[46]

These companies have had another effect upon the world economy. Many of them, if not most, do not produce a commodity from start to finish at a single site. Instead, they build some parts in some areas, export them to second subsidiaries where they are joined to other parts of the whole, and then exported to yet a third place. It is not at all unusual for an automobile, made by an American-owned corporation, to consist of a transmission made in one country, a motor made in a second, a body made in a third, and tires and fixtures made in a fourth. Twenty-five percent of

[46] Similar data are explored by Raymond Vernon, *Sovereignty at Bay: The Multinational Spread of U.S. Enterprises* (New York: Basic Books, 1971). The estimates

all American exports are to the overseas subsidiaries of American-based TNC's. Meanwhile, as much as one-fourth of all exports from Britain consist of international transactions within companies.[47]

More than merely uncloaking the enormity of these corporations, these characteristics reveal the extent to which they—largely unregulated by governments or by international agreement—are able to control the world economy and the economies of host states. Often their operations lead to political controversy, as in deGaulle's insistence upon de-Americanizing Europe, ITT's CIA-assisted *coup d'état* in Chile, and rampant scandals resulting from corrupt business practices abroad. In both developed and underdeveloped economies TNC's are able to penetrate fiscal policy and labor relations; they are able to profit by dispersing profits and losses among subsidiaries without regard for the host economy; and they are able to remove their economic activity to the detriment of the host. While they are able to contribute to economic development, they are also able to globalize such injurious phenomena as inflation and to use their economic might for political intervention. As a result, many governments have experimented with restrictions on foreign ownership of production, and the governments of the Third World have heightened their demand for international regulation of multinational corporate activity. Both the United Nations and the Organization for Economic Cooperation and Development are laboring toward that end at present.[48]

The *capital-lending institutions* also affect the world economy and the domestic economies of the host states. Though no one disputes the need for operating capital in industrial modernization, some would argue that the rapid growth of branch banks overseas is an instrument of neoimperialism. If American capital is the only available source of funds, then American banks and American fiscal policy actually regulate interest rates and growth rates overseas. Furthermore, both in the banking business and in commodity

used here are summarized in Elliot R. Goodman, "The Impact of the Multinational Enterprise Upon the Atlantic Community," *Atlantic Community Quarterly* 10 (Fall, 1972): 357–67. For a comparative review of the book-length literature on the multinational corporation, see Robert O. Keohane and Van Doorn Ooms, "The Multinational Enterprise and World Political Economy," *International Organization* 26 (1972): 84–120. The literature has grown substantially since this was published.

[47] Reported in Christopher Tugendhat, "Transnational Enterprise: Tying Down Gulliver," p. 503. See also Tugendhat, *The Multinationals* (London: Eyre and Spottiswoode, 1971).

[48] For reviews of recent progress in this regard, see particularly Robert O. Keohane and Van Doorn Ooms, "The Multinational Firm and International Regulation," *International Organization* 29 (1975): 169–212, and Paul A. Tharp, Jr., "Transnational Enterprises and International Regulation: A Survey of Various Approaches in International Organization," *International Organization* 30 (1976): 47–74.

American multinational business creates scandal in Japan: President of All Nippon Airways bows after offering testimony before the Budget Committee on receiving illegal "payoffs" from Lockheed, 1976.

UPI Photo

industries, profits are siphoned off and returned with minimal reinvestment, with the result that the principal gains from the multinational enterprise accrue solely to the country of origin.[49]

Looked at from political and economic perspectives, the multinational corporation is a mixed blessing. But what is it when viewed from the per-

[49] The most incisive critique of the political-economic effects is found in Harry Magdoff, *The Age of Imperialism: The Economics of U.S. Foreign Policy* (New York: Monthly Review Press, 1969). For a critical but less bleak European view, see J. J. Servan-Schreiber, *The American Challenge* (New York: Atheneum, 1969). For a study of U.S. banking abroad, particularly the growth of branch banks in other economies, see Table 1–1 of this book.

spective of transnationalism? What is its value as a nongovernmental actor capable of creating new intersocietal communications?

At present, the transnational corporation may contribute to integration through its ability to forge shared values among participating elites. There is a growing consensus that the managers of overseas subsidiaries must subordinate nationalistic attitudes to corporate profit, regardless of the country of central operations. Since the principal decisions are economic rather than political, and since the function of capitalist business is to achieve profit in competitive markets, the tendency in these corporations is to minimize national feelings.

Yet it is also probable that this attitude does not filter down very far within the company. Below uppermost management, few employees are aware of the full meaning of their participation in a multinational enterprise. Their objective in most cases is to progress in the plant rather than in the corporation, or in the industry rather than in the conglomerate. Furthermore, at the consumer level few who eat Cornflakes prepared in Britain realize that the company which made the product is a wholly-owned American subsidiary.

The multinational business enterprise has not had a deep overall impact upon national economic attitudes. There are many who feel that such organization is vital to efficiency in a technological world, and there are those who insist that regional supranationalism is dependent upon multinational business.[50] But there is little evidence to suggest its positive effect upon international stability through attitudinal change at the mass level. The opposite may be quite the case, in fact, because these huge operations tend to be exploitative and ready to use their considerable political weight. Often they become unwelcome by aggravating existing tensions. They sometimes force foreign governments to nationalize them, though this has proved a costly remedy.

To whatever extent transnational participation contributes to world stability, then, its virtue must be found in less visible places. Most such progress at present is found in the sociocultural sector. At its roots, the transnational process is one of awareness; and the indications are that at the individual level, maximum attitudinal change through awareness occurs through sociocultural contact only.

Governments naturally safeguard their prerogatives and prevent escape of political functions to nongovernmental agencies. But the intersocietal link-

[50] On the relation between the multinational corporation and the progress of European economic integration, see particularly Werner J. Feld, *Transnational Business Collaboration Among Common Market Countries* (New York: Praeger, 1970), and by the same author, "Political Aspects of Transnational Business Collaboration in the Common Market," *International Organization* 24 (1970): 209–38. See also a discussion of "The Multinational Corporation and World Economic Development," *Proceedings of the 66th Annual Meeting of the American Society of International Law*, September, 1972, pp. 14–22, especially remarks by Jack N. Behrman, pp. 14–15.

ages created by the movement of persons, information, goods, and capital across national boundaries challenges the purely state-centered model of international stability. It may ultimately alter the supremacy of the state as an actor in the international system, though to date such transformation is minimal. All in all, however, the several alternatives to absolute sovereignty which we have studied in this chapter and the last (international law, international organization, supranationalism, and transnational participation) all press in upon the nation-state and challenge its ability to remain the paramount actor in international relations.

13

Future

World Order

During the era of the Apollo moon probes, an American astronaut excitedly told mission control that the most remarkable thing about space travel is looking back upon earth as a planet without boundaries. From his vantage point deep in space, temporarily removed from armed conflict and the rhetoric of enmity, he voiced the long-standing view of many—that if enduring peace is to dawn, the international system must first be substantially altered. If war is a product of the nation-state system, then the role of the state must be diminished and that of other governing and social processes increased. Disillusioned with the balance of power, the balance of terror, and all known power distributions, observers ranging from nineteenth-century utopians to contemporary futurist scholars have sought alternative worlds, all focusing on one problem: how to supplant the nation-state's capacity for disruption.

But war-peace issues no longer monopolize scholarly examination of the future. On an overcrowded planet nearing depletion of resources and extinction of species, the dynamics of the international system have come upon new emergencies. Stability relies not alone upon the willingness of governments to put aside their arms, but upon their ability to correct anarchical ways. Consider briefly a few areas in which nation-states have compiled dismal records, and which now cry for international regulation.

Ecology

First among them is ecological anarchy. States have exploited the earth's natural riches, virtually without regard for the problem of exhaustibility and with little consideration of future generations or of the needs of others.

415

Environmental spoliation: clean-up of Santa Barbara, California, harbor after twelve days of leakage from an underwater oil well.

Growing energy demands threaten the imminent depletion of fossil fuels; deposits of hard metals have been used up; and supplies of fresh water are dangerously low. Meanwhile, we have poisoned the air, despoiled most of the major rivers of the world, toxified vast areas of the seas, made urban living a painful clatter, and outgrown designated dumping areas. These problems have become so nearly universal as to make clear that national regulation is too little and too late. Without new levels of cooperation, and without international regulation, we are bent upon ecological suicide.

Sadly, international cooperation on this issue has scarcely commenced, despite the best efforts of the United Nations system. Under its auspices, after fully four years of preparation, the Global Conference on the Human Environment was convened at Stockholm in 1972. Fraught with politics over the seating of East Germany (not then a member of the UN) and over Chinese charges against the use of defoliants in Vietnam, and beset by the insistence of the less developed states that environmental preservation is a luxury for the industrialized states, the Conference achieved but modest ends. It established the seeds of a global environmental monitoring system, promulgated an Action Program and a Declaration, and established UN oversight machinery. But beyond dramatic recognition of the need for international cooperation and establishment of functional machinery, the issue of preservation itself remains for the future.

Population

It took until the year 1800 for the world population to reach one billion. Thereafter, a level of two billion was reached in 1925, three billion by 1960, and four billion in 1976. It is predicted that by the year 2000, at current rates of reproduction, the global population will have reached nearly seven billion. Even more alarmingly, population densities are most stable in industrialized areas and least stable in the poorest sectors of the world. Current projections, for example, are that by 2000, the population density of North America will have increased by only four persons per square kilometer, while in South Asia there will be an increase of *one hundred-forty* persons in a similar space. [1]

Population control: Indian women await registration for tubal ligations.

Wide World Photos

[1] Mihajlo Mesarovic and Eduard Pestel, *Mankind at the Turning Point: The Second Report to The Club of Rome* (New York: The New American Library, 1974), chapter 6.

The world order consequences of these astounding projections are manifold, though not entirely clear. With respect to food, mineral resources, and other consumable commodities, there exists a spirited debate as to the world's capacity to sustain a growing population. [2] It is a demonstrable fact, nevertheless, that in the most overpopulated regions, even accelerating economic growth rates are being offset by population increases, with the result that per capita wealth continues to diminish. It is apparent, therefore, that apart from the global ability to sustain larger numbers of people, overpopulation retards economic growth, perpetuates squalor, and generally restricts the improvement of living conditions. In addition, poverty facilitates the spread of disease, limits educational opportunity, reduces life expectancies, and invites imperialism and autocracy. Despite efforts of contemporary international organizations to control population growth, effective progress on the issue remains a matter for the future. The seriousness of the problem is underscored by a decision in one of the states of India in 1976 to apply coercive sanctions, in which families will be penalized for the failure of at least one spouse to secure permanent sterilization after the birth of a third child. Despite efforts of contemporary international organizations to control population growth, effective progress on the issue remains a matter for the future.

Food

Recent preoccupation with the world's mineral distribution only temporarily obscured the global nutrition crisis. In November 1974, just one year after the major petroleum crisis, the United Nations convened the World Food Conference at Rome to deal with the long-term threat of dwindling food production in relation to need. The UN had projected that by 1985, an increase of production per year of 2.5 percent globally would barely offset the increased demand of the industrialized states, thus leaving none to contribute to the 3.6 percent increase in need from the industrializing states. [3]

Closely tied to the problem of population growth, global food shortages also present problems of their own. Aside from the obvious consequences —such as starvation, squalor, retarded economic growth—maldistribution of food resources introduces other potential difficulties. At present a major fear is that those states that enjoy plentiful foor supplies will use them coercively to ensure steady flows of mineral resources from the mineral-rich Third World countries. The introduction of food into the global

---

[2] See, for example, the debate as presented by *The Christian Science Monitor*, November 3, 1975, between Herman Kahn (optimistic view) and Dennis Meadows (pessimistic view).

[3] *Assessment of the World Food Situation: Present and Future,* Item Eight of the Provisional Agenda for the World Food Conference, p. 225.

"Food for Thought."

Courtesy of The Boston Globe

formula of competitive embargoes would represent a major change in the power resources of international politics, but with individually-measurable human costs.

Despite the declaratory efforts of the World Food Conference to establish an international food production program, most of the large producers, particularly the United States and the Soviet Union, have made it clear that food distribution will remain a matter of national policy for the foreseeable future. With respect to international planning and cooperation, the nutrition crisis remains a matter for the future.

Autocratic Government

From a humanistic viewpoint, another problem is just as large. Traditionally, each political system has determined its governing philosophy, and has established the quality of relations between the government and the governed. Many political systems—if not most—have justified stern restrictions on human freedoms and rights. Autocratic politics has been history's rule rather than its exception. In an era of growing literacy, improved mass communications, national liberation, and domestic protest, can the stability of the world be preserved against governmental brutality? Only new cooperation and international regulation that will deprive the state of absolute control of its subjects can ensure such stability.

World Economics

Yet another form of contemporary anarchy is the international economic system. Despite foreign aid and international development programs, the powerful few dominate the world economy, frequently at the expense of the less powerful many. Self-serving autocracy of the economically powerful states and of their political elites, together with central planning and allocation, is the guidepost of world economics. Imperialism, neoimperialism, exploitation, discrimination, and manipulation—these are the instruments used by the powerful to subordinate the weak. [4] Stability in economic relations cries out for international supervision and new modes of decision-making.

These examples and scores of others reveal our abiding problem: the forms of social and political organization which we have selected, particularly the state-centric international system, are bound for destruction. Only reform of basic attitudes, structures, and patterns of interaction can retard the process. Contemporary system dynamics are suicidal.

Furthermore, though statesmen have attempted through organization and integration to overcome these problems, the magnitude of the problems and the antiquity of national solutions further highlight the dilemma of traditional international remedies. So long as the unique sovereign attributes of the nation-state are preserved, the pace of deterioration will continue to outrun proposed solutions, rendering them always ideas *after* their times. Accordingly, research has centered upon wholly new approaches, though they vary considerably in scope. Some, labelled *maximalist* proposals, seek a fully structured world government; the *minimalist* proposals advocate upgrading existing international machinery; and the *reformist* proposals would generally retain the current systemic features, but would subject the nation-state to global law. Recently, through the auspices of the Institute for World Order in New York, scholars from many countries have

---

[4] Particularly with respect to Western capitalism, theories of imperialism and structural imperialism abound, which focus on the collusion between the elites of the industrial states with the oligarchs of the developing world to exploit the producing peripheries of the latter. See especially Johan Galtung, "A Structural Theory of Imperialism," *Journal of Peace Research* 13, no. 2 (1971): 81–118.

been participating in the World Order Models Project (WOMP).[5] This is the first systematic attempt to utilize modern social science techniques to design alternative world futures. Equally important, however, is the intent of this project to restore to the forefront of research the compelling normative and humanistic questions of all political systems—questions about the human condition and its future.

History of the World Order Idea

Though two world wars and the nuclear arms race have prompted new interest in the world order movement, the idea is an ancient one. It has arisen repeatedly in history, from peace groups, governments, philosophers, religious thinkers, imperialists, and nationalistic zealots. Until recently, the world order movement has been synonymous with the quest for world government. One of the earliest known forms was that of ancient Rome, whose imperial quest sought to bring all of the known world under Roman political control. Other imperial impulses to world domination have been grossly maniacal, such as that of Adolph Hitler, whose aim was to rule Europe and then the world.

Apart from these attempts at world domination, several other sources of universalist sentiment have also emerged. Theologians have posited concepts of control, though not through governmental superiority. St. Thomas Aquinas propounded the concept of a universal Christian spirit forging a human community, and supplying the ideals and benevolence of Christian rulers throughout the world. He distinguished the power of the state (*imperium*) from that of the church (*sacerdotium*), leaving room for separate governments in different lands, even though as a papist he viewed papal power as superior to secular power. Even in a Christian Europe, however, and writing a half-century later than Thomas (about 1310 A.D.), Dante saw the only hope for world peace (meaning essentially European peace) in the consolidation of all power in the Roman Emperor. In the words of one eminent student of political philosophy, "Neither by birth nor breeding was Dante a partisan of the imperial cause. His imperialism was purely an idealization of universal peace."[6]

Thinkers in more modern times have frequently revived these ideas. The Spanish theologian Francisco Suarez, writing in the absolutist era bridging the sixteenth and seventeenth centuries and imbued with Bodin's notions of sovereignty, moved from the concept of moral law to the hope of world

[5] Already available from this project are Richard A. Falk, *A Study of Future Worlds*; Rajini Kothari, *Footsteps Into the Future*; and Saul H. Mendlovitz, editor, *On the Creation of a Just World Order*, published by the Free Press (New York), 1975.

[6] George H. Sabine, *A History of Political Theory*, 3rd ed. (New York: Holt, Rinehart and Winston, 1961), pp. 257–58.

government. Later in the seventeenth century, the English philosopher Thomas Hobbes wrote in *Leviathan* that the political nature of society is that of war of every man against every man, and that through social contract men form governments to which they entrust the security of all. Applied to international relations, Hobbes' social contract extrapolates to a theory of world government.

The German thinker Hegel, whose dialectical method formed the basis of Marx's arguments about class conflict, included in his theory of history the concept of a world spirit of the governing class. Though Hegel was a nationalist, he nevertheless found a universal morality in political leadership, freedom, and even the arts. Despite his nationalistic fervor, he saw every state falling to the universal logic of the world spirit. Marx not only adopted Hegel's system of argument, he also made similar historical predictions. Rather than concentrate on a governing class and a mystical world spirit, Marx looked to the working class and the eventual elimination of class conflict. When power resides in the hands of the proletariat, states will wither away and all people will be ruled in classless harmony. In this utopian prediction, government becomes not state-centered, but spirit-centered.

But visions of universal political morality and utopian harmony have not arisen exclusively in philosophical abstraction. Indeed, the popularity of world government schemes has paralleled certain events: the frequency of war, the destructiveness of modern industrialized warfare, imperial competition, and the irrationality of ideological fears, to name only a few. There is at least impressionistic evidence of a correlation between world government enthusiasm and warfare. The activity and popularity of such proposals seem highest toward the ends of, and upon conclusion of, major wars; the longer and more tranquil postwar periods are, the more rapid the decline in popularity of world government ideals. This correlation seems guided by a simple rule of world politics: when states serve their functions satisfactorily and with minimal external disruption, only a handful of activists advocate world government; but when the nation-state system breaks down, more people share world government sentiment.

It follows from this "rule" that the present century has been one of consistently high interest in world government. The destruction from the First World War was unprecedented, and the vision of further industrialization of war potential forged a solid core of sentiment for some form of central government. In America, a group known as the League to Enforce Peace considered several alternative forms of international organization, with some of its adherents arguing for virtual international government. Intent upon retaining their sovereign prerogatives, however, national governments were willing to do no more than subscribe to President Woodrow Wilson's League of Nations. Predecessor to the United Nations, the League of Nations (1) prescribed mechanisms for the peaceful settlement of international disputes, (2) called upon its members to guarantee the territorial integrity and political independence of all other members, (3) looked forward to general arms limitation, (4) authorized its Council to undertake enforcement action against aggression, and (5) mandated member states to impose sanctions against violators of the peace.

The League of Nations was generally a disappointment to the advocates of world government as an instrument of world order. They viewed it as little more than a smokescreen for power politics. Its voting provisions, especially on matters of greatest interest to members of the Council, restricted progress toward effective international decision-making, and encouraged Great Power domination of policy. Though many saw in the Assembly, where all member states were represented, an opportunity to mature a sense of world community and to germinate the seeds of international society, there was general discouragement over the decentralization of sanction procedures and over the Great Power control of peace-war issues. But of major long-range interest was the network of functional organizations (single-purpose agencies with specific technical tasks) which seemed to promise greater person-to-person contact around the world, and to offer an opportunity for the development of loyalty to a political entity outside of nation-states. Ultimately, the problem of the nation-state system is not simply the existence of multiple sovereignties, but the ability of governments to monopolize the secular loyalties of individuals and to mobilize them for nationalistic rather than universalistic purposes. Any institutional structure which might erode this pattern is acceptable to the advocates of world government and to the proponents of most other doctrines of world order as well.

Some universalists viewed the League of Nations with even deeper suspicion, principally because of its collective security provisions. Collective security could not govern, they argued; it could only maintain peace by the threat of force. Thus it was a negative approach to international stability, still built upon nationalistic preferences. It did not address the causes of conflict; it was powerless to legislate preventative social, political, and economic changes; and it was impotent in the face of violations of international norms except by the unanimous consent of the Council members. Hence some saw the League not as a stepping stone between the nation-state system and world government, but as a threat to world government.

Although the League of Nations failed to prevent war, its history was partly successful from a world order perspective. It made modest but positive contributions to self-determinism, previously little more than a platitude. Its social, scientific, and economic projects made inroads in problems of squalor and disease. Postwar relief programs, assistance to refugees, and the League's management of intellectual exchanges all earned for the organization a reputation as a helpful intermediary among governments in matters not directly related to national security. One of the celebrated events of the League was its acceptance in 1939 of the Bruce Committee Report, which advocated a broad reorganization of authority for social and economic development. Though World War II prevented its immediate application, the report formed the rationale for establishing the Economic and Social Council as a permanent organ of the United Nations.

Despite these successes of the League, the concept of intergovernmental organization was not generally popular with advocates of world government during the interwar period. Like other critics of the League, they found its failings more notable than its successes. But more than that, the Second World War was testimony to the intrinsic weaknesses of collective security in particular, and of intergovernmental organization in general.

World War II and its aftermath further heightened the vigor of the world order movement. While the State Department was planning, at first secretly, for revitalizing collective security in an organization to be known as the United Nations, the United World Federalists were organizing the battle in support of world government. That the war was global rather than continental demonstrated the need for universal regulation. The unprecedented devastation, including the use of atomic weapons, accentuated to them the need for world government before technical advances led to world domination and centralized imperialism. The polarization of world politics and the Soviet-American standoff, along with the growing reality of a balance of terror, convinced many people that this might be our last half-century to achieve effective world order.

Vigorous advocacy was untimely. At the end of World War II, hopes were high for the United Nations, dedicated in part to the principle—called the Grand Design—that the major powers, despite their differences, could cooperate in peacetime to preserve stability as they had cooperated during wartime to establish it. Remembering the problems of 1918, advocates of world government had to contest this sentiment. Their first major effort occurred in October 1945, at a conference in Dublin, New Hampshire. Attended by both "world federalists" and proponents of a "world law" movement, the Dublin Conference derogated the adequacy of the United Nations; called for a world federal government of limited powers; and urged either that the United Nations Charter be amended into federalist form or that a world constitutional convention be called. Only five months later, in March 1946, a second conference was held at Rollins College in Winter Park, Florida. There, delegates reaffirmed the necessity for world federal government, but found the United Nations Charter the most practicable route.[7]

For the moment, the world government movement remained almost exclusively the province of a few committed activists. In the United States especially, sentiment seemed to lean toward intergovernmental organization, with the specific hope that this time, with the backing of American power, the UN experiment might prevent cataclysmic war. But the promise

---

[7] For a review of early events, see Edward McN. Burns, "The Movement for World Government," *Science* 25 (1948): 5–13.

collapsed with the onset of the cold war and the desire of like-minded nations to cluster into defensive alliances outside the United Nations. A new threat to the concept of world order emerged: the willingness of states to entrust the preservation of their sovereignty to their most powerful allies.

One result was the movement for a union of the Western democracies, which frightened the proponents of world government by the threat of a regional central government which, because of ideological inspiration, would harden the polarity of the world and further delay the universalist dream. There was fear that the North Atlantic Treaty Organization (NATO) might form the base of such a movement.

Faced with two competing movements—intergovernmental organization (UN) and the possibility of counterproductive regional supranationalism (NATO)—the universalists took to the offensive. In pursuit of the findings of the Rollins College meeting Cord Meyer, Jr., president of the United World Federalists, offered testimony before the House Foreign Relations Committee (May 1948) in which he called upon Congress to champion greater strength for the UN through Charter amendment, not to strengthen its intergovernmental quality but to advance it toward world government. A year later (October 1949) Grenville Clark, distinguished lawyer and later director of the World Peace Through Law Movement, sat before the same committee to testify on two bills: *for* the World Federation Resolution and *against* the Atlantic Union Resolution. The former called for an American initiative for the evolution of world government, and the latter for a union of Western democracies. In an eloquent plea, Mr. Clark argued that "The distinction is of basic importance. It marks, I believe, the difference between peaceful evolution and a probable or possible third world war." He concluded:

> We ought always to remember that there are only two ways for the West and the East to be brought into cooperation. One way is an enforced cooperation, following the conquest of one by the other. But we know that the West cannot be conquered in the foreseeable future. And we know that while the West might well completely subjugate the East, after unprecedented slaughter, the West has no wish to do so. We realize that, as Henry L. Stimson [former Secretary of State in the Hoover Administration and Secretary of War to President Franklin Roosevelt] has said: "Americans as conquerors would be tragically miscast."
>
> The only other way is that of cooperation by the free consent of both sides, to be achieved, slowly perhaps but steadily, by mutual toleration and without requiring either the sacrifice of honor or principle. That can be done and when it is achieved, the basis will exist to create the universal world federation by fundamental amendment of the United Nations Charter.
>
> One other thing we should never forget—that however necessary our present policy under the Atlantic Treaty (NATO) may be, that policy can be no more than a stopgap. It embodies no element of world order

under law. On the contrary, it is the essence of power politics. It may well be helpful in gaining time to seek the solution. It is in itself no stable solution at all.

The world federalism resolution fully recognizes this in calling for a more fundamental objective of our foreign policy, namely, the development of the United Nations into a world federation open to all nations.[8]

As the United States Congress entertained world government resolutions in its sessions of 1948 and 1949, private groups were busily drafting universal constitutions. Some of these, such as that of Grenville Clark, aimed at reordering the United Nations. Others started from scratch, constructing world constitutional models as though the experience of intergovernmental organization were not at hand.

It is one thing to propound the establishment of government, but quite another to equip it to achieve the desired ends in a heterogeneous world arena. How much power should there be? How should it be divided among governmental organs? To what extent should authority be left to "local" government of the former nation-states? What limitations on power ought to be prescribed? How can these limitations be preserved? What sorts of incentives to compliance should be arranged, and what kinds of punishment for violations? Even more fundamental, what aims and values is world government to pursue? One contemporary observer, a well-known international law scholar deeply concerned with problems of world order, has expressed his troubled feelings this way:

> I believe *that it is no longer a question as to whether or not there will be world government by the year 2000. The questions are rather, how will world government come into being and what form will it take?*[9]

Still, however, not all world order concepts embrace the idea of world government, though such a tendency is typical of maximalist proposals.

World Order: A Maximalist Proposal

Committed to the need to restructure international order, some students of the future have considered maximal alternatives. Inasmuch as many of the serious proposals have come from Americans, the federal model of gov-

---

[8] Mr. Meyer's testimony is reprinted in Julia E. Johnson, ed., *Federal World Government* (New York: H. W. Wilson Company, 1948), pp. 86–94. Mr. Clark's can be found in Appendix B of his *Plan for Peace* (New York: Harper and Brothers, Publishers, 1950), pp. 78–83.

[9] Saul H. Mendlovitz, "Models of World Order," in Richard B. Gray, ed., *International Security Systems* (Itasca, Ill.: Peacock, 1969), pp. 178–92, at p. 179. The emphasis is taken from the original.

ernment pervades most investigations. Harking back to U.S. constitutional heritage, the federal model has gained wider popularity through the United World Federalists and through implementation elsewhere. This is a system of government in which the total sovereignty of the state is cleaved in such a way as to make the central government sovereign over some transactions, other smaller units sovereign over some other transactions, and the two cooperatively sovereign over still other matters. This system is designed primarily to prevent absolutism or a drift toward full centralization. Moving from this model, Vernon Nash, then vice president of United World Federalists, wrote this disclaimer of absolute central world government:

> Conscious, sharp aversion to the idea of world government arises mainly from two false assumptions. The first is that national governments would be abolished, or entirely subordinated, in the creation of a world state. The second is that nationality would thereby be wiped out. Both fears are baseless. We do not need to end nationalism; *we need only modify the present absolute nature of national sovereignty.*[10]

Hence the movement for world federalism draws a distinct line between world government and the formation of a world state.

But in addition to its frontal assault upon absolute sovereignty, world federalism seeks to supervene strident nationalism. Effective peace through government requires more than changes in the political map. It means changing national perceptions, enlightening national views of the ideals and expectations of other peoples, and so on. In a symposium on the world community in 1947, one observer expressed a vivid notion which typifies the attack on nationalism:

> The person I cannot get out of my mind these days is the young man who dropped the first atomic bomb. I suppose he is a nice young man . . . yet the odd thing is that, if he had been ordered to go and drop it on Milwaukee, he almost certainly would have refused. . . . Because he was asked to drop it on Hiroshima, he not only consented but he became something of a hero for it. . . . Of course, I don't quite see the distinction between dropping it on Milwaukee and dropping it on Hiroshima. The difference is a "we" difference. The people of Milwaukee, though we don't know any of them, are "we," and the people of Hiroshima are "they," and the great psychological problem is how to make everybody "we," at least in some small degree. The degree need be only extremely small. I don't think we have to love our neighbor with any degree of affection. All that is necessary to create the psychological foundations of a world society is that people in Maine should feel the same degree of responsibility toward the people of Japan or Chile or Indo-China as they

---

[10] Vernon Nash, *The World Must Be Governed*, 2nd ed. (New York: Harper and Brothers Publishers, 1949), p. 44. Emphasis added.

feel toward California. That is pretty small, really, but it is apparently enough to create the United States.[11]

Though world federalists customarily place the formation of world government chronologically ahead of the formulation of a world society, their intention is to eradicate the nationalistic consequences of sovereignity as well as national sovereignty itself.

Separation of Powers

A second fundamental concept is also borrowed by the world federalists from the American constitutional model: *the separation of powers.* A concept traditionally ascribed to the French philosopher Montesquieu, separation of powers divides the power of the federal government into three branches: legislative, executive, and judicial. The intent is to avert tyranny by any single political authority. As James Madison argued in *Federalist Paper No. 47,* a pamphlet written to argue for ratification of the American Constitution, "The accumulation of all powers, legislative, executive, and judiciary, in the same hands, whether of one, a few, or many, and whether hereditary, self-appointed, or elective, may justly be pronounced the very definition of tyranny." Imbued with this spirit, major proposals for world federation usually include separation of powers.

The first attempt at world constitution-making emerged from the Committee to Frame a World Constitution, formed at the University of Chicago in 1945. Its chief author was an Italian emigré, G. A. Borgese. Equipped to reveal its work publicly through its publication *Common Cause* (in no way related to the contemporary American populist movement), this committee announced in 1947 and 1948, in serial fashion, a preliminary draft of a world constitution for the Federal Republic of the World.

In addition to prescription of the organs of government, the preliminary draft specified the areas of substantive power. In normal federal fashion the draft stipulated, after enumeration of specific powers, that "The powers not delegated to the World Government in this Constitution, and not prohibited by it to the several members of the Federal World Republic, shall be reserved to the several states or nations or unions thereof." This provision was intended to guarantee within the federal scheme the integrity of traditional governmental units and political communities. A few years later addressing the same point, another advocate of world federalism wrote,

The crucial need is for an effective division of the internal and external sovereignty of all nations. This would leave to each nation its internal

---

[11] Kenneth E. Boulding, "Discussion of World Economic Contacts," in Quincy Wright, ed., *The World Community* (Chicago: The University of Chicago Press, 1948), pp. 101–12, at pages 101–2.

sovereignty while helping all nations to pool their separately held frag-
ments of international sovereignty for transfer to world federal government. Generally speaking, any problem national governments are unable
to solve acting separately, requires international solution and ought to
become a responsibility of world government.[12]

Inis L. Claude, Jr., expressed this sentiment somewhat more succinctly
when he wrote that "Federalism symbolizes functionally-limited centralization, but centralization nonetheless. . . ." [13]

Highly institutionalized maximalist schemes such as the Borgese proposal have been rather common in the history of the world order movement.
Yet, in their ambition to restructure the international system, they have
run afoul of the same criticisms time and again. Principally, there have been
three attacks. One concerns the social practicability of these schemes. A
second relates to the slender probability of successful implementation. The
third deals with the issue of the philosophical desirability of world government at all.

The Social Practicability of World Government

The theologian and social observer Reinhold Niebuhr once wrote that
"Virtually all arguments for world government rest upon the simple pre-
supposition that the desirability of world order proves the attainability of
world government." [14] Even if one accepts the desirability of world government, which we will examine subsequently, what is the link between desirability and attainability?

The critical issue in addressing this question is the relation between society and government. World federalists tend to argue that if people will
look beyond their governments, they will be able to shape a supranational
government capable of maximizing social integration, effective compliance
with law, and perpetual peace. Critics hold, on the contrary, that governments have little capability to integrate communities; rather, the merger of
diverse value patterns and heritages is a socio-psychological process to which
governments may give direction, but which cannot be legislated into effectiveness regardless of the type of government. Integration is a matter of will
rather than of power.

Studies have been conducted in a number of countries on the images that
national peoples have of one another. Two of these, undertaken fifteen years

---

[12] Edith Wynner, *World Federal Government in Maximum Terms* (Afton, N.Y.:
Fedonat Press, 1954), p. 38.

[13] Inis L. Claude, Jr., *Power and International Relations* (New York: Random
House, 1962), p. 207.

[14] Rienhold Niebuhr, *Christian Realism and Political Problems* (New York: Charles
Scribner's Sons, 1949), as reprinted in Arend Lijphart, ed., *World Politics*, 2nd ed.
(Boston: Allyn and Bacon, 1971), pp. 71–80, at p. 72, "The Illusion of World Govern-
ment."

apart used essentially the same technique. Respondents to questions were asked to describe their feelings about their own nations and about people in other countries by placing in order several adjectives. In the earlier study, the frequency of selection of particular descriptive words was reported in percentages. For example, when Americans were asked to rate themselves, only 2 percent chose the word "cruel" and only 2 percent the word "backward." But when the same people were asked to rate the Russian people, no fewer than 50 percent selected "cruel" and 40 percent "backward." By the same taken, 39 percent of British questioned thought the Russians cruel, and 36 percent thought them backward. Only 12 percent of both British and Americans thought the Russian people intelligent. In the polling among people of eight different Western countries (Australia, Britain, Germany, France, Italy, The Netherlands, Norway, and the United States), positive adjectives were applied most frequently to the subject's own people. Consistently, the Soviet people and the Chinese people were assigned positive adjectives least frequently and negative adjectives most frequently.

But even among Western neighbors and allies there appeared to be social barriers to complete trust and mutual respect. Not surprisingly, given historical relations, the German people held the French in low regard. German respect for the French was only a fraction above that for the Russians and the Chinese, though Germans thought the French more intelligent, less cruel, and less backward than the Russians. However, Germans thought the French less brave, less self-controlled, and less peace loving than the Russians, even though the polling was done during the Korean War. [15]

A similar questioning technique presents subjects with pairs of adjectives which have opposite meanings, such as cowardly and brave, stupid and intelligent, lazy and industrious. In a study in which people were asked to select preferable adjectives first to describe foreign peoples and then to depict their governments, both ethnic images (people) and national images (governments) were determined. Among Americans polled, the results were tabulated in decreasing order of preference (see Table 13–1).

Note that in the ethnic ratings all non-Communist peoples rank higher than all Communist peoples with the exception of the Nationalist Chinese, who rank behind the European Communists but ahead of the Mainland Chinese. By contrast, in the national ratings there is no exception. *All non-Communist governments rate higher than all Communist governments.* The Soviet people and the Soviet government both rate consistently above the peoples and governments of the other communist states about which questions were asked. [16]

[15] For a full tabular report of results, see William Buchanan and Hadley Cantril, *How Nations See Each Other* (Urbana: The University of Illinois Press, 1953), pp. 46–47.

[16] For a full report of findings, see Richard H. Willis, "Ethnic and National Images: Peoples *vs.* Nations," *Public Opinion Quarterly* 32 (1968): 186–201, at 190.

TABLE 13–1   Ethnic and National Images Among Americans

Ethnic (people)	*National (governments)*
Finnish	United States
West German	Finland
American	West Germany
Russian	Nationalist China
East German	Soviet Union
Nationalist Chinese	East Germany
Mainland Chinese	Mainland China

Source: Adapted from Richard H. Willis, "Ethnic and National Images: People *vs.* Nations," 32 *Public Opinion Quarterly* (1968): 190. Reprinted by permission.

Finally, results concerning images and trust among allies have been substantiated even more recently. In a study reported by NATO in 1973, Europeans have the highest trust for the Swiss, with the United States ranking second. Although the polling was conducted prior to British entry into the European Economic Community, trust for Britain ranked third among people questioned in Belgium, France, Germany, Italy, and The Netherlands. Though engaged in the process of economic integration (see chapter 12), none of the Common Market members on the list received a majority expression of trust in all four other countries. [17]

These data underscore the fact that governments are not alone in their resistance to world government. Among allies as well as among enemies, there are still barriers to mass perceptions which are sufficient to rebut the assumption that if national governments were subordinated to a world government, antipathies among peoples would fade, and that an integrated world society would result. We must be cautious in presuming the social practicability of world government.

Probable Success Upon Implementation

What if the social and political barriers to the implementation of a world government were superable? Would the maturation of a world society be sure to deter further warfare? Most critics of the world government ideal argue that on the national level, central government has not invariably deterred civil war; they predict that even in a world state, to say nothing of a global federation, occasional warfare will erupt.

Advocates respond to this objection in a utopian way. On the assumption that an effective federation would achieve universal justice (though by

[17] For a full summary of findings, see "Swiss, then Americans Most Trusted by Europeans," *Atlantic Community News,* March-April, 1973, p. 2.

what value standards?) and adequate distribution of authority and goods, they insist that the contemporary causes of war would be eradicated. They assume that the absolute centralization of military force will provide adequate deterrence to the use of force by members. But this blanket assumption overlooks that hostilities often involve the use of power at other levels —that the ability of force to deter force is not absolute, but relative to conditions, situations, and perceptions. Furthermore, these assumptions trip upon the same snares as does collective security: those who threaten the peace are not always identifiable; self-defense may justify use of force, just as it may be used as camouflage for aggressive intentions; states sympathize with one another's interests and perceptions, thus minimizing the efficiency of global decision-making. The expectation that world government might invariably avert war is untenable in light of these observations. On this subject Claude concludes, "the hard fact is that the record does not support the generalization that the establishment of government, within a social unit of whatever dimensions, infallibly brings about a highly dependable state of peace and order." [18] The skeptics agree that world government and monopoly of force would not ensure perpetual peace.

Philosophical Desirability

Not all observers concur that world government is desirable. Some begin with the expectation that central government will gradually erode even the beneficial effects of different nation-states and of systems of governments, leading to a dreary, uncompetitive, and dull political community. More acutely, however, they differ with the universalist assumption that world government is necessarily good government, either in efficiency or in quality. In the American federal system the delicate balance between executive and legislative prerogatives has undergone fundamental change; why might not the same occur in a world federal system? If political conflict is capable of turning even ideal democracy into tyranny or constitutional authoritarianism, is there any prospect that global problems might produce a world government of universal tyranny? How would coalitions of like-minded states utilize their share of political power in a world system? Does world government *necessarily* eradicate the threat of worldwide absolutism?

These and scores of other related questions plague the theoretical integrity of the world government philosophy, just as does the claim that there is virtue in peaceful diversity. The critics of world government concepts agree that the idea carries an interpretation of Hobbes' social contract to logical absurdity. Inis Claude has observed,

Hobbes was right; when a community is so poorly developed that its pre-governmental condition is one of intolerable warfare, and its urge to

[18] Claude, *Power and International Relations*, p. 220.

establish government rests on no other foundation than a desperate desire to escape the perils of anarchy, the only theoretically adequate government is Leviathan, an omnipotent dictatorship. Locke, too, was right; when a community is held together by strong bonds of agreement concerning what is right and just, and common life is reasonably satisfactory, a limited and mild kind of government, based mainly upon consent, may suffice to supply its needs. World governmentalists describe the world's situation in Hobbesian terms, with a view to emphasizing the urgent need for a global social contract, but they depict the resultant government in Lockean terms, with a view to making the social contract palatable. It would be better to recognize that in so far as this is a Hobbesian world, it is likely to require a Hobbesian government.[19]

There are many, however, who argue that supranational world order short of total world government is both desirable and feasible. One such movement is that of World Peace Through World Law, and the other is the growing sentiment of globalism in the United Nations. We turn now to those alternatives of the future world order.

World Order: A Minimalist Proposal

The objective of the world order movement is the centralization of political authority for avoidance of war. However, because of the practical barriers to federation, other movements have proposed partial centralization of authority addressed to the specific problems of arms in international politics. The best known among these is the World Peace Through World Law movement, founded by Grenville Clark and assisted by Professor Louis B. Sohn of the Harvard Law School. The student is cautioned, however, that *world law* is not synonymous with *international law*. International law purports to interpose norms of behavior between states; the world law movement, in contrast, is concerned explicitly with the removal of arms from international politics, and the establishment of collective security. In the words of Saul Mendlovitz:

> World law thus ties together two very important notions: disarmament and a collective security system. It argues that the present system of international relations ... [is] based on unilateral decision-making sanctioned by armaments, and maintains that this situation results in a spiralling arms race that may very well set off a cataclysmic war. The world law model therefore posits the need for complete and general disarmament of all the states in the world down to the level of police forces,

[19] Inis L. Claude, Jr., *Swords Into Plowshares*, 4th ed. (New York: Random House, 1971), p. 429.

and proposes the establishment of a transnational police force that can maintain the territorial integrity and political independence of each state.[20]

The emphasis is upon elimination of arms, rather than their mere limitation.

The structural plans for the world law movement are found in the well-known volume *World Peace Through World Law*, prepared by Clark and Sohn. [21] The plan involves two steps. First, it calls for revision of the United Nations Charter to grant the General Assembly full authority for overseeing total disarmament, and with full power of enforcement through weighted voting. Thereafter, the General Assembly would establish an inspection commission which would begin by taking a world census on quality, quantity, and deployment patterns of national arms. The inspection would be accompanied by a truce on further arms production. Upon completion of this preliminary stage, actual disarmament would consist of a decade in which each state would reduce its national arms stockpile by 10 percent annually, all reductions being distributed evenly among the several military services so that all are reduced at the same rate. Verification of compliance both during and after the actual disarmament stage would be conducted by the United Nations Inspection Service, operating in national territories without governmental barriers. An alternative plan calls for the establishment of a special World Disarmament and World Development Agency with powers similar to those of the other plan.

Though the Clark-Sohn proposals would impinge only upon states' freedom to prepare for war, the plans run into several insuperable barriers. Can there *be* security without arms? Is international inspection trustworthy in a technological age? What are the possible political consequences of secret unilateral violations which result in clear military superiority, even monopoly? And there are still other problems. National armaments are the special possessions of arms manufacturers and certain elites in society, such as rival armed services. What are the prospects of weakening these groups to levels sufficient to make world disarmament proposals attractive to national governments? Do domestic political relationships bode well for the future of total disarmament? The skeptics—and they are legion—see little hope in current national perceptions. Thus the Clark-Sohn proposals, though humane, remain futuristic, persuading diplomats to concentrate their efforts on international law rather than world law, and upon arms limitation rather than arms abolition. The piecemeal attack on sovereignty remains the method of practical choice, despite the increasingly urgent need for major transformation of the international system.

[20] Saul H. Mendlovitz, "Models of World Order," p. 191.
[21] Grenville Clark and Louis B. Sohn, *World Peace Through World Law*, 3rd ed. enlarged (Cambridge: Harvard University Press, 1966).

World Order: A Reformist Proposal

In addition to the maximalist and minimalist proposals for world order, there have arisen other reformist ideas, each of which concentrates upon adaptation of existing national and international machinery. The prevailing idea at the moment is *globalism*, a movement which is tied to the United Nations by virtue of the UN's growing role as a center of international planning. While the UN has not achieved the level of authority proposed by Clark and Sohn, and while it has had little effect upon the world's armaments, its record as innovator and as a clearing house for planning and activity on other subjects has been a modestly good one. The UN has been most successful in economic development, through its Development Program (UNDP). Other areas to which globalism might spread are the allocation and preservation of natural resources and distribution of the world's produce.

But there is another dimension to globalism. As societies develop, they overcome problems; but at the same time they create new ones. Industry, the prime aim of underdeveloped states, is a case in point. While industrialization may eradicate poverty, disease, starvation and lack of the conveniences of life, it also causes environmental degradation, marked economic disparities of domestic social groups, problems of urbanization, depletion of natural resources and scores of other potentially critical problems. The philosophy of globalism attempts to transform concern for these issues from the national level to the global level. The UN began to attack these problems in the Stockholm Conference on the Human Environment (1972), which was to coordinate a global attack on ecological problems. Outside of the UN, the only coordinated attempts are regional, most important among them being the NATO Committee on the Challenges of Modern Society. The CCMS already has done significant work toward improving urban transportation, and is working on methods to contain and clean maritime oil spills. [22]

One globalist philosopher holds that the need for global planning is evident in a five-item "inventory of mankind's problems": environmental crisis, the widening gap between rich and poor, unemployment, urbanization, and malnutrition.

Given the scale and complexity of these problems, the remainder of the twentieth century will at best be a traumatic period for mankind, even with a frontal attack on the principal threats to human well-being. At worst it will be catastrophic. At issue is whether we can grasp the nature

[22] For an eloquent plea for development of a globalist philosophy, see Philippe de Seynes, "Prospects for a Future Whole World," *International Organization* 26 (1972): 1–17.

and dimensions of the emerging threats to our well-being, whether we can create an integrated global economy and a workable world order, and whether we can reorder global priorities so that the quality of life will improve rather than deteriorate. [23]

Although Brown sees the solution to this problem in part as one for supranational institutions (agencies that exercise the sovereignty of governments), he is principally concerned with the development of global planning which is acceptable to governments, and which does not alter their status as the principal actors in world politics. He looks ultimately to the creation of a globally planned economy and of a global infrastructure consisting of transport and communications systems. These, he suggests, will improve the quality of life through central planning, and will usher in a new world order—not through fear of threat, but through universal satisfaction.

Others who accept the philosophy of globalism have given more attention to its institutional needs. One well-known British author, for example, enumerates some of the social requisites to this globalist world order. [24] In fields of human rights, labor standards, and monetary controls, in particular, United Nations coordination is crucial to the implementation of the philosophy. It seems, therefore, that the development of globalism is tied to the future of some universal organization, most likely the United Nations. It is agreed that if the philosophy is to rise above futuristic platitudes about the human instinct for survival, then institutionalization is essential.

All of the proposals thus far studied have one thing in common: they are all *political-structural* concepts of world order; that is, each deals with international anarchy by adjusting the system's structural characteristics, and by prescribing mechanisms for addressing existing evils. More recent research, however, focuses upon the *universal cultural* aspects of international relations, recognizing that international events are often nongovernmentally motivated. It assumes that there are universal cultural similarities and, further, that cultural imperatives underlie many international events. Richard Falk characterizes the cultural perspective in this manner:

> The creation of a new system of world order must draw its animating vision from the long and widespread affirmation that all men are part of a single human family, that a oneness lies buried beneath the manifold diversities and dissensions of the present fractionated world, and that this latent oneness alone can give life and fire to a new political program of transformation.[25]

[23] Lester R. Brown, *World Without Borders* (New York: Random House, 1972), pp. 11–12.

[24] C. Wilfred Jenks, *The World Beyond the Charter* (London: George Allen and Unwin Ltd., 1969), especially chapter 4.

[25] Richard A. Falk, *This Endangered Planet* (New York: Random House, 1971), p. 296.

Contemporary research into the future of the international system rests upon the concept of universal culture as a basis for effective political co-operation.

The World Order Models Project typifies this new concern. To restore a humanistic view of the international system, WOMP focuses not only on peace and disarmament, but also on social justice and welfare. One participant argues that, "In a sense, social justice is prior to economic welfare and minimization of violence. Welfare will not be equitably distributed nor violence averted unless justice is done or is in prospect."[26]

Even if one accepts the need for conscious international transformation to achieve peace, justice, welfare, and ecological restoration, many troubling questions remain about transactions in a world without sovereign states. Historically, values have been allocated by power, conflict, and war. How will these ends be achieved in a warless world? Will merely eliminating absolute sovereignty necessarily be more effective for allocating global values? How will crucial value decisions be made? Will such a world be better than the one we have now?

The Problem of Sovereign Transfer

Whether by structural change or universal culture, the creation of world order requires fundamental alteration of individual states, especially the more powerful. The state, after all, serves many functions, both internally and externally. And while the international law of a nation-state system (see chapter 11) strives to *regulate* at least the external functions of statehood, effective world order may have to *deprive the state of control* over those functions. If contemporary international law is only modestly successful in its quest, the drive for comprehensive world order faces the same problems in far greater magnitude. While international law seeks to intrude in the exercise of functions with the consent of states, comprehensive world order attempts to abridge the absoluteness of states' sovereignty. And because this requires new institutional arrangements, world order schemes share with the world federalist notion the problem of transfer of loyalties away from the state to a culturally and politically heterogeneous entity.

But the picture need not be altogether bleak. Since world order ideas imply a rejection of world government, the transfer of loyalties, along with

[26] Ali A. Mazrui, "World Order Through World Culture," *Proceedings*, American Society of International Law (1972), pp. 252–53. A comprehensive study of the traditions and contemporary ideas of futuristic research, especially with the universal cultural orientation, appears in Louis René Beres and Harry R. Targ, *Reordering the Planet: Constructing Alternative World Futures* (Boston: Allyn and Bacon, 1974).

Comments by A. Michael Washburn, director of the university program of the Institute for World Order, have assisted in the preparation of this section of the text.

the readjustment of states' sovereignty, need only be both gradual and united. In this sense, the world order idea is consistent with the philosophy of functionalism, except the reassignment of public tasks and the redirecting of individual loyalties are determined not by the political innocuousness of issues, but by (1) the *importance* of the subject matter as a potential cause of war or as a preventative of war; and (2) *public and governmental support attainable* for transfer away from the nation-state.[27] Even so, unanimity on such issues is unlikely. If issues of transfer are decided by international conventions, it makes little difference whether delegates are appointed by governments or elected by publics. Sentiment to alter fundamental attributes of statehood is not rampant. In addition, delegates are likely to differ on whether or not certain issues cause war.

Mechanisms of Sanction

Under institutionalized world order by what means will the cooperation among nations be ensured? It is assumed that punishment of violators is the responsibility of all members of the community through both centralized and decentralized means. Besides the use of force by legitimized military control, however, the world order advocates prescribe various lesser sanctions. Foremost among these is the old-age technique of *ostracism*— economic boycott, censure, cultural isolation, and so on.

Power and Justice

There is probably universal agreement that power and war, the mechanisms by which international decisions have traditionally been made, have resulted in many unjust decisions. But what guarantee have we that some other mechanism will not occasionally be unjust? Presumably, core values of different national peoples will continue to collide. In the absence of war and traditional power struggles, what standards of justice are to be used? Whose concept of justice ought to prevail in a political process in the absence of coercion? International decision-making may require a functional equivalent to war, since we know that war has settled fundamental questions at critical historical moments. This is not to suggest that victory is the equivalent of justice; it suggests, rather, that war has been a prime instrument of decision-making and the allocation of values. Without it states will require a functional equivalent or they may be prompted to desert world order for their individual abilities to coerce.

---

[27] Norman L. Hill, "The National State and Federation," in Howard O. Eaton, ed., *Federation: The Coming Structure of World Government* (Norman, Okla.: The University of Oklahoma Press, 1944), p. 131. This world order standard is part of the world federalist intellectual tradition.

Furthermore, if states sacrifice their war-making ability by vesting central coercing authority in some supranational agency, we are confronted with the problem of that agency's capacity for justice. Might not such an authority be dictatorial, and thus prone to injustice? Alternatively, could it fall under the command of an influential minority of states? Or the converse, could it succumb to the avarice of a tyrannical majority of states which disdain the values and interests of others? These problems plague especially maximalist proposals for world order, but they are only relatively less critical for minimalist and reformist views.

Value Standards and Value Objectives

Underlying all other problems and questions is the matter of what standards are to be used and what objectives pursued in comprehensive world order. Order requires more than simple institutional mechanics; it reflects the value patterns which create it, and it is expected to perform in accordance with some values. The feasibility of world order is dependent largely upon the pertinence of the larger values to their particular political and social cultures, their economic systems and expectations, and their philosophies regarding rights, freedoms and other elements of public life. Proposals of world order cannot ignore the sociological imperatives of the international community.

Despite lingering sentiment for a world republic, most formal proposals have been products of the early cold war—an age of extreme ideological sensitivity. As a result, most of them lean heavily upon the philosophy of government which is broadly characterized as the Western liberal tradition, with emphasis upon civil liberties and economic individualism. At the same time, however, they attempt to attract socialist attention by including collective responsibility for economic development, allocation of natural resources, and distribution of wealth. Nevertheless, there is a distinct Western tone to them, with patent leanings toward an idyllic Western model. Proposals that call for upgrading the United Nations as an instrument of world order, on the other hand, are more realistic in accepting diverse domestic ideologies and political heritages. This realism has been imposed upon the Western world largely by the growing solidarity of the left-leaning Third World on economic issues at the UN.

The Problem of Internal War

Traditionally, students of international relations have distinguished sharply between international war and internal war, and a body of international law has arisen regulating each. In more recent years, especially in the revolutionary international system of the past quarter-century, the sharpness of the distinction has faded because of the tendency for internal wars to become international wars through intervention and third-party belligerency. It is by now evident that internal wars are a major threat to international peace and security. Can effective world order instruments avert this threat by resolving internal problems? How much authority ought the international community to have to intervene for such a purpose? Would the authority of centralized enforcement be tantamount to a dictatorial world state, or a menace of the majority?

A related problem—and from the viewpoints of justice and welfare perhaps a larger one—is the relation of world order to insurgent groups in strife-torn countries. If insurgency threatens world or regional peace, and if international agents have authority to intervene, are they *bound* to intervene in behalf of incumbents? Or ought they to act upon their judgment as to the relative merits of conflicting claims for social justice? What ideological and philosophical standards ought to be invoked? Who ought to create them? Furthermore, in internal situations, what will be the mechanisms for determining and executing value standards in the absence of unchallenged national authority?

Conclusion

In this section of the book, we have considered several approaches to world order, and we have concluded by exploring some existing proposals for alternative world futures. Despite the contributions made to international peace and stability by intergovernmental organization, international law, transnational participation, and regional integration, it is apparent that the international system presently points toward self-destruction. This is not due entirely to the potential for war in a balance-of-terror system. It is also attributable partly to the widening gap between the wealthy countries and the poor, with resulting social and political antipathies. Moreover, the presence of egalitarian ideals in the minds of virtually all peoples has heightened the demand for international protection of human rights in light of the failure of national governments in this matter. While all this political demand burgeons, the delicate balance of the human environment is deteriorating at an alarming rate. It is abundantly clear that the international system is in jeopardy unless statesmen and those whom they represent accept the critical need to rise above the narrow psychology of nation-states and of nationalism.

In deciding among alternative world futures, we are faced with several choices. We may proceed in the traditional political-structural manner, through maximalist, minimalist, or reformist means. But the social imperatives, the problems of loyalty transfer and fears about life in the future, retard progress on these choices even while the need becomes clearer. Our choice, it now appears, is *not* between perpetuation of the present structure and vague alternatives, but between (1) world order based on piecemeal erosion of states' sovereignty and (2) highly institutionalized and expansionist world government. The longer the choice is delayed, the more the alternatives narrow to two: expansionist world government and systemic destruction.

Index

E

East African Common Market, 154
Ecology, 415–17
  Global Conference on the Human
    Environment, 416
Economic Community, 78–84, 364,
  400, 402
European Economic Community,
  77–78, 377, 380, 383, 393
European Free Trade Area, 78
Economic determinism, 4
Egypt, 263, 357–58
Einstein, Albert, 298
Eisenhower, Dwight, 225
Engels, Freidrich, 4, 9
Equatorial African Customs Union,
  155
Equilibrium, 209–10
European Coal and Steel Community
  (ECSC), 385, 391
European Economic Community, 77–
  78, 276, 377, 380, 383, 393
European Free Trade Area, 78, 80
European Security Conference, 28
Europeanness, 228, 394–96
Expansionism, 63–65
Exploitation, 144
Extraterritoriality, 62, 99
Exxon, 408, 409

F

Fascism, 292–93
Fedayeen, 194
Fedorenko, N. T., 171
Feudalism, 4–5, 34
  and capitalism, 5
First Hague Conference, 272
First-strike capability, 244–45, 256
Five Principles of Peaceful Coexis-
  tence (Panch Shila Doctrine),
  106, 113, 123, 336
Food for Peace, 139, 151–52

Foreign aid, 118, 137–40, 150, 151–
  53, 158–59, 263
Foreign investment, 74, 80–81, 89–
  91, 137, 140–42, 149–51
Ford, Gerald R., 55, 116
Formosa. *See* Taiwan
Fourteen Points (Wilson), 335
Fragmentation bombs, 261
Functional satisfaction, 390

G

Gallup poll, 175–76
Gandhi, Mahatma, 299
General Agreement on Tariffs and
  Trade (GATT), 128, 264, 272,
  364
General Assembly (UN), 345–49, 369
General Motors, 141, 409
General Pact for the Renunciation of
  War (Kellogg-Briand Pact), 329
Global Conference on the Human En-
  vironment, 416
Globalism, 435–37
Gray Report, 90–91
Great Depression, 304
Greater East Asian Co-Prosperity
  Sphere, 103, 121
Green Revolution, 143–44, 152, 311
Group of Ten, 159
Guevara, Ché, 148

H

Helsinki
  Soviet-American agreement, 27, 28
Hiroshima, 205, 239
Hitler, Adolph, 184, 191, 199, 201,
  286, 292, 309
Hitler-Stalin nonaggression pact, 39
Ho Chi Minh, 194
Hobson, 7
Hoover, Herbert, 268

American occupation of, 65–66
balance of terror, 275–76
China, 68
expansionism, 63–65
integration, 400–401
international law, 332
international organization, 366
Nixon Doctrine, 69–73
Okinawa, 68
Pacific Treaties, 66–68
Vietnam, 69
Johnson, Lyndon B., 80, 197
Joint Chiefs of Staff, 197, 199
Jurisprudence, 318, 391

K

Kant, Emmanuel, 262
Kelsen, Hans, 324
Kennan, George, 45
Kennedy, John F., 139, 153
Khrushchev, Nikita, 224, 271, 274, 333
Kissinger, Henry, 42, 54, 195–96, 249
Korea and Korean War, 42, 53–54, 63, 72, 92, 100, 114–116, 121, 195–96, 199, 224–25, 227, 254, 257, 273, 278
Kuomintang, 101, 102, 104, 106, 118

L

Latin America, 19, 125, 135, 139, 150, 263, 380
Latin American Free Trade Association, 154
Laos, 70, 116
Law of community, 330
Law of reciprocity, 330
Law of the political framework, 330–31
League of Nations, 38, 62, 64, 75, 325, 326, 353, 361–62, 422–24

Lebensraum, 292, 309
Lenin, V. I., 4, 7, 12
Leninism, 21
Less developed countries. *See* Third World
Limited Nuclear Test Ban Treaty, 272
Lin Piao, 113
Lippmann, Walter, 312
Locke, John, 10
Long March, 102
Loring, Konrad, 300–301
Lotus Case, 318
Loyalty, 394–96, 437
Luxury consumption, 136, 139

M

Mackinder, Halford, 185
Mahan, Alfred T., 185
Major military powers, 192
Malaysia, 116, 121
Malik, Jacob, 172
Malthus, Thomas, 309–311
Manchu Dynasty, 99, 101
Manchuria, 63, 118
Mandates Systems, 353
Manifest Destiny, 62
Mao Tse-tung, 102, 112, 113, 118–19, 221, 370
Marshall, George C., 104, 120
Marshall Plan, 52, 76, 77, 400
Marx, Karl, 3, 114, 333
Marxism, 7
Marxism-Leninism, 4, 12, 112
Marxism-Leninism-Maoism, 95, 112
Massive retaliation, 274
Maximalist proposals, 420
McGovern, George, 266
McNamara, Robert S., 248–249
Middle East, 72, 73, 125, 140, 255, 359–61
Military-industrial complex, 305–307
imperialism, capitalism and, 22
Military expenditure, 132–136
Military preparedness, 191

Philippines-American Defense Treaty, 222
Poland, 44
Political socialization, 188–89
Polycentrism, 224, 225
Population, 127, 130–32, 187–88, 241, 417–18
Positivism, 318–19
Potsdam Conference, 43, 65, 277
Poverty, 125, 138
Power assymetrics, 284–85
Power, management of, 205
Power, source of
  natural, 184–188
  social and psychological, 188–91
  synthetic, 191
Pravda, 172
Pre-emptive attack, 214
Preventive attack, 214
Proletariat, 6, 7
Psychochemicals, 260–261

R

Rapacki Plan, 266
Realist school, 47–48
Realpolitik, 285
Reformist proposals, 420
Regional power balance, 234–35
Regionalism, 81
Regional integration, 154, 375–405
Relative deprivation, 307–309
Reparations Case, 363
Republic of China-America Defense Treaty, 222
Resources, natural, 127, 154–62, 185–87
Revolution, 7, 9, 11, 12, 34, 54
Rhodesia, 326–28
Roman Empire, 95, 108–109
Rousseau, Jean-Jacques, 10
Russian, 3, 13–14, 101, 104
  national interest, 11–12, 31
  revolution, 101

Russell, Bertrand, 298–99
Russo-Japanese War, 63, 103

S

San Francisco Conference, 363
Sanctions, 323–29
  collective sanctions, 325
Schelling, Thomas, 247
Schlesinger, James, 249, 251, 252
Seabed Treaty, 266
Second-strike capability, 244–45, 256
Security Council, 325–26, 349–53
Self-determination, 9, 75, 353
Separatism, 189, 287–88
Seward, William Henry, 297
Shanghai Communiqué, 109–111
Singapore, 121
Sino-American relations, 113–117, 227
Sino-Indian Declaration, 336
Sino-Indian War, 108
Sino-Japanese relations, 120–122
Sino-Soviet dispute, 54, 57, 119
Sino-Soviet relations, 117–120, 278
Sino-Tibetan conflict, 107–108
"Smart Bombs," 61
Social Contract, 34
Social controls, 6
Social Darwinism, 292, 295
Socialism, 30, 112, 165, 172
South-East Asian Treaty Organization (SEATO), 221
(South) Korea, 255, 326
(South) Korea-American Defense Treaty, 222
Soviet Union, 3, 14, 16, 43, 47, 52, 54, 57, 58, 64, 72, 75, 76, 82, 105, 107, 113, 117, 118, 158, 240, 250, 253, 254, 269, 277, 333, 347, 367–369
Soviet perspective, 3ff
  balance of terror, 277–78
  China, 28–30
  Europe, 24–28
  imperialism, 31

Soviet perspective (*cont.*)
  integration, 401–403
  international law, 333–35
  international organization, 367–69
  international system, 14
  World War I, 14
  World War II, 15–18
Stalin, Joseph, 9, 10, 118–19, 191, 274
State
  origins of, 5–6, 13
  withering away, 10
Strangelove, Dr., 258, 262
Strategic Air Command, 242
Strategic Arms Limitation Talks,
    (SALT), 55, 266, 268, 269, 272,
    275
Strategic Nuclear Weapons, 252–53
Suez War, 183
Sun Yat-sen, 101–102
Supranational Organizations, 340
Syria, 285

international organization, 371–72
luxury consumption, 136
military expenditure, 132
population growth, 130
terms of trade, 146
Tibet, 107–108
Tindemans Report, 380
Toynbee, Arnold, 195
Trade Expansion Act of 1962, 79,
    393
Transfer of loyalty, 394
Transnational corporations. *See* Mul-
    tinational Corporations
Transnational participation, 405–413
Treaties, 320
Treaty of Berlin, 9
Treaty of Nanking, 99
Treaty of Versailles, 64, 201
Truman, Harry S., 53, 199
Truman Doctrine, 45–51, 76, 273,
    320, 332
Trusteeship System, 353–354
Twenty-One Demands, 63

T

Tacitus, 301–302
Tactical nuclear weapons, 252–253
Taft-Katsura Agreement, 63
T'aip'ing rebellion, 99–100
Taiwan, 63, 72, 105–111, 114, 116,
    122, 369
Tanaka, Kakuei, 121
Taylor, Maxwell, 194
Technical assistance, 142–144
Terms-of-trade problem, 146–149, 158
Teheran Conference, 43
Thailand, 116, 121
Third World, 18, 57, 113, 128, 169,
    230, 279, 308, 337–338, 356,
    371–373, 404
Third World perspective, 125ff
  balance of terror, 279–280
  foreign aid, 137
  foreign investment, 141
  integration, 404–405
  international law, 337–39

U

Unconditional surrender, 203
Underwater Launched Missile Sys-
    tem (ULMS), 263
Unequal Treaties, 98
Union of Banana Exporting Countries,
    156
United Nations, 40, 43, 66, 113, 115,
    225, 269, 322, 325, 326, 328,
    332, 343, 346, 424–26, 435
United Nations Conference on Trade
    and Development (UNCTAD),
    138, 147, 338, 372
United Nations Development Pro-
    gram, 372
United Nations Security Council, 112,
    115, 261, 325, 349–352, 357–360
United Nations Special Committee on
    Peacekeeping, 348